Becoming Madam Chancellor

Angela Merkel and the Berlin Republic

JOYCE MARIE MUSHABEN

CAMBRIDGE
UNIVERSITY PRESS

CAMBRIDGE
UNIVERSITY PRESS

University Printing House, Cambridge CB2 8BS, United Kingdom

One Liberty Plaza, 20th Floor, New York, NY 10006, USA

477 Williamstown Road, Port Melbourne, VIC 3207, Australia

4843/24, 2nd Floor, Ansari Road, Daryaganj, Delhi – 110002, India

79 Anson Road, #06–04/06, Singapore 079906

Cambridge University Press is part of the University of Cambridge.

It furthers the University's mission by disseminating knowledge in the pursuit of education, learning, and research at the highest international levels of excellence.

www.cambridge.org
Information on this title: www.cambridge.org/9781108417730
DOI: 10.1017/9781108278232

First published 2017

Printed in Great Britain by Clays Ltd, St Ives plc

A catalogue record for this publication is available from the British Library.

ISBN 978-1-108-41773-0 Hardback
ISBN 978-1-108-40563-8 Paperback

This book is dedicated to girls everywhere, looking for positive political role models, who are committed to the proposition that women's rights are human rights, and human rights are women's rights.

It is also dedicated to my late husband, Harry F. Few, who had a hard time understanding why his wife insisted that the words "same" and "equal" are not synonyms, and that sometimes we actually need to be treated "differently" to achieve equality when it comes to reconciling family and career.

Contents

Tables, Figures, and Boxes

TABLES

FIGURES

BOXES

Abbreviations

AfD	Alternative for Germany (party)
BAMF	Federal Ministry for Migration and Refugees
BL	Basic Law (Constitution)
BND	*Bundesnachrichtendienst*/Federal Intelligence Agency
CEAS	Common European Asylum System
CDU	Christian Democratic Party
CEE	Central East European states
CHP	Combined Heat and Power
CSU	Christian Social Union
DA	*Demokratischer Aufbruch*/Democratic Awakening
DAX	*Deutsche Aktien Index*/German Stock Exchange
DG	Directorate-General (European Union)
EC	European Community
ECJ	European Court of Justice
ECtHR	European Court of Human Rights
ECB	European Central Bank
ECSC	European Coal and Steel Community
EU	European Union (post 1991)
EURODAC	European Dactyloscopy (European Union registry)
FAZ	*Frankfurter Allgemeine Zeitung*
FCO	*Bundeskanzeramt*/Federal Chancellor's Office
FDJ	Free German Youth (East Germany)
FDP	Free Democratic Party
FRG	Federal Republic of Germany (West Germany, and post-unty)
FRONTEX	European Border and Coast Guard Agency
GC	*Gro-Ko* Grand Coalition
GDP	Gross Domestic Product
GDR	German Democratic Republic (former East Germany)

GHG	Green-house Gases
GM	gender mainstreaming
IMF	International Monetary Fund
INF	Intermediate-Range Nuclear Forces
ISIS	Islamic State in Iraq and Syria
KGB	Committee for State Security (Soviet Union)
LNG	Liquid Natural Gas
NATO	North Atlantic Treaty Organization
NIP	National Integration Plan
PDS	Party of Democratic Socialists
PLO	Palestine Liberation Organization
R&D	research and development
RE	Renewable Energy
Red-Green	Social Democratic/Green Party coalition
SDS	Students for Democratic Society (West Germany)
SED	Socialist Unity Party (East Germany)
SME	social market economy
SPD	Social Democratic Party
SS	*Schutzstaffel* (Nazis)
Stasi	Secret Police (East Germany)
STEM	Science,Technology, Engineering, and Math; known in German as MINT for Math, Computing, Natural Sciences, Technology
Treuhand	State Privatization and Holding Company (unification)
UN	United Nations
WMPW	"World's Most Powerful Woman"

Acknowledgments

As I regularly advise my students, once you "discover" gender, you are destined to spend the rest of your career looking for it (and usually finding it) under every policy rock, as well as in every institutional nook and cranny. For those of us who secured our jobs in the 1980s, it was a case of learning-by-doing. For most of my younger colleagues and undergraduates, identifying the many sources of inequality shaping the lives of women and minorities has become second nature.

Had I not been able to share *the personal and the political* with the people recognized here, I would not have made it this far. The ability to w(h)ine, dine, write, co-edit and critique each other's work has helped us all to weather a long march through the institutions. It has been an honor and a privilege to share this field, along with countless literature tips, conference panels, hotel rooms, special issue deadlines, speaking venues, and classroom experiences with treasured colleagues like Gabriele Abels, Louise Davidson-Schmich, Friederike Eigler, Lily Gardner Feldman, Sabine Lang, Christiane Lemke, Ann Philipps, Jonathan Olsen, Helga Welsh, Ruth Wittlinger, and Jennifer Yoder. Gabi and Sabine provided especially detailed feedback regarding parts of this manuscript. Other women who have inspired me, based on their special roles in gendering the European Union, include Agnes Hubert, Barbara Helfferich, and Maria Stratigaki. Jeff Anderson and Eric Langenbacher supplied multiple opportunities to hone my arguments (and power-point skills) by inviting me to speak at the BMW Center for German and European Studies at Georgetown University, as did the past and present directors at the European Studies Center at the University of Illinois. I extend further thanks to special friends who have served as moral supporters and discussion partners over the years, namely, Susanne Müller-Menckens, Eddi Ditscheck, and Asiye Kaya.

Nor could this project have been completed without the help of the many professionals who supplied me with data, documents, and a place to take a daily Diet-Coke break. I am especially grateful to Renate Körber, Maria Hahn, Doris Schawaller, and the other kind librarians at the Bundestag Bibliothek in Berlin, where I not only enjoyed a "welcoming culture" and peaceful work environment but also a fabulous view of the Spree, the Reichstag, and the Chancellor's Office for three summers in a row. My deep appreciation likewise goes to many unsung interview partners and millions of German taxpayers who have so generously financed my research over the last decade, in addition to paying for the books, journals, and printer paper I used at university libraries in Tübingen and Berlin. Katje Hartmann and the staff of the Alexander von Humboldt Foundation not only supported my field work financially but also allowed me to indulge in memorable musical interludes known as the Open Air Classics. Sara Doskow's enthusiastic response to this project as well as help from Robert Judkins and Lyn Flight at Cambridge University Press also kept me going, particularly during the later stages. Mary Angelica Painter gets heaven points for relieving me of the need to spend days, if not weeks, rendering my tables and graphs comprehensible to normal mortals, given my lack of computer skills beyond word processing, "snipping tool," and Skype. I also owe many thanks to Alexandra Löhr, my favorite house-sitter and indexing wizard.

Last, but not least, I express my heartfelt thanks to Joshua, the son who had no choice but to put up with his Mom's itinerant academic existence, including the semesters he spent with me in Erfurt and Berlin. Josh was my rock when brain cancer overtook my very strong, very handsome, and very smart husband. I can assure any good woman who might want to marry Josh someday that he has learned what it means to engage in very hard but very sensitive care work, seven days a week, twenty-four hours a day. He may not openly admit that he is a feminist but he has made his equality obsessed Mom very proud.

Introduction: "Becoming Madam Chancellor"

Man is the hidden reference in language and culture; women can only aspire
to be as good as a man; there is no point in trying to be as good as a woman.
                          Dale Spender (1984)[1]

On November 22, 2005, Angela Merkel made her way to the Sophie
Charlottenburg Palace, where Federal President Horst Köhler presented
her with a certificate of appointment for the chancellorship, after she had
secured 397 of 611 parliamentary votes. The usual venue for presidential
acts of state, Schloss Bellevue, was undergoing renovations; it was quite
fitting, however, that modern Germany's first female leader got her start in
the palace named for the first Prussian Queen (1688–1705). During her
marriage to Frederick I, the well-educated Sophie Charlotte, Duchess of
Braunschweig-Hannover, founded the Berlin Academy of Science. Equally
committed to scientific progress as a former physicist, Dr. Merkel
proceeded to the Bundestag, where she solemnly swore to dedicate
herself "to the well-being of the German people." She promised further to
"promote their welfare, protect them from harm, uphold and defend the
Basic Law and the laws of the Federation, perform [her] duties
conscientiously, and do justice to all," concluding her oath with the
optional phrase, "so help me God."

In contrast to the orderly transition that usually follows Germany's
mercifully short election campaigns, this one had not produced a done
deal by the time the polls closed on September 18, 2005. Along with many
other academics, foreign journalists, and party workers who had gathered
at the North Rhine-Westphalian mission in Berlin, I was stunned by the
official projections posted on the TV monitors at 6 pm sharp: it was a race

too close to call. Both the Christian Democrats and the Social Democrats had lost votes to a number of smaller parties, but neither the Free Democratic Party (FDP) nor the Greens had garnered enough seats to join either major party as a junior partner in a "normal" coalition. During the traditional, post-election "Elephant Round" discussion televised later that evening, Social Democratic Party (SPD) Chancellor Gerhard Schröder (who had called for early elections), aggressively insisted that he would remain in power while hammering away at his shell-shocked CDU opponent: "Do you seriously think that my party will consider an offer to discuss [options] with Ms. Merkel when she says that *she* would like to be Chancellor?"[2] Although it would take another six weeks of fierce negotiations, the woman no one ever really expected to rise to the top achieved her goal.

Angela Merkel has accrued a long list of political "firsts," rendering her an exceptional leader worthy of investigation on many fronts. Not only does she stand out as the first postwar politician to have ascended the party ladder without having completed the traditional German *Ochsentour*.[3] Divorced and childless, she was the first Easterner to serve as the Federal Minister of Women and Youth, and later as Minister for the Environment, Nature and Nuclear Reactor Safety. She rose through the party ranks in less than a decade, becoming the national CDU Deputy-Secretary in 1991 and chair of the Mecklenburg-Vorpommern conservatives in 1993. Named CDU General-Secretary in 1998, she led the Opposition during the Red–Green government years; she was elected CDU party chief in 2000 and chaired the CDU/CSU Bundestag caucus (*Fraktion*) as of 2005.[4]

The 2005 elections secured Merkel's place in history as the first woman, Easterner, physicist, and even the first pastor's daughter to take charge of the world's fifth largest economy. As the youngest person to hold that office to date, she is also the only chancellor since 1949 to have led her party to a "normal" victory after managing a Grand Coalition (GC, *Gro-Ko*) for four years, featuring the two largest parties with opposing ideological orientations. In December 2013, she became the first person to head a *second* Grand Coalition, garnering 462 out of 621 Bundestag votes. Domestically speaking, Merkel thus provides a one-woman laboratory for comparing the special impact of GC politics on the chancellor's powers (2005–2009) with traditional limitations on her ability to rule under a conservative–liberal coalition of her own making (2009–2013), followed by another exceptional CDU–SPD government (2013–2017).

Given her preeminent role in European Union (EU) affairs, Angela Merkel's three terms as chancellor also supply a unique opportunity to assess the impact of changing international dynamics on her performance. Germany is clearly a country in which the past continues to shape the present, but unification marked a profound break with the post-1945 order. The end of the Cold War saw the restoration of its national sovereignty, coupled with significant EU enlargements, new forces of economic globalization, and major technological change. Merkel stands as the personal embodiment of demographic transformation processes that have taken root across the country and the continent since the fall of the Berlin Wall in 1989. After forty years of national division, the sudden merger of two ideologically opposed polities would have generated major challenges for *any* post-1990 leader. This chancellor has also encountered multiple global crises, for example, the 2008 financial melt-down, the Fukushima disaster, the Euro crisis, and Russia's annexation of Crimea, all of which have allowed or, more accurately, required her to play a unique role in redirecting the course of European history.

Almost before the ink had dried on the 2005 interparty agreement, pundits began predicting that Merkel's first Grand Coalition would not last; completing her first term, she emerged as the voters' clear favorite during the next set of national elections.[5] Critics continued to insist throughout her second term, starting in 2009, that her conservative–liberal government was also likely to collapse. Opposition members regularly complained that "she just doesn't lead," while people in her own party attacked her for being "too presidential." Bombarded by new crises at every turn, Merkel continued to steer the ship of state with an unflappable, pragmatic, self-confident demeanor.

Shortly after she was re-elected for a third term in September 2013, the usual suspects predicted that Merkel would probably retire in 2014, as soon as she turned sixty. Reflecting on her first two stints as chancellor, one journalist noted that the need to address several crises in rapid succession "can wear down even a woman with an iron constitution and an inexhaustible appetite for work ... She has led Germany for longer than anyone ever expected ... but from the first day after re-election she would also be burdened with the knowledge that time is running out ..."[6] Throughout his sixteen-year reign (1982–1998), Helmut Kohl encountered major anti-nuclear energy protests, mass mobilizations against Pershing II deployments, a collapsed East German economy necessitating average annual "transfers" of €140 billion, three years of unprecedented xenophobic violence, and a widely critiqued *Reformstau* (gridlock). Yet no one had dared to suggest that the male chancellor might have been "worn down" by the time he left office at age sixty-eight.

As the country's first woman chancellor qua eastern physicist, it was inevitable that Merkel would be treated as an exotic species by the male-dominated political and media establishments during the early stages of her career. Her rapid rise to power and her effectiveness to date make it difficult to argue, however, that either her sex, her GDR upbringing, or her lack of a strong Land-level base have subjected her to serious discrimination. Indeed, one could argue that Merkel's unique experiences supplied some distinct advantages not available to other would-be women rulers. So what lessons, if any, might her three terms as a very powerful chancellor hold for the future of gender equality in Germany?

FROM "RESEARCH PUZZLE" TO CLEAR CASE: WHY I WROTE THIS BOOK

Persuaded that generational change had already triggered a fundamental transformation of West German political culture by the mid-1980s, I decided to take closer look at the "national identities" of older, middle, and younger cohorts as they had evolved from 1949 through unification. In addition to drawing on forty years of survey research, I interviewed ninety members of the Bundestag and other elites through the mid-1980s.[7] By May 1989, I was ready to investigate identities on the other side of the Wall, but that project was soon overtaken by historical events. The collapse of the German Democratic Republic (GDR) made it possible for me to conduct interviews with over fifty members of the first, and last, freely elected *Volkskammer* during the summer of 1990. One of my discussion partners was a woman about my own age who had just decided to switch from physics to politics as deputy press speaker for the new prime minister, Lothar de Maizière. His primary task was to negotiate the conditions under which the GDR would cease to exist; her job was to explain that process to hordes of foreign and domestic journalists, an eye-opening experience for someone unacquainted with a free press and "fractious democracy."

Two days after my June 12 discussion with thirty-five-year-old Angela Merkel, I met with a former GDR pastor, Joachim Gauck, who had secured a parliamentary seat on the Bündnis 90/Greens ticket. My first interviewee moved on to become chancellor of a united Germany;

the second served as federal president, after directing the agency tasked with evaluating "100 miles of *Stasi* (secret police) files." Although I have moved from the rank of Assistant to Associate to Curators' Professor over the years, I still occasionally wonder what went wrong with my own career strategy. Had I known back then that my discussion partner would become "the World's Most Powerful Woman" ten times over, I would have asked very different questions, and maybe even pursued political office myself.

I have followed Merkel's career trajectory since 1990, reading every book written about her to date during my summer research leaves at the Humboldt University and the Bundestag Library in Berlin. Curiously, all but one of those texts have been written by journalists.[8] Most offer biographical treatments, question her leadership style, or critique her "lack of vision." Few, if any, have assessed Merkel's actual *performance* in ways that incorporate the diverging imperatives imposed by different coalition configurations, a changing party landscape, and disruptions of the global sort. Noteworthy exceptions include studies addressing broad policy changes under Merkel's first two governments.[9] This is one factor that inspired me to write a scholarly book on this fascinating political personality.

Second, I find it quite curious that no feminist scholars in Germany have taken up this book challenge, perhaps out of a reluctance to identify with a woman whose party has long espoused a gender regime limited to *Kinder, Küche und Kirche*.[10] Still waiting for a first woman president in the United States, I am less encumbered by party-political considerations. It is impossible to predict *a priori* what leadership style, mobilization strategies, or policy priorities any powerful woman is likely to pursue. Because prescribed gender norms differ from country to country, as well as from North to South and East to West, the only way to explain why some identity traits prevail over others in any woman's success is to execute detailed case studies. My qualitative approach infers that "success," by definition, is context- and policy-specific.

A third reason for this book derives from my earlier work on youth movements, generational dynamics, and political cultural change in both East and West Germany prior to 1990. My familiarity with the ideological, societal, and economic conditions that shaped Angela Merkel during the first thirty-five years of her life, renders me better equipped than many mainstream scholars to interpret the motives, values, priorities, and behaviors evinced by this particular chancellor. Having spent nearly eighteen years living in Germany as a scholar, my peculiar insider–outsider status enables me to assess the "everyday" consequences of complex policy processes. Several of my German academic peers note, only half in jest, that I understand their West–East identities better than they do.

While my research has been informed by many conceptual frameworks utilized by comparative and gender politics experts, this will not be a theoretically driven or hypothesis-heavy work. My approach is unabashedly qualitative and eclectic, offering *thick description* and *process tracing*; I draw on interdisciplinary sources covering historical events, socioeconomic data, cultural variables, gender dynamics, and policy analysis. Those sources include Merkel's speeches, government publications, campaign materials, media reports, refereed publications, formal interviews, and hundreds of conversations with expert colleagues. With all due respect to countless scholars investigating women's paths to power, the institutional barriers they face, the stereotypical role expectations that hinder their progress, and new mechanisms equalizing their participation in politics, my primary interest lies in analyzing the ways in which *one woman has actually used her power* to improve the human condition across three terms.

My final motive for writing this book began with an ostensible paradox: having completed her first stint as Grand Coalition leader in 2009, Merkel enjoyed great popularity among voters and was well respected on the international stage, yet German pundits routinely described her as weak, faltering, and doomed to fail. I recalled the words of George W. Bush, who complained in 2000 of being regularly "misunderestimated" as president of the United States.[11] His lack of rhetorical skills aside, the term Bush used suggested an intensified form of *being underestimated*.

As a woman operating in a world historically reserved for powerful men, Merkel has encountered more than her fair share of skepticism and resistance. As an inexperienced "thirty-something" assuming a Cabinet post in 1990, she was quickly written off by established politicians as "Kohl's Girl." By the time she was sworn in as chancellor, she had accumulated eight years of ministerial experience, moved up the CDU executive ladder at warp speed, and led the conservative opposition in the Bundestag for four years. By the end of her first term as chancellor, Merkel had already been designated "the World's Most Powerful Woman" (WMPW) four times straight, yet her adversaries kept insisting that she lacked vision, charisma, and leadership skills. That was the puzzle: how could someone so successful be accused of "not leading?"

Looking back, it seems that her initial WMPW rankings had a lot to do with the fact that she was the first female chancellor, running a very big country with a very strong economy. *Forbes* selection metrics include net worth, company revenues, GDP, media presence, potential spheres of influence, and one's impact inside or outside a personal "field." Europeans awarded Barack Obama the Nobel Peace Prize shortly after he was first inaugurated, largely because they were happy to see the Bush years end, not because the new president had really stopped any wars at that point. Merkel did not evince the same leadership skills back then that we all take for granted today.

My original plan was to cover Merkel's first two terms, allowing me to compare how she performed under two governmental configurations, one involving an *exceptional* Grand Coalition (CDU/CSU–SPD), the other a *traditional* dominant party–junior partner majority (CDU/CSU–FDP). Critics continued to underestimate Merkel's popularity with voters well into her second term, as well as her uncanny ability to move hardliners to embrace societal reforms that they had vociferously resisted for decades. By 2013, however, the original puzzle had evaporated into the thin air of "polycrisis": given her tough stance on austerity policies, her response to climate change, and her willingness to chastise Vladimir Putin over the Ukraine, few could question this chancellor's leadership.[12]

The onset of her third term provided the breathing space I needed to focus on the larger "lessons" Merkel had ostensibly drawn from each crisis she encountered. As one of Europe's longest serving leaders since 1990, she has certainly juggled more than her fair share of global messes, so she has obviously learned a lot. Her third term has seen a rational, *pragmatic* Merkel taking some very *principled* human rights stances, regarding asylum seekers and Chinese dissidents, for example. These decisions have required a degree of self-confidence and international clout that she simply did not possess in 2009. She would be the first to admit, as her earlier interviews with Herlinde Koelbl attest, that she is a very different person today than when she first came to politics. At present, Angela Merkel really *is* the World's Most Powerful Woman, although given her favorite virtue – humility – she probably would not have minded ceding her title to Hillary Rodham Clinton for a few years, had the 2016 US presidential elections ended differently.

Neither *power* nor *leadership* are static components of governance, especially within democratic systems. Both require constant adjustment to changing political stakeholders, policy contexts, and environmental conditions. This study presents Merkel's three terms as an extraordinary learning process that has allowed at least one woman to make a significant difference in a united Germany: hence, the emphasis on "becoming" Madam Chancellor. Although she refuses to label herself a feminist, I maintain that Merkel has done more to modernize gender roles in united Germany than all of her predecessors. Exposed to a very different gender regime during her "35 years in the waiting room of GDR history," the chancellor has relied on female cabinet members like Ursula von der Leyen, Annette Schavan, and Maria Böhmer to leverage EU policies in ways that have opened doors to the balanced participation of women and men in political, economic, and community life.

I argue that the secret of Chancellor Merkel's success to date rests with three factors: first, although she was initially "misunderestimated" by political elites at home, she has derived strength from the unprecedented respect she enjoys among key actors abroad. Second, she has learned how to leverage domestic and supranational developments better than any previous chancellor, largely as a function of significant political and demographic changes across Europe. My third contention is that both her eastern socialization and her training as a physicist have outfitted her with hybrid political values and a unique set of analytical skills that make it very difficult for even her sharpest rivals to out-strategize her. As a former CDU official opined over a decade ago, "she learns faster than others think."[13]

THEORETICAL FRAMING, CORE CONCEPTS, AND THE PROBLEM OF "N = 1"

Merkel's tenth year in power, 2015, marked the seventieth anniversary of Germany's unconditional surrender, the fiftieth anniversary of diplomatic relations with Israel, the twenty-fifth anniversary of unification, and various centennial commemorations linked to the First World War. As a western born, eastern educated woman, Angela Merkel appears to embody, literally and figuratively, a wide array of social modernization processes that have reshaped the nation since 1949. While her contributions to this transformation are rooted in broader processes of European integration, globalization, and generational change, I believe that one can disaggregate her personal efforts to shape policy outcomes from those external forces. In order to do so, I need to present a bigger picture of what policies prevailed before and after unification. As a result, this is not only a book about Angela

Merkel; it also amounts to a brief history of the Federal Republic of Germany since unification.

Drawing on *historical institutionalism* in a broad sense, my study incorporates postwar background, institutional detail, and policy analysis testifying to continuity and change in the united Berlin Republic. Institutional factors include the formal and informal powers of the chancellor as they have evolved under two types of coalitions, as well as the changing nature of Bund–Länder relations. Proportional representation and the rise of new parties have rendered German state governments testing sites for kaleidoscopic coalitions not seen in the United States. I moreover concentrate on substantive issues ranging from the convergence of East–West identities and changing German–Israeli relations to Merkel's role in the Eurozone crisis, her orchestration of a major energy turn-around, and her efforts to expand citizenship rights to millions held hostage to the "foreigner" label for four decades. Each of her three terms has exposed Merkel to different coalition dynamics, offering at least a few control variables for assessing the impact of her unique socialization experiences.

A second construct framing this project, *intersectionality*, raises the core question: *what difference does difference make?* Intersectionality stresses "intra-category diversity – that is, the tremendous variation within categories such as ... 'woman-hood' ... and their role in politics ..."[14] The intersectionality paradigm uses the life experiences of "real women" to examine the ways in which gender interacts with race/ethnicity, religion, class, and other traits that shape an individual's access to, use of, and (re)presentation of power. One cannot simply take note of Merkel's sex, add her religion, her profession, and finally stir in her "eastern-ness" to theorize about her performance as a leader; for starters, "each social division has a different ontological basis, which is irreducible to other social divisions."[15] Working with a sample of one poses a further problem: counterfactuals are of little value in detailed case studies, the aim of which is to establish a significant baseline. Men are also subject to intersectionality, but, as Louise Davidson-Schmich observes, few scholars analyze the gender experiences of males.[16] The only other German to head a Grand Coalition, Kurt Georg Kiesinger (1966–1969), adopted a meditating style as chancellor that differed significantly from the "dominant leader" approach he embraced as Minister-President of Baden-Württemberg.[17]

Without attempting to review, critique, or reinvent the existing feminist–theoretical literature, my study also builds on the concept of women's political *representation*. I focus on three types – descriptive, substantive, and transformative – each of which I associate with a different kind of "extreme makeover."[18] The first type, *descriptive representation*, goes beyond the numbers; I use it here to deconstruct the physical images and stereotypes inflicted on female candidates for high political office (Chapter 1). While she was initially reluctant to campaign as a woman, much less as a feminist, Merkel's status as Germany's first female chancellor has rendered the executive branch more representative in numerical terms. Although women had already achieved "critical mass" (over 30 percent) in the Bundestag by the time she took charge, Merkel has significantly expanded the roles available to women at the national executive level, though only five women have headed state governments to date. This raises the question as to whether, given her unusual staying power as a three-term chancellor, Merkel has helped to eliminate long-standing gender stereotypes at the highest levels of government, enhancing the prospects for parity democracy.[19]

The second mode, *substantive representation*, pertains to women's ability to reshape policy in the legislative sense. Justified or not, female politicians are expected to do a better job of advocating for conjoined *women-and-children*; male leaders are rarely expected to do special things for all men. Female executives are perceived as natural experts in matters of health, education, and family, but those who actively pursue feminist policies are often accused of favoring "special interests." The question here is whether *this* female chancellor has indeed produced better policies for women.

The evidence is positive so far: "Angie" has bridged the gap between antithetical East–West gender regimes, for example, through policies supporting the reconciliation of work and family life.[20] She gradually embraced a quota system to increase women's presence on corporate management boards, leveraging EU mandates against Germany's looming demographic deficit. Her tough approach to the Euro crisis, however, has trapped more women outside Germany in part-time or precarious work. What are the trade-offs? Should we really expect Merkel, just because she is a woman, to be more gender-sensitive to policy consequences than her predecessors?

A third type, *symbolic representation*, invokes the reconstruction of women's proper place in society, public and private. Questions here center on the extent to which Merkel's life experiences have led her to open up new spaces for women and men, even if her motives disappoint orthodox feminists. I prefer to label this *transformative representation*, arguing that many of the reforms she has introduced since 2005 go well beyond the symbolic. By leaving his "super-ministry" (Economics and Energy) early on Wednesdays to pick up his daughter at nursery school, Vice-Chancellor Sigmar Gabriel sends a powerful signal to employers about the government's family-friendly expectations. Better yet: in 2013, Merkel appointed a physician-mother of seven, Ursula von der Leyen, to serve as Germany's first female Defense Minister; she immediately introduced day-care options for Bundeswehr troops and staff. I will assess the extent to which Merkel's "politics of small steps" has triggered a cultural revolution of sorts, as she pushes her country from concerns about role equity to bona fide role change, especially among men.

Since 2005, the nation united has undergone multiple institutional, cultural, and economic makeovers, resulting in new definitions of what it means to be German. Here, too, Merkel's representation of the Federal Republic has been transformative. Her first appearance on the national ministerial stage in 1990, responsible for Women and Youth, subjected her to waves of criticism and derision over her hair, her clothing, and her "humble" demeanor. Digging deeper, one could argue that the aim of these gendered assaults was to affirm the superiority and know-how of the wealthy, "masculine" Western states vis-à-vis their poor Eastern counterparts. Having subjected herself to a new hairdo, make-up, and wardrobe, Merkel's emergence as a three-time chancellor testifies to a dramatic reversal of fortunes: while younger Easterners willingly embraced a new, free-market way of life, older Westerners are now anxious about changes in their own living standards, imposed by EU enlargement and regional crisis management. Equally significant, Merkel's effectiveness on the international stage has not only rendered Germany a normal state capable of pursuing national interests but has also raised expectations that her country will assume greater global responsibility; it can no longer confine itself to the role of "good European."

My choice of policy domains grew out of the realization that new "multi-level governance" constraints, born of accelerated EU integration, could have made it easier, or harder, for Merkel to achieve her preferred outcomes. As noted earlier, the criteria one can use to judge a leader successful or not depend heavily on the issues involved, as well as on the degree of autonomy she might enjoy in a specific decision-making context. I therefore analyze Merkel's performance at four different levels. I begin with the "meta" or *historical–psychological level*, exploring this chancellor's efforts to foster a positive, united national identity (Chapter 2), as well as her efforts to "come to terms" with the country's traumatic past vis-à-vis Israel (Chapter 3). Born in 1954, Merkel is the first national leader to benefit directly from "the blessing of late birth," according her new opportunities to redefine Germany's historical responsibility toward the past and the future.[21] These chapters demonstrate Merkel's effective use of key anniversaries, historical sites, and cultural institutions, enabling her to bridge the gap between East and West interpretations of the past, both domestically and internationally. The qualitative indicator used to assess her performance at this level centers on *reconciliation*. I argue that the chancellor's success in reconciling antithetical historical legacies in these two cases derives from her socialization experiences as a pastor's daughter raised under an authoritarian regime. I contend that her willingness to speak out about her personal efforts to "come to terms" with two traumatic German pasts renders her a credible source of identification for post-Wall Easterners and Westerners, as well as for postwar Germans and Israelis.

Second, Merkel's foreign policy savvy and recognized mediator skills have helped her to balance conflicting sets of national interests at the *international level*, despite being wedged between two nuclear superpowers and one supranational actor: the United States, Russia, and the European Union (Chapters 4 and 5). Although she was in no position to control the first two players, she was perceived as very effective at this level during her first term, despite her lack of foreign policy experience. She received high praise for securing crucial support for climate-change initiatives as the G8 hostess at Heiligendamm in 2007, as well as for securing ratification of the 2009 Lisbon Treaty following the French and Dutch rejection of the EU Constitution. Her second and third terms brought new trials and tribulations at these levels. Two developments, in particular, have radically redefined the foreign policy context: Putin's increasingly aggressive stance regarding "the Near Abroad" (Crimea, Ukraine), and the ongoing Euro crisis, subjecting her to vehement attacks for refusing to bail out core debtor nations.

At this level I use *containment*, the chancellor's ability to re-establish regional stability, as a key indicator of her effectiveness. Realizing that efforts to bring Putin "back from the dark side" are futile, Merkel has done more than all of her transatlantic counterparts to keep Russia engaged in various dialogues with Europe. The chancellor's GDR upbringing, her language skills, her East-bloc travels, and her physics background supply her with a deeper understanding of Putin's multiple security dilemmas, rendering her a fit sparring partner for a sexist, authoritarian president.[22] In my judgment, Merkel's interventions in the Georgian and Ukrainian crises prevented the onset of worst-case scenarios, restoring enough stability for her to pursue dialogues in other arenas, no matter how tense or constrained they might be.

The Euro crisis case reveals that tactics and skills proving useful in one domain do not necessarily work in another. Merkel's post-1989 faith in ordo-liberal market principles did not prepare her for the Byzantine world of global banking, credit debt swaps, or massive sovereign debt. Assuming an equally assertive stance on austerity policies, she overestimated the ability of debt-plagued countries to embrace structural change, and underestimated the extent to which those states might play the old Nazi card against a strong, prosperous Germany. Chronic shortages in the GDR had taught her the importance of "living within one's means," leading her to a gendered affinity with the proverbial Swabian housewife mentioned in her speeches. While she was effective in calming German citizens and markets, her need to master complex financial data in 2008–2009 while campaigning for re-election left little time for empathizing with vulnerable groups in other countries. While she may have won the war and saved the Euro by forcing the EU to adopt her preferred structural changes, she clearly lost the public opinion battle in many quarters, giving rise to new populist parties with an anti-EU bent. Those antagonisms, in turn, undermined European solidarity in response to the 2015 refugee crisis.

Third, Merkel's commitment to migration, refugees, and human rights has required her to negotiate *a new balance between the supranational and national levels.* The standard I apply to the next two cases targets her ability to secure *fundamental policy change.* Building on citizenship reforms adopted by the Red–Green government (Chapter 6), Merkel utilized her six months as EU Council president to launch national initiatives, pushing Germany to accept itself not only as *a land of immigration* but also as a country of *proactive integration.* I would rate her as very successful at this level, although most citizens are unaware of how much she has leveraged EU developments to induce domestic reforms. Policies introduced during Merkel's first two terms, especially from 2007 to 2013, afforded a solid foundation for managing a second, post-Wall refugee influx. I argue again that her socialization as a pastor's daughter in a state that denied its people fundamental freedoms, coupled with her recollections of 1989, have shaped her principled response to waves of desperate refugees entering Europe after 2014. Despite a few ugly pockets of resistance at home, Angela Merkel has unquestionably transformed the nation united into a "welcoming culture."

Finally, I focus on energy and climate-change policies to test Merkel's skills in mediating between *the national and state levels*, reshaping *Bund–Länder relations* (Chapter 7). Her first Grand Coalition adopted two sets of federalism reforms, but these have not constrained her ability to reconcile national needs with those of sixteen diverging states to the same extent as the shift to a multi-party system, denying her a stable Bundesrat majority. I began this project based on the assumption that despite her reputation as the *Climate Chancellor*, Merkel was likely to encounter tough resistance to policy change from powerful "state-princes" intent on defending their sovereignty. I also predicted that her lack of a strong Land constituency would expose Merkel to greater partisan conflict during the conservative–liberal period (2009–2013) than seen under the Grand Coalition (2005–2009).

Enter Fukushima Daiichi in March 2011: the Law of Unanticipated Consequences granted this chancellor a unique opportunity to eliminate state opposition to an unprecedented national energy turn-around. Merkel's decision to shut down all nuclear energy plants, based on her physicist-reading of the Japanese tea-leaves, has enabled her to overcome deeply entrenched environmental versus economic interests, on the one hand, and to foster proactive "cooperative federalism," on the other. Germany is currently enjoying a job-creating export boom, based on climate-friendly technologies. Conflicts over specific energy subsidies notwithstanding, Merkel has deployed FRG strength in this arena to "upload" tougher emission standards at the EU level to the extent that they do not contravene other national interests, given its powerful automobile industry. This domain also amounts to a Merkel-driven success story.

Although she has learned a lot along the way, it still seems paradoxical that a shy, apolitical pastor's daughter from the East would prove to be "the right person at the right time, in the right place," compelling Germany to face the challenges of twenty-first-century globalization. This brings us back to sex and politics: gender and intersectionality go a long way in explaining why politicians and pundits occasionally still underestimate Angela Merkel's charisma, staying power, and "vision." The concluding chapter summarizes Merkel's most noteworthy achievements to date, before addressing the ultimate question: does gender still matter with regard to perceptions and patterns of women's leadership?

I begin with reflections on the chancellor's use of "hard" and "soft" powers (ascribed to men and women, respectively), in order to define the nature of *transformational leadership*. My aim is to transcend the stereotype that "all women lead alike." In fact, as Merkel's three terms attest, one woman may be forced to lead in different ways over the years: a lot depends on the time, the place, the structures, and the circumstances, not just on a willingness or reluctance to "play the gender card." One nonetheless discerns a high degree of normative and behavioral consistency across the policy courses she has pursued, which I summarize under the heading, "Merkel's Fifteen Laws of Power " (Chapter 8). My own feminist values lead me to argue that better policies for women are usually better policies for everyone. Although our priorities differ in some cases, Merkel's "holistic" approach suggests that our everyday orientations tend to overlap.

The next question is whether Germany's first woman chancellor has lived up to our sometimes conflicting expectations regarding descriptive and substantive gender representation. At least two cases (the Euro crisis and refugee policies) show that a specific policy choice may benefit females at home while negatively affecting women beyond the national borders. Crises, by definition, do not leave much time for collecting detailed, sex-disaggregated statistics where none existed. As a former physicist, Chancellor Merkel has introduced "implementation monitoring" schemes and data-banks that will remain in place, even when she decides to spend more time "baking plum cake" or heading some global organization.

I believe that institutions and context still matter, and that only detailed studies such as this one can help us to sort out the differences. Unless otherwise indicated, all translations are my own. The wise counsel of friends notwithstanding, I assume full responsibility for any missing data, questionable interpretations, overt value judgments, bad puns, or Teutonically long sentences the reader might encounter in the pages that follow. We now turn to consider the direct application of gender stereotypes and role expectations that plagued Angela Merkel during the first two stages of her career, prior to assuming the chancellorship.

NOTES

1. Dale Spender, *Time and Tide Wait for No Man* (London: Pandora Press, 1984), p. 201.
2. "Der Tag an dem die Wähler Amok liefen," *Die Welt*, September 16, 2007.

3. The *Ox-tour* refers to the path a would-be politician must follow, tediously plodding through lower-level positions, often starting with the party's youth organization, then moving through various communal, district, and Land-level positions before being declared fit for national office by party gatekeepers.

4. The conservative camp consists of two parties, the Christian Democratic Union (CDU) and its heavily Catholic, arch-conservative Bavarian sister, the Christian Social Union (CSU); together they are known as the Union.

5. Sirimavo Bandaranaike, Golda Meier, and Indira Gandhi were also presumed to be "transitional figures" who outlasted their male detractors.

6. Stefan Kornelius, *Angela Merkel. Die Kanzlerin und ihre Welt* (Hamburg: Hoffmann & Campe, 2013), pp. 275, 278–279.

7. Joyce Marie Mushaben, *From Post-War to Post-Wall Generations. Changing Attitudes towards the National Question and NATO in the Federal Republic of Germany* (Boulder, CO: Westview Press, 1998).

8. The late Gerd Langguth taught at Bonn University but doubled as a CDU functionary. His biography focuses more on the "abuses of communism" than on Merkel's own motives. Journalists Evelyn Roll, Mariam Lau, Margaret Heckel, and Stefan Kornelius offer more thoughtful analyses and policy considerations (see Chapter 2).

9. Sebastien Bukow and Wenke Seemann (eds.), *Die große Koalition: Regierung – Politik – Parteien* (Wiesbaden: Verlag für Sozialwissenschaften, 2010); Christoph Egle and Reimut Zohlnhöfer (eds.), *Die zweite Grosse Koalition: Eine Bilanz der Regierung Merkel 2005–2009* (Wiesbaden: Verlag für Sozialwissenschaften, 2010); also, Reimut Zohlnhöfer and Thomas Saalfeld (eds.), *Politik im Schatten der Krise: Eine Bilanz der Regierung Merkel, 2009–2013* (Wiesbaden: Springer, 2015).

10. In 2011, several US scholars produced a special issue of *German Politics*, concentrating on Merkel's first four years. See Louise Davidson-Schmich (ed.), "Gender, Intersectionality, and the Executive Branch: The Case of Angela Merkel," *German Politics*, 20(3) (2011): 325–341. A few US and UK scholars, cited in Chapter 2, initially analyzed her path to power.

11. Speaking in Bentonville, Arkansas, Bush complained on November 6, 2000: "They misunderestimated me."

12. EU Commission President Jean-Claude Juncker introduced the term "polycrisis" at the annual meeting of the Hellenic Federation of Enterprises in Athens, June 21, 2016.

13. Hajo Schumacher, *Die Zwölf Gesetze der Macht. Angela Merkels Erfolgsgeheimnisse* (Munich: Heyne, 2007), p. 25.

14. Ange-Merie Hancock, "When Multiplication Doesn't Equal Quick Addition: Examining Intersectionality as a Research Paradigm," *Perspectives on Politics*, 5(1) (2007): 67.

15. Nira Yuval-Davis, "Intersectionality and Feminist Politics," *European Journal of Women's Studies*, 13(3) (2006): 195.

16. Davidson-Schmich, "Gender, Intersectionality, and the Executive Branch."

17. Joyce Marie Mushaben, "The Best of Times, the Worst of Times: Angela Merkel, the Grand Coalition and 'Majority Rule' in Germany," *German Politics and Society*, 34(1) (2016): 1–25.
18. US gender scholars often cite four levels – formal, descriptive, substantive, symbolic – but the lines begin to blur when one assesses real-world developments.
19. Gabriele Abels, "Das 'Geschlechterdemokratiedefizit' der EU. Politische Repräsentation und Geschlecht im europäischen Mehrebenensystem," in Eva Kreisky, Sabine Lang, and Birgit Sauer (eds.), *EU. Geschlecht. Staat* (Vienna: WUV, 2001), pp. 185–202.
20. Sabine Lang, "Gender Equality in post-Unification Germany: Between GDR Legacies and EU-level Pressures," *German Politics*, forthcoming 2017.
21. Gerhard Schröder also lacked personal experience with the Second World War but joined New Leftists in charging the parental generation with Nazi collaboration.
22. Valerie Sperling, "Putin's Macho Personality Cult," *Communist and Post-Communist Studies*, 49(1) (2016): 13–23.

PART I

"THE PERSONAL IS THE POLITICAL"

Most early biographical accounts of the future chancellor mention the fact that she rarely wore GDR-typical clothing while growing up; maternal relatives in Hamburg sent regular "care packages" to Templin, giving her privileged access to blue jeans and other highly valued Western goods. Aside from one unfulfilled request for a yellow blouse (when retailers were dictating other color choices), the young Angela Krasner seemed unencumbered by high-fashion thoughts. Once she took up her post as a quantum chemistry expert in Berlin-Adlershof, her primary clothing concern was not ruining her sleeves while conducting various experiments. The overwhelming presence of male elites in both German states provided few fashion clues for women bold enough to enter the power arena prior to 1990.

Entering politics shortly before unification, Merkel experienced her first culture shock when she was indirectly advised by her boss, interim GDR premier Lothar de Maizière, to get rid of her long hippie-style skirts, baggy hand-knitted sweaters, and "Jesus sandals" before traveling to Moscow for the Two plus Four Treaty negotiations that would restore German sovereignty. For the next fifteen years she would face more public criticism over her hair and clothes than for her policy choices as a two-term minister in the Kohl cabinet. This section analyzes two fundamental "makeovers" – one physical, the other political – that set Merkel on the path to becoming Madam Chancellor. Incorporating basic biographical background, it attempts to unpack various gendered images ascribed to Merkel prior to 2005, and hints at some of the new problems of image management that awaited her, as she moved on to become "the World's Most Powerful Woman."

The Extreme Makeover of Angela Merkel: Gender, Style, and Substance

Western female candidates are all too familiar with the media's tendency to spend more time critiquing their hair, clothing, make-up, and facial expressions than explaining their policy positions in the heat of an election campaign. Both Geraldine Ferraro and Elizabeth Dole were dogged by detailed assessments of their physical appearance along the US campaign trail. The media displayed a similar obsession with the many hairdos of Hillary during her years as First Lady, but those treatments were harmless compared to the downright misogynist assaults Clinton faced during her first run for the presidency in 2008.[1] Curiously, neither Condoleezza Rice nor Elaine Cho faced much scrutiny along these lines, perhaps because reporters fear charges of racism more than complaints regarding sexism.[2]

Having followed gender themes in the American and German press since the 1980s, I would argue that the "lipstick watch" tends to be less intense in the Federal Republic for historical as well as systemic reasons.[3] For starters, women played a crucial role in literally digging a shattered Third Reich out of its own rubble, while the exercise of male-power-as-usual was circumscribed by de-Nazification and a decade of military occupation. The female politicians who helped to rebuild the nation during the 1950s and 1960s derived certain benefits from the "good mother" stereotype tied to the restoration of traditional gender roles after the war.[4] Finding their voices by way of a radical student movement in the 1960s, a new generation of women aligned themselves with second-wave feminism, joining their male counterparts in bigger battles against "the Establishment." Drawing legitimacy from the UN Decade of Women, the 1970s saw the rise of autonomous book stores, presses, and journals, allowing some equality activists to establish themselves as cool, if exceptional, "power-women."[5] Building on proportional representation and internal party quotas adopted by the Greens and Social Democrats in the 1980s, women increased their share of seats faster than journalists could invent frilly, derogatory nicknames.[6] Reinforced by a growing number of "femocrats," "velvet triangles," and positive action programs in Brussels, a new wave of gender policy experts impelled the media to accept women as a normal part of the political landscape in the 1990s.[7] By then women had crossed the 30 percent threshold in two-thirds of the EU member state parliaments, although the East European states admitted after 2004 (with two exceptions) still fall short of "critical mass."[8]

Systemic factors also play a role: German newspapers offer an array of political viewpoints, offering less space for sensationalized personality contests. Political campaigns are still publicly financed, while televised "duels" among the candidates require high levels of policy expertise, in contrast to US efforts to "stay on message." The 2009 debate between Angela Merkel and her *Gro-Ko* (short for Grand Coalition) SPD foreign minister, Frank Walter Steinmeier, was so harmonious and boring that it was labeled a "duet."[9] Comprising 37 percent of the Bundestag, female parliamentarians have learned to deploy their differences strategically, as more honest, family-friendly, and environmentally conscious consumers, although it still helps a female candidate to "look like she's 20, have a head as all-knowing as City Hall, and to work like a horse."[10] The life-style magazine *Men's Health* still urges its readers to "vote" for a Miss Bundestag at the beginning of each legislative period.[11]

Between 2001 and 2005, many journalists shifted toward gender-neutral reporting, at least partly attributable to the "Merkel Factor." Disparaged for nearly a decade as "Kohl's Girl," the young eastern physicist who served as a powerless family minister, then as a visible environmental minister, shocked the political establishment in 1999 by using the mighty *Frankfurter Allgemeine Zeitung* to knock the Unity Chancellor off his party pedestal. Assuming the role of opposition leader for the remaining Red–Green years, Merkel filled a CDU leadership vacuum long enough for editors and reporters to get used to the idea that a woman could exercise power. If there is one thing the media respect, it is power. Further factors included her lack of vanity, her skill at working behind the scenes, her patience in watching events unfold, and her ability to outlive rivals.

As Germany's first female chancellor, Angela Merkel has shattered multiple gender stereotypes. Counted among the *losers* of unification after 1990, East German women witnessed more than their fair share of unemployment, benefit cuts, and marginalization. Despite Helmut Kohl's 1991 promise that all women would "have it better than before," unity brought the re-criminalization of abortion and ended state-provided childcare.[12] As one of the few female winners, Merkel's capacity for substantive representation assumes a significance greater than the power of one. This is not to say that all of the mocking, know-it-all, or malicious descriptions of her as a "zone pigeon" (Merkel: "I didn't find that nice") have ceased. No other leader qualifying for various "most-powerful" lists has encountered so many questionable tributes; in addition to the Merkel "Barbie Doll," she has witnessed a never ending stream of before/after hairdo montages, paper-doll sets, a comic book, animated "dance" videos, a "Blazer Watch," and the inevitable pants-suit jokes. Her evening-gown appearance at the Oslo Opera House in April 2008, for instance, unleashed a wave of cleavage-commentaries, including rather offensive UK tabloid headlines, "Merkel's Weapons of Mass Destruction" and "Deutschland boober alles."[13] Over time the chancellor has learned that her best defense against sexist onslaughts is to combat them with humor. When the SIXT rental car company featured her in an ad looking like Medusa riding in a convertible (caption: "Want a new hairdo?"), she countered that her hair was standing on end because she had just read the Red–Green government's budget proposal.[14] She is also known to use her sardonic wit to put others in their place.

This chapter centers on two fundamental Merkel makeovers, one physical, the other political. Both processes evince ironic twists and turns relevant to the transformation of post-unification gender relations. Orchestrated by image consultants between 1990 and 2005, Merkel's physical transformation, in my judgment, proved less extreme than the political makeover she experienced while moving up the CDU leadership ladder at warp-speed. Managing one's political image is more difficult than adding highlights, mascara, and pastels, however. The media have assigned Merkel many disparaging monikers with strong gender undertones, implying that mostly male critics found it difficult to accept her as the real leader of a powerful nation well into her second term as chancellor. Among the more memorable labels are: "Kohl's Girl," "Joan of Arc," the "Iron Maiden," "Father-Murderer," "Angie the Sleeper," the "Sphinx," *Angela Ahnungslos* (the "Clueless"), the "Black Widow Spider," "Maggie Merkel," the *Trümmerfrau* ("Rubble Woman"),

"Deutsche Queen," "Alice in Wunderland," "Madam Europe," the "Harmony Chancellor," the "Crisis Chancellor," "Mrs. Cool," the *Alpha-Kanzlerin*, the "Power-Physicist," the "Lost Leader," "Merkiavelli," and, of course, that all-time French favorite, "Madam Non." She has also graced the covers of many publications drawing on Terminator, Muslim, Nazi, and Mother/Mommy themes. Although most of these were coined in an effort to downplay Merkel's strength as a female leader, the specific labels chosen suggest just the opposite.

STAGE ONE: THE EARLY YEARS OR "TOTO, I'VE A FEELING WE'RE NOT IN TEMPLIN ANYMORE"

Born on July 17, 1954 in Hamburg (West Germany), Angela Dorothea Kasner was the daughter of a Lutheran pastor who voluntarily relocated to the East shortly before the Victorious Powers ended military occupation. Despite strong reservations, her mother Herlind, from Danzig, joined East Berliner Horst Kasner in the small village of Quitzow eight weeks later.[15] After moving to Templin, the Kasners supplemented family food rations with goats, chickens, and a vegetable garden. The parsonage sat next to Waldhof, a center housing persons with various disabilities; Angela thus learned about "difference" at an early age. Her father conducted special seminars for theologians, known for their open dialogue despite his curiously close ties with key state officials. Supplied with clothing and food packages from the West, Angela grew up in a politically engaged household that "gave the children space."[16] Although her husband's profession barred Herlind from teaching English and Latin in state schools, Angela belonged to an Eastern baby boom that acquired political consciousness just as the GDR began subsidizing "women-friendly" benefits, hoping to raise birth rates and increase female employment simultaneously, to counter postwar labor shortages.

Despite her father's engagement with "the Church in Socialism," Angela's childhood was uneventful; a school friend later described her as an early *CdU* (Club of the Unkissed) member. She participated in the Young Pioneers but opted for Lutheran confirmation over a state-sponsored Youth Dedication ceremony. Two years younger than the other contestants, she came in third during her first Russian-language "Olympics," taking first place the following year; her prize was a trip to Moscow, where she bought her first Beatles album and was asked about "reunification" – around the time of *Ostpolitik*. She would later hitch-hike through southern Russia, Armenia, Georgia, and Azerbaijan; she practiced English by reading the *Morning Star*, a communist newspaper from the UK. Spending time with her grandmother in Berlin, she met American, Bulgarian, and British tourists in various museums, "telling them about the GDR." Though she saw herself as apolitical, she memorized the names of West German cabinet members. She was vacationing in Czechoslovakia with her family when the Prague Spring erupted: thirty years later she would engage in acrimonious debate with Green minister Joschka Fischer over the consequences of "1968." Despite her father's job, her own church involvement and a close-call with school officials over a provocative class presentation (involving a poem about a wall), Kasner completed her *Abitur* with high marks in 1973.[17]

Majoring in physics at Leipzig University, Angela served as campus "cultural secretary" for the Free German Youth (FDJ) but later insisted that she had avoided *Stasi* recruitment by declaring she could not keep secrets.[18] In 1976, she moved in with fellow student Ulrich Merkel, whom she had met during a 1974 student trip to Leningrad and Moscow; they married in Templin in 1977, aged 23, hoping to get jobs in the same city. She landed a privileged research assistant slot at the Central Institute for Physical Chemistry (GDR Academy of Sciences) in 1978 but left Ulrich a few years later, illegally occupying an abandoned apartment in Prenzlauer Berg. Divorced by 1982, she completed her doctorate in 1986. She joked later that she received a lousy grade on the Marxist–Leninist thesis required as part of her doctoral exam because her essay on class relations between workers and peasants put "too much emphasis on the peasants." Having once taken 45 minutes to jump off a 3-meter diving board to pass a school swimming test, just as the class bell rang, she admits that she was never particularly courageous. Her fear of dogs would return to haunt her later.

Existing Merkel biographies stress her Eastern Protestant upbringing more than her sex, a curious tribute to the official *equal rights stance* characterizing GDR gender relations. Her Prussian sense of duty, her Protestant work ethic, and her fascination with Marie Curie helped her to make it as a female scientist in a man's world; her political role model is Catherine the Great of Russia. Conceding that she had avoided dissident groups prior to 1989, Merkel deflected questions regarding her participation in regime-friendly associations like the FDJ through the 1990s. Addressing Western audiences, she often referred to her mother's promise that when the Wall fell, they would "go eat oysters at Kempinski's," a five-star hotel in West Berlin. When news spread that checkpoints had opened on November 9, she kept her usual Monday-night sauna appointment with a friend, before crossing the border at Bornholmerstrasse later that evening. As chancellor she stresses Westerners' lack of understanding for the lives of Easterners, recognizing that her family circumstances had given her the luxury of not having to identify with the state: "I never felt that the GDR was my natural home ... but I always made use of the opportunities."[19]

Angela's political engagement commenced with meetings involving religious activists in summer 1989. After the Wall collapsed, she joined *Democratic Awakening* (DA), a group that initially included Pastor Rainer Eppelmann, theologian Edelbert Richter, Church Synod member Erhart Neubert, and lawyer Wolfgang Schnur. DA advocated constitutional reform, ecological renewal, and a new European peace order; it did not call for dissolution of the socialist state. By November 1989, it had more than 10,000 members. A right–left split led author Daniela Dahn, pastor Friedrich Schorlemmer, and other progressives to leave the association; it was quickly absorbed by the *Alliance for Germany*, a surrogate for the East-CDU that had collaborated with the Socialist Unity Party (SED) by way of the National Front. Merkel's initial contribution to DA involved assembling computers and fax machines generously supplied by Westerners, pushing to garner future electoral support. Impressed by her organizational skills, Schnur elevated her to the post of press secretary. The DA secured only four mandates in the first free elections of March 1990, right after Schnur had been outed as a Stasi informant.

Merkel, then 35, became deputy spokesperson for Lothar de Maizière's interim CDU government; she then worked briefly at the Federal Press and Information Office, worried that she would not qualify for a permanent civil service job due to high blood pressure. I interviewed her on a very hot June 12, 1990. Her brown hair was short, her attire nondescript, and her answers to my questions brief, due to very loud traffic outside and a constantly ringing telephone. Stressing that she had never been "political," she explicitly supported rights/benefits enjoyed by GDR women, including legal abortion. The surprising political savvy she displayed over the next ten years, one pundit noted later, derived from a reservoir of energy "that she had managed to save up through 35 boring years in the GDR, before she was cast into the typhoon of reunification, and then spun and hurled to the top."[20] The image of Dorothy being propelled by a tornado from Kansas to Oz comes to mind.

STAGE TWO: "KOHL'S GIRL"
OR "GUT GEMACHT, ANGELA!"

The fall of the Wall played a seminal role in the collapse of socialist regimes, but instead of evoking deep feelings of sisterly solidarity, the unification process precipitated disillusionment, frustration, and very hard feelings between GDR and FRG feminists.[21] Long excluded from positions of political responsibility for the Fatherland, German women were ill-prepared for a coming to terms with two dictatorial pasts, much less with each other, having been socialized under opposite ideological paradigms for forty years.[22]

Merkel was initially mentored by Easterner Gunther Krause, a leading unification treaty negotiator, who charged her with manipulating a state election after corruption charges forced him to resign as Minister of Transportation. Elected to the Bundestag by a conservative landslide in December 1990, the new parliamentarian from Mecklenburg-Vorpommern was whisked off to the ball as a member of the Kohl cabinet. As the plain but unknown girl-next-door who could also fill more than one CDU "quota," the 36-year-old divorcee became the Minister for Women and Youth, not exactly areas of expertise for a childless physicist. After Kohl's ostensible crown prince, Wolfgang Schäuble, was partially paralyzed by a would-be assassin in October 1990, Merkel assumed the CDU Deputy-Chair position in 1991. The rising star from the East also took on the job of CDU-chair in Mecklenburg-Vorpommern as of 1993.

As an Easterner, Merkel had learned early on to avoid conflict with the state, and to keep critical thoughts to herself; she stresses, "It is a great advantage . . . that one learned to keep quiet. That was a survival strategy then. It still is."[23] Westerners, by contrast, have few qualms about directly confronting their opponents in ways that East citizens perceived as arrogant or offensive. Merkel's definition of perseverance and assertiveness includes cooperation and compromise. She perceived the self-serving, tough-guy behavior of Western politicians as "unpleasant," noting that politics should be about service; she prefers "calm analytical men who keep their distance."[24]

Ironically, a young woman who had rarely worn GDR clothing, thanks to care packages from Western relatives, was soon harshly criticized regarding her attire. More concerned about her lack of political experience, Merkel was shocked by the media's obsession with her looks throughout the 1990s. As Monika Maron noted at the time, "West women have styles, East women have hair."[25] In 1992, she complained that journalists "idiotically judge any politician who wants to bring a little order into the country according to external appearances. It is completely irrelevant whether or not I am wearing lipstick."[26] GDR prime minister Lothar de Maizière had been the first to have a co-worker advise his young press secretary to "get rid of the Jesus sandals" and buy a few outfits befitting her role before he took her to Moscow for the Two plus Four negotiations.[27] Kohl assigned his wife and his secretary the same task before his new Minister for Women and Youth accompanied him to meet with Ronald Reagan in California.

Uncomfortable with the feminist label, Merkel learned a great deal about Western women's movements while recovering from a broken leg in 1992, a "lucky break" that provided her with many visitors, time to read, and a chance to grasp the conflicting gender expectations invoked by her appointment. Many older women comprising the CDU/CSU caucus found it hard to accept her approach to women's policies: "Many had plowed through and struggled for 10, 15 years, then German unification came and suddenly I'm sitting in the armchair as the Women's Minister." Not that party men were any more supportive: when she tried to outlaw sexual harassment at the workplace and to fill half of all civil service positions with women (as foreseen by the unification treaty), CSU Carl-Dieter Spranger told Merkel "You know, girl, if I didn't find you so nice, I wouldn't vote for any of this rubbish."[28]

Over time she did embrace policies demanded by FRG feminists, including an Equal Rights Law, but she was sooner motivated by GDR experiences where women "worried most about very practical things," such as a legal right to nursery and kindergarten places (subsequent family-friendly reforms were initiated in response to EU mandates).[29] Because abortion was the one issue that threatened to stop unification dead in its tracks, Kohl postponed a final decision for two years but hoped that Merkel's presence in the conservative cabinet might reframe the debate. Her compatriots expected her to lobby on behalf of Eastern women suddenly facing mass unemployment, the loss of subsidized childcare, and other *socialist achievements*. Surveys show that 69 percent of GDR women and 57 percent of FRG women supported legal abortion in 1990; the ratio was 79 percent to 71 percent among those aged 18–29.[30] Various draft proposals triggered vehement debates within the party. "The pressure from all sides, also the public pressure, was so strong that at the end I hardly knew what I wanted myself," Merkel declared; "in the Bundestag I made myself speak out in favor of the CDU proposal, though in one important point it did not correspond with my position."[31]

Despite her reluctance to ban the procedure after twenty years of legal abortion in the GDR, the Women's Minister toed the party line in 1992. The *Leipziger Zeitung* carried a front-page photo of Kohl patting her hand after the vote, with the caption: "Good job, Angela." She nonetheless refused to join hardliners who appealed to the Constitutional Court to overturn the "tri-partisan law" warranting women's right to choose. Abortion was judged "illegal but unpunishable" in 1993.[32] Merkel was soon replaced by a rare practicing Catholic from Thüringen, Claudia Nolde, who was only 24 and radically opposed to any abortion exemptions. She told me in a June 1990 interview that her husband was staying at home with their children while she pursued politics.

Merkel initially "wanted nothing to do with quotas," which she saw as "degrading and defamatory" but did vote for a CDU "quorum" after seeing the barriers women faced in her own party. Her rapid ascent up the party ladder (in her words: "because they needed a woman") rendered her a "de-territorialized female-token" for the party as a whole: women accounted for only 44 of the 319 Bundestag conservatives in 1990.[33] Her conversations with Herlinde Koelbl reveal that Merkel did reflect on her special status in a man's world. Beyond lacking time to bake *Pflaumenkuchen* (plum cake), praising her own potato soup, and asserting that marriage would not change her long-term relationship, she admitted that having a child would have forced her to give up politics.[34] The fact that she was married and divorced at a young, GDR-typical age does not appear in her official CDU biography. Archbishop Joachim Meisner's denunciation of her "wild" cohabitation, along with pressure from conservative hardliners, induced her to wed her partner of seventeen years, chemistry professor Joachim Sauer, in December 1998, prior to becoming CDU General-Secretary. Former pastor Joachim Gauck faced few pressures regarding his unsanctified relationship with Daniela Schadt when he became federal president in 2012.[35]

Ostensibly a lateral move, Merkel's next position as Minister for the Environment, Nature Protection and Reactor Safety at least fell within her area of expertise. She assumed control of a traditionally male policy domain from 1994 to 1998, although many of its core functions were soon transferred to the Science and Technology Ministry. Her predecessor, Klaus Töpfer, had been forced out for sharing safety concerns voiced by anti-nuclear energy protesters. Merkel immediately fired an arrogant state secretary who claimed she "would need his help," giving rise to charges that she was a "hardliner who suddenly strikes out" at staff, coupled with assertions that, as an Easterner, she "lacked experience with democracy." New gender challenges surfaced, despite her physics background: "Many thought because I was a woman I didn't know what I was talking about ... since I lacked a deep male voice and a big physique."[36]

Her effort to introduce packaging regulations and ozone limits engendered hostility on all sides: "The states were against me, Cabinet members thought it wasn't important, the Bundestag opposed me, the industrialists thought they knew it all, the EU and the anti-trust agency clashed, and in case of other doubts, there was the Constitutional Court." Pushed to tears during a cabinet meeting over her proposed Ozone Law, she turned it to her advantage: "They weren't used to me having an emotional outbreak since I didn't shout like the men ... but it helped. I probably wouldn't have gotten a majority without it."[37]

Within a year, the Environmental Minister was entangled in a major scandal over the transport of leaking nuclear waste containers. Although her security detail advised against it, she won grudging respect for her willingness to visit Gorleben (a proposed storage site) to debate with protestors. She had her first run-in with Gerhard Schröder, who later tried to deny her the chancellorship; governing Lower Saxony, he invited her to meet over the storage issue, then immediately leaked their discussion. She apprised Koelbl: "I told him that one day I would corner him in the same way. I will need some time, but one day it will happen. I'm already looking forward to it." In fact, she managed to "kick him in the shins" in 1997 by finding a way to pass the Nuclear Law without Länder consent. Schröder, she noted, "just can't stand it when a woman, in particular, manages to ruin his game. He's not very good at accepting failure ..."[38] She did give him credit for working with her on car recycling and packaging regulations later on.

Merkel's second ministerial portfolio allowed her to go global on environmental issues. In spring 1995, she hosted delegates from 170 countries at the first UN Climate Summit in Berlin, which she describes as the highpoint of her time in Kohl's cabinet. Her staying power was all the more remarkable, given that her first eight years involved the two ministries most conservatives loved to hate, covering areas in which "the public is way ahead of the politicians": gender rights and climate change. Though pundits continued to mock her modest demeanor and dull attire, Merkel's talk-show appearances attested to her rapid learning curve regarding Western politicking. Her Mecklenburg-Vorpommern constituents began to complain that they saw her more often in Bavarian beer gardens on the nightly news than at constituency events in Rostock, chairing the state CDU.

Commenting on a few humiliating experiences of her earlier years, Merkel claimed to be "sometimes irritated, sometimes amused" by the label "Kohl's Girl": "I became what I am because of him, had to learn to stand my ground ... sometimes with a fast-beating heart ... I can easily say thank you." More frustrating was the fact that "half of the German press feels constantly obliged to evaluate my haircut ... to vent their snarkiness. I used to think this was because I am a woman, but I have come to see it as an *Ossi* (Easterner)-syndrome. They make fun of Thierse [Bundestag president] due to his beard and clothes, and because he lives in Prenzlauer Berg."[39]

By 1997, Merkel realized that "the more I take on this political role, the more I change as a private person. I am no longer who I used to be."[40] Her apprenticeship ended abruptly in September 1998 when the conservative–liberal coalition was forced into opposition for the first time since 1982. Her appointment as CDU General-Secretary at age 45 coincided with breaking news of a campaign finance scandal implicating Kohl's inner circle. By late 1999, Angela would emerge as the CDU's dominant standard bearer, becoming its parliamentary-caucus chair at 48. Adding color and accessories to her wardrobe would not stop her rivals from inventing further gendered labels with darker overtones, for example, the "Black Widow," the "King-Killer," and "Merkiavelli."

STAGE THREE: CHALLENGING THE OLD BOYS AND THE "ANDES PACT"

Neither her sex, her Eastern roots, nor her physics training guided the next stage of Merkel's career, but rather her "humble" Protestant ethics. As the first Easterner to secure the CDU's second highest position, she over-estimated "how far unity had come": she remained a sample of one. The new General-Secretary faced the glaring spotlights when her patriarchal mentor refused to admit culpability and reveal the names of secret contributors; his presumed successor, Schäuble, had also accepted funds for a Swiss account transfer before the Wall fell. Shocked by these revelations, Merkel broke with Kohl through an open letter to the *Frankfurter Allgemeine Zeitung* on December 22, 1999, urging him to make room for a new generation of leaders. Impressed with her courage, party members elected her national Party Chair in April 2000.

By 2002, Merkel had not only become the "Mistress of Spin" who visited one of Berlin's top hair salons run by Udo Walz; she also enjoyed significant support among CDU voters, based on regional conferences and membership surveys she initiated to renew the party, to compensate for her lack of a strong state base. Still the insults continued; men in her own party called her *die Ossi-Biene mit der Pokermiene* ("the East-bee with the poker-face") and *die Zuckerpuppe aus der Schwarzgeldtruppe* ("the sugar doll of the dirty-money gang").[41] Although her position should have automatically entitled her to seek the chancellorship, younger male rivals rallied in support of Bavaria's old-boy minister-president, Edmund Stoiber (CSU). Under the heavy influence of Chevas Regal, a young group of ambitious CDU males calling themselves the "Andes Pact" had agreed on a flight en route to Santiago, Chile, never to rival each other for key party positions.[42] A dozen up-and-coming conservatives, including Christian Wulff (Lower Saxony), Friedbert Pflüger (Berlin), Jürgen Rüttgers (North Rhine-Westphalia), and Roland Koch (Hesse) conspired to block her candidacy in 2002. Merkel outwitted them by undertaking a secret trip to Stoiber's home in Bavaria for Sunday breakfast, to "approve" his candidacy in exchange for leadership concessions. Stoiber's uncanny ability to offend women (mixing up their names during TV talk-shows) and Easterners (referring to them as "dumb calves choosing their own butchers") turned his national campaign into a catastrophe. This cleared the way for Merkel to pursue the chancellorship three years later, when Schröder called for early elections.

Politics, Merkel discovered, "is a bit like playing sink-the-ships. When I hit one, it's really great."[43] By 2004, she had out-maneuvered Kohl, Schäuble, Stoiber, and Friedrich Merz, and outlasted popular state leaders like "King Kurt" Biedenkopf (Saxony), Manfred Stolpe (Brandenburg), and Bernhard Vogel (Thuringia). Eastern dissidents, actively courted to testify against the repressive "SED dictatorship" in the early 1990s, had also vanished from the CDU scene, for example, Gerd and Ingrid Poppe, Vera Langsfeld, Erhart Neubert, and Angelika Barber. Mirroring the GDR slogan *überholen ohne einzuholen* ("overtaking without catching up"), Merkel bypassed pastors-turned-politicians like Rainer Eppelmann, Wolfgang Thierse, Marcus Meckel, and Hans Misselwitz, who continued to stress the flailing Eastern economy a decade after unity. The only other GDR carry-over to evince similar staying-power is Joachim Gauck, who became federal president in 2012.

Rather than try to beat the collusive Andes Pact head-on, Merkel used the next few years to co-opt individuals like Volker Kauder, Ronald Pofalla, and Peter Altmaier; the rest fell on their swords in the wake of self-induced scandals. Wulff, for example, was forced to resign the federal presidency (secured with Merkel's support) for having taken questionable personal loans while governing Niedersachsen. Pflüger, Röttgen, and Oettinger all lost key Land elections, while Koch and Rüttgers fell prey to state scandals. One *Spiegel* reporter opined, "Never before has a woman in Germany had as much political power as Angela Merkel. For many Westerners the CDU-boss from the East is still eerie; her promoters are amazed as to how skillfully she wins over or uses people for her own purposes." Another writing for *Die Zeit* observed: "Many wonder now, how Angela Merkel was able to assert herself so well in the men-and-power party CDU. I don't wonder. Anyone able to live through Honecker's power, could also deal with Kohl, and with Stoiber in any case."[44] When a sighing Michael Glos (CSU) asked, "Oh, Angela ... who will be your next victim?," she replied: "What should I do, when there are only men in politics? Men are constantly murdering men."[45]

STAGE FOUR: ELECTIONS AS A POWDER-PUFF DERBY

After flirting very briefly with neo-liberalism at the 2003 Leipzig CDU party congress (quickly rejected by the masses), Merkel mastered the discourse of tax cuts, family values, and castigating the Red–Green government for *its* failure to create jobs in the East – something Kohl had not accomplished in eight years. She turned 50 in 2004 but rather than invite 1,000 party stalwarts to the usual champagne and appetizer reception, she hauled them into the CDU's headquarters for a guest lecture by a German neuroscientist, Wolf Singer, on "the functions of the brain as an example of a self-organized system." That year also marked the start of her dramatic physical makeover, precipitated more by hopes of sharpening her image for a really big election than by a post-estrogen urge to "look great for her age."

In summer 2005, Angela Merkel became the first woman in postwar Germany to seek the chancellorship. A new haircut, highlights, make-up, and pastels gave her a "softer, more sophisticated look," but she showed no interest in "running as a woman" even when her spin-team labeled her

Angie, at least until the Rolling Stones threatened to sue over use of their song in campaign ads.[46] Although the CDU is known as the "black" party, Merkel's managers used orange to market their candidate (blue would have been more flattering). I pointed out during a discussion at the CDU's Berlin headquarters that orange was a politically loaded color, suggesting the problematic Ukrainian revolution, unrequited soccer love in the Netherlands, "the Troubles" in Northern Ireland, and a high state of alarm at the Department of Homeland Security, but our speaker was too young to see the connections. That, in itself, signified that Merkel was capable of mobilizing a new generation. Prior to campaigning, she had asked Swabian hardliner Georg Brunnhuber, "Am I conservative enough for all of you in the South?" He responded: "Forget that. We are already conservative enough on our own. You should see to it that our daughters stick with us." That was the deal.[47]

Merkel's handlers pursued a gender-neutral campaign, not an easy feat when the candidate is the proverbial pink elephant in the china shop, about to crash through the glass ceiling of patriarchal power in a country of 81 million – blame the mixed metaphors on the chaos of the times. One surprising endorsement came from Western *Über-Feminist*, Alice Schwarzer. As the first campaign to utilize the Internet, this one produced mixed results: one video labeled Merkel *Die Kandidatin*, followed by the question: *Kann die dat?* ("Can she do it?"); Schröder appeared under the rubric, *Der Kanzler*, followed by another play on words: *Der Kanz!* ("He can!").

While the media focused on her sex, voters worried about Schröder's privatized pension scheme (*Riester Rente*) and tough labor market reforms (Hartz IV) that challenged job security and introduced low-wage jobs. Surviving Andes Pact rivals recognized the need for the fundamental reforms Merkel advocated but viewed her as a placeholder until one of their own could position himself for higher office. The vote tallies reported at 6 pm on September 18, 2005 rendered the outcome far from clear. Both the 2005 and 2009 elections raised constitutional questions regarding a complex system of "overhanging mandates" that might be reallocated to ensure a Bundestag majority. The results were so close that the *Bild Zeitung* featured half-page, upside-down images of each candidate as the "winner" on page one. Schröder's aggressive, alpha-male TV performance that evening (Elephant Round) featuring both candidates united CDU/CSU stalwarts behind Merkel.[48] Stoiber and others immediately inferred that her powers would be limited, however, once the CDU and SPD agreed on terms for a Grand Coalition. The lady-in-waiting replied: "The constitutional guideline powers [Art. 65 GG] also apply to a female chancellor."

At age 51, Merkel not only became Germany's first woman leader, but also its youngest. Within days, *Die Zeit* featured a front-page photograph of a serious-looking leader crossing a big stage, wearing a black pant-suit: gone was the smiling, blonde-haired, blue-eyed, pastel image. My first reaction was that instead of celebrating Merkel as their first woman chancellor, conservative elites had decided to present her as an *honorary man*. By the end of her second term, the stereotypical image of women as an exception to the rule had yielded to their acceptance as real players in the power-politics game. Ministers Ursula von der Leyen, Ulla Schmidt, and Annette Schavan, to name a few, have contributed to real change in the reception of female politicians. Significant differences with respect to their family status, religious beliefs, professional training, and regional roots have impelled reporters to concentrate on women's policy priorities and subject competence, despite a few left-over references to their personal lives or clothing.[49] By October 2010, the *Frankfurter Allgemeine Zeitung* was speculating again about "the end of Merkel's career," predicting that her young, charismatic CSU Defense Minister would become the next chancellor candidate.[50] Within two months Karl-Theodor zu Guttenberg would be forced to resign, following revelations that he had plagiarized parts of his dissertation. As of this writing, no other major CDU rivals are on the horizon.

While most of the earlier gender monikers have faded into oblivion, the image of *Mutti Merkel* ("Mommy") has prevailed, although its meaning has shifted dramatically since 2005. CSU minister Michael Glos first used the term to discredit her as a frumpy yet overly solicitous GDR figure; his characterization was quite at odds with the economically independent working mothers in the East who had out-(re)produced their stay-at-home counterparts in Bavaria. Critics on both sides used to it attack her economic policies. The initial media images bordered on the obscene, featuring Merkel nursing querulous politicians like the Kaczyński brothers in Poland.[51] During the 2014 World Cup soccer games in Rio, it took on positive "mother of the nation" connotations (*Muttivierung der Mannschaft*). At the peak of the 2015 refugee crisis, Merkel was featured as a political Mother Teresa on the cover of *Der Spiegel* (September 18, 2015). She has learned to grin and bear it.

Nearing the end of her third term, Angela Merkel remains an intriguing female politician, despite her reluctance to view herself as such. She has extended her grip on power, paradoxically, not by disaggregating *the personal* and *the political*, the prerogative of male politicians but by frequently drawing on her GDR experiences to justify major policy turn-arounds. Through it all she has managed to keep her private life amazingly private, although she is occasionally spotted at a local discount grocery store in *Stadt-Mitte* or at the Chinese restaurant close to her unpretentious apartment. We now consider a few ways in which Merkel has contributed to the descriptive, substantive, and transformative representation of women in united Germany, irrespective of her intentions.

PRESENTING AND REPRESENTING WOMEN
IN POLITICS: THE POWER OF PANT-SUITS

It is the fate of every women who has ever been the first to achieve something to be compared with other "firsts," leading earlier pundits to label the chancellor "Maggie Merkel" during her first term. Although both were trained as natural scientists, identified with conservative parties, and enjoyed special status as the first women to lead G7 countries, Merkel rejects direct comparisons with her British counterpart; she has never ascribed to unfettered capitalism or indignant Euroskepticism. The institutional parameters defining each woman's ability to exercise power also differ significantly: Thatcher controlled a first-past-the-post, unitary government, domi-nated by the House of Commons. Merkel has to secure the approval of two federal chambers based on proportional representation, one of which (the Bundesrat) is subject to asynchronous elections and shift-ing coalitions. She is further constrained by a powerful Constitutional Court. What nonetheless binds these women is the fact that Thatcher and Merkel drew on personal, albeit different, gender resources in their efforts to swim against an often misogynist media tide. Both have fundamentally transformed the "postwar order" in their respective countries.

As the UK's first female prime minister, Margaret Thatcher was never accused of being a weak, visionless leader, even by those who vehemently opposed her policies. Dubbed the Iron Lady, she was forced out of power after eleven years, having served longer than any prime minister since 1945. For Thatcher, class concerns trumped gender: she took diction lessons at an early age to secure a proper accent, fearful that being tutored by a female Nobel Prize winner and completing a chemistry degree from Oxford were insufficient to qualify her for UK politics. Thatcher dressed impeccably at all times, even changing into a new outfit immediately after the attack on her life at Brighton, for example, so that she would appear to be in charge, rather than look like a "victim," during her first remarks to the press.[52] It is unclear as of this writing how the chancellor will get along with Theresa May, another pastor's daughter, as the Brexit negotiations proceed.

Merkel embodies *intersectionality* to a degree not seen among most female leaders. Attempting to understand her leadership style and motives in varying policy domains is comparable to peering into a kaleidoscope: the colors remain the same, but the pattern is always different, depending on which earlier experiences she draws upon to shape her decision-making processes. "Class struggle" ceased to be an issue the day the state of workers and peasants collapsed. Unlike Thatcher, who insisted "there is no such thing as society," Merkel uses inclusive language and, at times, pension increases to coincide with key elections. When it comes to German–Israeli relations, the pastor's daughter takes the lead, pursuing lessons of reconciliation and forgiveness, although her GDR experiences lend support to human rights issues involving Palestinians. Under the Eastern gender regime, she accepted policies like subsidized childcare as a natural part of paid female employment. Her training as a physicist drove her to abandon nuclear energy after Fukushima, just as her data-driven analysis causes her to link Germany's imminent demographic crisis to integration projects for youth of migrant descent. The Euro crisis brings out her typical German preference for *ordered liberalism* blended with social protection policies. Her private baking activities lead her to stir in the favorite ingredient of every Swabian *Hausfrau*, "living within one's means."

Descriptive representation pertains to those traits that allow members of a particular group to recognize a candidate as someone who embodies their specific needs and interests. At the national executive level, women's strong presence in the Red–Green government (50 percent in 2004) granted Merkel a legitimacy in the Grand Coalition she might not otherwise have enjoyed, lonely as it is at the top of her own party. Her three cabinets have held at least 40 percent women (fluctuating with departures). Women's share of Bundestag seats has risen as well, despite occasional declines when conservatives and liberals prevail (Chapter 8): until Merkel and von der Leyen entered the arena, neither of those parties accepted gender-friendly policies.[53]

But this raises a further question: to what extent have Merkel's life experiences rendered her an effective role model for other women aspiring to politics? Does she evince typically gendered personal traits and skills, despite her exceptional path to power? Regarding her family status, the chancellor resembles Western women: she was raised by a stay-at-home mom, true of only 10 percent of GDR females. Among her Eastern cohorts, 90 percent were mothers, averaging two children by their late twenties; only 60 percent of the Western Baby Boomers gave birth, usually producing fewer offspring at older ages.[54] Prior to 2000, women were more likely to enter politics either as widows, divorcees, or after their children were grown.

Her physicist background makes Angela Merkel a rarity in both worlds, although Eastern women were more likely than Western females to pursue mathematics and natural science careers, due to a shortage of postwar men. She is also exceptional in that she was religiously engaged in a country dominated by atheists. By 1989, only 3 percent of GDR residents were practicing Christians; 70 percent of Eastern youth are non-believers. Despite her father's role in supplying a forum (Weißenseer Circle) for system-critical theologians, Merkel secured a university degree, a privilege denied to many clerical offspring. More typical was her earlier decision to create an apolitical niche for herself, guaranteeing her a relatively comfortable GDR life. While former dissidents and human rights activists also tried to take advantage of new political opportunity structures after 1990, they proved less capable of adapting to Western elite ways.

There is limited evidence that the female chief executive has dramatically increased descriptive representation at the national level beyond the boundaries of her own cabinet. But we should not underestimate the longer-term impact of her twelve-year rule. Journalists with privileged access highlight the strong women comprising her inner circle, who are changing the culture of the Federal Chancellor's Office (Chapter 8). Nor should we underestimate Merkel's appointments of von der Leyen as the first female defense minister and Aydan Özogu as the first federal integration commissioner of migrant descent.

Substantive representation centers on a leader's ability to promote women's interests in a parliamentary democratic sense. Prior to 2005, Merkel made no effort to champion either Eastern or gender causes. Emphasizing freedom and personal responsibility, she distanced herself from delegates in her own party calling for special measures (*Aufbau Ost*) to counter the collapse of the Eastern economy. Her performance as Minister of Women disappointed Western CDU, SPD, and Green activists alike, although many rallied to support her later on. Easterners construed her refusal to actively defend legal abortion based on the right to choose (in contrast to Bismarckian "indicators") as an outright betrayal. Of course, her lack of experience and inability to put up a real fight is exactly why Kohl chose her for this post; the responsibility for drafting that legislation was turned over to other ministries headed by female hardliners at the outset.

Merkel freely admits that she has changed a great deal since 1990, physically as well as politically. Power will do that to a girl. During a ceremony marking the twentieth anniversary of the Women's Ministry, she noted that while she had "gladly" spoken out against quotas at first, she understood by the time she became chancellor that without a 25 percent CDU quorum, she "would not have made it in." As a physicist, she stressed, "I thought about everything but not about the fact that I was a woman. The longer I have been in politics, the more I become conscious of the significance of this topic."[55]

Merkel recalled her surprised relief when CSU parliamentarian Michaela Schreyer advised her in the early 1990s, "you know, you can wear pant-suits." Although no formal dress code exists, parliamentarians are expected to "preserve the dignity and honor" of the Bundestag. The seventeen men from Bavaria who showed up in Lederhosen in 1949 were not reprimanded for violating the parliamentary dress code; by the 1950s, however, men were required to replace their suspenders with belts. The first time a woman – Lenelotte von Bothmer, a Social Democratic mother of six – dared in 1970 to address the Bundestag wearing a beige pant-suit, the *Hannoversche Alllgemeine* headline quoted an outraged parliamentarian: "You are a dishonored dame."[56] Conservatives later railed against the tennis shoes Joschka Fischer wore the day he was sworn in as foreign minister; the Greens, in turn, raised complaints when a CSU parliamentarian appeared at the podium in a traditional, cleavage-exposing Bavarian dirndl.[57]

Formerly indifferent to fashion, Merkel has joined an elite club known as the "Sisterhood of the Traveling Pantsuits," but younger men who ought to know better still use sex stereotyping to put powerful women in their place. Replacing gay Vice-Chancellor Guido Westerwelle in Merkel's second cabinet, FDP Minister Philipp Rösler, an adoptee born in Vietnam in 1973, was no stranger to prejudice. Yet in 2010, he joked at the Gillamoos-Volksfest in Bavaria that his coalition boss "is also now available as a Barbie Doll . . . It costs 300 Euros. That is, the doll only cost 20 Euros. But the 40 pant-suits are really expensive."[58] He said nothing about the exploding costs of healthcare, for which he was responsible. For the record: €70 does not seem like a lot to pay for a pant-suit worn by the World's Most Powerful Woman.

The Euro crisis, war in Syria, the rise of ISIS, and the NSA phone-tapping scandal notwithstanding, bloggers and fashionistas used Merkel's sixtieth birthday to quantify, color-code, and otherwise analyze her "designer blazer" collection, along with her "rules" for when to wear what.[59] These self-appointed experts noted she never wears red when negotiating with the SPD; blue is best for state visits; pink, orange, or yellow conveys optimism to the public. Green is her favorite color, perhaps explaining her commitment to a national energy turn-around. Whether her preference for three-button models ("76 percent of the time") is indicative of her support for the EU Troika's hardline approach to the Greek bailout is open to debate. While reports on high-level meetings between Chancellor Merkel and Secretary of State Hillary Clinton stressed their necklaces, black slacks, practical shoes, and compatible colors ("Merkel in lilac, Hillary in cornflower-blue"), their descriptions of each other emphasize intelligence, determination, and honesty.[60] During her 2016 campaign, Clinton described Merkel as her favorite world leader, stressing her strong leadership, steadiness, and bravery in the face of multiple crises.[61]

Rather than go shopping on her sixtieth birthday in 2014, the chancellor invited her compatriots to a lecture by historian Jürgen Osterhammel, outlining the ways in which Europe and Asia perceived each other during the nineteenth century, another era of global change. She spent her vacation reading the work of Russian economist Nikolai Kondratieff, who reflected in the 1920s on technological innovations and long-term economic cycles (K-waves), resulting in 40–60-year cycles of high and low growth.[62] Perhaps it is her advancing age, or her ability to master complex economic data, as demonstrated during the 2008 financial meltdown, that led major media outlets to stop commenting on her hair during the 2013 campaign. Her handlers nonetheless promoted her "softer" side, for example, comments on her husband's desire for more "cake crumbles" when she bakes, and reflecting on her "private life" in a *BRIGITTA* interview.[63] The truth is: traditional gender stereotypes just do not fit a woman with this kind of staying power.

Empirical studies attest that Merkel's three terms as chancellor have induced changes in media culture vis-à-vis female politicians; few reporters comment on their appearance.[64] The "Chancellor bonus," coupled with her popularity, guarantees Merkel more substantive media coverage than most politicians. She has largely escaped the double bind that requires women to display compassion, patience, and caring, only to be deemed unfit for deviating from male-normed qualities like determination, assertiveness, or independence. Critics still charge that Angela Merkel lacks charisma and vision, a theme to which we return in later chapters.

Easterner Jana Hensel was only 13 years old when the Wall fell, hardly old enough to comprehend why the products, shows, and routines that had made the GDR feel like home disappeared overnight. Unification granted her the chance to study in Leipzig, Marseilles, Berlin, and Paris; she published a best-selling memoir, *Zonenkinder* (*Children of the Zone*) in 2002, describing the efforts of younger cohorts to adjust to Western cultural dictates. A Theodor Wolff Prize recipient, Hensel represents a new generation of journalists, writing for *Freitag, Der Spiegel, Die Welt,* and *Die Zeit.*[65] This beneficiary of increasing *gender representation* effectively summarized the ambivalence countless women initially felt toward their first female chancellor: "I don't agree with her politically on all matters, but ... I really have to confess, that I admire Angela Merkel for many, many things and that she is a very important figure for me personally ... as a woman, as an East German woman in the public sphere, she is a real role model for me."[66]

It is harder to demonstrate one woman's real-world impact than theoretical constructs like *descriptive* and *substantive representation* might lead us to believe. Merkel's legacy is likely to be greater than the sum of the parts, given the paradigm shifts her policies will engender in the longer run. Nor can we assess the *transformative* impact of her three terms to date without detailing the policy changes she has sought to institutionalize across the Federal Republic. For the populist demagogues now dominating the headlines, "the word reform sounds like a root canal without anesthetic," suggesting Merkel's victories have not come easily.[67] In Chapter 2, we explore another ironic development resulting from her "extreme makeover": this western-born, eastern-educated female chancellor has come to personify not only a legally united but also a pluralistically *unified* Germany.

NOTES

1. Susan J. Carroll, "Reflections on Gender and Hillary Clinton's Presidential Campaign: The Good, the Bad, and the Misogynic," *Politics & Gender*, 5(1) (2009): 1–20.
2. For concrete examples, see https://genderandsocs13.wordpress.com/2013/05/01/gender-bias-in-the-media-coverage-of-hillary-clintons-2008-presidential-campaign.

3. Diane J. Heith, "The Lipstick Watch: Media Coverage, Gender and Presidential Campaigns," in Robert P. Watson and Ann Gordon (eds.), *Anticipating Madam President* (Boulder, CO: Lynne Rienner, 2003), pp. 123–130.
4. Gabriele Abels, "90 Jahre Frauenwahlrecht: Zum Wandel von Geschlechterverhältnissen in der deutschen Politik," in Gabriele Abels (ed.), *Deutschland im Jubiläumsjahr 2009: Blick zurück nach vorn* (Baden-Baden: Nomos, 2011), pp. 197–219.
5. Mechthild Jansen (ed.), *Frauenwiderspruch – Alltag und Politik* (Cologne: Pahl-Rugenstein, 1987).
6. Eva Kolinsky, "Political Participation and Parliamentary Careers: Women's Quotas in West Germany," *West European Politics*, 14(1) (1991): 56–72.
7. See Alison E. Woodward, "From Equal Treatment to Gender Mainstreaming and Diversity Management," in Gabriele Abels and Joyce Marie Mushaben (eds.), *Gendering the European Union: New Approaches to Old Democratic Deficits* (Basingstoke: Palgrave Macmillan, 2012), pp. 85–103.
8. Joyce Marie Mushaben, "The Politics of *Critical Acts*: Women and Leadership in the European Union," *European Studies Journal*, 15(2) (1999): 51–91; Drude Dahlerup, "The Story of the Theory of Critical Mass," *Politics & Gender*, 2(4) (2006): 511–522.
9. Mariam Lau, "Merkel trifft Steinmeier: Mehr Duett als Duell," *Die Welt*, September 14, 2009.
10. Birgit Meyer, "'Nachts, wenn der Generalsekretär weint' – Politikerinnen in der Presse," *Aus Politik und Zeitgeschichte* 50 (November 2009): 9–15.
11. "Schönste Abgeordnete: *Men's Health* – Jana Schimke ist Miss Bundestag," *Bild Zeitung*, February 11, 2015.
12. Joyce Marie Mushaben, "Second-Class Citizenship and its Discontents: Women in United Germany," in Peter Merkl (ed.), *The Federal Republic of Germany at 45* (New York: New York University Press, 1995), pp. 80–98.
13. "Posters of Angela Merkel's Cleavage Spice up German Election Campaign," *The Telegraph*, August 11, 2009.
14. "Merkel darf jetzt eine Runde Cabrio fahren," *Die Welt*, May 8, 2001.
15. Born in Posnen (now Poland), Angela's grandfather did not change his surname from Kazmierczak to Kasner until 1930.
16. Kornelius, *Angela Merkel: Die Kanzlerin und ihre Welt*, p. 20.
17. This biographical background draws on Jacqueline Boysen, *Angela Merkel* (Munich: Ullstein, 2001); Evelyn Roll, *Die Erste. Angela Merkel's Weg zur Macht* (Reinbek: Rowohlt, 2005); Hugo Müller-Vogg, *Angela Merkel: Mein Weg* (Hamburg: Hoffmann & Campe, 2005).
18. Two authors argue polemically that Merkel was more loyal to the party and state than she admits. See Ralf Georg Reuth and Günther Lachmann, *Das erste Leben der Angela M.* (Munich: Piper, 2013).
19. Kornelius, *Angela Merkel: Die Kanzlerin und ihre Welt*, p. 21.
20. Nina Grunenberg, "Und was nun, Männer?" *Die Zeit*, September 9, 2000.
21. Katrin Rohnstock (ed.), *Stiefschwester: Was Ost-Frauen und West-Frauen von einander denken* (Frankfurt: Fischer, 1994).

22. Joyce Marie Mushaben, "Collective Memory Divided and Reunited: Mothers, Daughters and the Fascist Experience in Germany," *History and Memory* (1999): 1–34; Christiane Lemke, *Die Ursachen des Umbruchs. Politische Sozialisation in der ehemaligen DDR* (Opladen: Westdeutscher, 1991).
23. Roll, *Die Erste*, p. 58.
24. Kornelius, *Angela Merkel: Die Kanzlerin und ihre Welt*, pp. 43, 75.
25. Grunenberg, "Und was nun ..."; Gerhard Schröder sued one pundit for alleging during the 2005 campaign that he had dyed his hair to look younger.
26. Herlinde Koelbl, *Spuren der Macht. Die Verwandlung des Menschen durch das Amt* (Munich: Knesebeck, 1999), pp. 49, 51.
27. Grunenberg, "Und was nun ..."
28. Mariam Lau, *Die letzte Volkspartei: Angela Merkel und die Modernisierung der CDU* (Munich: Deutsche Verlagsanstalt, 2009), p. 53.
29. Koelbl, *Spuren der Macht*, p. 52.
30. Spiegel Spezial, *Das Profil der Deutschen. Was sie vereint, was sie trennt*, No. 1 (1991), p. 64.
31. Koelbl, *Spuren der Macht*, p. 51.
32. Joyce Marie Mushaben, "Concession or Compromise? The Politics of Abortion in United Germany," *German Politics*, 6(3) (1997): 69–87.
33. The quorum ensures women one of every three candidate slots for party office, in theory. Koelbl, *Spuren der Macht*, p. 53; Louise Davidson-Schmich, *Gender Quotas and Democratic Participation: Recruiting Candidates for Elective Offices in Germany* (Ann Arbor, MI: University of Michigan Press, 2016).
34. Koelbl, *Spuren der Macht*, p. 50.
35. Meißner blamed GDR childcare policies for the decline in birthrates *after* unification; Gauck has been separated since 1991, but his wife of fifty-three years will not agree to divorce. I interviewed him in 1990, and again in 1992 at the agency processing Stasi files.
36. Koelbl, *Spuren der Macht*, pp. 55–56.
37. Ibid., pp. 54–55.
38. Ibid., p. 58.
39. Ibid., p. 60.
40. Ibid., p. 57.
41. Wolfgang Stock, *Angela Merkel: Eine politische Biographie* (Munich: Olzog, 2000), p. 11.
42. Roll, *Die Erste*, pp. 308 ff.
43. Koelbl, *Spuren der Macht*, p. 58.
44. Michael Biedowicz, "Angela und ich," *Die Zeit*, June 9, 2005; also *Der Spiegel*, August 8, 2005.
45. Grunenberg, "Und was nun ..."
46. Susan Ferraro, "The Prime of Pat Schroeder," *New York Times*, July 1, 1990.
47. Lau, *Die letzte Volkspartei*, p. 9.

48. Matthias Geis, "Angezählt, aber noch nicht ausgezählt," *Die Zeit*, September 22, 2005.

49. The first two books on Ursula von der Leyen mocked her for borrowing her daughter's clothes, but most mothers of seven would be thrilled to be so trim. See Ulrike Demmer and Daniel Goffart, *Kanzlerin der Reserve: Der Aufstieg der Ursula von der Leyen* (Berlin: Berlin Verlag, 2015); Peter Dausend and Elisabeth Niejahr, *Operation Röschen: Das System von der Leyen* (Frankfurt: Campus, 2015).

50. "Konservative K-Frage: 'FAZ' spekuliert über Merkels Karriere-Ende," *Der Spiegel*, October 13, 2010.

51. Norbert Wallet, "Mutti lädt zum Essen ein," *Stuttgarter Nachrichten*, November 20, 2013; see the title page, "Machoca Europy," *Wprost*, June 28, 2007.

52. Clare Becket reported this at a Conference of Europeanists panel in Barcelona, June 22, 2011.

53. Women's average Landtag share rose to 20 percent after 1990, reaching 30 percent in 2004. Baden Württemberg has yet to top 22 percent, even under a Green government. Women fare better in local councils representing 500,000 or more residents. See Gender Data Report, available at: www.bmfsfj.de/doku/ Publikationen/genderreport/6-politische-partizipation-und-buergerschaftliches-engagement.html.

54. Joyce Marie Mushaben, "Ost–West Identitäten: Generationen zwischen Wende und Wandel," *Berliner Debatte INITIAL*, 12(3) (2001): 74–87.

55. Lau, *Die Letzte Volkspartei*, p. 51.

56. "Sie sind ein würdeloses Weib," *Hannoversche Allgemeine*, April 15, 1970; Petra Kipphoff, "Mutprobe in Hosen, na und? Bei uns bleibt der Protest aus," *Die Zeit*, May 22, 1970.

57. Rainer Woratschka, "Die K-Frage," *Der Tagesspiegel*, May 19, 2015.

58. "Volksfest: Rösler verspottet Merkel," *Der Spiegel*, September 6, 2010.

59. See "Kanzlermode-Hochrechnung zur Outfit Wahl," compiled by "color expert" Silvia Regnitter and "fashion psychologist" Kate Nightingale, available at http://stylite.de/Love/Kanzlermode.

60. "Merkel und Clinton: Im Hosenanzug der Macht," *Der Spiegel*, April 14, 2011.

61. Nolan D. McCaskill, "In Swipe at Trump, Clinton names Merkel as her Favorite World Leader," *Politico*, September 29, 2016.

62. His thesis did not find favor with Stalin; sent to the gulag, Kondratieff was executed in 1938.

63. Susanne Merkle, "Personalisierung und genderspezifische Berichterstattung im Bundestags wahlkampf 2013 – 'Ausnahmefall' Angela Merkel oder typische Frau," in Christine Holtz-Bacha (ed.), *Die Massenmedien im Wahlkampf. Die Bundestagswahl 2013* (Wiesbaden: Springer, 2015), p. 241.

64. Dana Dülcke and Sascha K. Futh, "Die 'Mutter der Nation' gegen den 'Panzerkandidaten': Geschlechterbilder in der Berichterstattung der Printmedien zum Bundestagswahlkampf 2013," in Christine Holtz-Bacha

(ed.), *Die Massenmedien im Wahlkampf. Die Bundestagswahl 2013* (Wiesbaden: Springer, 2015), pp. 249–273.

65. Hensel's *Zonenkinder* (Reinbek: Rowohlt, 2002) remained on the *Spiegel* best-seller list for a year; her second book was titled *Achtung Zone: Warum wir Ostdeutschen anders bleiben sollten* (Munich: Piper, 2009).

66. Thea Dorn, Jana Hensel, and Thomas Brussig (eds.), *Sind wir ein Volk? 25 Jahre nach dem Mauerfall* (Freiburg: Herder, 2015), p. 73.

67. Lau, *Die letzte Volkspartei*, p. 34.

2

A Pastor's Daughter in a "Difficult Fatherland": Reconciling East and West German Identities

As authors ranging from William Faulkner to Christa Wolf have stressed, Germany is a country in which "the past is far from dead … it's not even past," as many commemorative events of the last few years testify.[1] The year 2015 marked the seventieth anniversary of unconditional surrender, fifty years of diplomatic relations with Israel, and the thirtieth anniversary of Federal President Richard von Weizsäcker's eloquent May 8 address to the Bundestag, which Duchess Marion von Dönhoff at *Die Zeit* once described to me as "the best speech ever delivered in Germany." Topping off the year were countless exhibits, conferences, and speeches celebrating twenty-five years of unification. The present, however, inevitably serves as the frame of reference for shaping any citizen's understanding of the past.

The path to peaceful revolution that ended forty years of national division in Germany drew inspiration and reinforcement from protest movements in other "fraternal" socialist states. Once the dust began to settle, scholars noted that it had taken ten years in Poland, ten months in Hungary, ten weeks in the GDR, ten days in Czechoslovakia, and a mere ten hours (ending badly) in Romania to topple long-entrenched dictatorships, the Baltic states included. The Soviet Union itself would not implode until August 1991. In retrospect, these regimes were a lot more fragile than citizens realized, despite many pundits who tried to claim afterwards that they had predicted their collapse. Timur Kuran offers a succinct explanation as to why these revolutions, so surprising at the time, seemed so inevitable once they were over. Attributing regime durability to *preference falsification*, he argues that once the number of citizens courageously voicing their discontent reached a critical mass, the silent majority found it easier to jettison its fears and join in.[2] In another retrospective analysis, Albert O. Hirschman ascribed these revolutions to the dynamics of "exit, voice and loyalty."[3] Exploring "the unbearable lightness of authoritarianism" in relation to Arab Spring developments, Andrea Teti and Gennaro Gervasio offer a third type of explanation: they suggest that decades of coercion, corruption, and co-optation often convey a false image of regime stability, due to the lack of solid opposition. Political observers erroneously conflate the ferocity evinced during occasional state crackdowns with real political strength.[4] My own work highlights the quintessential role of *generational change* in system break-down as well.[5]

Western opinion polls executed from the 1950s through the 1980s usually featured German *Wiedervereinigung* (reunification) as an all-or-nothing proposition, eliciting responses "for" or "against"; the number of "don't knows" grew over time. Publications summarizing the results focused on an *abstract desire* for unification (mandated by the Basic Law) but revealed little about citizens' *realistic expectations* as to when or how it might occur. Nor were they questioned about the *material sacrifices* they would willingly make to bring it about. Re-assessing thirty-five years of survey research data, I demonstrated in an earlier book that most pre-1989 studies of attitudes toward reunification were simplistic at best, or consciously partisan at worst.[6] By the mid-1980s most West Germans no longer believed that unification was particularly desirable, few thought it likely to occur, and no one imagined that making the nation whole again would eventually require €2 trillion in tax-funded transfers.[7]

When the Wall opened on November 9, 1989, former Berlin Mayor Willy Brandt declared emotionally, "now that which belongs together can grow together." While he might have been a brilliant statesman, the ex-SPD chancellor was not an expert demographer: had he reflected a bit on generational change, his prognosis would have been a lot more pessimistic. By 1989, two-thirds of all Westerners and three-fourths of all Easterners had been born after the Second World War, meaning that most had never consciously experienced a whole nation. The German experience proves that while a single currency, a common language, and a shared history may constitute the necessary conditions for resuscitating a unified national identity, they are clearly not sufficient. This is especially true in places where citizens on both sides have been subjected for decades to hostile propaganda and diverging ideological interpretations of a history once shared.

On the surface, the events of 1989–1990 required 15 million East German residents to make a complete break with their own way of life, while 60 million Westerners outside Berlin were free to pursue business and politics as usual. GDR citizens were immediately expected to reassess who they were, why they had "arranged" themselves with the SED regime, whether they had suffered or benefited from state activities, and how they might best adapt to a new world. Those who did not quickly renounce all aspects of "the dictatorship," erroneously equated with their daily lives, were soon accused of embracing an illusory *Ostalgie* (Eastern nostalgia). Almost no one reflected critically on its logical counterpart, *Westalgie*.

New surveys revealed that after the first five years of unity, Germans on both sides felt they had grown farther apart, despite CDU assertions that "internal unity" had become a reality.[8] By 1996, 62 percent shared this perception in the East, compared with 30 percent in the old Länder, explained by the fact that most Westerners outside Berlin live far from the FRG–GDR border. Their only real association with unification involved higher taxes, used to finance massive "transfers" to the new states; they erroneously assumed that Easterners were exempt from the so-called *Soli* (solidarity surcharge). Unequal treatment, like lower wages, consolidated perceived differences over a span of two decades: By 2004, 73 percent still felt strongly connected to the East, while only 38 percent identified with the Federal Republic as a whole. Correspondingly, 36 percent construed unification as a win, 30 percent as a loss, and 30 percent as a bit of both.[9] Westerners were likewise ambivalent, affirming Dieter Thomä's earlier characterization: "There are two cultures in Germany: a German one and a German one."[10]

Unified is not synonymous with *united*. Throughout the 1990s, many scholars focused largely on *winners* and *losers*, but unification was not a zero-sum game. Imposing a single set of political and economic institutions is only the first step in eliminating disparate opportunity structures. Despite Helmut Kohl's promise that everyone would be better off than before, GDR citizens quickly learned that "greater freedom" meant fewer rights for women, starting with abortion and unemployment. In 1994, the Unity Chancellor signaled to Easterners that he was no longer committed to "blossoming landscapes": the constitutional right to uniform or "equal" living conditions (*Einheitlichkeit*) under Article 72/2 of the Basic Law was reduced to a guarantee of *Gleichwertigkeit*, living conditions of "comparable worth," at best.

For those of us who recall the vehement debates between *Besserwessis* (know-it-all Westerners) and *Jammer-Ossis* (whiny Easterners) over the SED dictatorship, Stasi collaborators, *Ostalgie*, and the "leading culture," the last ten years have been remarkably quiet on the topic of German identity, anti-migration protestors notwithstanding. According to Karl Mannheim, twenty-five years is long enough for new cohorts to jettison the "historical ballast" of older generations, raising the question as to whether it has merely been the passage of time that has put this subject to rest. Alternatively, have hefty criticisms invoking Nazi imagery from less fortunate, debt-challenged Euro states forged *Ossis* and *Wessis* into a united, defensive front, given their own export and job boom? Have the thousands of refugees dying at sea, trying to escape violence and hunger in Syria, Afghanistan, Somalia, and the Sudan made both sides realize how privileged they really are? What, if anything, has Germany's first Eastern, female chancellor contributed to this reconciliation process?

I contend that Germany has taken a great leap forward in the direction of *internal unity* over the last decade, owing largely to various reform courses pursued by Angela Merkel. Over time, the Eastern chancellor has increasingly drawn on her own biography to persuade Westerners that they, too, must adapt to rapidly changing socioeconomic conditions. In contrast to all her predecessors, Merkel has succeeded in combining rhetorical concepts such as *fatherland* and *homeland* (familiar to Easterners) with "the politics of small steps" (trusted by Westerners), as part of a much larger plan to modernize the CDU. As the leading lady on the European stage, she calls for regional solidarity but also defends national interests. These practices have gone a long way toward making Germans a healthier, happier, satisfied people. Three generations removed from the war atrocities that divided them, Easterners and Westerners have internalized a more realistic assessment of their shared national identity, even though neither side got what it prayed for.

This chapter explores Merkel's contributions to a slow but steady reconciliation of East–West differences along three axes, allowing Germans to "come to terms" with the past, the present, and a prospective united future. Beginning with their respective pasts (*Vergangenheitsbewältigung*), I highlight key systemic factors that contributed to the evolution of separate FRG and GDR identities across forty years of division. Next, I describe the Chancellor's own efforts to master three historical narratives, subject to antithetical East–West interpretations. They center on: (1) assigning blame for the Third Reich and the Holocaust; (2) explaining "collaboration" with the SED regime; and (3) ascribing radical meaning to the events of "1968."

The next section on "mastering the present" (*Gegenwartsbewältigung*) addresses two policy domains, economic restructuring and gender policies, that have allowed Merkel to modernize the "Christian" parties by leveraging EU initiatives, while depoliticizing competing left–right factions over these issues. Many reforms of the last decade have ostensibly reinstated Eastern policies for women, including a right-to-choose abortion, family–work reconciliation, and guaranteed childcare.

Two further issues will play a key role in Germany's mastery of future challenges (*Zukunfstbewältigung*): the energy turn-around and securing millions of skilled workers to replace retiring Baby Boomers. As Mother of the Nation, Merkel is acutely aware of her country's looming demographic crisis: its population is expected to plunge from 82.5 million to 69 million by 2050, while the retiree-to-worker dependency ratio will rise from 32 per 100 (2005) to 60–64 per 100. Pushing personal responsibility along with technological innovation, Merkel wants both sides to scale back their expectations of Father State, as well as to develop normal feelings of affection for the land that has given them so much already. Her clear commitment to migration reform and climate-change mitigation has fostered more inclusive identity feelings among many societal groups, not only those positioned along the East–West divide. To appreciate her contributions to a new, shared national identity, we first need to consider the cultural gaps that emerged between the two populations from 1949 through 1989.

A DIFFICULT FATHERLAND: FROM ONE VOLK IN TWO STATES, TO TWO NATIONS IN ONE STATE

Writing on the *Social Origins of Dictatorship and Democracy*, Barrington Moore, Jr. observed that "to maintain and transmit a value system, human beings are punched, bullied, sent to jail, thrown into concentration camps, cajoled, bribed, made into heroes, encouraged to read newspapers, stood up against a wall and shot, and sometimes even taught sociology."[11] This eclectic array of political socialization methods, some more coercive than others, implies that the goal of any state is not only to transform official political culture but to have it internalized by its citizens as well. The difficulties leaders face in inculcating *new* identities indicate how hard it must be to wipe out old ones; the picture becomes more complicated in places where, by some curious twist of fate, people who shared a history, language, and currency long ago suddenly find themselves sharing those three things again.

In his first speech as federal president during a very turbulent political era, Gustav Heinemann declared on July 1, 1969 that: "There are many difficult Fatherlands. One of them is Germany. But it is our Fatherland."[12] Active in the Confessing Church, Heinemann had strongly opposed the creation of the Bundeswehr, German rearmament, and initial NATO nuclear deployments in the 1950s. The Adenauer government nonetheless managed to absorb over 12 million refugees and expellees, many of whom would pursue recognition of their own postwar victimization for decades to come.[13] From 1949 to 1989, those trapped behind the Oder–Neisse border paid a very different price for Nazi atrocities.

Also reflecting on the *difficult fatherland*, Theodor Adorno broadcast his seminal talk, "Working through the Past," on Hessian State Radio in February 1960, following a disturbing wave of anti-Semitic vandalism. He argued that German society was still infected with National Socialism, uncertain as to whether it was "merely the ghost of what was so monstrous" that it lingered on after its own death, or whether it had "not yet died at all." He warned that the people's "readiness for unspeakable actions" was most likely to re-emerge should FRG society "[fail] to live up to the norms and ideals it ascribes to itself."[14] Germans had recovered so quickly from the material devastation of war that they were "covered up by the slick façade of everyday life" which prevented them from facing up to "pathological nationalism" and "the rage of the Hitlerian world against everything that was different" to which they had personally ascribed.[15]

Rather than fade with time, the *difficult fatherland* debate intensified with the rise of a new generation. In 1967, Alexander and Margarete Mitscherlich published their landmark text, focusing on Germans' "inability to mourn" peoples victimized by a megalomaniacal Führer to whom they had willingly turned over their "collective ego." Their postwar refusal to follow the Freudian formula, "remember, repeat, then work through the past" had resulted in emotional rigidity, psychosocial immobilism, and a refusal to accept new political realities such as the Oder–Neisse border.[16] Immersed in the emotive paranoia of anti-communism, they impeded their own ability to internalize real democracy. Hermann Lübbe would counter in 1983 that *Verdrängung* (memory suppression) proved essential for integrating and stabilizing the fledgling republic. Tilmann Moser would insist even later, in 1992, that the Mitscherlichs had led youth to rebel against "a communicative reconciliation" with their parents' generation.[17]

My own studies of the vehement rebellion of "fathers against sons," a fractured student movement, second wave feminism, the peace, environmental and human rights campaigns running from the 1960s through the 1980s leads me to side with the Mitscherlichs.[18] Reflecting further on the writings of Moore and Mannheim, I see the chaotic, political–cultural revolution initiated by the so-called "68ers" as an absolutely necessary *historical break with the past*. These movements heralded a new era, reflecting a broader societal willingness to cast off revanchist authoritarianism in favor of empathy, tolerance and, above all, the ability to "dare more democracy."

The détente era, associated with Willy Brandt, also saw the emergence of a new generation of academics willing to tackle the past head-on in their research. The 1979 TV series "Holocaust" unleashed an unprecedented public debate over statutes of limitation, leading new cohorts to hunt down surviving Nazi perpetrators to a degree not seen before or after the Eichmann trial in 1961, the year the Wall was built.[19] Marking the FRG's thirtieth anniversary in 1979, Martin and Sylvia Greiffenhagen published a six-part *Spiegel* series, subtitled "A Difficult Fatherland."[20] Their work featured extensive survey data and broader social science reflections on the identity complex of West Germans. Reading these texts in early 1980s, I was struck by the fundamental transformation of FRG political culture that had taken hold during the first twenty years of national division. Yet as late as 1985, Western pundits wedged between the "Historians' Controversy" and the anti-Pershing II protests were still debating whether May 8 marked a day of "liberation" or "occupation."[21]

It was much harder to access empirical evidence regarding cultural changes on the other side, despite Easterners' shared experiences with authoritarian rule under Otto von Bismarck, the collapse of the Weimar Republic, and twelve years of National Socialist barbarity.[22] Blaming capitalists for the rise of fascism as of 1949, the SED avoided major historian controversies but faced its own problems with prominent GDR figures challenging its interpretation and implementation of socialism, including the philosopher Rudolf Bahro, scientist Robert Havemann and singer Wolf Biermann.[23]

From these studies I derive three traits useful for defining *the difficult Fatherland*: it entails a collective inability to mourn; an unwillingness to empathize; and a societal rejection of difference. By the time the Federal Republic turned forty in 1989, Western elites had yet to agree on their own identity parameters, based on a simple survey of my own bookshelves. After four decades of division, it was still hard to determine what *Germany as a Whole* (Zieger), much less what *German Identity Today* (von Berglar) was supposed to mean. In order to answer *Three Questions regarding Germany* (von

Häussling), namely, *Are We Really One Nation?* (Moersch), *What Will Become of the Germans?* (Bahr), and *Can We Still be Saved?* (Petersen), one first had to determine *Where Germany Lies* (Gaus).[24] If neither in the East or West, then maybe it was somewhere in the middle of Europe.

For many debate participants, including *The Wall-Jumper* (Schneider) and others benefiting from *The Blessing of Late Birth* (Heidenreich), the *Attempt to Explain the Federal Republic to Ourselves and Others* (Brückner) required countless hours of *Meditating over Germany* (Weidenfeld). Some found their answer in *Perplexed Normality* (Weidenfeld), while others actively tried to promote *Germany as Our Mission* (Gradl), or clung to the optimistic perspective, *German Unity Will Surely Come!* (Venohr). Despite the hope that *Without Germany, Nothing Goes* (Venohr), the querulous persistence of *The German Neurosis* (Peisl) and *The Fear of Germans* (Leinemann), many Westerners had already accepted their *Germany as a Provisional State* (von Bredow), knowing that *German History Moves On* (von Weizsäcker). Contemplating *The Rise and Fall of the Third Reich* (Shirer), they still asked, *Is National-Socialism Just History?* (Diner), while routinely reassuring their allies that *The Germans* (Craig) were unlikely to take "two steps forward, one step backwards," should the Wall ever fall.[25]

President Richard von Weizsäcker's speech of May 8, 1945, forty years after the Nazi capitulation, rounded out the picture. Perhaps unwittingly, it applied the Freudian formula: *remember* all victims "honestly and without distortions"; *repeat* the lesson that their own actions had caused German suffering; and *work through the past* by mobilizing for peace, which had given FRG citizens a "priceless opportunity to live in freedom." Although the western republic had become more tolerant of leftists, ecologists, feminists, and gays, it still had a long way to go in accepting difference along ethnic lines. *Ausländerfeindlichkeit* (anti-foreigner hostility) became a household word, despite Kohl's failed attempt to repatriate guestworkers who had overstayed their welcome by fifteen to twenty years. He also gutted an unqualified right to political asylum, anchored in the Basic Law (Chapter 7).

Five years before the Wall fell, I set out to explore the identities of FRG citizens, convinced that generational change had already radically redefined what it meant to be German since 1949. Curiously, most of my interview partners, including seventy-five Bundestag members, denied that they possessed a "West German" identity back then. Instead,

I discovered a spectrum of national identifications, which I classified along demographic lines: namely, the *Economic Miracle Generation*, the *Long March Generation*, and the *Turn-around* or *Wende* (I) *Generation*, respectively.[26]

While the Old Guard lived to see unification, the younger generations saw their identities most rattled by its occurrence. Citizens born between 1945 and 1964, the Baby Boomers who still control the establishment, were deeply divided among themselves. Their ranks included: self-proclaimed *internationalists*, who held that "no national identity was a good national identity"; *Europeanists*, subdivided into enthusiastic supporters and resigned integrationists (distrustful of Brussels technocrats); and *rapprochement activists*, who discovered how German they really were through interactions with European peace groups.[27] The youngest set consisted of *pragmatic frequent-flyer Germans*, who viewed their nationality as a matter of administrative–technical necessity for securing passports, pensions, etc.[28] Although my sample was not statistically representative, survey data confirmed that as late as 1988, Westerners still found it hard to declare they were "proud to be German."

FRG citizens who visited the GDR before the Wall fell often described it as "more foreign" than Austria or Switzerland. As a system, the GDR epitomized all that was theoretically bad or good about life in their own country. The Wall, Peter Schneider wrote, "became a mirror for the Germans in the West, which told them day by day, who was the fairest in the land. Whether there was life on the other side of the death-strip is something that soon interested only pigeons and cats."[29] Western curiosity about the *other* Germany rose in response to sensational events (June 17, 1953, building of the Wall in 1961, Prague Spring 1968) but faded from consciousness in times of relative stability. More likely to be grandchildren or distant cousins than "brothers and sisters" by 1989, Westerners were constitutionally obliged to view Germans as "one people," divided only by the ideological forces of good and evil. But they were regularly exposed to "enemy images" challenging the other system's right to exist, as were their Eastern counterparts.

Rather than leave citizens free to define their relationship(s) to the past, the GDR developed a framework of *regulated anti-fascism*. Since the FRG claimed to be the Reich's legitimate successor, the SED could assign all blame for the Holocaust, slave labor, the Cold War, and other consequences of the Second World War to its capitalist nature. GDR efforts to break with the national past took place in various doctrinal stages. SED leaders initially appealed for the restitution of the *united German state*, albeit one purged of all capitalist-imperialist structures. The 1952 SED Party Conference decreed that "a new reality" had emerged with the creation of two sovereign states embracing diametrically opposed social orders.³⁰ It openly rejected future unification in 1955, when the FRG acquired full NATO membership (resulting in the Warsaw Pact Organization). A new constitution promulgated in April 1968 identified the GDR as *the socialist state of the German nation* (Article 1), a designation that immediately lost favor when Willy Brandt embraced *two states in one nation* as Bonn's new leitmotif in 1969.

The SED then switched to *the socialist German nation-state*, proclaiming at its eighth Party Congress (1971) that "the national question has disappeared from German soil."³¹ Further doctrinal rebooting in the 1974 constitution expunged all remaining references to a "gradual growing-together" and established the GDR as the *state of workers and farmers* (Article 8). This ironically coincided with the Brandt government's adoption of the formula "change through rapprochement" (*Wandel durch Annäherung*) as the basis for *Ostpolitik*. A new premier (Erich Honecker), acquisition of a United Nations seat, and the SED's decision to host the World Youth Games raised hopes that other liberalizations would follow; instead, GDR citizens witnessed a sudden, intensified "demarcation." Over the next five years, leaders moved to rename all official organizations and publications, replacing the adjective *German* with the words *GDR national* or *of the GDR*; noteworthy exceptions were the *Deutsche Reichsbahn, Neues Deutschland*, and the *Sozialistische Einheitspartei Deutschland* per se.

Hoping to instill emotional identification, loyalty, and legitimacy, the 1974 formula, *citizenship: GDR, nationality: German* was accompanied by new policies like state-provided day-care and abortion rights. It drew a fine line between identity's objective and subjective components, defining *the nation* as an "historical community of human beings which derives from the formation of community based on its economic relations, its territory, its language, its specifics of culture, its character."³² The "inherited, subjective" components, rooted in a shared past, language, and ethnicity, did not comprise the essence of a nation. National groups that had grown together at earlier points in time could also grow apart, based on new political, economic, social, and legal–structural realities.

In May 1989, I initiated a parallel study of East German identities; few people "over there" thought they had one, until they were asked to compare themselves to FRG relatives. Building on demographic data,

I classified my Eastern interview partners (including fifty members of post-Wall *Volkskammer*), as the *Reconstruction Generation*, the *Born-Here Generation*, and the *Wende II Generation*, respectively, but I soon discovered that Western and Eastern demographics were out of synch. While GDR woman gave birth, on average, between the ages of 19 and 23, FRG females produced their offspring between 27 and 30: fertility rates also diverged: 90 percent of GDR women were mothers, while only 60 percent were in the FRG. Eastern births plunged dramatically after unification: sterilizations rose by 500 percent, but 90 percent of those involved women 36 or older, over 60 percent of whom had two or more children. This was not a "birth strike," as reported by Western analysts; 1990 seemed to mark the end of an Eastern birth cycle, occurring at twenty-year intervals.[33]

This also means that Western and Eastern Baby Boomers came of political age at different points in time: 1968 invoked different memories not only because FRG youth were taking to the streets as part of a national student movement, while GDR citizens saw Soviet tanks moving into "counter-revolutionary" Prague. Because one Eastern boomlet had peaked earlier, followed by a second one twenty years later, these "key events" acquired different salience on each side. Some GDR interviewees cited the World Youth Games (1973) with the same reverence that Westerners mention Woodstock (1969).[34] Angela Merkel turned 14 two weeks before the Czech uprising of 1968; street-fighter Joschka Fischer was already 20.

By the time I completed my eastern interviews, the SED regime had collapsed, the Deutsche Mark (DM) had become the coin of the realm, and unification was set for October 3, 1990. Although Westerners rejected the idea of a state-imposed identity for themselves, they made no effort to distinguish between official "GDR identity" and the daily *habitus* ("local patriotism") of Easterners, better known as peer culture.[35] West politicians quickly convened a Committee of Parliamentary Inquiry not to construct a memory of the GDR "in its entirety but rather as the 'SED dictatorship.'" As stressed by premier Lothar de Maizière, "perhaps two percent [had been] victims, and perhaps three percent perpetrators. But 95 percent were ordinary people," just trying to secure a good life for themselves and their families.[36] As Angela Merkel herself admits, her life as a pastor's daughter in Templin had granted her the luxury of not being forced to identify with the state: "I never felt that the GDR was my natural home ... but I always made use of the opportunities."[37]

Oblivious as to how stodgy their own republic had become, Westerners began to demand that Easterners change everything at a time when their own state was being described as "the sick man of Europe," in light of 8 percent unemployment (2.2 million by 1986). Wallowing in *Reformstau* (gridlock), Kohl's popularity had plunged after sixteen years in power (compared to Honecker's eighteen years).[38] Completing my western book and my eastern monograph in the early 1990s, I concluded that re-establishing a *united state* would prove easier than restoring a *unified nation*, and that it would take years to reweave the ties binding the German people. I got it right.

FROM PARTY TO HANGOVER: REACTIONS TO THE FALL OF THE WALL

In May 1989, Hungary agreed to uphold the free-passage provision of the Geneva Convention on Refugees, a decision that overlapped with growing criticism over fraudulent communal elections in the GDR. On June 27, 1989, the Austrian and Hungarian foreign ministers posed for journalists as they symbolically "cut the fence" constituting their mutual border.[39] Giving little thought to long-term ramifications, officials on both sides temporarily opened the border for a Pan-European Picnic Day on August 19. By nightfall over 600 not-so-happy GDR campers had abandoned their vacation spots along Lake Balaton near Budapest to cross the green frontier. On September 11, Hungary opened the entire border, becoming a path to freedom for over 25,000 East German citizens. The SED responded by terminating visa-free travel to Czechoslovakia where first hundreds, then thousands began seeking refuge in the FRG embassy compound. By the time the Wall collapsed, over 225,000 had exited via other fraternal socialist states.

Protests back home began with competing chants in summer 1989: would-be exiters in Prague and Budapest shouting "We want out!" were soon countered by others declaring "We're staying here!" in hopes of moving their state in a democratic direction. Building on the Monday night peace-prayer tradition of the early 1980s, Easterners started reconvening at the Nikolaikirche in Leipzig; the first mass demonstration, attracting 5,000 participants, took place on September 25. On October 4, roughly 7,600 "embassy refugees" leaving Prague for Bavaria were forced to stop in the GDR for exit visas, triggering a riot at Dresden's central train station. As the number of Monday-night protestors grew from 20,000 (October 2) to 70,000 (October 9), to 120,000 (October 16), and then 300,000 (October 30), they spilled over into other cities like Magdeburg, Jena, Plauen, and Zwickau. By month's end, the mantra had shifted to

Wir sind das Volk! ("We are the people!"). The intellectuals, artisans, religious, peace and ecology activists who participated in the first-wave demonstrations through early November wanted to transform the GDR into a democratic system based on *socialism with a human face*. Even after Honecker was forced to resign on October 18, they rejected the idea of a rapid fusion with the other Germany, preferring interim premier Hans Modrow's call for a *Community of Treaties* and an eventual federation between the two.

Western witnesses to the 1989 protests were not the same Germans who had hoped for unification prior to August 13, 1961; they were, in fact, Federal Republicans, with too many of their own problems, for example, nuclear proliferation, to care about the GDR, although they realized that Easterners deserved the same rights – political freedom, quality consumption, foreign travel – that they took for granted As noted earlier, we need to deconstruct their pre-1989 attitudes along three axes, regarding the *desirability of unification*, their realistic *expectations*, and the *conditions* most would accept to achieve it. By 1984, the minority who still "desired" national unity were largely over 60; only 5 percent of all respondents *expected* to see it happen. The sudden arrival of 400,000 eastern resettlers in 1984 under a liberalized GDR exit law had offered a kind of "test of unification," but as Anne Köhler and Volker Ronge discovered through interviews, the results were not encouraging: five years prior to the real thing, most "re-enfranchised" Easterners found it hard to integrate into Western culture, despite generous state and local assistance.[40]

Still, the initial FRG response to the 1989 "wall jumpers" was one of warm welcome, amidst a scramble for housing and jobs. Easterners recounting their "day-to-day misery" made them acutely aware of their own good fortune. During the first stage, August–November, Westerners were quite willing to take in kindred spirits from the other side. On November 9, 1989, the Federal Republic was suddenly rendered a chaotic country in a very good mood. During a guest lecture in St. Louis a year later, Peter Schneider observed, "After the party comes the hangover, and the hangover usually lasts longer."

Rather than stem the flow, the Wall's opening brought a new wave of Easterners who had waited long enough for a share of the national pie. The arrival of 2,500–3,000 per day between November and January aggravated housing shortages, traffic jams, and budget deficits for city administrators in Giessen, Hannover, Berlin, and Bremen. Westerners worried about labor market competition, given media reports describing the new arrivals as young, highly skilled workers; many felt that resettlers were receiving "too many" benefits. New groups joined the protests, radically redefining the goals. Waving imported FRG flags on November 25, demonstrators in Plauen called for *Germany, united Fatherland*, a line from the GDR anthem. Kohl announced his Ten-Point Program for a confederation on November 28; by December Easterners in many cities were proclaiming *Wir sind ein Volk!* ("We are ONE people!"). About to face unification without so much as a vote, many West Germans responded: *Wir auch!* ("So are we!").[41]

Sitting in a Paris hotel room the night the Wall fell, Patrick Süskind experienced an identity crisis typical of FRG '68ers. Reading that West Berlin mayor Walter Momper had described the Germans on November 9 as "the happiest people in the world," he responded: "Had the man lost his marbles? Was he drunk? . . . What did he mean by 'the German *Volk*'? Citizens of the Federal Republic or the GDR? West or East Berliners? All of them together? Maybe even Bavarians? Me too? . . . And why 'happy'?" Stunned by Willy Brandt's declaration, "Now what belongs together will grow together," Süskind wrote: "Different societies, different governments, different economic systems, different educational systems, different standards of living, different bloc memberships, different histories, different levels of alcohol permitted for drivers – nothing at all will grow together there, because nothing at all belongs together."[42] For the 40-year-old playwright, unification overlapped with his own Baby Boomer midlife crisis:

we find ourselves in that interval of life where a human being tends to call for a time-out, to look inwards, to reflect back, to draw a balance and gradually to orient himself towards the second half of life ... Just when we thought we had gained control of our own existence and comprehended the world ... now suddenly we're rolled over by this midlife crisis in the form of German unity! We might have been prepared to deal with impotence problems, with prostate disease, false teeth, menopause and a second Chernobyl, with cancer and death and the devil – but never with *Deutsch-land-ei-nig-Va-ter-land*! ...[43]

Bundestag Vice-President Antje Vollmer (Greens) labeled the call for a united Fatherland "the dream of old men" who had neglected a core task of nation-building:

These men meant well. They have already done a lot for us. They built a free and democratic Republic. They built a free and critical press. They built a political opposition capable of governing. Now they want to do one last thing for us. They want to return Germany to us forty-five years after the war's end, and not even a nationalistic one. No, simply a civilized one. For the happiest people in the world from the happiest politicians in the world.

But they had skipped a crucial step:

It certainly counts as a major act of negligence of German politics over the years, that [the old men] never made the feeling [of eventually encountering] the sensational, historical happy-event the core of a new, more modest and more satisfied German identity ... the political Right thought that they were only getting out of this happy-event what was ours all along. The political Left ... to which I belong ... construed it as a case of bad luck that, without a doubt, is really good luck for many people. Both sides have missed the chance to form a positive identity.[44]

The culture shock of unification was not confined to Westerners. Born in 1944, Pastor Friedrich Schorlemmer (aligned with *Demokratische Aufbruch*, later joined by Merkel) observed:

Wonderful that there was such a thing as the Basic Law. The West Germans had to take us. And we gladly allowed ourselves majority-wise to be swallowed whole. Now we lie rather heavily in the stomach of the well-nourished and groomed Federal Republic – with our heavy metals, asbestos-palaces, rotted landscapes, kaput cities, Stasi-snares that reach all the way to Bonn, with broken-down, unsellable factories. Now it's a question of digestion. Cramps are unavoidable. For many it is a gall-bladder attack.[45]

Former SED member and lawyer, Gregor Gysi expected the illness to be a long and painful one; citing GDR author Stefan Heyme, he also described unification in visceral terms: "The snake that swallows the porcupine is likely to experience serious digestion problems."

The speedy pursuit of unification reflected great international uncertainty, given the unstable conditions in Russia. Bundesbank experts had opposed a full-fledged currency union (given big productivity and "competitiveness" gaps), but few politicians considered the psycho-cultural problems likely to ensue from demographic shifts. Easterners saw the negotiations as an arrogant exercise of Western power, devoid of the grassroot values that characterized the FRG's own social movements.

It was not Merkel's grasp of western power politics that has helped her to bridge the cultural gap between *Ossis* and *Wessis* since 2005; in my judgment, her ability to effect a gradual reconciliation of conflicting identities owes more to her pragmatic Protestant upbringing. As a pastor's daughter in a godless state, she was never at liberty to accept GDR doctrines at face value. Although she escaped the heavy discrimination experienced by other pastoral offspring, she evinces a capacity for empathy that "difficult fatherland" critics had found lacking among earlier generations. One key to her success in helping her compatriots come to terms with difference has been her personal effort to assume responsibility for its collective moral failings and to find her own place in the national past. We turn now to the complexities of *Vergangenheitsbewältigung*.

RECONCILING THE GERMAN–GERMAN PASTS

There are three "German" histories and interpretation frameworks at stake in the wake of unification; the first involves the horrors associated with the Holocaust; the second pertains to suffering linked to authoritarian SED rule; and the third centers on two forms of political violence linked to 1968. The speed with which western conservatives pounced on the "SED dictatorship," along with their biased selection of experts and topics, suggested to outsiders like myself that they cared more about downplaying FRG policies that had sustained the eastern regime (like "buying out" prisoners) than about reconciling the two cultures. The Commission's portrayal of the GDR as a land of victims and perpetrators did more to alienate Easterners than to foster meaningful exchanges between the two sides. Exposing East Germans with alleged Stasi ties (Lothar de Maizière, Gregor Gysi) after 1989 further obscured the western state's quick reintegration of former Nazis into prominent leadership positions (Hans Globke, Kurt Georg Kiesinger, Hans Filbinger) after 1945.

Swirling into the Kohl cabinet like Dorothy landing in Oz, Merkel probably did not see the first historical battle as hers to fight. She had not participated in dissident or human rights movements, nor did she join a civil society group before the Wall had collapsed. Although Kohl appointed her to the cabinet because she was eastern and female, she avoided journalists' attempts to place her in either one of those boxes. As she moved up the party ranks, Merkel rarely referred to her earlier life, unless others charged that she had been part of the system, for example, as the FDJ Secretary for Agitation and Propaganda at the University of Leipzig.[46] As Richard von Weizsäcker noted later, Westerners would have behaved no differently had they found themselves on the other side of the Wall. Merkel had to study the world-views of Westerners before she could challenge their moral inconsistencies head-on, for example, Kohl's refusal to name illegal campaign contributors as a matter of "honor." Her annual discussions with Herlinde Koelbl testify to her rapid learning curve in this respect. By the time she spoke with Hugo Müller-Vogg in 2005, she had become quite fluent in CDU *politician-speak*.[47]

As Peter Reichel discerned, efforts to process the Nazi past have grown more complicated over time: "Out of the ongoing confrontation with the NS dictatorship and its crimes of violence ... there has emerged a multi-faceted history of [the disputes] themselves. ... the second history of National Socialism has meanwhile become longer, many times over than the first one. And it is still going on."[48] Initially confined to Nuremberg Tribunal participants, the stakeholders now include lawyers, researchers, museum directors, archivists, textbook writers, youth exchange coordinators, Israeli intelligence forces, and even urban anthropologists.

Merkel's engagement with Holocaust themes predated her activities as chancellor. In order to embrace Western framing of Nazis and the *Shoah*, she first had to reject the socialist *Staatsräson*: "I myself spent the first 35 years of life in the German Democratic Republic ... where National Socialism was considered a West German problem." The freely elected *Volkskammer* formally apologized to Israel on April 12, 1990 for decades of SED hostility. Among its first official acts, the resolution expressed "sadness and shame" for Easterners' "co-responsibility" for deportations and murder; it sought forgiveness from Israel and Jews worldwide for the "hypocrisy and animosity" of GDR policies. Its promise to provide just reparations for material losses, a major sticking point for the United States, was subsequently rejected by FRG politicians.

As a teenager, Merkel had visited the Ravensbrück concentration camp not far from her home in Brandenburg. Her father's Templin parish stood next door to the Waldhof home for the disabled, a group directly victimized by the Nazis. Having read a contraband copy of von Weizsäcker's emotionally compelling speech in May 1985, she echoes its themes in her own speeches, adamantly asserting that no matter what groups try to re-contextualize Third Reich activities, German history remains "indivisible," as does the responsibility her people continue to bear regarding Israel. In her words: "It is because we have recognized the Holocaust as a singular event that we can say today: we are free, we are united. That recognition has made us what we are today."[49] Having paid homage at Buchenwald in 2009, she became the first German chancellor to visit Dachau in 2013, returning in 2015. Helmut Kohl, by contrast, insisted on taking Ronald Reagan to the Bitburg Cemetery, known to contain SS graves.

Merkel's ethical convictions have been put to the test multiple times, for example, concerning CDU Bundestag member Martin Hohmann, who inferred in a 2003 speech that the "dark side" of Jewish behavior had "perpetrated" a godless ideology during the Russian Revolution. After some hesitation as CDU Chair, she expelled him from the party, along with Reinhard Günzel, the Special Forces Commander who publicly praised the speech. In August 2006, the literary "moral authority," Günter Grass, admitted to having served in the Waffen-SS in 1944–1945.[50] He raised hackles again in April 2012 with his poem, "What Needs to be Said," warning against the delivery of dual-use submarines to Israel.[51] Although Grass subsequently attacked the chancellor for *her* FDJ past, Merkel held back, perhaps reluctant to deny dissenting authors freedom of speech because of her GDR upbringing.[52]

A further incident involved Hermann Schäfer, an assistant to CDU Culture and Media Commissioner Bernd Neumann. At a major arts festival in Weimar memorializing concentration camp internees at Buchenwald, Schäfer stressed the suffering of German victims, hardly mentioning the Nazis' primary targets. Allegedly "unaware" that Buchenwald survivors were in the audience, the historian apologized the next day.[53] The next debacle involved a powerful CDU "state prince" in Baden-Württemberg; Günther Oettinger insisted in a 2007 eulogy that former leader Hans Filbinger, a navy judge who had sentenced many deserters to death after the war had ended, had been "an opponent of the National Socialist regime . . . not a Nazi."[54] Merkel forced Oettinger to apologize, but when he lost his state post in the next election, she appointed him EU Commissioner for Energy, hardly a harsh penance.[55]

Perhaps her finest moment was when the chancellor admonished Pope Benedict XVI for his 2009 reinstatement of four excommunicated bishops who denied the reality of the Holocaust. Lacking any ecclesiastical authority beyond her standing as the daughter of a Lutheran pastor, Merkel declared: "I believe that a fundamental question is at stake, when a Vatican decision conveys the impression that one can conceivably lie about the Holocaust . . . about how anyone at all should handle fundamental questions involving the Jews." As a Protestant Christian, she found it "very encouraging that many voices inside the Catholic Church also demanded a clear position from the Vatican on this issue."[56] A former Hitler Youth member, the German Pope claimed to have "known nothing" about the denials, a crime under federal law; the Catholic Church admitted to "miscommunication." This is one instance in which the chancellor was far ahead of her critics.

Rather than exonerate herself by invoking "the blessing of late birth," Merkel has used such incidents to link the past and present as guideposts for the future. Her first term provided multiple opportunities to rethink her GDR-inculcated view of the Nazi past, giving her the courage as well as the right, to challenge powerful Western figures for not adhering to FRG moral imperatives. In doing so, she makes it easier for citizens on both sides to re-process more than one German past, even if both sides apply different memories of "suffering" to this effort.

REVISITING THE CULTURAL REVOLUTION(S) OF 1968

Despite mocking assaults on her "hippie clothing," Angela Merkel was too young to experience flower-power, student movements, and the sexual revolution first-hand. As chancellor, she has nonetheless helped to bridge the diverging East–West meanings ascribed to 1968 and the democratic lessons each side drew from contradictory experiences. Eastern youth were not oblivious to radical protests on the other side of the Wall. As Annette Simon, daughter of Christa Wolf, noted: "The Sixty-Eighters of the GDR [were] shaped just as much by the music of the times and the life-feelings it transported as their sisters and brothers in the west."[57] What they lacked were alternative channels for expressing their discontent. The SED banned avant-garde music in 1965, along with jeans and long hair. The Leipzig *Beat Rebellion* of October 31, 1965 produced the first mass demonstration since June 17, 1953, drawing roughly 2,500 adolescents: 267 were arrested, 100 of whom subsequently endured weeks of hard labor in the coal mines, without trials or convictions.[58]

This did not stop eastern youth from borrowing western protest symbols; while FRG students mobilized against the "Emergency Laws," fearing they would be pulled into the Vietnam War, GDR youth called for a conscientious objector/alternative service option, later known as *Bausoldaten* (construct-ion soldiers). In January 1968, the GDR began restricting access to the Chinese Embassy in East Berlin, as marginalized youth developed an interest in Maoism.[59] More than 100 people gathered in early summer to oppose the SED decision to blow up the University Church in Leipzig, where Merkel would later study and participate in a Protestant youth group.[60]

Practicing "repressive tolerance" against its own youth, the Stasi min-istry intensified police surveillance of Humboldt University students debating differences between Karl Marx and Herbert Marcuse. The SED-sponsored meetings between SDS and FDJ functionaries to win over Western youth, only to discover that their own emissaries used them for personal, system-critical discussions. Socialist leaders exploited FRG opposition to Bundeswehr rearmament and the Vietnam War but declared pacifism at home a state crime. In March 1968, the SED openly attacked reforms advocated by the Czech Communist Party, banning newspapers, artworks, and musical recordings from Prague. By spring it was restricting tourist travel between the two states, which it needed to pay its Czech trade debts. It arrested Frank and Florian Havermann, sons of an SED functionary, for distributing leaflets against the Soviet invasion.

The Kasners counted among a few privileged GDR families allowed to vacation outside Prague in August 1968; Angela's parents traveled into the city for a day as the crisis unfolded. When she returned to school, the 14-year-old model student realized that talking about her summer vacation would probably cause trouble. The SED crackdown on potential protestors clearly targeted youth: 66 percent of those arrested from August to November were under 25, including workers and apprentices. Strongly represented in the freely elected *Volkskammer*, this generation later sought forgiveness from the Czech people for GDR participation in the Warsaw Pact invasion in its April 1990 resolution.

Given the violent crackdown she had witnessed in the East, Merkel failed to grasp the significance of New Leftists' efforts in 1968 to confront the Nazi past and the complicity of their parents. The SED's repressive response, coupled with the Czech hardliners who replaced Dubček, also blinded her to the democratizing currents driving their "extra-parliamentary" associations, some of which would outlive the radical violence. This became clear during a 2001 Bundestag debate, when CDU opposition leader Merkel denounced Green minister Joschka Fischer, demanding that he "atone" for physically attacking a Frankfurt policeman in 1973 as well as for his "totally twisted view of the Federal Republic."[61] She was shocked by the angry response that ensued, "even within her own party," over the audacity of an Eastern woman trying to impart a history lesson to Westerners.[62]

Ironically, the Red–Green government, including ex-SDS members who used to attack "the system," laid the foundation for Merkel's later migration and gender policy reforms. By then politicians of all stripes had come to see 1968 as a part of a larger cultural revolution, united in part by the music of the times (she also liked the Beatles). As an outsider Merkel had not been privy to its liberalizing effects on FRG views of women's rights, Third World solidarity, personal expression and sexual relations. She observed later:

I used to believe that the 1968 movement was a total disaster for Germany. But there came a time when I discovered, to my astonishment, that there were people in the CDU who opposed the 1968 contingent in the Party but now think there ought to be a monument to Rudi Dutschke ... This threw me off balance, but today I can understand their attitude ...[63]

The western "'68 generation" likewise served as the vanguard of another reform favored by the chancellor after Fukushima: "One day I heard Joschka Fischer speaking about the *Scheiss-Plutonium* (shitty-plutonium) economy ... I said to myself: 'the what?' Only then did I realize that for many people there are close associations between nuclear power stations and nuclear weapons production, and thus with NATO and our alignment with the West. I understand those sensitivities better now."[64]

Potential GDR rebels turned to literature, the arts, and church-based environmental initiatives, but most avoided direct confrontations with the state. They would take the lead in a second cultural revolution twenty years later, however, making up for lost time between August and November of 1989. We turn now to Merkel's efforts to master a crisis-ridden present in relation to two further issues: economic restructuring and redefining gender relations.

MASTERING THE PRESENT: THE EASTERN ECONOMY AND GENDER RELATIONS

On July 1, 1990, Unity Chancellor Kohl, promised to turn eastern states into "blossoming landscapes in which it paid to live and to work again," insisting that no one "would be worse off than before – many would be better off."[65] Millions of Germans expected to see rejuvenated cities, industrial modernization, and environmental makeovers in just a few years. Instead of immediate peace and prosperity, GDR citizens were blown away by a "gale of creative destruction."[66] Between 1990 and 1994, more than 600 factories closed, industrial production plunged by 60 percent, and the East German labor force declined from 8.9 million to 5.8 million.[67]

Instead of accruing major profits from the sale of state assets (to cover restructuring costs), the privatization agency (*Treuhandanstalt*) accumulated DM 256 billion in debts by 1994. Rather than list the 1,000 biggest companies for public auction, it engaged in "discrete bargaining."[68] Staff were barred from selling a third of the agricultural land so as not to "disrupt" western prices.[69] The *Treuhand* strategy was plagued by "many bad decisions, corruption and stupidity," turning privatization into a fire-sale for West Germans; the latter bought whole factories for 1 DM, then demanded subsidies to clean up environmental messes. While its own staff grew to 4,200, 72 percent of those working in liquidated enterprises lost their jobs. Western producers pursued "oligopolistic self-interest," focusing more on eliminating potential competition than on improving eastern production capacities.[70]

Social security payments to the new states, equivalent to 20 percent of eastern GDP, were immediately rechanneled into consumption. Billions in financial transfers turned into a huge subsidy program for stagnating *western* companies that quickly expanded production; these funds passed through the eastern states "like a boomerang," leading Rudiger Frank to ask: "Now, who benefited from all that investment? It was West German companies who expanded to the east. So that was a subsidy to West German industry. Infrastructure projects, highways, roads, telecommunication networks, who did that? West German companies, because all the East German construction companies were either bankrupt or bought up by West German competitors."[71] Kohl even allowed them to sub-subcontract laborers from Poland and Italy, cheaper than jobless East Germans, to build the new government center near the Brandenburg Gate. The so-called ABM (job creation) funds subsidized wages for western employers, who fired "trainees" as soon as subsidies ended; some of my friends, all women, lost such jobs four times, then gave up. State monopolies were replaced by private ones in relation to hotel and grocery chains.

Forty percent of the non-earmarked funds went to local authorities who, like liquidated businesses, were required to pay off DM 350 billion in old GDR debt that was turned over to Western banks; these windfall credit-assets entitled the latter to DM 16 billion in future interest payments on those debts. Banks in Bonn received nearly DM 70 billion in assets.[72] Kohl's insistence on property restitution over compensation allowed Western "inheritance communities" (descendants of formerly expropriated owners) to file 2 million claims. Winning their cases with the help of savvy Western lawyers, they immediately re-sold the properties to real-estate speculators who raised rents to levels that long-term inhabitants could not pay. Lacking Western forms of collateral, entrepreneurial Easterners could not get loans to start their own businesses.

In 1994, lawmakers amended Article 72 BL, which had granted the government special powers to ensure "equal" living conditions throughout the federal territory since 1949. By 1995, SPD Bundestag Vice-President Wolfgang Thierse declared that the Eastern economy was "on the brink of disaster."[73] Although the first Solidarity Pact supplied €7.1 billion through to 2001, then €10.5 billion per year, aggregate stagnation continued. The last Solidarity Pact, running through 2019, foresees €105 billion for special needs, and €51 billion to promote economic growth. All told, unification has cost about €70–80 billion ($118 billion) per year, a bargain compared with the $750 billion George W. Bush handed over for the first Wall Street bailout. Total unification costs for the first twenty years ran upwards of €2 trillion. Of course, freedom is priceless.

Merkel never criticized Westerners' erroneous belief that they alone financed reconstruction; employed Easterners also paid taxes. Most "transfers" actually involve normal federal responsibilities, like highway construction, railway upgrades, and disaster relief; the SED did not "cause" the massive floods of 1997. Hessen, Baden-Württemberg, Bavaria, North Rhine-Westphalia, and Hamburg are net contributors to the constitutionally mandated revenue-sharing and VAT re-allocation, but the beneficiaries also include Berlin, Bremen, Lower Saxony, Rhineland-Palatinate, Schleswig-Holstein, and the Saarland. Stricter EU competition rules on subsidies imposed in the early 1990s restricted direct state investment in Eastern firms but did not stop the indirect subsidies to Western firms.

Eastern infrastructure and productivity have dramatically improved since 1990: unit labor costs run at about 88 percent, wages average about 81 percent of Western norms, but neo-liberal deregulation and EU enlargement now enables employers to hire Poles and Czechs, even cheaper. By 2005, 21 percent were still jobless in Leipzig, despite its Boom Town status. Unemployment decreased by half a million after 2005, but only 60 percent of Easterners found steady work. Though only 5 percent of federal research and development (R&D) funding flows into the East, "Silicon Saxony" has generated real growth in the IT and chemical sectors. Dresden alone has added 200 companies, generating 20,000 new jobs. Youth unemployment has dropped by a third, thanks to a 13.7 percent decline in population: younger, better educated citizens have headed west for work.

Things have blossomed in the East in unanticipated ways and places: weeds and wildflowers took over once crowded labor sites after whole industries shut down; job losses were disguised as short-term layoffs until workers qualified for early retirement. Resembling ghost towns, those areas hardest hit have torn down entire housing complexes (*Abbau Ost*). Losing 20,000 jobs, open-cast coal mines throughout the Lausitz have been flooded with rainwater, resulting in a chain of lakes covering 130 km²; another 50,000 hectares (124,000 acres) were privatized as nature preserves. An economic growth spurt kicked in after 2008, courtesy of an accelerated "renewable energy turn-around" that has added forests of profit-producing wind turbines and fields of photo-voltaic panels to the eastern landscape, especially in northern and rural regions (Chapter 6). Bucolic Mecklenburg-Vorpommern, for example, collects

€162 million in subsidies for wind energy, although it only consumes a fraction of the power it produces.[74]

The shrinking gap between older and younger states results from more than the green technologies export boom. Westerners have been forced to identify with their Eastern relatives in another sense: the Hartz reforms introduced by SPD Chancellor Schröder subjected many *Wessis* to the same bitter, neo-liberal medicine dosed out to *Ossis*. They, too, have encountered low wage mini-jobs, temporary contracts, and endless retraining programs. In 2012, the Constitutional Court admonished lawmakers for cutting benefits to levels that no longer supported human dignity. Twenty years after the Wall collapsed, writer Daniela Dahn observed: "When something warm and something cold flow together, the warm element becomes colder and the cold one becomes warmer. That's nature. When rich and poor are unified, the rich become richer and the poor become poorer. That's how humans are."[75] Not all Westerners draw DAX-CEO salaries, and not all Easterners are desperately hunting for jobs and partners in *Mezzogiorno-Mecklenburg*.

Another shared experience derives from the fact that economic crises usually allocate a disproportionate share of austerity costs to women, leading us to examine Merkel's contribution to the reconciliation of those identities.[76] Eastern women were hit hard by unemployment and the elimination of socialist benefits, and were less likely to be rehired by Western employers. When younger, educated females headed west in search of jobs, state officials in Mecklenburg-Vorpommern started a public campaign in 2007 to find wives for its "abandoned" rural men, the Eastern equivalent of Norwegian bachelor farmers in Lake Wobegon. Conservatives blame women, especially academics, for the big drop in fertility rates over the last three decades, but, as noted earlier, GDR women produced more children at an earlier age, then continued to engage in paid labor.

Not that Western and Eastern feminists have found it easy to get along: they differed on everything from motherhood, abortion rights, and employment to attitudes toward men, identity politics, and state funding. Women's identities were the result of a gendered socialization process that pitted them against each other, so that each side could "stabilize and support its own ideology."[77] Male leaders and interests dominated the politics of unification, construed as "the triumph of the Fatherland," but Western feminists were just as quick to assert their superiority vis-à-vis their Eastern "stepsisters."[78] The SED's motives were more pro-natalist than emancipatory, but it did provide many work–family reconciliation benefits lacking in the West. During the first stage of their own difficult relationship, Eastern equality activists accused women in the old states of domination, while Western feminists dismissed the former as "theoretically naive" with regard to state patriarchy. Both sides pulled back into their respective epistemological shells, avoiding the real problems facing those whose benefits and jobs rapidly disappeared as neo-liberal pressures pummeled Germany as a whole.

Fresh from the GDR, Merkel observed that in 1989, before joining the Kohl Cabinet, she had "thought about everything, except about the fact that I was a woman. The longer I am in politics, the more I become aware of the significance of this topic."[79] In 1992, her efforts to legislate penalties against sexual harassment and to fill half of all civil service vacancies with women were blocked by conservative hardliners intent on preserving "natural" gender roles. As a data-driven scientist, Merkel quickly recognized the potential economic consequences of an imminent demographic deficit; her GDR socialization moreover helped her to identify one of its root causes: a lack of childcare facilities allowing for work–family reconciliation, a path preferred by 80 percent of all women. From 1998 to 2005, Herta Däubler-Gmelin, Christine Bergmann, and Renate Schmidt (all SPD ministers) pushed for an anti-discrimination law, gay partnerships, expanded childcare, and even corporate quotas, but they were blocked by Chancellor Schröder who socialized with CEOs, wore designer suits, and smoked expensive cigars before he went off to work for Putin at Gazprom.[80] It took a childless Eastern physicist to enact most of these reforms, irrespective of family structure: "Family is there where parents assume responsibility for their children and children for their parents."[81]

The EU adopted *gender mainstreaming* in 1996, but most FRG officials were clueless as to its meaning; many still are, but that has not stopped Easterners from interpreting it as something they had experienced for years. For them, the EU emphasis on family–work reconciliation, childcare, and promoting women in science and technology is a return to things past. Adding twelve EU new member states in 2004–2005 also mitigated the perception that Easterners were the odd ones out. Realizing that Sweden, Denmark, Finland, France, and the Netherlands provide the same services that they had once enjoyed, it became clear to Eastern women that they were part of the progressive mainstream: West Germans and their antiquated breadwinner models were the ones wallowing in a modernization deficit.

These differences, too, have diminished with time, thanks to new policies introduced under an Eastern chancellor and a Western working mother of seven. Thanks to EU directives, their "social achievements" have become the norm across the united Germany. In fact, the biggest attitudinal changes regarding gender roles – let us call them positive mood swings – have taken hold in the West. First, post-unity feminists are less skittish about state regulation in gender-specific domains because they are no longer ruled by Father State but rather by *Mutti Merkel* and her Minister-Mom side-kick, von der Leyen. Second, earlier hostility toward the patriarchal state is fading insofar as Merkel's reforms have produced real changes in the rights and responsibilities of men, for example, paternity leave. Third, presented as a means for improving early education outcomes among children of migrant descent, utilizing childcare facilities no longer renders women vulnerable to branding as "Raven Mothers."[82] Fourth, demographic projections of population decline, from 81 to 69 million by 2050 (a third of whom will be over 65), makes it easier to present women's paid labor as quintessential to Germany's economic sustainability.

PROVIDING FOR A SUSTAINABLE FUTURE: DEMOGRAPHIC CHANGE

Gender is not the only arena in which the chancellor has pulled off a spectacular CDU modernization. Two other policy domains figure prominently in Merkel's hopes of coming to terms with the future. She wants to meet the challenges of climate change by becoming No. 1 in renewable energy and green technology production. Eastern economic recovery is rooted in the energy turn-around introduced in 2008 under the first Grand Coalition but its rapid acceleration owes to Merkel's reading of the Japanese tea-leaves after the Fukushima Daiichi nuclear disaster of 2011. While "Silicon Saxony" had already established itself as a base for high-tech start-ups in the 1990s, based on the industrial concentration and reputable technical universities found there in GDR times, less urbanized areas have also found new productive niches; laggards like Mecklenburg-Pomerania have moved forward with New Economy ventures such as "Biocon Valley." Rather than produce wind turbines and solar cells, Easterners are specializing in the design and maintenance of eco-friendly equipment (described in Chapter 6).

The second challenge is to move Germans to support the integration of millions of new migrants as permanent members of society. As an

Easterner, Merkel had no direct exposure to Italians, Greeks, Croatians, and Turks recruited by Western industries as of the 1950s. The SED compensated for its "missing generation" after 1949 by pulling women into the paid labor force. It later recruited 190,000 temporary laborers from fraternal states like Vietnam and Mozambique, but they were isolated from the population at large under dire conditions. Irene Runge and Landolf Scherzer demonstrate that, despite official May Day speeches hailing solidarity under international proletarianism, average GDR citizens had few chances to learn about "living with difference."[83] Western politicians were quick to blame "life under the SED dictatorship" for a wave of xenophobic violence between 1990 and 1993, but three-fourths of the anti-foreigner arson attacks took place on Western soil: thirteen Turkish women and children were burned alive in Mölln and Solingen. Youth from Hamburg, Kiel, and Berlin were among those arrested for attacking an asylum hostel in Rostock in summer 1992.[84]

Heading two Grand Coalitions, Merkel has fundamentally redefined citizenship, migration, and asylum rights in Germany (Chapter 7). "Failed integration" can no longer be blamed on "foreigners"; persons with migration background account for 20 percent of the population. Advocating sustainable integration, she expects Germans themselves to adapt to new demographic realities, under the motto "Unity is the Goal, Diversity is the Way." She made that quite obvious in August 2015 when she suspended the Dublin regulations and opened her country to over 800,000 refugees fleeing civil war, terrorism, and sectarian violence stretching from Libya to Afghanistan. Thousands of her compatriots rallied to assist them at 14,000 volunteer centers across Germany.

Curiously, many NPR, BBC, and even *Deutsche Welle* reporters attributed citizens' helpful reactions to the thousands of refugees pouring into their towns to memories of the 12 million forced to flee their homelands in 1945. Most of today's Germans were not even born then. The image I have in mind is June 27, 1989, when two foreign ministers symbolically cut the fence between Austria and Hungary.[85] The pictures of countless men, women, and children trying to climb over or under new razor-wire barriers along the Hungarian and Slovakian borders reminds me of thousands of GDR citizens scaling the walls of FRG embassy compounds in Poland and Czechoslovakia. As I watched huge crowds pressing to enter the Budapest *Ostbahnhof* in August 2015, I did not imagine trains deporting millions of people to concentration camps, doomed for extermination; instead, I recalled rioting Dresdeners trying to jump on to trains heading for Bavaria from Warsaw and Prague on October 4, 1989. The images of

Hungarian police beating and tear-gassing women carrying infants should have reminded all Germans of the world's positive response to unification.

The 2015 references to the millions forced to flee during the Second World War were troubling for another reason. Merkel has repeatedly stressed that Germany must become a "welcoming culture." Old frameworks of guilt and shame associated with Nazi atrocities offer a lousy foundation for a *positive*, united identity. It makes more sense to base this new culture on postwar German pride in having mobilized the biggest Eastern and Western peace movements witnessed in Europe and in pulling off two extraordinary economic reconstructions.[86] It should draw on the values of freedom, democracy, opportunity, and international cooperation that their country has come to represent. It should recognize their contributions to ecological sustainability, and a new willingness to assist others who have never enjoyed "freedom, solidarity and justice." The chancellor stressed those very themes in her eloquent remarks of August 31, 2015, when she declared, "German unity is not something we achieved with normal effort."[87]

CONCLUSION: LEARNING TO LIVE WITH DIFFERENCES

The Berlin Wall fostered the illusion that only the geo-physical barrier, not forty years of systemic, ideological opposition, changing life-styles, and communication structures separated the Germans. While politicians assumed that a common constitution, currency, and borders would do the trick, Schneider unwittingly prophesied in the early 1980s that, "To tear down the Wall in the head will take longer than any undertaking required to tear down the visible Wall."[88] It has taken both sides twenty-five years to realize, citing Egon Bahr, that "reunification is not a single act that can be put into practice on the basis of an historical resolution on an historical day at an historical conference but is rather a process with many steps and many stations."[89] Angela Merkel may be the only exception: "I can only say, if I am a political product then I am one [produced] by German unity, and I am proud that I am an all-German politician with east German roots; otherwise I am a product of my parents, and I am also proud of that."[90]

Merkel grew up with two father figures, Pastor Kasner and the SED state, both difficult in their own way. The first instilled in her not only the virtues of hard work but also the need for ethical principles to ensure that "tolerance does not become indifference, that freedom does not mean thoughtless laissez-faire, that individuality does not foster a society without solidarity."[91] Attributing her decisions to her Christian upbringing, she cites seven precepts guiding her behavior: preserving human dignity; acting with moderation and proportion; treating things that are the same equally, and things that are unequal differently; fostering solidarity and citizen inclusion; thinking beyond today; exercising personal reliability; and last but not least, practicing more humility.[92] Her socialization under an authoritarian state supplied her with other unusual skills for confronting a querulous all-German Fatherland. She regularly expresses appreciation for the everyday improvements brought by unification. When asked what she loved about Germany she responded, "I think about air-tight windows. No other country can produce such thick and attractive windows."[93]

To reunite Easterners and Westerners slow to internalize the empathy, tolerance, and respect for difference denied to them by their two difficult Fatherlands prior to 1990, Merkel has had to shepherd her compatriots through four critical stages. First, although unification initially produced little "internal unity" *between* east and west, it did unify each side *from within*. The '68ers, now sixty and seventy-somethings, had mellowed significantly by 1989; most had abandoned fierce, all-night debates over the ideological fallacies of New Left or Springer Press antagonists. They preferred to wax "westalgic" over the good old days of protest while drinking red wine from Tuscany. After October 3, 1990, "previous Maoists found common ground with Hanseatic business executives, former *Spontis* bonded with southern German liberals and long-term *Jusos* joined with Rhineland conservatives in shaking their heads together over the East Germans. Nothing has unified the West Germans so much as the admission of the East Germans."[94]

Given their lack of free expression under an authoritarian state, East Germans were more unified from the start, *ein Volk*. They were nonetheless surprised to learn that dramatist Peter Hacks was correct, having alleged decades earlier that "in the GDR there are fewer Communists than they say but also more than they think." Although many had been at odds with the state, unification solidified their sense of shared peer identity by collectively subjecting them to radical changes in their life-styles, beliefs, and opportunities.

The second stage involved learning to live with differences *between East and West Germans*, once both sides registered that they did not comprise an organic community based on history, language, and lineage.[95] The Hartz IV reforms subjected Westerners to the neo-liberal medicine that had been dosed out to their GDR counterparts, pushing them out of Adenauer's comfortable "no experiments" paradigm into the Hegelian world of the dialectic. It took citizens of the old Federal Republic ten years longer to adjust to structural changes, but the impact has been just as profound. In the final analysis, thesis met its antithesis; a new generation will become the standard-bearer of an identity synthesis.

A third stage of learning to live with difference directly affected women. Deeply divided across the 1970s as liberal reformists, socialists, autonomous separatists, and lesbians, many West feminists took refuge in epistemological debates over Judith Butler, professional networking, post-structuralist theorizing, and campaigns targeting male-normed nouns during the 1980s. East women were too busy trying to restore the real-existing support systems that their childless counterparts could afford to ignore. Ironically, a substantial part of the GDR gender regime has become "the new normal."

Women on both sides had moreover exonerated themselves from the hypernationalism and racism of the Fatherland, despite systemic differences. Once GDR women charged FRG feminists with "domination," they all began to face up to racist proclivities in their encounters with women of migrant and Muslim descent. Both sides were shocked to see younger women, *Femi-Nazis*, joining right extremist groups.[96] Merkel has created an opening for women to carry their share of a German historical burden (Holocaust) she deems "indivisible" despite the sex of the perpetrators. She expects all Germans to engage in the cultivation of a positive national identity, including youth of migrant descent.[97]

This brings us to the fourth step, learning to live with ethnic diversity and religious pluralization. I spent 2006 teaching at Berlin's Humboldt University, close to the Fan Mile that attracted nearly 1 million World Soccer Cup revelers under the motto, "the world, a guest among friends." Sometimes the crowd sang the FIFA theme song, *Arriba, Arriba!*, composed by Jorge Luis Piloto; but many also learned the national anthem, hearing it played whenever their own team took to the field. The sad truth is that as late as 2009, only 51 percent of Westerners knew the words.

The stretch between the Brandenburg Gate and the *Siegessäule* (Winged Victory), commemorating other highs and lows in German history, was packed with young people sporting FRG flags, black/red/gold face-paint and wigs. Many of my peers were horrified by the joyful display of "national symbols." Non-Germans thought they looked like "the united faces of Benetton" featured in clothing ads. Turkish-German youth headed the car-caravans cruising up and down the Ku-damm, honking incessantly after the FRG's first two victories. Thousands cried, literally, as the party came to an end with the closing ceremony on July 10. To me, this was compelling visual testimony that the nation is finally "normal." And what better image of national unity could we desire than 2006 and 2014 photographs of a powerful Eastern woman in the middle of a smelly soccer locker room, cheek to cheek with guys named Muller, Khedira, Steinschweiger, Boateng, Neuer, Podolski, Klose, Özil, or Götze?

Now it is time to top off the relative accomplishments of unification with a final step. Remembered more for his peace activism than for his presidential accomplishments, Gustav Heinemann was asked point blank by a *Spiegel* journalist in 1969 if he loved Germany, to which he responded curtly, "Ach, I don't love any state. I love my wife." If there is one thing that the SED accomplished over a span of four decades, it was to have its citizens internalize the ability to combine "love" and "fatherland" in a single phrase: *Love for the socialist Fatherland*. Many Westerners interviewed by Marie Louise Janssen-Jurreit in the mid-1980s had a cathartic reaction to her simple question: "Do you love Germany?"[98] Love of Fatherland was an absolute anomaly in the West German pyramid of affections.

Ultimately, there is not some unique, peculiar way in which Germans can define their national identity by not having one. A lack of personal identification with one's country holds many consequences for system stability. It is precisely a measure of internalized, sentimental attachment that ensures a reservoir of legitimacy and loyalty in times of crisis. In Merkel's words: "If Germany can find its identity and stand by it, that will be good for democracy ... A great deal of damage is done by what remains unsaid, concealed. We must develop a sense of our history as a whole, and then say: We are happy to be German. That already rolls easily off my tongue!"[99]

When critics charged that she had not reflected enough on that difficult word, *Vaterland*, she responded:

You are only thinking about this from a west German perspective – I [think in] all-German terms ... when I use a word like Fatherland, I am not using it in some over-elevated sense. I don't find the Germans particularly bad or extraordinarily great. I'm a great fan of döner and pizza ... I don't use the word Fatherland based on the judgment that we are the pivot and linchpin of the world. I use it in the sense that I can say, this is my language, over there stand my trees, there is my lake, and that is where I grew up. I like living here. I have confidence in this country, and I am part of its shared history – with all of its pains and its good sides.[100]

Do twenty-five years of unification guarantee that the Germans of East and West are ready to live happily ever after with each other? The short answer is probably no more than one would expect people in Hamburg, Berlin, or Schleswig Holstein to love CSU politicians in Bavaria. After all, these are the people who invented the terms *Weltschmerz, Schadenfreude,* and *Wutbürger.* But I do believe that Merkel has helped them to see that differences are normal, non-antagonistic, necessary, and even welcome in a pluralist democracy.

As ex-FRG President Christian Wulff once said of Merkel: "The good shepherd leads the herd from behind; he [sic] does not lose a sheep but still the herd goes in the direction that he wants."[101] That analogy would not be lost on a chancellor raised as a pastor's daughter in an otherwise top-down, ideologically driven system. Angela Merkel entered national politics with a faith in dialogue and democratic processes that had been lost among traditional politicians. She is not afraid to discuss her personal values, and though she could do a better job of practicing what she preaches in some domains, her pragmatic performance record is substantially better than her partisan reputation. For that reason, I see Angela Merkel as the personification of something we all came to realize on that incredible day the Berlin Wall fell: miracles happen.

NOTES

1. William Faulkner, *Requiem for a Nun* (1951), was also cited by Christa Wolf in *Kindheitsmuster,* originally published in 1976.
2. Timur Kuran, "Now Out of Never: The Element of Surprise in the East European Revolutions of 1989," *World Politics,* 44(1) (1991): 7–48.
3. Albert O. Hirschman, "Exit, Voice and the Fate of the German Democratic Republic," *World Politics,* 45 (1993): 173–202.
4. Andrea Teti and Gennaro Gervasio, "The Unbearable Lightness of Authoritarianism: Lessons from the Arab Uprisings," *Mediterranean Politics,* 16(2) (2011): 321–327.
5. Joyce Marie Mushaben, "Youth Protest and the Democratic State: Reflections on the Rise of Anti-Political Culture in Prewar Germany and the German Federal Republic," *Research in Political Sociology,* 2 (1986): 171–197; Joyce Marie Mushaben, "Cycles of Peace Protest in West Germany: Experiences from Three Decades," *West European Politics,* 8(1) (1985): 24–40; Joyce Marie Mushaben, "Anti-Politics and Successor Generations: The Role of Youth in the West and East German Peace Movements," *Journal of Political and Military Sociology,* 12 (1984): 171–190; Mushaben, "Ost–West Identitäten."
6. Beyond reviewing hundreds of surveys conducted by Allensbach, Emnid, Forschungsgruppe Wahlen, and Infratest, I also drew on specialized government surveys shared by "insiders." See Mushaben, *From Post-War to Post-Wall Generations.*

7. For extensive summaries, see Mushaben, *From Post-War to Post-Wall Generations*, ch. 3.

8. Günther Rüther, "Politische Kultur und innere Einheit in Deutschland," Konrad Adenauer Stiftung, Sankt Augustin, 1995.

9. Gunnar Winkler (ed.), *Sozialreport 2004. Daten und Fakten zur sozialen Lage in den neuen Bundesländern* (Berlin-Brandenburg: Trafo, 2004), pp. 13–15.

10. Dieter Thomä, "Keine nationalen Töne!" *Die Zeit*, April 29, 1994.

11. Barrington Moore, Jr., *On the Social Origins of Dictatorship and Democracy: Lord and Peasant in the Making of the Modern World* (Boston, MA: Beacon Press, 1966), p. 486.

12. Gustav Heinemann, available at: www.heinemann-bildungsstaette.de/48.html.

13. Klaus J. Bade and Jochen Oltmer (eds.), *Aussiedler: Deutsche Einwanderer aus Osteuropa* (Osnabrück: Universitätsverlag Rasch, 1999).

14. The original essay appeared as "Was bedeutet Aufarbeitung der Vergangenheit" (Frankfurt: Suhrkamp, 1959); for an English version, see Theodor W. Adorno, "What does Coming to Terms with the Past Mean?" in Geoffrey Hartman (ed.), *Bitburg in Moral and Political Perspective* (Bloomington, IN: Indiana University Press, 1986), pp. 114–129.

15. Adorno, "Coming to Terms with the Past," p. 124.

16. Alexander Mitscherlich and Margarete Mitscherlich, *Die Unfähigkeit zu trauern: Grundlagen kollektiven Verhaltens* (Munich: Piper, 1967).

17. Hermann Lübbe, "Der Nationalsozialismus im politischen Bewußtsein der Gegenwart," *Historische Zeitschrift*, 236 (1983): 579–599; Tilmann Moser, "Die Unfähigkeit zu trauern: Hält die Diagnose einer Überprüfung stand? Zur psychischen Verarbeitung des Holocaust in der Bundesrepublik," *Psyche*, 46 (1992): 389–405.

18. Charles Maier, *The Unmasterable Past: History, Holocaust and German National Identity* (Cambridge, MA: Harvard University Press, 1988).

19. Hannah Arendt, "Eichmann in Jerusalem," *The New Yorker*, February 16, 1963.

20. Martin Greiffenhagen and Sylvia Greiffenhagen, *Ein schwieriges Vaterland – Zur politischen Kultur der Bundesrepublik Deutschland* (Frankfurt: Fischer, 1981).

21. *Historikerstreit: Die Dokumentation der Kontroverse um die Einzigartigkeit der nationalsozialistischen Judenvernichtung* (Munich: Piper, 1987).

22. Rudolf Hirsch and Rosemarie Schuder, *Der gelbe Fleck: Wurzeln und Wirkungen des Judenhasses in der deutschen Geschichte* (Berlin: Rütten & Löning, 1987): Lutz Niethammer, *Die volkseigene Erfahrung: Eine Archäologie des Lebens in der Industrieprovinz der DDR* (Berlin: Rowohlt, 1991).

23. Rudolf Bahro, *Die Alternative: Zur Kritik des real existierenden Sozialismus* (Cologne: Europäische Verlagsanstalt, 1977).

24. Gottfried Zieger, Boris Meissner, and Dieter Blumenwitz (eds.), *Deutschland als Ganzes. Rechtliche und historische Überlegungen* (Cologne: Wissenschaft & Politik, 1985); Peter von Berglar, Hans Filbinger et al., *Deutsche Identität*

heute (Weikersheim: Hase & Koehler, 1983); Josef von Häussling, Klaus Held et al., *Drei Fragen zu Deutschland–58 Antworten* (Munich: Albrecht Knaus, 1985); Karl Moersch, *Sind wir denn eine Nation? Die Deutschen und ihr Vaterland* (Bonn: Bonn Aktuell, 1982); Egon Bahr, *Was wird aus den Deutschen? Fragen und Antworten* (Reinbeck: Rowohlt, 1982); Peter Petersen, *Sind wir denn noch zu retten? Der Bundestagsabgeordnete schreibt an seinen 19-jährigen Sohn, der sich Sorgen um die Zukunft macht* (Stuttgart: Burg, 1984); and Günther Gaus, *Wo Deutschland liegt–Eine Ortsbestimmung* (Hamburg: Hoffmann & Campe, 1983).

25. Peter Schneider, *Der Mauerspringer* (Darmstadt: Luchterhand, 1982); Gert Heidenreich, *Die Gnade der späten Geburt* (Munich: Piper, 1986); Peter Brückner, *Versuch, uns und anderen die Bundesrepublik zu erklären* (Berlin: Klaus Wagenbach, 1984); Werner Weidenfeld (ed.), *Nachdenken über Deutschland* (Cologne: Wissenschaft & Politik, 1985); Werner Weidenfeld, *Ratlose Normalität–Die Deutschen auf der Suche nach sich selbst* (Osnabrück: Interfrom, 1984); J. B. Gradl, *Deutschland als Aufgabe* (Cologne: Wissenschaft & Politik, 1986); Wolfgang Venohr (ed.), *Die deutsche Einheit kommt bestimmt!* (Bergisch Gladbach: Gustav Lübbe, 1982); Wolfgang Venohr (ed.), *Ohne Deutschland geht es nicht–7 Autoren zur Lage der Nation* (Drefeld: SINUS, 1985); Anton Peisl and Armin Mohler (eds.), *Die deutsche Neurose–Über die beschädigte Identität der Deutschen* (Frankfurt: Ullstein, 1980); Jürgen Leinemann, *Die Angst der Deutschen. Beobachtungen zur Bewußtseinslage der Nation* (Reinbeck: Rowohlt, 1982); Wilfried von Bredow, *Deutschland–Ein Provisorium?* (Berlin: W. J. Siedler, 1985); Richard von Weizsäcker, *Die deutsche Geschichte geht weiter* (Munich: Deutscher Taschenbuch Verlag, 1985); Dan Diner (ed.), *Ist der Nationalsozialismus Geschichte? Zu Historisierung und Historikerstreit* (Frankfurt: Fischer, 1987); and Gordon A. Craig, *The Germans* (New York: Putnam, 1982).

26. The term *Wende-Jugend* signified youth's shift to more conservative values during the Reagan, Thatcher, and Kohl eras, in reaction against the leftist ideals of the '68 generation.

27. French peace activists wanted nuclear disarmament that excluded their own *force de frappe*.

28. Mushaben, *From PostWar to Post-Wall Generations*, p. 40

29. Schneider, *Der Mauerspringer*, p. 13.

30. Jürgen Hofmann, *Ein neues Deutschland soll es sein: Zur Frage nach der Nation in der Geschichte der DDR und der Politik der SED* (Berlin: Dietz, 1989).

31. Hofmann, *Ein neues Deutschland*, pp. 251 ff.

32. Thomas Heubner, "Nation und Nationalität – Staatsbürgerschaft: DDR – Nationalität: Deutsch – oder wie entwickeln sich Nationen?" *Junge Generation*, 35(10) (1981), p. 34.

33. Irene Dolling, with Daphne Hahn and Sylka Scholz, "Biomacht – Biopolitik," *Potsdamer Studien zur Frauen- und Geschlechterforschung* 2 (1998). Editor Konrad H. Jarausch misinterprets this decline in his introduction to *United Germany. Debating Processes and Prospects* (New York: Berghahn, 2013).

34. Mushaben, "Ost–West Identitäten."
35. Lemke, *Die Ursachen des Umbruchs. Politische Sozialisation in der ehemaligen DDR.*
36. Heinrich Bortfeldt, "United yet Separate: A View from the East," in Konrad H. Jarausch (ed.), *United Germany. Debating Processes and Prospects* (New York: Berghahn, 2013), pp. 55–56; also, Jennifer Yoder, "Truth without Reconciliation in post-Communist Germany: An Appraisal of the Enquete Commission on the SED Dictatorship in Germany," *German Politics*, 8(3) (1999): 59–80.
37. Kornelius, *Angela Merkel: Die Kanzlerin und ihre Welt*, p. 16.
38. Thomas Ahbe, "Die Konstruktion der Ostdeutschen. Diskursive Spannungen, Stereotype und Identitäten seit 1989," *Aus Politik und Zeitgeschichte*, 41/42 (2004), p. 21. Further, Karl-Siegbert Rehberg, "Ost–West," in Stephan Lessenich and Frank Nullmeier (eds.), *Deutschland, Eine gespaltene Gesellschaft* (Bonn: Bundeszentrale für politische Bildung, 2006), p. 219.
39. The electrified cables and barbed wire used for the Soviet SZ-100 signaling system had rusted, but because Hungarians had been free to travel since 1988, the interior minister did not waste valuable hard currency reserves replacing them. See Walter Mayr, "Hungary's Peaceful Revolution: Cutting the Fence and Changing History," *Der Spiegel*, May 29, 2009.
40. Martin Ahrend (ed.), *Mein Leben, Teil Zwei* (Cologne: Kiepenheur & Witsch, 1989); Anne Köhler and Volker Ronge, "Ein Test auf Wiedervereinigung? Die Reaktion der Bundesdeutschen auf die Übersiedlerwelle aus der DDR von Frühjahr 1984," *Deutschland Archiv*, 18(1) (1984): 52–59.
41. The first free GDR elections took place on March 18, 1990; FRG leaders introduced the currency union on July 1, 1990; Kohl's one-to-one exchange rate produced an immediate liquidity crisis. The first Western vote took place in December, two months after unification had been signed, sealed, and delivered.
42. Peter Süskind, "Deutschland – Eine Midlife Crisis," *Der Spiegel*, September 17, 1990.
43. Süskind, "Deutschland – Eine Midlife Crisis."
44. Cited in Mushaben, *From Post-War to Post-Wall Generations*, p. 372.
45. Friedrich Schorlemmer, "Graben statt Mauer: Wir brauchen euch – Ihr braucht uns nicht," *Die Zeit*, July 5, 1991.
46. Roll, *Die Erste*.
47. Müller-Vogg, *Angela Merkel*.
48. Peter Reichel, *Vergangenheitsbewältigung in Deutschland: Die Auseinandersetzung mit der NS-Diktatur in Politik und Justiz* (Hamburg: Beck'sche Reihe, 2007), p. 199.
49. "Verantwortung, Vertrauen, Solidarität." Rede von Bundeskanzlerin Angela Merkel am 18. März 2008 vor der Knesset in Jerusalem.
50. Günter Grass, "Ich war Mitglied der Waffen-SS," *Der Spiegel*, August 11, 2006.
51. Avi Primor, "Peeling Günther Grass' Israeli Onion," *Israel Journal of Foreign Affairs*, 6(2) (2012): 101–106; Wolfgang Kraushaar, *Wann endlich beginnt*

bei Euch der Kampf gegen die heilige Kuh Israel? Über die antisemitischen Wurzeln des deutschen Terrorismus (Reinbeck: Rowohlt, 2013).

52. "Günter Grass nennt Bundeswehr Söldnerarmee," *Die Welt*, June 26, 2013. *Spiegel* editor Jakob Augstein's support drew an equally vehement Israeli response. Both Jürgen Mölleman's (FDP) 2002 endorsement of Palestinian violence against Israelis and Martin Walser's 1998 complaint about using the Holocaust as a "moral cudgel" were more troubling in their intent.

53. "Buchenwald Rede: Schäfer entschuldigt sich bei KZ-Opfer," *Der Spiegel*, August 28, 2006.

54. *Spiegel* Dokumentation, "Hans Filbinger war kein Nationalsozialist, Oettinger Trauerrede im Freiburger Münster," April 12, 2007.

55. Gunther Hoffmann and Bernd Ulrich, "Was haben wir uns angetan?"*Die Zeit*, August 28, 2003.

56. "Holocaust-Debatte: Merkel fordert Papst zur Klarstellung auf," *Der Spiegel*, February 3, 2009.

57. Annette Simon and Jan Faktor, *Fremd im eigenen Land?* (Gießen: Psychosozial-Verlag, 2000), p. 9.

58. Bernd-Lutz Lange, *Mauer, Jeans and Prager Frühling* (Berlin: Aufbau, 2006), p. 121.

59. Bernd Gehrke, "*Die 68er-Proteste*," Bundeszentrale für politische Bildung, Bonn, March 18, 2008.

60. Lange, *Mauer, Jeans and Prager Frühling*.

61. Roll, *Die Erste*, p. 48; "Prügel-Affäre: Joschka Fischer zieht das Büßerhemd an," *Der Spiegel*, January 6, 2001.

62. Kornelius, *Angela Merkel: Die Kanzlerin und ihre Welt*, pp. 24–25.

63. Ibid., p. 26.

64. Ibid.

65. Kohl's TV address of July 1, 1990, reported in *Bulletin des Presse- und Informationsamts der Bundesregierung*, No. 86, July, 3, 1990.

66. Joseph Schumpeter coined this term in *Capitalism, Socialism and Democracy* (New York: Harper & Row, 1942).

67. Rainer Land, "East Germany, 1989–2010: A Fragmented Development," in Konrad H. Jarausch (ed.), *United Germany. Debating Processes and Prospects* (New York: Berghahn, 2013), p. 109.

68. Jörg Roesler, "Privatization in East Germany," *Europe Asia Studies*, 46(3) (1994), pp. 505, 508.

69. Uwe Siegmund, "Was Privatization in Eastern Germany a Special Case? Some Lessons from the Treuhand," Davidson Institute, Working Paper No. 85, University of Michigan, September 1997, p. 23.

70. Land, "East Germany, 1989–2010," p. 114.

71. Rudiger Frank, cited in an interview with John Feffer, "The Cost of Unification," August 21, 2014, available at: www.johnfeffer.com/the-costs-of-reunification.

72. "Finanzen: 'Da fällt die Guillotine,'" *Der Spiegel*, p. 41.

73. Christoph Dieckmann, "Ostdeutschland steht auf der Kippe," *Die Zeit*, January 4, 2001.

74. Erik Gawel and Klaas Korte, "Regionale Verteilungswirkungen und Finanzierungsverantwortung: Bund und Länder bei der Strom-Energiewende," in Thorsten Müller and Hartmut Kahl (eds.), *Energiewende im Föderalismus* (Baden-Baden: Nomos, 2015), p. 155.

75. Daniela Dahn, "20 Jahre Mauerfall – oder das Vermächtnis des demokratischen Aufbruchs," talk delivered at Lafayette College, Pennsylvania, October 2010 (personal copy).

76. Anna Elomäki, *The Price of Austerity: The Impact on Women's Rights and Gender Equality in Europe* (Brussels: European Women's Lobby, 2012).

77. Ingrid Miethe, "Women's Movements in East Germany: Are We in Europe Yet?" in Konrad H. Jarausch (ed.), *United Germany. Debating Processes and Prospects* (New York: Berghahn, 2013), p. 158; also, Ingrid Miethe, "Die 89er als 68er des Ostens: Fallrekonstruktive Untersuchungen in einer Frauenfriedensgruppe der DDR," in Annegret Schüle, Thomas Ahbe, and Rainer Gries (eds.), *Die DDR aus generationsgeschichtlischer Perspektive – eine Inventur* (Leipzig: Uni-Verlag, 2006), pp. 355–376.

78. Brigitte Young, *Triumph of the Fatherland: German Unification and the Marginalization of Women* (Ann Arbor, MN: University of Michigan Press, 1999); Rohnstock, *Stiefschwestern*.

79. Lau, *Die Letzte Volkspartei*, p. 51.

80. Joyce Marie Mushaben, "Girl Power, Gender Mainstreaming and Critical Mass: Women's Leadership and Policy Paradigm Shifts in Germany's Red–Green Coalition, 1998–2002," *Journal of Women, Politics, and Policy*, 27(1/2) (2005): 145–182.

81. Lau, *Die Letzte Volkspartei*, p. 55.

82. "Raven mothers" are accused of forcing their offspring from their nests when they are too young.

83. Irene Runge, *Ausland DDR. Fremdenhass* (Berlin: Dietz Verlag, 1990); also Landolf Scherzer, *Die Fremden: Unerwünschte Begegnungen und verbotene Protokolle* (Berlin: Aufbau, 2002).

84. Mushaben, *From Post-War to Post-Wall Generations*, pp. 329 ff.

85. Mayr, "Hungary's Peaceful Revolution."

86. Joyce Marie Mushaben, "Swords to Plowshares: The Church, the State and the East German Peace Movement," *Studies in Comparative Communism*, 17(2) (1984): 123–135; Mushaben, "Cycles of Peace Protest in West Germany."

87. See at: www.bundesregierung.de/Content/DE/MitschriftPressekonferenzen/2015/08/2015-08-31-pk-merkel.html.

88. Schneider, *Der Mauerspringer*, p. 102.

89. Egon Bahr, speech delivered at the Evangelische Akademie, Tutzing, July 15, 1963.

90. Cited in Marcus Mauerer, Carsten Reinemann, Jürgen Maier, and Michaela Maier, *Schröder gegen Merkel. Wahrnehmung und Wirkung des TV-Duells 2005 im Ost-West-Vergleich* (Wiesbaden: VS Verlag, 2007), p. 75.

91. Cited in Robin Mishra, *Angela Merkel – Machtworte: Die Standpunkte der Kanzlerin* (Freiburg: Herder, 2010), p. 107; also, Volker Resing, *Angela Merkel. Die Protestantin* (Leipzig: St. Benno, 2009).

92. Mishra, *Angela Merkel – Machtworte*, pp. 109, 110–114; Sebastian Fischer, "Christliche Kanzlerin: 'Umfangen von der Liebe Gottes,'" *Der Spiegel*, July 21, 2009.

93. Lau, *Die letzte Volkspartei*, p. 9.

94. Ahbe, "Die Konstruktion der Ostdeutschen."

95. Annette Leo, "Keine Gemeinsame Erinnerung: Geschichtsbewusstsein in Ost und West," *Aus Politik- und Zeitgeschichte*, 40/41 (2003): 27–32.

96. Joyce Marie Mushaben, "The Rise of *Femi-Nazis?* Women and Rightwing Extremist Movements in Unified Germany," *German Politics*, 5(2) (1996): 240–275; also Mushaben, "Collective Memory Divided and Reunited"; Joyce Marie Mushaben, Memory and the Holocaust: Processing the Past through a Gendered Lens," special issue, *History of the Human Sciences*, 17(2/3) (2004): 147–185; and Birgit Rommelspacher, *Dominanzkultur. Texte zu Fremdheit und Macht* (Berlin: Olanda, 2006).

97. Viola B. Georgi, "Jugendliche aus Einwandererfamilien und die Geschichte des Nationalsozialismus," *Aus Politik- und Zeitgeschichte*, 40/41 (2003): 40–45.

98. Marie Louise Janssen-Jurreit, *Lieben Sie Deutschland? Gefühle zur Lage der Nation* (Munich: Piper, 1985).

99. Kornelius, *Angela Merkel: Die Kanzlerin und ihre Welt*, p. 95.

100. Ibid., pp. 95–96.

101. Mishra, *Angela Merkel – Machtworte*, p. 11.

3

From *Staatsräson* to *Realpolitik*: Reconfiguring German–Israeli Relations

Commemoration events focusing on national tragedies often result in iconic photographs that seem to "humanize" national leaders. Two that stand out in postwar Germany are the image of Willy Brandt falling on his knees at the Warsaw Ghetto site in December 1970, as well as the picture of François Mitterrand and Helmut Kohl, holding hands at Verdun in September 1984. Perhaps such images evoke emotional responses because one normally expects male leaders to appear strong and decisive, standing above the fray of personal responses. The photograph of Angela Merkel expressing her gratitude in Hebrew for the privilege of addressing the Knesset on March 8, 2008, the fiftieth anniversary of Israel's founding, is far from iconic: just a woman dressed in black, speaking at a podium, foregrounded by an Israeli flag.[1] Although she was the first head of government to bring her personal experiences to bear on very complex German–Israeli relations, the chancellor displayed her usual cool, calm, and collected demeanor.

In addition to her other "political firsts," Angela Merkel will likely go down in history as Germany's most highly decorated leader (see below) regarding her efforts to "work through" the barbaric National Socialist past. She is also the first chancellor to have been labeled *Israel's best friend*, and its "second best ally" after the United States. Her ability to secure the trust and respect of a tough crowd of Jewish elites stems from her clear declaration early on that Israel's right to exist remains a core component of her own country's "reason of state" (*Staatsräson*). Repeatedly testifying to the singularity of the *Shoah* and Germany's never-ending historical responsibility for its crimes against humanity, Merkel is also the first FRG leader to embrace Israel's identity as a "Jewish" state.

84

The chancellor reinforced those sentiments while standing before the Knesset, declaring that Israel's security would "never be negotiable."[2] In my judgment, this was more than an official affirmation of long-standing precepts of German policy toward Israel. Over the last few years, the Israeli media have reported on Merkel's fierce telephone exchanges with Prime Minister Benjamin Netanyahu, castigating him for expanding illegal settlements in the Occupied Territories. It is hard to imagine any of her predecessors launching such a strong public critique of Israeli policies, much less surviving the inevitable political fall-out.

The year 2015 marked the seventieth anniversary of unconditional surrender as well as the fiftieth anniversary of diplomatic relations between Germany and Israel, but it is not only "the blessing of late birth" that has granted Merkel greater flexibility in shaping her country's Middle East engagement.[3] Global developments ranging from the Arab Spring to the rise of ISIS (Islamic State) pose new dangers but also extend new opportunities to a German leader willing to engage in *Realpolitik* beyond her own region. This chapter argues that Angela Merkel is "the right person, in the right place, at the right time" for moving German–Israeli relations to a new stage, due to three factors. First, she has clearly deepened ties with Israel across many policy domains, based on the foundation established by earlier chancellors. Second, her personal effectiveness is directly, if paradoxically, rooted in the earlier trust cultivated by her erstwhile "moral" adversary, Foreign Minister Joschka Fischer. Finally, I attribute the chancellor's quick mastery of the conundrum of German–Israeli relations to her personal socialization experiences as the eastern daughter of a Lutheran pastor.

This chapter begins by defining three core concepts that have been used to shape German policies toward Israel dating back to the 1950s: *Staatsräson, Realpolitik,* and *special relationship.* I then review key stages and turning points in German–Israeli relations between 1945 and 1989, followed by a treatment of FRG policies since unification, in an effort to determine what is and remains unique about their mutually recognized "special relationship." Next, I review curious biographical parallels that have led both a '68 radical turned Green minister and a pragmatic, Protestant CDU Chancellor to engage more personally with Israelis *and* Palestinians than any of their respective national predecessors. The fifth section outlines an emerging Merkel Doctrine in response to the never-ending spiral of violence afflicting the Middle East. I conclude with several paradoxes that could precipitate even further changes in German–Israeli relations over the next decade.

UNDERSTANDING "MERKIAVELLIAN" DISCOURSE: HISTORY, MORALITY, AND SPECIAL RELATIONSHIPS

Even when translated as "reason of state," the German term *Staatsräson* holds little meaning for Americans who have long embraced the premise, "that government is best which governs least." For Europeans, *the state* entails more than a concrete set of institutions exercising legal authority over a clearly defined territory: it stands as a reification of a specific ethnonational culture that transcends the identities or needs of individuals, particularly in countries relying on *jus sanguinis*. It represents a closed, organic community, a concept all too easily abused by leaders intent on purging their territory of ethnic, religious, or other minority groups.

Variously translated as *Staatsräson, ragion di stato*, or *raison d'état*, the concept was first used by diplomat-politician Niccolò Machiavelli in the early 1500s. He asserted that in order to ensure its survival and legitimacy, the state had to be able place its own interests above those of individual citizens, justified in terms of *voluntas, necessitas, utilitas* (will, necessity, utility). Giovanni Botero elaborated on the concept in 1589, positing that the state required the means to exercise stable, permanent power over its people for "the founding, the preservation and expansion" of its own dominion. Such actions could not be measured in terms of the "ordinary reason" guiding average subjects; cultivating the will, understanding the necessity, and assessing the utility of certain (authoritarian) behaviors to this end would require "excellence in a ruler." The term *Staatsräson* entered German discourse in conjunction with the Thirty Years War (1618–1648).

Realpolitik, introduced by Ludwig von Rochau in 1853, was likewise rooted in "the study of the powers that shape, maintain and alter the state." It was construed as "the basis of all political insight," in the belief "that the law of power governs the world of states just as the law of gravity governs the physical world." "To bring down the walls of Jericho," Rochau observed, the *Realpolitiker* – often (con)fusing papal with earthly authority – "knows the simple pick-axe is more useful than the mightiest trumpet."[4] The first practitioner was Otto von Bismarck, whose ruthless process of national unification worked its way into a tendency to equate the term with "power politics." Distancing themselves from the absolutist powers defining "the state" in Europe, American founding fathers embraced the power of market-liberalism and limited government over the notion of a higher organic, moral order. "The national interest" associated with *Realpolitik* in the United

States became inextricably intertwined with capitalist spheres of influence and thus the material interests of the dominant group. International relations theorists largely assume that the needs of citizens, often pitted against each other in terms of gender, race, class, ethnicity, and religion, can all somehow be subsumed under a single national interest.

By the early 1970s, the German understanding of *Realpolitik* began to diverge from the heavier concept of *Staatsräson* as well. Stripped of sovereignty until 1990, Germany faced special problems precipitated by the Cold War and national division. Shedding the emphasis on assertive state power, its leaders focused on pragmatic steps to preserve other national interests, for example, possible reunification. *Realpolitik* was goal-oriented, limited only by practical exigencies; it was best exemplified through the step-by-step Eastern policies (*Ostpolitik*) of Willy Brandt.

Dealings between Germany and Israel are likewise routinely characterized in terms of a *special relationship*. Offering the first concrete definition of this concept, Lily Gardner Feldman points to three conditions that render a bilateral relationship "special."[5] At issue are processes of *historical intertwining*; a high degree of *intensity* giving rise to regular interactions; and the presence of a mutual, *psychological resonance* between two peoples. While the first two play a key role in creating and operationalizing the relationship, the third factor must persist to render the final product "special." For Gardner Feldman, *intertwining* is conditioned by the unique nature of the historical event that links the two countries, not the duration of their interactions as measured in years or decades. Neither the maintenance nor the endurance of their relationship depends on the commitment or behavior of individual leaders. It becomes self-sustaining.

The *intensity* of their relations "depends more on ... what nations do than on ... what they say."[6] At issue is how their interactions deviate from the bilateral norm: do they pursue some courses of action with each other that they would not regularly undertake with other states? Special in this context implies not just "difference" but also a clear "preference" for interacting with the other, even when alternative countries might be available to fill a need. They may also draw on special instruments, secret courses of action, and the use of code words to demonstrate their respective motives for engagement. Intensity also suggests a "mutual preoccupation" with each other, reflecting a deeper psychological implication (*Befangenheit*). Their exchanges evoke strong emotions on both sides, positive and negative, that would not color their respective dealings with a third party. External responses to the actions of one or the other need not be symmetrical: Germany was a pariah on the international stage when it first approached the new state of Israel, while the latter enjoyed broad support and sympathy. Today Germany evokes global respect, while Israel draws hostile criticism for its treatment of Palestinians and Israeli Arabs.[7]

STAGES AND TURNING POINTS: "FROM ENMITY TO AMITY"

German and Jewish histories began to intertwine long before the National Socialists met in Wannsee to draw up plans for a "Final Solution" in January 1942. An 1812 edict recognizing all Jews in Prussia as citizens comprised the first step toward legal emancipation. The parliament of the North German Confederation adopted its Equality Law in 1869, abolishing restrictions on Jewish residency and property rights, guaranteeing freedom of occupation. Bismarck's consolidation of the Second Reich extended emancipation (including military duty for Jews) to all states in 1871. The next four decades were nonetheless marked by resurgent anti-Semitism as well as by contradictory stereotypes, featuring Jews both as the money-mongering drivers of capitalism and as ruthless conspirators fomenting Bolshevik revolution. Hitler's henchmen pursued the institutionalized extermination of 6 million Jews, together with countless leftists, homosexuals, disabled or mentally impaired persons, alcoholics, Roma, Sinti, and other ethnic minorities. Rounded up across Europe, Jews nonetheless comprised the primary target group. Despite the collaboration of many national governments in the deportation, asset confiscation, and denial of refuge to those who fled, Germany was and remains uniquely responsible for these "crimes against humanity."[8]

Gardner Feldman offers an extensive list of symbolic breakthroughs shaping German–Israeli relations, starting with concrete reparation gestures, followed by material exchanges and, ultimately, a steady institutionalization of positive relations between the two states. Comprising the first of five stages, the immediate postwar period, 1945–1961, extended from the Nuremberg Trials through the Eichmann Trial; early initiatives were German–Jewish in orientation insofar as neither state existed prior to 1948 (first Israel, then the FRG and GDR in 1949). This era focused on capturing and punishing individual perpetrators, establishing national accountability and collective guilt (a term Adenauer avoided). Contacts were limited to behind-the-scenes events like study groups and Action Reconciliation projects, until Erich Lüth and Rudolf Küstermeier opted to "end the silence" on August 31, 1951, as founders of the Peace with Israel Movement. Adenauer responded with a Bundestag speech on September 27, 1951, calling for moral and material indemnity regarding crimes committed not *by* but rather *in the name of* the German people. The speech ended with "a minute's silence – to end the silence."⁹

Dire economic conditions impelled Israel to enter into negotiations with Germany, resulting in the Luxembourg Reparations Agreement of September 1952. Both sides were motivated by "morality" and "mutual need." Germany's willingness to recognize its responsibility to Holocaust survivors became "the acid test for readmission to the international community."¹⁰ Israeli leaders argued that reparations (*Wiedergutmachung*) were nothing more than payment for what had been stolen from Jews, completely divorced from "forgiveness." Science and technology programs featured prominently in the Agreement, leading to friendships within these communities, despite non-fraternization rules. Heading the Bundestag opposition, Erich Ollenhauer (SPD) delivered the first public talk by a German leader in Israel in 1957. Konrad Adenauer and David Ben-Gurion met for the first time, unofficially, at the Waldorf Astoria in New York City in March 1960. Most analysts credit strong personal chemistry between those two leaders with the onset of positive relations. Ben-Gurion displayed great courage in moving a country full of *Shoah* survivors to accept economic support from the perpetrators to build the fledgling nation from scratch.

The second stage, 1965–1980, brought treaty formalization and the establishment of diplomatic relations. Israel had lobbied for ambassadorial ties much earlier, but German officials were reluctant to antagonize Arab states, given Cold War tensions and national energy concerns. In August 1965, Golda Meir received Second World War veteran Rolf Pauls as the first German Ambassador to Israel.¹¹ The trajectory continued with a number of other diplomatic firsts: the pioneering FRG visit by a Knesset delegation in March 1969; the inaugural trip by an Israeli foreign minister in February 1970; and the first visit by a German foreign minister in June 1971. Chancellor Willy Brandt undertook his first state visit in July 1973 (Adenauer only traveled there *after* his 1966 retirement), followed by the first top-level visit by Prime Minister Yitzhak Rabin in July 1975.

Although it vehemently attacked the older generation for collaborating with the Nazis, core elements of the '68 generation paradoxically turned away from Israel after the Six Day War (1967), out of sympathy for the Palestinians. This decade was marked by tragedies, ranging from the murder of Israeli athletes at the 1972 Munich Olympics, to the 1976 hijacking of an Air France flight, ending at Entebbe, Uganda. Rising domestic and international terrorism led to ever more security, intelligence, and (secret) defense cooperation. Positive German–Arab relations predated the Second World War, but the OPEC oil boycott and the 1973 Yom Kippur War led the energy-dependent FRG to multilateralize its relations with other Middle Eastern polities. Germany, in turn, helped Israel to secure "friendly state" status vis-à-vis the European Economic Community, culminating in a 1975 Free Trade Agreement. Israel joined the French-sponsored Euro-Arab dialogue, and found new sources of industrial investment to stabilize energy supplies, initiating further defense and intelligence ties. Brandt and Schmidt also forged good personal connections with Israeli leaders (though not the same ones), but the change from a Labor to a Likud government in 1977 weakened those relationships.

The third phase, 1981–1989, saw the institutionalization of many new policy exchanges, linking more ministerial officials on both sides. October 1985 marked the first visit by a German president, Richard von Weizsäcker, paving the way for the high-level talks on "culture." Chaim Herzog undertook the first Israeli presidential visit in April 1987. This period also brought new tensions, not always subject to German control. Israel took offense at the European Community's (EC) 1980 Venice Declaration, despite FRG efforts to tone down the wording; its support for Palestinian self-determination and a PLO role in negotiations was a "defining moment" in fostering Israeli distrust of the EC.[12] The 1982 invasion of Lebanon and Israel's response to the First Intifada (1987) alienated the EC in turn.

One outcome of the nuclear disarmament campaign and the Greens' move into the Bundestag was a renewed German ban on supplying weapons exports to combat or conflict zones, leading to subsequent secret delivery scandals. German scientists had helped Egypt to build rockets for use against Israel in the 1960s, triggering a serious crisis at that time. As Yves Pallades and Werner Sonne document, Germany relied on top-secret deals to supply weapons. It refused to provide offensive Fuchs armored personnel carriers but did deliver Cerberus jammers and "loaned" Israel a defensive Patriot anti-missile system, largely at German expense. Despite the awful memories rekindled by the hostage killings at the 1972 Munich Olympics, Israel has increasingly come to rely on Germany for hostage and prisoner negotiations with modern rogue states.

Stage four, 1989–2004, was driven by a new kind of "politics of memory," once national sovereignty was restored under the Two plus Four Agreement (1990).[13] Unification challenges were accompanied by the rise of Hamas and Hezbollah, making PLO leader Yasser Arafat look like a seasoned diplomat. Additional factors were Germany's *visible* military cooperation with Israel, member state divisions on the EU front over two Gulf wars, and a shift to orthodox–conservative politics in Israel. While Helmut Kohl viewed unification as his greatest historical achievement, Prime Minister Yitzhak Shamir, a militant veteran of the Israeli Defense Forces, deemed it the commencement of "the Fourth Reich."[14]

When the United States commenced its attack on Iraq in January 1991, Saddam Hussein launched a number of Soviet Scud missiles against Tel Aviv and Haifa. The day after, Kohl was presented with a secret military report revealing that German electronics had been used in the steering system of 860 modified Scuds: "Without German technology, no 'Scuds', without 'Scuds', no dead Israelis."[15] Messerschmitt-Bölkow-Blohm had used a Swiss front company (Consens), and German engineers had been paid up to $3,000 per day for their know-how. The Federal Intelligence Service (BND) had known about the sales but alleged that Bonn "didn't want to hear about it."[16] Because the components had civilian as well as potential military value, the Germans had rejected American and Israeli complaints regarding illegal technology exports.

Even worse, FRG firms had delivered chemicals to Iraq during its war against Iran; as one ministerial official noted, "You know, of course, that the words gas and Germany don't sound very good together."[17] Germany immediately approved DM 250 million in humanitarian aid and delivered military materials worth DM 1.2 billion to Israel, along with a promise to pay the entire DM 880 million bill for two Dolphin submarines. In 1994, Kohl agreed to "sell" Israel a third submarine during a personal meeting with Rabin, purchased with another DM 220 million subsidy. This one was outfitted with four additional torpedo-launch tubes based on Israeli specifications, revealed to be nuclear-capable.[18] Following the logic of "don't ask, don't tell," Kohl noted that "If the Israelis demand it, we give it to them."[19] Since 1992 Germany and Israel have exchanged military chiefs of staff, conducted top-level meetings between their respective military branches, and instigated joint training exercises. They agreed to mutual exchanges of military force members in 1995.

The FRG's six-month EU Council presidency in 1994, and again in 1999, afforded new opportunities for broader engagement in Middle East peace processes, or at least in efforts to jump-start initiatives stemming from the Oslo Process. The 1994 Essen Declaration granted "special" EU standing to Israel, resulting in the 1995 EU–Israel Association Agreement; the latter included preferential trade terms, along with special access to EU

R&D technology programs. Ironically, this also rendered Israel eligible to compete against Germany for one of the temporary regional seats on the UN Security Council for 2019 (a seat it usually holds once every eight years). Having emphasized Palestinian rights since 1969, Germany became the first EU member to open a permanent representation in the Occupied Territories in 1994. It actively lobbied to include the Palestinian Authority in the Euro-Mediterranean partnership in 1995, to counter illegal migration, organized crime, and regional instability.[20]

In January 1996, Ezer Weizman became the first Israeli president to speak to the Bundestag; his counterpart, Johannes Rau, was not invited to address the Knesset until February 2000, which also saw the first formal protocol on cultural cooperation. Although the FRG formally terminated its "development assistance" (DM 140 million per annum) to the new state that year, Israel has not gone empty-handed, thanks to German lobbying within the EU. Tempus and Erasmus programs have brought ever more EU students to Israel, which joined Galileo in 2004, followed by the Copernicus initiative (involving civilian satellites). Israeli leaders then "demanded" inclusion in EU programs linked to transport and outer-space, despite strong European Parliament opposition to the brutal staging of Operation Defensive Shield in the Palestinian Territories during April 2002.

German support for Israel's right to self-defense increasingly put it at odds with EU players such as France, the United Kingdom, and Spain. Collectively rejecting the "separation barrier" and housing demolitions as violations of international law, the EU began training Palestinian police, prosecutors, and judges in the West Bank (EUPOL-COPPS); it also supplied a majority of the UNIFIL troops in southern Lebanon. Extending "an invitation nobody wanted," Israeli Prime Minister Ehud Olmert went so far as to request active FRG support: "We would have no problem accepting German soldiers in southern Lebanon – [there is] no country friendlier to Israel than Germany and would therefore welcome its participation."[21] The Bundestag and the public disagreed, however, demanding that there should be: "No German boots on Israeli soil." The FRG provided a sea blockade to back up UN troops instead.

The period 2005 to the present marks a new phase, beginning with the formation of Merkel's first Grand Coalition. Beginning with the fortieth anniversary of diplomatic relations, this stage has triggered some deep thinking about the "special relationship," understood as one that is both unique and preferential. Mindful of the generational change driving both nations, Merkel has introduced discursive shifts to German–Israeli relations, not all of which have been welcomed by the public at large, or even by her own federal president.[22] The process of historical reconciliation and commitment to a "common destiny" has reached another turning point. This has opened the door to new characterizations noted by Gardner Feldman: "friendship," "partnership," and "alliance" are terms that stress common values as the new bedrock of German–Israeli relations.[23]

This stage evinces four new features. First, while *the past is not yet past*, it is clearly being pushed aside by present and future concerns. As the witness generation succumbs to mortality, Merkel has no choice but to establish a new framework for those relations, despite paying homage to her country's historical responsibility. Second, in moving from *reparations* to *reconciliation* to *special relationship*, Germany has multilateralized ties between the two states. This is not the only domain in which Merkel has learned to leverage EU developments, by "uploading" her preferences to counteract policy deficits at the national level. Since the mid-1990s, Germany has sought "to develop more 'even-handed' positions on the Israeli–Palestinian issue under the cover of EU declarations."[24] Applying a two-edged sword to this Gordian knot creates conflicts of another sort among member states.

The third element consists of Germany's now overt military support and intelligence cooperation with Israel, best demonstrated by Schröder's 2002 declaration: "Israel gets whatever it needs for maintaining its own security, and it gets it whenever it needs it."[25] Indeed, weapons exports to Israel increased in 1999, rising to DM 1.29 billion by 2000, although the first two Dolphins had been approved by Kohl.[26] Weapons transfers, including many left over from the GDR army, were put on hold following Operation Defensive Shield (Second Intifada) but resumed in 2003.[27] By mid-decade, the value of these military procurements reached €100 million, including the "long-term loan" of Patriot anti-aircraft systems. Foreign trade between the two states grew from US$3.33 billion in 1998, to US$4.43 billion in 2005, to US$6.1 billion by 2014.[28]

The fourth change linked to this stage is the growing number of voices in Germany directly criticizing Israeli policies and actions.[29] Transparent arms deals concurrently gave rise to stronger domestic criticism of Germany's willingness to supply rogue states with dual-use technologies as part of its broader export strategy.[30] The next section addresses other policy shifts toward Israel introduced by German leaders who have been the real beneficiaries of "late birth," chancellors Schröder and Merkel.

STAATSRÄSON AS THE DEFENSE OF ISRAEL

The responsibilities associated with *Staatsräson* depend not only on the prevailing world order but also on dominant national discourses and shifting interpretations of history. Prior to 1989, the avenues open to German and Israeli leaders were over-determined by the Cold War push for *Western integration*. After unification, politicians' responses became situational: foreign policy options became "less pre-determined, more contradictory in their goals, and less committed to traditional lines."[31] The pulls of transatlantic and European institutions no longer completely overlap; East Germans express stronger affinities for the Arab states, and right-wing governments in Israel are more inclined to engage in the pre-emptive use of force.[32]

The SPD–Green government formed in 1998 was the first to include bona fide '68 activists like Schröder, Fischer, Wieczorek-Zeul, Schily, and Däubler-Gmelin, as well as two individuals born after 1949 (Trittin and Beck). The partisan realignment marked a generational sea-change, with advancing politicians able to pursue foreign policies consciously aligned with "German interests." While Schröder and Merkel have consistently recognized the atrocities perpetrated by the Nazi regime as "irrevocable" components of German memory and identity, both have applied other aspects of historical responsibility to re-configure foreign policy discourse, rendering them "less inhibited ... in a positive sense" in their dealings with the Israeli state.[33]

By 1998, old questions of historical responsibility were beginning to merge with new security concerns rooted in fears of Islamicization. Unification also precipitated a shift in expectations regarding Germany's role on the world stage. Political elites still evince broad consensus regarding four policy ingredients in the Middle East. They collectively recognize: (1) Israel's unquestionable right to exist; (2) the need to maintain a balance between Israeli security and Palestinian rights to self-determination; (3) a preference for a European peace-keeping framework, as opposed to unilateral action; and (4) a firm belief that US engagement remains indispensable for achieving all of the above.[34]

Genocidal practices ("ethnic cleansing") witnessed in a fractured Yugoslavia had already challenged two unshakeable postwar postulates governing German military engagement, pitting *Never again war* against *Never again Auschwitz*. The first Gulf War, marked by Scud missile attacks against two Israeli cities, undermined Germany's clandestine approach to meeting Israeli security needs. The Red–Green government inherited an astounding array of secret arms deals from its conservative predecessor, initiated shortly after the fall of the Wall. Initially blocked by Defense Minister Moshe Dayan as too expensive, Kohl's promise to deliver two Dolphin submarines to ensure a second-strike capability met long-term Foreign Minister Genscher's core criterion: "Anything that swims is allowed." Bribes associated with arms dealer Karlheinz Schreiber would return to haunt Kohl in 1999.

Israel's subsequent request for three more dual-use submarines violated the 1982 combat-zone export ban, however. Deeming it a continuation of earlier policy, Schröder signed the contract on his last day in office, subsequently approved by Chancellor Merkel and her SPD Foreign Minister, Frank Walter Steinmeier. The rationale was to "preserve German jobs and export German know-how."[35] According to Sonne, supplying offensive weapons to a high-conflict zone turned the German "reason of state" into the art of "looking away."[36]

The sixth submarine showed just how complicated the *Staatsräson* question could become, as Federal President Joachim Gauck had warned.[37] Israeli cabinet hardliners overruled their own navy, which did not want another boat. Merkel hoped to use her submarine decision to pressure Netanyahu into peace-process concessions for the Palestinians. His half-hearted response led to a ten-month moratorium on settlement construction. The chancellor was incensed when he nonetheless refused to transfer promised tax revenues to the Palestinian Authority, after the latter secured UN Non-Member Observer State status. Merkel forced Netanyahu to pay up and to allow construction of a German-financed water treatment plant in Gaza. The deal was signed in March 2012, but no peace progress ensued. German taxpayers again picked up a third of the €400 million price tag.[38] Arab states also began to request U-boats "made in Germany." Israel and the Saudis now have a common enemy: Iranian Shiites. When Germany began to export Leopard tanks to Saudi Arabia, Israeli officials "just kept quiet."[39]

Two new priorities gained momentum as of the second Gulf War: first, the "Jewish" state had to be protected against a Holocaust-denying Iranian regime seeking to acquire nuclear weapons, despite German business interests. Second, the two-state solution was recognized as the only hope for achieving sustainable peace within the region. Germany has emerged as Europe's largest national donor to the Palestinians; between 1992 and 2006, it pumped €500 million into their economy and infrastructure.[40] Since 2009, the EU and Israel have resorted to a "double game of economic passion and political hostility."[41] Despite overwhelming member state support for a two-state solution foreseen by the EU Road Map and the Israeli Action Plan (both 2004), EU leaders have vociferously denounced Israel's excessive use of force, extrajudicial killings, its barriers to humanitarian assistance, and refusal to ban new settlements. Unprecedented tensions over the Second Intifada, partial reoccupation of the West Bank, and Israel's raid on the Gaza flotilla (2012) led even the Swedish foreign minister to declare "it's time the EU told Israel that enough is enough."[42]

Despite Germany's active provision of military support and equipment, negative public reactions to Netanyahu's intransigence over illegal settlements and peace negotiations have ironically evoked new charges of anti-Semitism among ultra-Orthodox communities.[43] From 1949 to 1989, the moral imperatives underlying Germany's "reason of state" were historically intertwined with its *Realpolitik*, subject to clear military constraints. Israel is not alone in demanding that a sovereign, powerful FRG now play an active role in Afghanistan, the Balkans, North Africa, and the Middle East. The need to redefine its *real-political* national interests is driving a wedge between what used to be overlapping normative precepts: *Never again war* versus *Never again Auschwitz*. The chancellor recognized as Israel's "best friend" faces the task of reconceptualizing the "special relationship" in between these two dicta. We now consider personal factors shaping Merkel's trusting relationship with Israel that renders "a few honest words" possible.[44]

FINDING SYNERGY IN STRANGE PLACES: JOSCHKA FISCHER AND ANGELA MERKEL

As Matthias Zimmer writes, "An understanding of the reason of state without its power-political components would be empty; without the ethical components it would remain blind."[45] Although Merkel brings many personal strengths to the German–Israeli table, she also benefited from SPD–Green government policies, and the good will established by Joschka Fischer, in particular. Both politicians have blended *idealism and values* with *realism and interests*. They stress dialogue as quintessential to the pursuit of Palestinian human rights, while highlighting core values: "peace, democracy, freedom, trust, solidarity, the rule of law, friendly competition, respect, and tolerance."[46] Each has lent new emphasis to the singularity of the Holocaust and to German responsibility "in perpetuity." While earlier leaders also tried to balance their criticisms of regional actors, Merkel and Fischer have conveyed a stronger *personal* commitment toward the Middle East, according them greater recognition inside Israel.

Merkel has already received more awards for her commitment to Jewish culture and the Israeli state than any of her predecessors. She received her first honorary doctorate from the Hebrew University in April 2007, where she pledged to uphold "the fight against racism and anti-Semitism" at home and "Israel's right to live in security and honor." The Central Council of Jews in Germany bestowed its Leo Baeck Prize in November 2007, followed by B'nai B'rith's Europe Award of Merit-Medal, which she received in March 2008 for challenging anti-Semitism and racism. In 2011, the American Jewish Committee (Berlin) accorded her its Light unto the Nations Prize on January 20, a date marking the start of Himmler's infamous Wannsee Conference; Tel Aviv University granted her a second honorary degree in February; in April, Berlin honored her with its Capital City Prize for Integration and Tolerance; by October she had also taken home the Prize for Understanding and Tolerance, marking the tenth anniversary of the Jewish Museum. As the chancellor noted on that occasion, "Jewish life has always been a part of Berlin."

In November 2012, the Jewish Community of Berlin presented the chancellor with the Heinz Galinski Prize for helping to rebuild Jewish life in Germany and supporting Israel, as she says, "in words and deeds." Merkel is only the second person to have received the Lord Jakobovits Prize of European Jewry; in May 2013, she was singled out by the European Conference of Rabbis for her strong statements and fast-track legislation guaranteeing Jewish and Muslim parents the right to circumcise their sons.[47] In February 2014, President Shimon Peres conferred Israel's highest civilian award on Merkel, the Presidential Medal of Distinction. The *laudatio* read: "Your commitment to Israel's security and to the cause of peace is set in stone." In December 2015, she accepted another prize from the Abraham Geiger College, University of Potsdam, the first liberal academy to train European rabbis and cantors since Hitler closed down its predecessor in 1942. The US Holocaust Memorial Museum Extended its Elie Wiesel Prize to Merkel in march 2017. Missing from this list are countless "freedom prizes" extended by other foreign entities over the last ten years.

The chancellor's closest competitor for awards received when it comes to supporting Israel and Jewish life in Germany is her erstwhile adversary, Joschka Fischer.[48] The street-fighter-turned-diplomat who never finished college was granted an honorary doctorate by Haifa

University in May 2002. He received the Heinz Galinski Prize in October that year, then the Buber–Rosenzweig Medallion from the German Society for Christian–Jewish Cooperation in March 2003. Like Merkel, he was accorded the Leo Baeck Prize in May 2005, and acquired his second honorary degree from Tel Aviv University in May 2006. Despite his post-retirement engagement with various ecological, European, and Middle Eastern foundations, he is unlikely to match the rest of her record.

Although two previous FRG presidents had delivered speeches to the Israeli parliament, Merkel became the first chancellor to address Knesset members in chamber on March 8, 2008 (Kohl spoke to lawmakers in 1984 outside the plenary hall). The mere act of inviting a German head of government required a special act of parliament. Like presidents Johannes Rau and Horst Köhler, Merkel was granted permission to speak in German, "the language of the perpetrators." In contrast to her predecessors, however, she began and ended her speech with expressions of gratitude and peace in Hebrew. Her address was very well received; in fact, the chancellor drew a standing ovation. In all three cases, some Israeli MPs boycotted the event.

The personal commitment exhibited by Fischer and Merkel derives from a few curious biographical parallels that have rendered them mirror opposites. First, both leaders experienced family lives that were directly reconfigured in the wake of the Second World War, despite a six-year gap in their respective ages. As members of the German ethnic minority in Hungary, Fischer's parents were forced to flee in 1946. As the son of expellees, he was very familiar with discussions of "German suffering" that had occurred following the collapse of a dictatorial regime responsible for world war and the Holocaust. Held as a prisoner of war at age 19, Merkel's father studied in the West but moved his wife and daughter to the eastern zone in 1954, exposing her to a different kind of German suffering. Her family was torn apart by national division after 1961, leaving her to grow up under another regime that denied its citizens the freedoms that Fischer took for granted on the other side of the border.

A second commonality has shaped their respective leadership styles. Because neither hailed from well situated, professional families, they both began their political careers as outsiders. While each was quick to learn the political ropes, both bring their personal experiences into the public arena, indicating the special role that earlier encounters have played in their later deliberations and decisions.

The third parallel is a bit more complicated, rooted in the fact that both witnessed a major paradigm shift regarding "leftist" attitudes toward Israel during the 1960s, well before they entered politics. Critical of their parents' active collaboration or passive complicity with the Nazis, New Leftists like Fischer were initially supportive of Israel. Somewhere between the Six Day War (1967) and the Yom Kippur War (1973), the Western '68ers did a radical about-face; turning against Israel in the fight against US imperialism, they championed Palestinians as the "Newly Oppressed." Indeed, some sympathizing with the Baader–Meinhof gang and the Red Army Faction (RAF) would later join terrorists in attacking Jews inside and outside Germany. Fischer himself attended a Palestinian rally in 1969 calling for a "final victory" over Israel. His cohorts compared the latter's camp massacres at Sabra and Shatila in Lebanon to the Warsaw Ghetto, even describing Palestinians as "victims of the victims."[49] Horst Mahler's rabid anti-Semitism led his former defense lawyer, a recently elected Chancellor Schröder, to renounce his old friend.[50]

The Greens' efforts to prove their reliability as a potential coalition partner after 1983 required another about-face; their eventual acceptance of the transatlantic alliance and Western support for Israel made them "fit to govern," just as the SPD's embrace of NATO and the social market economy at Godesberg had done in 1959. Two events solidified the second leftist reversal: the 1976 Air France hijacking, ending in Entebbe, Uganda, produced the first moment of truth for Fischer and *Realo*-Greens, impelling them to embrace Germany's special historical responsibility as their own.[51] In 1985, PLO terrorists hijacked an Italian cruise ship, the MS *Achille Lauro*, deliberately executing an elderly, disabled Jewish-American. This completed the paradigm shift.

On the other side of the border, GDR policy toward the Middle East followed erratic swings in Soviet doctrine. Explicitly recognizing the Holocaust, Stalin supported Israel's founding in 1948 but quickly came to oppose "Zionist imperialism" and "Jewish cosmopolitanism" backed by the United States and Great Britain. USSR purges of Jewish socialists were accompanied by equivalent SED purges in the 1950s. By the mid-1960s, the Soviet Union and its minions were supplying high-tech military support to Arab states against the "aggressor-state Israel." The East German approach to "victims of fascism" centered on compensating communist resistance fighters. GDR leaders accused Israel of mass pogroms, racism, *Blitzkrieg*, and genocide against the Arab world for nearly four decades. The tide turned again in April 1990, when the freely elected *Volkskammer* issued a formal apology "for the hypocrisy and animosity" of GDR policies toward Israel. Ironically, the united Germany opted to transfer Soviet-made weaponry left over from the National People's Army (NVA) for use by the Israeli Defense Forces after 1991.

A fourth parallel pertains to their stress on history as an ongoing motive in their dealings with Israel. Born in 1948 and 1954, respectively, neither Fischer nor Merkel possess personal war memories, yet neither invokes "the blessing of late birth" in defining national interests. During his 2003 visit to Yad Vashem, for example, Fischer cited Willy Brandt in his visitors' book entry: "Memories are the key, not to the past but to the future." Before she aced her *Abitur*, Merkel and her classmates had been required to visit the women's concentration camp at Ravensbrück. In 2008, she visited the grave of David Ben-Gurion at the Sde Boker Kibbutz, then became the first chancellor to visit the Buchenwald and Dachau camps (2013, 2015). This puts her ahead of her predecessors with regard to homage paid at Nazi death sites. Although she delivered a speech on the seventieth anniversary of the liberation of Auschwitz-Birkenau, she had yet to visit Europe's most infamous death camp by 2017. Merkel makes explicit use of the Hebrew term *Shoah* ("catastrophe") rather than *Holocaust*; the latter derives from a Greek term, inferring the *sacrificial burning* of an animal for *a holy purpose*, completely at odds with Nazi crimes against humanity.

A fifth commonality derives from the intense, *personal soul-searching* in which first Fischer, then Merkel publicly engaged, hoping to rectify distorted "leftist narratives" of the past. Growing up in the West and East, respectively, these leaders had been exposed to very different interpretations of their shared history. Western radicals knew little about the price GDR citizens paid for all-German atrocities, based on forty years of "real-existing socialism." Easterners, by contrast, escaped New Left charges of personal guilt directed at parents and politicians, having been exonerated by officially mandated anti-fascism, the GDR's *Staatsräson*. Yet both reach the conclusion "that the political agenda must be accompanied by an emotional one," manifested in their respective "words and deeds."[52]

Concentration camp images from Yugoslavia and the 1995 Srebrenica massacre raised the specter of Auschwitz for Fischer, moving him to accept military intervention in Kosovo. As the Green foreign minister declared in 1999:

Bosnia has shown itself to be a victory for those who rely on brutal and barbaric forms of violence, while the politics of the peace movement have proved helpless and those of the United Nations carrying it disunified . . . This bitter recognition forces all of us into a fundamental reassessment . . . I have great respect . . . for positions that reject violence. I also reject violence in the deepest way. And this is said by someone who for weeks, yes for months, really made an effort to bring about a peaceful solution . . . it was one of the saddest days of my political life when the Rambouillet process finally broke down.[53]

He continued: "I would have to question the very things that comprise my political biography, if I were to turn my back on political developments one could rightfully characterize as barbaric fascism . . . I belong to the generation that asked its own parents, why? Why did you allow it to happen?"[54] Turning against fundamentalist-pacifists in his own party, Fischer applied the same mental framing to Israel's right to exist. Linking this to later genocidal developments (Rwanda, Bosnia), he recognizes Germany's potential obligation *to engage in armed force* in order to preserve key components of its *Staatsräson*.

Merkel had to reject the socialist reason-for-being to "catch up" with the Western approach to historical intertwining: "I spent the first 35 years of my life in the German Democratic Republic . . . where National Socialism was considered a West German problem . . . It took more than 40 years before Germany as a whole acknowledged and embraced both its historical responsibility and the State of Israel."[55] Breaking with the GDR required her to accept "personal responsibility" for coming to terms with the past; to do that she first had to grasp the role New Left protesters had played in opening the Western Holocaust debate. As CDU opposition leader, she had attacked Fischer for his protests, demanding in 2001 that he "atone" for physically attacking a Frankfurt policeman (ironically named Marx) in 1973.[56]

The CDU Chair was shocked by the angry response that ensued, even among conservatives, when an Eastern woman historically chastised a Westerner by dictating the wording of his apology. Even Adenauer had avoided the word "atonement" (fraught with religious overtones) in his September 1951 declaration of regret, a speech that fell very short of asking for forgiveness. As noted in Chapter 2, Merkel's struggle to accept cultural differences over "1968" helped to bridge the East–West interpretation gap concerning Nazi history. Recognizing Israel's right to exist in a way that implicates citizens on both sides granted her new legitimacy in accepting historical responsibility for the nation as a whole. If absolutely necessary, she would risk armed force to preserve Israel.

Particularly striking is a sixth factor linking these leaders: both display a tendency to use direct, personalized language: neither shies away from the pronoun "I." As a result, their declarations strike a different chord with Israeli audiences. Each conveys the feeling that upholding Israel's right to exist is not just a "rule to live by" memorized in school, nor a party-political mantra used to win elections. Usually exuding self-confidence, Fischer (raised a Catholic), may have found it harder to admit past transgressions.[57] Merkel, by contrast, is credited with "self-confident modesty"; her favorite virtue is humility (*Demut*).[58] The only other leader to strike this personal chord was Johannes Rau, during his Knesset speech of February 2000: "I bow my head in humility before those who were murdered, those who have no graves at which I could ask their forgiveness."[59] Like Rau, Merkel was raised in the Protestant tradition of "forgiveness and reconciliation." In fact, she borrowed his phrase while addressing the British House of Commons in February 2014, commemorating the start of the First World War: "As German Chancellor, I bow my head before the victims of these horrible wars."[60]

A seventh factor connecting Fischer and Merkel centers on the "good chemistry" each has cultivated with Israeli leaders over time; "the personal is the political," as earlier cases show. The special German–Israeli relationship grew out of the mutual respect displayed by Adenauer and Ben-Gurion; it was reinforced by the positive chemistry between Willy Brandt and Abban Eban. Former *Wehrmacht* officer Helmut Schmidt established personal ties with Golda Meir, Moshe Dayan, and Shimon Peres (with no love lost on Menachem Begin). Helmut Kohl's lack of a close connection to an Israeli ruler may have been due to his controversial Bitburg visit (1985) and his refusal to ban Waffen-SS veteran reunions, despite intensified military and intelligence cooperation through the 1990s. Schröder continued Kohl's policies but otherwise relied on his foreign minister to cultivate German–Israeli relations.

Fischer exchanged fourteen visits with Likud's Ariel Sharon over his seven years in office. Merkel forged friendships with Prime Minister Ehud Olmert, Foreign Minister Tzipi Livni, and Israeli Ambassador Shimon Stein, the only diplomat ever invited to her private weekend home in the Uckermark. Olmert labeled the chancellor Israel's "helpful friend" in the face of growing EU criticism over human rights violations in Gaza (2006). For the record: both Fischer and Merkel enjoyed positive relations with US Secretaries of State Madeleine Albright and Hillary Clinton.

An eighth parallel linking Fischer and Merkel is that both treat efforts to secure Israeli trust as a *prelude* to reaching a two-state solution for the Middle East conflict.[61] The 1999 "Berlin Declaration" was the first explicit EU call for a Palestinian right to self-determination. As the primary author of the EU Road Map adopted in 2004, Fischer focused on concrete steps – timetables and benchmarks – to move both parties toward a permanent settlement.[62] Merkel was likewise adamant about the need for a two-state solution in her 2011 Light unto the Nations speech: "It is about [achieving] a secure Israel, a Jewish state of Israel, and ... a Palestinian state." Although she was the first chancellor to stress the concept of a "Jewish" state, she points to demographics (high Arab birth rates), inferring that only a separate state will allow Israel to maintain itself as such.

Finally, Fischer and Merkel have shared a "yes, but ... " style regarding Israeli behavior. Fischer consistently matched criticisms of Israel with admonitions regarding the PLO: "both sides are a hundred percent right, and ... one hundred percent wrong."[63] Although not as active as Merkel within the EU context, Fischer worked to soften Community language that was overly critical of Israel. He helped to establish the German–Israeli Future Foundation for young leaders; his interest in peace plans spiked after he witnessed a terror attack in a Tel Aviv disco across from his hotel in June 2001. He claims to have personally dissuaded Ariel Sharon from undertaking a full-scale retaliation and pushed Yasser Arafat into at least one ceasefire.

Merkel has displayed no hesitation in admonishing Olmert's hardliner successor, Benjamin Netanyahu, for violating their agreement regarding the ban on new settlements. In February 2012, the Israeli paper *Haaretz* reported on the chancellor's fiercely critical telephone exchanges with the prime minister over illegal construction in the Occupied Territories. Michael Mertes claims that her outspokenness reflects "a new communication style but no change in the substance" of German–Israeli relations.[64] She fired back in a paradoxically self-righteousness manner when Netanyahu tried to blame Hitler's genocidal acts on Palestinian Haj Amin al-Hussein, then Grand Mufti of Jerusalem: "I can say for the Federal Government and myself, we know the responsibility that National-Socialists bear for the civilization break of the *Shoah*: For our part we therefore see no reason to change our picture of history, particularly regarding this question."[65]

More recently she has admonished Netanyahu for misconstruing her comments to support positions she does not share. He asserted, for example, that she had abandoned the two-state solution when she noted at a joint press conference, "Now is certainly not the time to make really comprehensive progress, but you can achieve improvements in certain places."[66] She probably gave him one of her famous (ex-GDR) grimaces when he declared, "If Israel weren't there, the Middle East's entire western part would be flooded by the forces of Islamic fanaticism: Together with this flood, many millions more [refugees] would come to Europe: Israel is Western civilization's iron wall in the heart of the Middle East."[67]

Historical intertwining, intensity, and *psychological resonance:* the odd couple Fischer and Merkel consciously personify the three elements used to define Germany's "special relationship" with Israel. Representing significant processes of political cultural and generational change, Merkel faces the more challenging task of reconciling her country's historically rooted *Staatsräson* with new *Realpolitik* imperatives. She bears the equally heavy burden of persuading her own citizens that no matter how critical they may be of the latter, their state must always prevail as the embodiment of a higher order vis-à-vis Israel, "to ensure its own survival and legitimacy."

THE MERKEL DOCTRINE

Constrained by the realities of national division, the Cold War, and the active pursuit of special relationships with Israel and the United States, German leaders could ignore the kind of theoretical distinctions that usually preoccupy political scientists. This section argues that Chancellor Merkel does draw a line, however, between Germany's "reason of state," grounded in a unique moral qua historical responsibility toward Israel, and the day-to-day business of *Realpolitik*. In her Knesset address of March 8, 2008 she declared:

Here of all places I want to explicitly stress that every German Government and every German Chancellor before me has shouldered Germany's special historical responsibility for Israel's security. This historical responsibility is part of my country's *raison d'être* (sic). For me as German Chancellor, therefore, Israel's security will never be open to negotiation.[68]

As discussed earlier (Chapter 2), the chancellor has encountered many day-to-day opportunities to uphold memories of the *Shoah* and "Israel's right to live in security and honor" as a central component of German identity. Merkel was not directly involved in the debate following Martin Walser's October 1998 admonition not to use Auschwitz as a "tool of intimidation" or a "moral cudgel" to constrain the exercise of German power. She also maintained a curious silence when Günter Grass used poetic license to criticize Israel's aggressive stance toward neighboring states.[69] Her Eastern socialization has undoubtedly shaped her reluctance to limit freedom of expression among intellectuals and writers. She is much less hesitant to take on public officials who seek to relativize or close the book on the Nazi past, as her responses to Martin Hohmann, Reinhard Günzel, Günther Oettinger, and even Pope Benedict XVI testified.[70] In these cases, moral and political imperatives appear to overlap.

The Merkel Doctrine that has emerged since 2005 encompasses three components. The first entails an unambiguous acknowledgment of historical responsibility that precludes any attempt to normalize the German past. Second, it offers a clear recognition of German suffering, albeit rooted in the fact that expulsion, expropriation, and national division occurred because of aggressive Nazi expansionism. Although his own family faced harsher treatment during the immediate postwar period, Fischer rarely addressed this topic.[71] Finally, Merkel consistently posits a link between the past, the present, and the future with regard to discourse and policy. All three components reflect her familiarity with Richard von Weizsäcker's speech of May 1985, which she read shortly after it was delivered. As a GDR physicist, she had a harder time securing articles from Israeli journals; she depended on US or UK contacts to forward items of scientific interest.

Although the FRG has long favored multilateralism, the Merkel Doctrine concentrates heavily on the EU as a primary vehicle for consolidating bilateral efforts. She often draws smaller powers like Poland and the Czech Republic into wide-ranging reconciliation processes. She has "trilateralized" youth exchanges, for example, leading Germans to interact simultaneously with Poles, Israeli Arabs, and Palestinians since 2008. Merkel has supported Fischer's (stalled) European Road Map, the EU Action Strategy for the Middle East, and countless scientific exchanges.[72] Although she blocked EU moves to declare East Jerusalem the capital of a future Palestinian state in 2009, the chancellor was so furious over Netanyahu's breach of faith regarding settlement policies that Germany abstained during the UN vote that granted the Palestinian Authority "non-member observer state" status in 2012.[73] Although she lacks the emotional ties displayed by Adenauer, Schmidt, and Kohl, Merkel appreciates France's role in the capacity-building processes of the EU Mediterranean Partnership.[74] She sees social cohesion as key to internal reconciliation processes.

As in other policy domains, Merkel emphasizes practical modalities, pushing institutional capacities and infrastructural improvements to "cement reconciliation." Her support for the two-state solution comes with three prerequisites: (1) Hamas must unconditionally recognize

Israel's right to exist; (2) it must accept all existing Israeli–Palestinian accords; and (3) it must reject all forms of terrorism. A 2008 Berlin conference on Palestinian Civil Security and the Rule of Law specifically addressed supplies and infrastructure in Gaza. Israel's 2010 attack on the humanitarian flotilla heading for the Occupied Territories alienated the EU and grossly antagonized Turkey, its last friend in the region.[75] Merkel joined Palestinian president Mahmoud Abbas in calling for a transparent, comprehensive investigation into the raid.[76]

In March 2008, the chancellor had introduced direct consultations between the German and Israeli cabinets, chaired jointly with Ehud Olmert. These meetings have been used to add new projects involving business collaboration, joint investment, venture capital, energy efficiency, climate change, technology, waste/water, and shared training for African agricultural irrigation experts. She used the third direct German–Israeli consultation session (2011) to declare that "stand-still stand and stagnation" regarding the peace process are unacceptable: "I say this as a friend of Israel: the situation in Egypt is not an excuse for not continuing the peace process ..." Asked by an Israeli journalist if Germany would take "further measures" against Israel for the new settlements, an irritated chancellor responded: "I am not someone who threatens."[77]

The restoration of German sovereignty, coupled with a growing military–industrial complex hungry for new export markets, has presented the post-unity chancellor with a modern Pandora's box. Less than a year into her first term, Merkel admonished lawmakers,

> If it belongs to Germany's *Staatsräson* to guarantee Israel's right to exist, then we cannot simply say: When Israel's right to exist in this region is endangered – and it certainly is – then we will just keep out of it. If we want to participate in the necessary humanitarian and political processes, then it will be very hard to say: Others should please take over all of the military components.[78]

The FRG suspended military transfers to Israel in April 2002 following the attack on Palestinians at the Jenin refugee camp; its Fuchs tanks can be used in Lebanon but not in Gaza or the West Bank. The Bundestag debate over "an invitation nobody wanted," following Israel's 2006 anti-Hezbollah campaign, revealed substantial party divisions but not along traditional lines.[79] The FDP and the Left party opposed any direct involvement; the SPD argued for "help yes, shooting no." The CSU only wanted to "train security experts," while the CDU and Greens supported a sea blockade for UN troops.

Merkel prefers UN actions over EU measures when it comes to Iran. In May 2006, Germany joined five UN Security Council members in demanding that Iran cease all uranium enrichment measures by August. Its failure to comply by December 2006 brought new sanctions on trade-sensitive nuclear technology. The chancellor was initially hesitant to restrict Germany's lucrative trade deals with that rogue state, knowing that Russia and China were eager to take its place. A Siemens subsidiary, KRAFTWERK, designed and constructed its Bushehr nuclear facility in 2006; by 2007, FRG exports (e.g., turbines, water treatment equipment, monorails, windmill farms) were valued at US$5.7 billion. When her Economics Ministry scaled back credit guarantees from US$3.3 billion to US$1.2 billion, Chinese exports to Iran rose by 44 percent. When Commerzbank and Deutsche Bank pulled out, the Bank of China hustled to fill the gap; Sinopec, for example, signed a US$2 billion deal to develop the Yadavaran oil field.[80]

Israeli hardliners interpreted trade with Iran as "a clear sign that for all its Holocaust memorializing, for all its anti-Nazi legislation and for all its protestations of friendship with Israel and the Jewish people," Germany had not yet mastered the real lessons of *Shoah*.[81] Merkel's attempt to walk a fine line between trade relations and historical responsibility has been undermined by intermittent reports of illegal German exports.[82] The United States, the United Kingdom, and France were frustrated by Merkel's reluctance to accept tougher sanctions through 2014, but she strongly supported the 2016 Iranian nuclear deal. Netanyahu accused the United Nations of trying to turn a tiger into a kitten. Her reaction to Russia's Ukrainian exploits (Chapter 6) demonstrated a new willingness to place principles before profits.

More problematic is the renewed public debate concerning German weapons sales not only to Israel but to other Arab states, bringing us back to Pandora. The chancellor announced in 2011: "If you don't want to send troops yourself, then you have to send weapons so that these countries can defend themselves. It is no longer enough to extend 'words of encouragement' to such countries."[83] Her admonition coincided with a CDU/CSU–FDP decision to sell 270 Leopard 2 tanks (worth €5 billion) to Saudi Arabia, just as the Arab Spring kicked in. Ranked 160th on the UK-based "Democracy Index," Saudi men can now steer German tanks in a place where women cannot even drive cars. When Economics Minister Phillip Rösler put the sale on the Federal Security Council agenda, Foreign Minister Guido Westerwelle (both FDP) asked for Israeli objections but heard none. The mushrooming of Islamicist terrorist groups is turning adversaries into allies of expediency.[84]

THE DILEMMAS OF GENERATIONAL CHANGE

As Lily Gardner Feldman observes, "the transition in German–Israeli relations from enmity to amity in less than a generation is nothing short of miraculous."[85] Now several cohorts removed from the Nazi experience, both sides face new challenges. The paradox is that the more self-sustaining and institutionalized their cooperative ties become, the harder it will be to maintain public commitment to the *specialness* of this relationship. Both countries must search for new ways to preserve the memory of the historical tragedy that underlies their bond.[86]

Representative surveys only offer a "Kodak moment" of German–Israeli attitudes, increasingly influenced by current events. In 2009, 67 percent of FRG respondents were "proud" of national reconciliation, but few saw Israel as their "most important partner." While 65 percent classified their relationship as special, only 35 percent still held Germany uniquely responsible for Israel's security. Average citizens no longer see Israel as little David defending himself against the Arab Goliath.[87] They define their "historical responsibility" as the need to prevent war and protect human rights. In 2013, 89 percent stressed individual rights, while 80 percent deemed the protection of ethnic and religious minorities a pressing social task; figures for Israelis were 63 percent and 66 percent, respectively.[88] As of 2013, 55 percent of Germans preferred to "leave the past behind," compared with 22 percent among Israelis.[89]

Right-wing fringe groups still engage in anti-Semitic activities (demonstrations, desecrating Jewish cemeteries), but Germany responds more rapidly and decisively than most EU member states. Secondary anti-Semitism is a further problem: the group labeling Jews "unsympathetic" due to Israeli policies grew from 30 percent in 2007 to 41 percent in 2013; 41 percent saw parallels between Nazi practices and Israel's treatment of Palestinians.[90] By 2009, 77 percent of Israelis agreed that their government was heading in the wrong direction, versus 50 percent in 2007.[91] Indeed, the Second Intifada induced a wave of Israelis to "reclaim" their German passports.[92] Likud leaders urged Jews to abandon Europe after the 2015 "Charlie Hebdo" attack in France, but young, single Israelis in Berlin invited peers to join them, using *Aliyah*, a term exhorting Jews to "ascend" to the Promised Land. Roughly 400 migrate north each year; 35 percent of Palestinians also associate Berlin with "coolness" and "fun," though less than 4 percent have visited.[93]

Generational change is also producing serious memory loss. Among secularist Israelis, 70 percent have a positive and 28 percent a "very positive" image of Germany. Only 31 percent concur among the ultra-Orthodox; Russian-born residents are also more critical, possibly due to Cold War socialization. Men (76 percent) are more favorable than women (62 percent), admiring FRG technology, innovation, and product quality.[94] Volkswagen ranks among the top five foreign auto importers, while Lufthansa outpaces all foreign carriers landing in Tel Aviv. Sociologist Natan Sznaide observes, "You can advertise German goods as efficient without people fainting, and when Israelis talk about German efficiency, they have Bayern Munich in mind where hardly any German players play."[95] Helene Bartos contrasts this to earlier Israeli responses: when the FRG beat Croatia at the UEFA Euro 1996 soccer championship, Israel's second largest daily, *Ma'ariv*, ran the headline: "To our regret – Germany won."[96]

Another positive sign: in July 2015, seventy years after Nazi capitulation, Jewish sports activists held the European Maccabi Games ("Jewish Olympics") in Berlin. The games featured 2,000 athletes from thirty countries, "a sign that the Jewish Community takes for granted that it has become a vital and visible part of this country." Honored guests included descendants of Jewish athletes who had qualified for the 1936 Olympics but were barred from attending due to Hitler's deal with then US Olympic Committee president, Avery Brundage. Despite "friendship games" scheduled with German professional teams, organizers did not secure a single corporate sponsor listed on the DAX exchange, but the Berlin police were "open and helpful."[97]

Perceived as a modern, democratic state among secular, better educated and more affluent Israelis, Germany ranks first among their favorite European nations. In 2005, 78 percent of 16–34 year olds agreed that it bears no resemblance to Nazi Germany; rather than fearing a Fourth Reich, 59 percent view unification as having improved their relations (by ending hostile GDR policies).[98] Up from 50 percent in 2007, Chancellor Merkel enjoyed a 70 percent approval rating in 2014 (80 percent among Labor, 56 percent Likud, 46 percent among Arab party voters). Aware of her stance against settlements, they credit her government with submarine deliveries and freeing kidnapped soldier Gilad Shalit, in 2011.[99] Labeling her an "honest broker," 83 percent see her country actively securing Israel's right to exist, leading 57 percent to express "complete trust and reliance" in the FRG; 62 percent also see it as defending their interests in the EU. Only a tenth still consider "all Germans" guilty, perceptions rooted largely in Orthodox and religious extremist communities.[100] Israelis and Palestinians would like Germany to play an active role in international conflict resolution, although Israelis are mindful of its aid to Palestinians: in 2014 it poured €104 million into the Occupied Territories. The latter are likewise cognizant of Germany's special responsibility toward Israel; 64 percent of Fatah voters, versus 37 percent of Hamas sympathizers, view Germany positively.[101]

Contradictory attitudes are also emerging in Israel. The 1990s saw a controversial intellectual debate over its "founding narrative," reminiscent of the West German *Historikerstreit* of the 1980s. The "New History" debate arose in conjunction with the 1993 Oslo peace process: to advance negotiations, Israelis had to acknowledge that their 1948 War of Independence had inflicted mass suffering on Palestinians, who describe the period as "The Catastrophe." Declassified documents proved that the Israeli Defense Forces responsible for mass expulsions had themselves engaged in war crimes. Officials revised the educational curriculum in 1995, rewriting textbooks and issuing a twenty-two-part documentary (*Tekuma*) in 1998 testifying to Arab deaths and "dispossession."[102] The 1995 assassination of Yitzahk Rabin by a Jewish extremist elevated the Likud Party, enabling Netanyahu to become prime minister (the first born in Israel). His government banned the revised textbooks and the film, introducing a new school curriculum known as "Heritage." The Knesset then passed the *Naqba* Law, prohibiting official acts of mourning on Israeli Independence Day.

Former Knesset president Avraham Berg contends that Netanyahu uses "the trauma of the *Shoah*" as a political strategy, because it makes things possible that an "intact people would not undertake and that no other state could get away with."[103] But the ironies do not stop there. As Muriel Asseburg argues, in the land of the perpetrators, the dictum "never again war" has fostered a political culture based on military self-restraint and a preference for multilateralism; in the land of the victims, the cry "never again Auschwitz" has resulted in demands for military strength, unilateral action, and nuclear deterrence.[104] Second, insistence on a state rooted in *ethnos* led the Nazis to exterminate Jews as the embodiment of European cosmopolitanism. Today Germany is the locomotive of European integration, reflecting openness and diversity (see the national soccer team). Under mounting Orthodox influence, Israel is becoming a closed society, insisting on ethno-religious purity and discriminating against Arab citizens and Ethiopian Jews. As Berg observes, the presence of the *Shoah* in Berlin has turned it into a tolerant city, but in Israel, which wants to live in the past, Palestinian history has been erased.

A final irony rests with the fact that a growing number of Israeli youth, living testimony to Jewish survival, could make it even harder for their German counterparts to uphold their special relationship. High birth rates among ultra-Orthodox and illegal settler communities are contributing to the success of militant right-wing parties. Viewing Germany more negatively than secularists, three-fourths of those youth would support a military strike against Iran, should sanctions prove ineffective. This could unleash a regional war that would horrify Germans, who would be expected to provide the weaponry. Yet over 80 percent of the latter reject weapon deliveries, compared with 16 percent among Israelis.[105] Would the German *Staatsräson*, including a chancellor's promise that "Israel's security will never be open to negotiation," supersede the right of citizens in a democratic polity to block a potential "nuclear Holocaust" in the Middle East? How far will the miracle of reconciliation extend?

Christoph Schult, a Hebrew-speaking journalist with twenty-seven years of personal ties to Israel, cautions that "those who get caught in the fog of absolute loyalty to Israel ... despite all of the nonsense coming out of the current government," run the risk of undermining its future. A true friendship, he notes, "thrives on the courage to give criticism – and on the ability to accept it."[106] Schult offers one example involving KaDeWe (*Kaufhaus des Westens*), an upscale store in Berlin that featured goods imported from the Occupied Territories. Because neither the Golan Heights nor the West Bank have been recognized internationally, EU regulations dictate that products from those areas cannot be labeled "made in Israel." Temporarily removing mislabeled items from its shelves in order to re-tag them, store executives were immediately accused by (now) pro-Israeli Greens of "boycotting" Jewish products. Social networks posted images of Nazi paramilitaries standing in front of Jewish businesses in 1933. Within hours Netanyahu declared, "This department store had been owned by Jews, the Nazis took it ... We strongly protest this step, which is unacceptable morally, practically and on its merits. We expect the German government to act on this grave matter." Shocked by the response, KaDeWe workers returned the goods to the shelves, despite EU requirements. Like Berg, Schult sees Netanyahu as willing to exploit the *Shoah* to shore up his own electoral base, as if "friends can only be real friends if they support his policies 100%."

CONCLUSION: GENDER AND THE SHOAH REVISITED

A rapidly changing international environment can pose new challenges to any special relationship, even one as morally, institutionally, and psychologically intertwined as this one. Angela Merkel's effectiveness in managing historically overdetermined German–Israeli relations stems, in large part, from her experiences as a pastor's daughter, raised in the East. Pragmatic Protestantism, drawing on the Confessing Church framework advanced by theologians who had witnessed Nazi persecution, stresses the role of individual responsibility in seeking "forgiveness and reconciliation." This chancellor's efforts to work though conflicting elements of her own past have granted her a unique right to speak for Germany united. As Gardner Feldman writes, "Merkel completed the circle through her dedication to the principle of reconciliation even though, as an East German citizen, she had no opportunity to participate earlier in its conceptualization or practice."[107] She embodies a sense of individual as well as collective responsibility rarely witnessed among postwar politicians.[108]

Merkel's affirmation of Germany's postwar *Staatsräson* recognizes the permanent nature of its moral responsibility to Israel. Her desire to preserve the Jewish state by creating a sustainable Palestinian state is driven by pragmatic *Realpolitik* concerns, and her ability to read the demographic writing on the wall: radical-right religious groups in Israel (evincing the highest birth rate among OECD countries) are confronting ever more radical Palestinian youth. Responsible for 750,000 refugees in 1950, the UN Relief and Works Agency now assists 5 million displaced Palestinians, 1.5 million of whom are held in fifty-eight refugee camps.

Beyond the maternity dimension, what does gender have to do with the future of German–Israeli relations? On the surface, not much, and therein lies the problem. The gender implications of any policy, historical or contemporary, assume many forms. Women have long been excluded from official discourses involving Nazi atrocities, historical memory, compensation deals, and reconciliation processes. They were disproportionately rounded up, deported, and exterminated, along with their children, in Nazi death camps after thousands of men had fled.[109] Early studies posited that women embraced a Nazi ideology rooted in masculine notions of racism and anti-Semitism; but they also pursued their own interests in rejecting cooperation with Jewish women's organizations starting in 1933.[110] Housewives boycotted Jewish stores, shunned or denounced non-Aryan neighbors, allowed their children to join the Hitler Youth, sent their sons to war, and accepted their churches' collaboration with the Nazis.

Women in powerful positions, such as Hitler cabinet member Gertrude Scholz-Klink (found living under a pseudonym in 1950), received milder prison sentences, connoting their secondary status.[111]

Women nonetheless seemed more remorseful after the war: a 1950–1951 survey found that 60 percent shared feelings of personal or collective responsibility, compared with 44 percent among men.[112] Despite increasing numbers of feminist scholars, women played no part in the Historians' Controversy of 1986–1987, a debate characterized by Charles Maier as an intellectual confrontation between "fathers-turned-grandfathers and sons-turned-fathers."[113] When Germany established a new fund in 1998 to compensate neglected groups of slave laborers, women who had been forced to serve as domestics and agricultural workers were deliberately excluded from the settlement.[114] While pre-1990 writings overwhelmingly ignored female anti-Semitism, younger feminist scholars began to stress links between sexism, racism, and cultural dominance after unification, triggered by xenophobic violence at home and "ethnic cleansing" in Yugoslavia.[115] Israel could also use a feminist-scholarship jolt: ultra-Orthodox bullies are now forcing women to the back of the bus and attack those attempting to pray at the Wailing Wall in Jerusalem.[116]

Merkel remains firmly focused on generic, gender-neutral formulations regarding human rights issues in the Middle East. The bigger question is whether her personal engagement with *Staatsräson* issues might move German women to reflect more on their own national historical responsibility for keeping the *Shoah* memory alive. Merkel neither walks on water nor is she capable of parting the Red Sea, but it is pretty amazing that a Lutheran pastor's daughter from Templin can harshly critique Israeli policies without undermining their special bond. Unable to control processes of generational change, she can ensure that other reconciliation efforts take institutional root, for example, through her dealings with Poland and the Czech Republic. One way to transfer her strong support for religious diversity at home to the negotiating table would be to re-involve Germany in Middle East peace processes (á la Fischer's Road Map). She is a master at managing "the politics of small steps."

The 2015 re-election of Benyamin Netanyahu has made the chancellor's job a lot tougher. Fluent in Russian, she would have gotten along much better with one of his predecessors, a Jewish girl from Kiev (Ukraine) who likewise spent her youth without democracy and human rights, and years of her political life trying to prove that she was more than a "transitional" leader. Israeli Prime Minister Golda Meir (1969–1974) noted, "One cannot and must not try to erase the past merely because it does not fit the present." Meir also declared with respect to female leadership: "Whether women are better than men I cannot say – but I can say they are certainly no worse."[117] Imagine how the Middle East might look ten years from now, under the combined efforts of German Chancellor Merkel, an Israeli prime minister named Tzipi Livni, Palestinian leader Hanan Ashrawi, and a new US president, Hillary Clinton. Their two-state solution might not immediately bring peace but it would certainly improve the prospects for democracy, freedom, trust, solidarity, the rule of law, friendly competition, respect, and tolerance across the region in the long run.

NOTES

1. "Merkel in the Knesset: 'We Would Never Abandon Israel,'" *Der Spiegel*, March 18, 2008.
2. Rede von Bundeskanzlerin Dr. Angela Merkel vor der Knesset in Jerusalem, March 18, 2008.
3. Introduced by diplomat Günther Gaus, Kohl used this phrase before, during, and after his 1983 visit to Israel to suggest that he and others born after 1930 were not implicated in the events of the Second World War; aged 15 when it ended, he was directly exposed to Nazi propaganda during his formative years. Gaus later complained that he had used it in the Lutheran confessional sense, while Kohl used it to signify an "accident of birth." Born in 1944, Schröder would have been the first to lack personal memories of the war and its aftermath.
4. Ludwig August von Rochau, *Grundsätze der Realpolitik angewendet auf die staatlichen Zustände Deutschlands* (1853).
5. I owe a great deal to Lily for her insightful scholarship and moral reflections on Germany's postwar reconciliation with many states since the 1980s. See Lily Gardner Feldman, *The Special Relationship between West Germany and Israel* (Boston, MA: Allen & Unwin, 1984), and Lily Gardner Feldman, *Germany's Foreign Policy of Reconciliation: From Enmity to Amity* (Lanham, MD: Rowman & Littlefield, 2012). Drawing on Gardner Feldman, Yves P. Pallade presents a wealth of data regarding their trade, military and cultural exchanges in *Germany and Israel in the 1990s and Beyond: Still a "Special Relationship"?* (Frankfurt: European University Studies, 2005).
6. Gardner Feldman, *Germany's Foreign Policy of Reconciliation*, p. 87.
7. Gardner Feldman, *Germany's Foreign Policy of Reconciliation*, p. 263.
8. William Drozdiak, "Facing Up to Some Unsavory History," *Washington Post*, February 10, 1997.
9. Gardner Feldman, *Germany's Foreign Policy of Reconciliation*, p. 40; further, Stefan Engert, "A Case Study in 'Atonement': Adenauer's Holocaust Apology," *Israel Journal of Foreign Affairs*, 4(3) (2010): 111–122; and Karin Beindorf, "Feinde, Freunde, Fremde: 50 Jahre deutsch-israelische Beziehungen," *Deutschlandfunk – Essay und Diskurs*, aired on May 10, 2015.

10. Gardner Feldman, *The Special Relationship*, pp. 52–53.
11. Asher Ben Natan and Niels Hansen (eds.), *Israel und Deutschland: Dorniger Weg zur Partnerschaft – Die Botschafter berichten über vier Jahrzehnte diplomatischer Beziehungen, 1965–2005* (Cologne: Bohlau, 2005).
12. Raffaella Del Sarto, "Plus ça change ... ? Israel, the EU and the Union for the Mediterranean," *Mediterranean Politics*, 16(1) (2011), p. 118.
13. Ruth Wittlinger, *German National Identity in the Twenty-first Century. A Different Republic After All?* (Basingstoke: Palgrave Macmillan, 2010).
14. Gardner Feldman, *Germany's Foreign Policy of Reconciliation*, p. 170.
15. Hans Christian Ströbele (Greens) placed the blame elsewhere, declaring that Scuds were a "logical, almost compelling consequence of Israeli offensive policies in the region." See Andrea Humphreys, "Die Grünen and the Israeli–Palestinian Conflict," *Australian Journal of Politics and History*, 50(3) (2004), p. 411.
16. Werner Sonne, *Staatsräson? Wie Deutschland für Israels Sicherheit haftet* (Berlin: Propyläen, 2013), p. 190.
17. Ronen Bergman et al., "'Made in Germany': U-boats to Israel," *Der Spiegel*, June 4, 2012, p. 27; Pallade, *Germany and Israel in the 1990s and Beyond*.
18. Bergman et al., "*Made in Germany*," pp. 20–32.
19. Sonne, *Staatsräson?* pp. 188, 193 ff.
20. Patrick Müller, "The Europeanization of Germany's Foreign Policy toward the Israeli–Palestinian Conflict: Between Adaptation to the EU and National Projection," *Mediterranean Politics*, 16(3) (2011): 385–403.
21. Sonne, *Staatsräson?* p. 115.
22. "Gauck distanziert sich von Merkels Haltung zu Israel," *Die Zeit*, May 30, 2012.
23. Lily Gardner Feldman, "What's in a Name? The German–Israeli Partnership: Is It a Special Relationship, a Friendship, an Alliance or Reconciliation," AICGS, March 6, 2014.
24. Gardner Feldman dates this process back to the 1970s, *Germany's Foreign Policy of Reconciliation*, p. 386; Sharon Pardo, "Going West: Guidelines for Israel's Integration into the European Union," *Israel Journal of Foreign Affairs*, 3(2) (2009): 51–62.
25. Schröder's original declaration stems from 2002. See "Israel Debatte: Feigheit vor dem Freund: Der umstrittene U-Boot-Deal," *Die Zeit*, April 13, 2012.
26. Muriel Asseburg and Jan Busse, "Deutschlands Politik gegenüber Israel," in Thomas Jäger, Alexander Höse, and Kai Oppermann (eds.), *Deutsche Außenpolitik, Sicherheit, Wohlfahrt, Institutionen, Normen* (Wiesbaden: Verlag für Sozialwissenschaften, 2011), p. 697.
27. Christiane Hoffmann and René Pfister, "Diplomatie: Im Sprachkorsett," *Der Spiegel*, January 14, 2013.
28. Cited in Asseburg and Busse, "Deutschlands Politik," pp. 698–699. The German Foreign Ministry reports trade figures in US$.
29. Kraushaar, *Wann endlich beginnt bei Euch der Kampf gegen die heilige Kuh Israel*; "Manifest der 25: Freundschaft und Kritik: Warum die 'besonderen Beziehungen' zwischen Deutschland und Israel überdacht werden müssen," *Frankfurter Rundschau*, November 15, 2006.

30. Yves P. Pallade, "Antisemitism and Right-Wing Extremism in Germany: New Discourses," *Israel Journal of Foreign Affairs*, 2(1) (2008): 66–67.

31. Matthias Zimmer, "Der Staatsräson der Bundesrepublik Deutschland vor und nach 1989," *Zeitschrift für Außen- und Sicherheitspolitik*, 6(2) (2009), p. 68.

32. Thomas Haury, "Die DDR und der 'Agressorstaat Israel' – Das 'unschuldige Deutschland' im Nahostkonflikt," *Tribüne*. 173 (2005): 202–215; Efraim Inbar and Eitan Shamir, "'Mowing the Grass': Israel's Strategy for Protracted Intractable Conflict," *Journal of Strategic Studies*, 37(1) (2014): 65–90.

33. Ruth Wittlinger, "The Merkel Government's Politics of the Past," *German Politics and Society*, 26(4) (2008): 9–27.

34. Humphreys, "Die Grünen and the Israeli–Palestinian Conflict," p. 410.

35. Bergman et al., "Made in Germany," p. 26.

36. Sonne, *Staatsräson?* p. 201.

37. "Gauck distanziert sich von Merkels Haltung zu Israel," *Die Zeit*, May 30, 2012; also Sonne, *Staatsräson?* pp. 202 ff.

38. Sonne, *Staatsräson?* p. 204.

39. Sonne, *Staatsräson?* pp. 183–184.

40. Sonne, *Staatsräson?* pp. 393–394.

41. Pardo, cited in Del Sarto, "Plus ça change … ?" p. 121.

42. Pardo, "Going West," p. 124.

43. Heiko Beyer and Ulf Liebe, "Antisemitismus heute. Zur Messung aktueller Erscheinungs formen von Judenfeindlichkeit mithilfe des faktoriellen Surveys," *Zeitschrift für Soziologie*, 42(3) (2013): 186–200; Yves P. Pallade, "Delegitimizing Jews and the Jewish State: Anti-Semitism and Anti-Zionism after Auschwitz," *Israel Journal of Foreign Affairs*, 3 (2009): 63–69.

44. Jörg Lau, "Deutschland braucht eine andere Nahostpolitik," *Die Zeit*, November 10, 2011.

45. Zimmer, "Der Staatsräson der Bundesrepublik Deutschland," p. 67.

46. Gardner Feldman, *Germany's Foreign Policy of Reconciliation*, pp. 62–63.

47. "Neue Regeln: Regierung legt Gesetz zur Beschneidung vor," *Der Spiegel*, October 3, 2012.

48. Deutscher Bundestag, Stenographischer Bericht, 142. Sitzung, Berlin, January 17, 2001.

49. Humphreys, "Die Grünen and the Israeli–Palestinian Conflict," p. 415.

50. Hans Kundnani, *Utopia or Auschwitz. Germany's 1968 Generation and the Holocaust* (New York: Columbia University Press, 2009), pp. 221 ff.

51. Mushaben, *From Post-War to Post-Wall Generations*, ch. 5.

52. Gardner Feldman, *Germany's Foreign Policy of Reconciliation*, p. 60.

53. Fischer press conference of April 7, 1999, cited in Joyce Marie Mushaben, "*Nie wieder Krieg! Nie Wieder Auschwitz!* Germans, Generations and NATO Participation in the Balkans," German Studies Association Meeting, Houston, Texas, October 5–8, 2001.

54. Fischer, April 7 press conference.

55. Rede von Bundeskanzlerin Dr. Angela Merkel vor der Knesset in Jerusalem, March 18, 2008.

56. "'Prügel-Affäre': Joscka Fischer zieht das Büßerhemd an," *Der Spiegel*, January 6, 2001.
57. As late as 1990, the Vatican report, "We remember the Shoah," still blamed Nazi atrocities on "the sins of her children," rather than on its own Concordats with Mussolini and Hitler that eliminated channels for Catholic resistance.
58. Gardner Feldman, *Germany's Foreign Policy of Reconciliation*, p. 62.
59. Helene Bartos, "Israeli–German Relations in the Years 2000–2006: A Special Relationship Revisited," Master's thesis, University of Oxford, 2007, p. 10.
60. Reported by the BBC, available at: www.bbc.com/news/uk-politics-26368783.
61. "Von der Zwei-Staaten-Lösung überzeugt," Gespräch mit Bundesaussenminister Joschka Fischer," *Tribüne* (2008), pp. 24–32.
62. Marco Allegra and Paolo Napolitano, "Two States or Not Two States? Leadership and Peace Making in the Israeli–Palestinian Conflict," *Mediterranean Politics*, 16(2) (2011): 261–278; Jan Busse, "Zwischen historischer Verantwortung und Zweistaatenlösung: Die Nahostpolitik der Bundesregierung unter Kanzlerin Merkel," *SWP-Studie*, 8 (March 2009); Khaled Elgindy, "The Middle East Quartet: A Post-Mortem," Analysis Paper No. 25, February 2012, Saban Center, Brookings Institution; and Matthias Kuentzel, "A Dubious Achievement: Joschka Fischer, the Road Map, and the Gaza Pullout," *Der Spiegel*, August 22, 2005.
63. Humphreys, "Die Grünen and the Israeli–Palestinian Conflict," p. 417.
64. Michael Mertes directed the Konrad Adenauer Stiftung office in Jerusalem. His comments derives from a *Deutsche Welle* interview (December 6, 2012) that, "there is a new style of communication, but no change in substance."
65. Klaus Remme, "Netanyahu-Besuch. Merkel kritisiert Siedlungspolitik," *Deutschlandfunk*, October 21, 2015; Peter Beaumont, "Anger at Netanyahu Claim, Palestinian Grand Mufti inspired Holocaust," *The Guardian*, October 21, 2015.
66. "Treffen mit Merkel in Berlin: Netanyahu preist Israel als Festung gegen den Islamismus," *Der Spiegel*, February 16, 2016.
67. Ralph Ahren; "Merkel: Now's Not the Time for Major Progress to Palestinian State," *The Times of Israel*, February 16, 2016.
68. The official English translation curiously uses the French term, "reason for being," not "reason of state."
69. "Total Normal?," *Der Spiegel*, November 30, 1998; also, Lily Gardner Feldman, "What Really Must Be Said," AICGS Advisor, Washington, DC, April 10, 2012.
70. "Holocaust-Debatte: Merkel fordert Papst zur Klarstellung auf," *Der Spiegel*, February 3, 2009.
71. Hoffmann and Ulrich, "Was haben wir uns angetan?"
72. Elgindy, "The Middle East Quartet."
73. Ralph Neukirch, "An Affront from Berlin: Israeli–German Relations Strained after Abstention," *Der Spiegel*, December 3, 2012.
74. Del Sarto, "Plus ça change … ?" pp. 117–134; Yoel Guzansky, "Israel's Periphery Doctrine 2.0: The Mediterranean Plus," *Mediterranean Politics*, 19(1) (2014): 99–116; Müller, "Europeanization of Germany's Foreign Policy."

75. Matthew S. Cohen and Charles D. Freilich, "Breakdown and Possible Restart: Turkish–Israeli Relations under the AKP," *Israel Journal of Foreign Affairs*, 8(1) (2014): 39–55; Oded Eran, "Turkey and the European Union: An Israeli Perspective," *Israel Journal of Foreign Affairs*, 2(2) (2008): 65–71; Trude Strand, "Tightening the Noose: The Institutionalized Impoverishment of Gaza, 2005–2010," *Journal of Palestine Studies*, 43(2) (2014): 6–23.

76. "Merkel Calls for a 'Comprehensive and Transparent' Probe into Flotilla Raid," *The Hindu*, June 4, 2010.

77. Severin Weiland, "German–Israeli Relations: Merkel and Netanyahu Seek to Play Down Differences," *Der Spiegel*, December 6, 2012.

78. Sonne, *Staatsräson?* p. 120.

79. Sonne, *Staatsräson?* p. 115.

80. Benjamin E. Power, "The Berlin Connection: Locating German–Iranian Relations within the Current Understandings of Post-Unification German Foreign Policy," *Journal of International Relations*, 10 (2008), pp. 15–16.

81. Caroline Glick, "Germany's Honored Guest," *Jerusalem Post*, May 2, 2006.

82. Cathrin Gilbert, Holger Stark, and Andreas Ulrich, "Nuclear Technology for Iran: German Investigators Uncover illegal Exports," *Der Spiegel*, October 1, 2012.

83. Rede von Bundeskanzlerin Dr. Angela Merkel, "50 Jahre Bergedorfer Gesprächskreis" der Körber Stiftung am 9. September 2011 in Berlin, available at: www.bundes-regierung.de/Content/DE/Bulletin/2011/09/89–3-bk-bergedorfer.html.

84. Holger Stark, "Tank Exports to Saudi Arabia Signal German Policy Shift," *Der Spiegel*, October 14, 2011.

85. Gardner Feldman, *Germany's Foreign Policy of Reconciliation*, p. 182.

86. Poland also worries about memory losses: in 2007, it pushed UNESCO to rename Auschwitz-Birkenau the "Former Nazi German Concentration Camp of Auschwitz," fearing that future visitors will attribute historical atrocities to Poland because of its geographic location. "Poland seeks Auschwitz Renaming," BBC News, March 31, 2006.

87. Muriel Asseburg, "50 Jahre deutsch-israelische diplomatische Beziehungen," *SWP-Aktuell 40* (Berlin: Stiftung Wissenschaft und Politik, 2015), p. 4.

88. Steffen Hagemann and Roby Nathanson, "Germany and Israel Today: Linked by the Past, Divided by the Present," Bertelsmann Stiftung, Berlin, January 2015, p. 18. The survey covered 1,000 Germans and 1,001 Israelis; it was conducted in late 2013, with a summer 2014 follow-up, after Israel launched a further attack on Hamas.

89. Ibid., p. 23.

90. Ibid., p. 36.

91. Mitchell Barack, Sharon Pardo, and Lars Hänsel drew on a smaller sample (500 Israeli Jews, 100 Israeli Arabs). See "Measuring the Attitudes of Israelis towards the European Union and its Member States," Konrad Adenauer Stiftung and KEEVOON, 2009.

92. Bartos, "Israeli–German Relations," pp. 64–68.

93. "Jewish Migration: Next Year in Berlin," *The Economist*, October 11, 2014. Also, Michael Borchard and Hans Maria Heyn, "*Das Heilige Land und die Deutschen*," Konrad Adenauer Stiftung, Jerusalem and Ramallah 2015, p. 10. This poll involved 1,000 Jews, Arab Israelis, and Russian Jews, as well as 1,270 Palestinians.

94. Borchard and Heyne, "Das Heilige Land," p. 3.

95. Bartos, "Israeli–German Relations," pp. 66–67.

96. Ibid., p. 68.

97. Jens Schneider and Javier Cáceres, "Einzug in den Park," *Süddeutsche Zeitung*, April 4–5, 2015.

98. Borchard and Heyne, "Das Heilige Land," p. 5.

99. Ibid., p. 6.

100. Mustafa Mohanad and As'Ad Ghanem, "The Empowering of the Israeli Extreme Right in the 18th Knesset Elections," *Mediterranean Politics*, 15(1) (2010): 25–44.

101. Borchard and Heyne, "Das Heilige Land," p. 10.

102. Lisa Strömbom, "Identity Shifts and Conflict Transformation: Probing the Israeli History Debates," *Mediterranean Politics*, 18(1) (2013): 79–97. The 1953 State Education law stressed Jewish culture, love for the homeland, loyalty to the Jewish state, and the "voluntary flight" of Palestinians. Arabs were consistently depicted as primitive, underdeveloped, culturally inferior, or invisible people prior to 1948, and later as "blood-thirsty killers and rioters, aggressively continuing the anti-Semitism of the Holocaust."

103. *Deutschlandfunk* interview, May 10, 2015, available at: www.deutschland funk.de/ex-knesset-praesident-burg-offene-kritik-an-israel-gefordert.868.de .html?dram:article_id=319403.

104. Asseburg, "50 Jahre," p. 3.

105. Hagemann and Nathanson, "Germany and Israel Today," p. 51.

106. Christoph Schult, "Polemics have No Place in True Friendships," *Der Spiegel*, December 11, 2015.

107. Gardner Feldman, *Germany's Foreign Policy of Reconciliation*, p. 65.

108. Willy Brandt constitutes another exception, for example, when he fell to his knees at the Warsaw Ghetto site in December 1970.

109. Dalia Ofer and Lenore J. Weitzman (eds.), *Woman in the Holocaust* (New Haven, CT: Yale University Press, 1998).

110. Mushaben, "Collective Memory Divided and Reunited."

111. This minister-mother of eleven children was the only cabinet member not sentenced to death at Nuremberg; banned from her profession and stripped of her pension, she was released after two years in prison, and lived off donations from neo-Nazi groups until her death in 1999.

112. Mushaben, "Collective Memory Divided and Reunited."

113. Maier, *The Unmasterable Past*.

114. Mushaben, "Memory and the Holocaust."

115. Frigga Haug was labeled a "nest-dirtier" for chipping away at the traditional victim–perpetrator dichotomy, though she did not challenge male agency. Christine Thürmer-Rohr's work on "female co-perpetrators" (1983) held that women's culpability rested in capitulating to men's designs, a form of

active self-victimization. In 1987, Karin Windaus-Walser refuted "the blessing of female birth," claiming that the "murderous normality" witnessed under fascism was due not only to the evil actions of men but also to the reactive accommodation of women.

116. "Israeli Rosa Parks' Receives Death Threats after Refusing to Move to Back of ultra-Orthodox Bus," *Haaretz* online, January 4, 2012, available at: www.haaretz.com/israel-news/israeli-rosa-parks-receives-death-threats-after-refusing-to-move-to-back-of-ultra-orthodox-bus-1.405463.

117. Golda Meir Center for Political Leadership, available at: www.msudenver .edu/golda/goldameir/goldaquotes.

PART II

FROM UNDERSTUDY TO LEADING LADY: ANGELA MERKEL ON THE GLOBAL STAGE

This Section moves beyond the "meta-level" of national identity and moral responsibility vis-à-vis the German past in order to examine Chancellor Merkel's performance as she attempts to balance global imperatives with regional commitments and national interests. Having spent the first thirty-five years of her life in the "GDR waiting room of democracy," Merkel claims to have long idealized the "American Dream," conveyed by way of second-hand sources which were inevitably subject to strong ideological filters. Her view of the United States was colored by the socialist critiques of her home government as well as by the conflicting images featured in the West German media prior to the Wall's collapse. Joining the cabinet in 1990, "Kohl's Girl" knew almost nothing about the European Union that would make her life so difficult once the 2008 global financial crisis morphed into an ongoing Euro crisis. Nor did Merkel's direct exposure to Soviet-style secret policing prepare her for the fact that her own phone would one day be tapped by the US National Security Administration. She later discovered that her own intelligence services also spied on friends and allies, while missing out on right-wing terrorism at home.

Lacking direct foreign policy experience prior to 2005, Germany's first female chancellor nonetheless took to the international stage like a duck to water. In less than four years, she emerged as a very effective mediator among three competing forces: the United States, the European Union, and Russia. Merkel's refusal to embrace rigidly ideological positions is countered by her fervent commitment to human rights, democratic values, slow but steady deliberations, and occasionally dramatic all-night negotiating sessions, resulting in surprising agreements. Named *Time*

Magazine's "Person of the Year" in 2016, the first woman featured in thirty years, Merkel has carved out a new role for Germany as a global player that no longer strictly limits itself to *civilian power*. Taking advantage of generational change, a thriving economy, and a lack of leadership in many European quarters, this chancellor has worked hard to keep all major parties engaged in dialogue but she does so in surprising ways – with the result that friends and foes rarely get what they bargained for.

4

Checkmate: Angela Merkel, Vladimir Putin, and the Dilemmas of Regional Hegemony

In February 2005, nine months before she became Germany's first female chancellor, Angela Merkel delivered the *laudatio* for then-Senator Hillary Clinton, who had traveled to Baden-Baden to receive the prestigious German Media Prize. At the end of her speech, the CDU opposition leader cited one of my favorite lines from Eleanor Roosevelt, which she erroneously attributed to Hillary: "A woman is like a tea-bag: you only know how strong she is when she's in hot water."[1] Rarely inclined to discuss the gender challenges she has encountered while climbing the political ladder, Merkel does pay homage to two women she claims as personal role models. The first is a two-time Nobel Prize recipient, physicist Marie Curie; the second is Russia's longest reigning empress, Catherine the Great. Indeed, journalists familiar with Merkel's seventh floor sanctum in the Federal Chancellor's Office report that she keeps a small portrait of Catherine on her desk. The only other painting on prominent display there is that of Germany's first postwar chancellor, Konrad Adenauer.

The two women Merkel admires most were both born in Poland but later adopted new homelands, where each managed to shatter the glass ceiling of her day. Each was unusually well educated for her time, preferring reason and evidence over passion and rhetoric; both women, in turn, successfully established themselves in domains historically reserved for men. Despite her Nobel Prizes in physics and chemistry, respectively, Marie Curie was denied admission to the French Academy of Sciences in 1911 but later served on the Committee for Intellectual Cooperation at the League of Nations.[2] In 1995, her remains were transferred to the Pantheon Mausoleum in Paris, the first woman to be nationally honored "in perpetuity" based on her own accomplishments.

Characterized as an "enlightened despot," Catherine began her life as Princess Sophie of Anhalt Zerbst; she was baptized as a Lutheran in Stettin (Pomerania), less than 50 miles away from Templin, where Merkel was later raised. At 15 Sophie acquired a new name when she embraced the Russian Orthodox faith, a precondition for her marriage to the grandson of Peter the Great. Fluent in German, French, and Russian, Catherine read vociferously and promoted the arts; she also expanded the Russian empire to include much of modern Poland, Ukraine, and the Crimea. She published two manifestos inviting farmers, miners, and traders (excluding Jews) to relocate from her homeland to help develop Russia. Later known as the Volga Germans, they were granted the unusual privilege of maintaining their own culture, language, and religions, as Lutherans, Catholics and Mennonites, contributing to her reputation as a supporter of religious tolerance.

Merkel's paternal grandparents, as well as her mother, were likewise born in Poland; her family moved from the Western city of Hamburg to the Eastern state of Brandenburg in 1954, requiring Angela to adapt to a "foreign" culture in unified Germany thirty-five years later. As a Lutheran pastor's daughter fluent in German, Russian, and English, Merkel frequented museums and collected art postcards in her youth; she still attends concerts, theater, and opera performances. She has moreover positioned unified Germany as a key actor on the global stage. Deeply committed to democratic freedoms, Merkel claims to admire Catherine as a woman "who had accomplished many things under difficult circumstances" and "as a reformer, nothing more."[3] As someone who has almost single-handedly impelled CDU/CSU hardliners to cross that bridge to the twenty-first century with modernized family policies, the chancellor's idea of "nothing more" says a lot about an unusual political virtue she shares with the former empress: humility (*Demut*). Both leaders have had to master political environments falling under the proverbial curse, "May you live in interesting times." As Catherine noted during her reign, 1762–1796, "A great wind is blowing and that either gives you imagination ... or a headache." She observed further, "I shall be an autocrat: that's my trade. And the good Lord will forgive me: that's his." Perhaps Merkel drew some comfort from those words as she worked behind the scenes to impose a very unpopular austerity package on Greece.

However circumscribed Merkel's admiration for Catherine the Great may be, the latter's accomplishments offer crucial historical insights to those trying to comprehend the chancellor's turbulent relationship with the current Russian leader, Vladimir Putin. Like no other couple on the contemporary political stage, Merkel and Putin have experienced parallel lives. Fate required them to share a geo-political space until 1990, one as a GDR citizen, the other as a KGB operative in Dresden; like parallel lines, however, their values and world-views are unlikely to intersect any time soon. After the Wall's collapse, these two political outsiders pursued national leadership tracks at equivalent speeds; while both have evinced impressive political staying-power, Putin's notion of "sovereign democracy" differs significantly from Merkel's rights-based, rule-of-law version.

Ever since her first speech at the Munich Security Conference in 2003, Angela Merkel has sought to balance her unwavering commitment to the North Atlantic Alliance with Germany's *Realpolitik*-need to keep Russia engaged in international negotiations and dialogue. Her personal affection for the United States rarely translated into an easy time for George W. Bush or Barack Obama, whose policies she candidly challenged. Presenting herself as a critical friend, Merkel has taken issue with their respective violations of fundamental American values concerning torture, rendition, the Guantanamo Bay prison camp, and the intrusive nature of National Security Administration spying; the latter included the tapping of her personal cell-phone. Despite her steadfast support for NATO, Merkel is painfully aware that US entanglements over the last twenty years have taken their toll on that country's reputation as the defender of the free world.

The end of bipolarism, a European shift from *hard* to *soft power* responses to global conflict, public demands for nuclear disarmament, and new forms of violent insurgency have undermined traditional NATO doctrines and strategies, long fixated on nuclear deterrence. Generational change has also reconfigured views about Germany's contemporary partners and adversaries, particularly since unification. The first Western chancellor, Konrad Adenauer, experienced the atrocities of two world wars, as did his short-term successor Kurt Georg Kiesinger. The next FRG leader, Willy Brandt, spent several years as a member of the anti-Nazi resistance in Norway; his successor, ex-*Wehrmacht* officer Helmut Schmidt, served on the Eastern front, and later in the Ardennes offensive. Although too young to fight, Helmut Kohl also witnessed the war first-hand in Ludwigshafen, later incorporated into the French occupation zone. All of these chancellors focused on "West integration," collective security via NATO, a special Franco-German friendship, and outright rejection of military engagement in any place where German boots had once marched between 1939 and 1945.

Only a toddler when the war ended, Gerhard Schröder quickly turned his back on a contentious French president, Jacques Chirac, in favor of a personal friendship with Vladimir Putin; following his 2005 electoral defeat, he accepted a highly paid job advising the Russian energy conglomerate, Gazprom. Born after the Korean War and forced to turn eastward as a GDR citizen, Angela Merkel never developed the emotional tie to France evinced by her predecessors, nor did she inherit an intuitive understanding of the European Community. Having hitch-hiked extensively across Eastern Europe and parts of the Soviet Union prior to 1989, she naturally gravitated toward the new democracies after unification, emphasizing reconciliation with Poland and Israel. By the time she became chancellor, Merkel understood better than any other Western leader why it was essential to bring the Russians back into any dialogue involving Europe. She has been no less candid in her dealings with Putin than she was with Bush and Obama, especially concerning Russian incursions into Georgia, the Crimea, and eastern Ukraine.

My original aim was to offer a number of short case studies, illustrating Merkel's efforts to keep the United States and Russia engaged in regional discourses by way of "triangulation." Like my chapter on her approach to migration and integration policies, however, this one has been overtaken by current events. As of this writing, the Merkel–Putin relationship offers more than enough fertile ground for exploring Germany's increasingly assertive behavior on behalf of national interests, as well as for ascertaining what makes "the world's most powerful woman" tick in the foreign and security policy domain.

The chapter begins with a brief historical review of Germany's transition from an international pariah, to a steadfast NATO partner, to an increasingly independent civilian power. It then considers the rules of "power physics" that have shaped Merkel's personal relationship with Putin, rendering them subject to *the irresistible force paradox*. Next, I consider Germany's efforts to walk a fine line between its energy security concerns and divisions between "old" and "new" European Union members. I then describe Merkel's efforts to mediate with regard to Putin's aggressive approach to the Georgian, Crimean, and Ukrainian conflicts. The concluding section reflects on the kind of "hard" versus "soft" power dilemmas that recent out-of-area crises raise for a German chancellor, seeking a modicum of Russian cooperation, for example, in the global war on terrorism.

I argue that despite her extensive exposure to forced solidarity with the Soviet Union and its Warsaw Pact minions, Merkel had no problem internalizing a traditional FRG commitment to multilateralism and collective security under NATO. While she prefers détente to deterrence, she recognizes that German responsibility for securing the peace now extends beyond regional boundaries.[4] This chancellor displays little tolerance for despotic nationalism, but her "double-track" approach to Putin has complicated her relations with Central East European states also displaying national-populist tendencies in these "interesting times."

BECOMING A RELUCTANT HEGEMON: WEST INTEGRATION, OSTPOLITIK, AND CIVILIAN POWER

The restoration of national sovereignty under the 1990 Two plus Four Treaty had little immediate impact on the extraordinary bipartisan consensus that has characterized German foreign and security policy dating back to 1949. For nearly four decades, FRG citizens and elites shared a commitment to NATO membership as the lesser of two evils in the face of possible Warsaw Pact encroachments. They nonetheless played a vanguard role in searching for alternative approaches to European security. By the early 1970s, the Federal Republic's commitment to regional integration and East–West cooperation would endow postwar Germans with a source of positive identification with their own state, matched only by pride in their "miraculous" economic recovery.[5]

Mutually exclusive reconstruction plans advanced by the victorious powers following Germany's unconditional surrender in May 1945 soon gave rise to four decades of "cold war and hot peace." The first postwar chancellor, Konrad Adenauer (CDU), defined the contours of national policy from 1949 to 1963. In the spirit of "rather half of Germany completely than the whole with half-control," Adenauer pursued a masterful consolidation strategy focusing on economic reconstruction and the cultivation of unshakable ties to the West in communion against the Soviet Union. Following short-lived de-Nazification efforts, US policy toward the new Western state centered on "keeping the Germans down, the Americans in, and the Russians out."[6] Despite vehement protests, FRG citizens eventually accepted rearmament and nuclear weapons on their territory under an integrated NATO command, to prevent a military confrontation along the inter-German border. The Basic Law placed strict limits on Bundeswehr deployments, however, linked to collective security mandates.[7] Adenauer visited Moscow for the first time in 1955, resulting in diplomatic relations with the Soviet Union and the return of the last surviving prisoners of war.

Prior to 1998, FRG security policy was driven by two key postulates, "never again war, never again Auschwitz," pursued by way of a threefold strategy known as *Westbindung*. Germany's full integration into the transatlantic camp rested, first, on its responsible participation in the NATO alliance; second, on the cultivation of a special Franco-German relationship, initiated by Adenauer and de Gaulle; and, third, on its willingness to strengthen (and pay for) a fledgling European Community. West integration was viewed as "a lifeline for gaining equal status among the family of nations, for pursuing economic recovery, and for establishing internal and external stability."[8] Erected in 1961, the Berlin Wall symbolized the nation's "permanently provisional" division, lending a paradoxical stability to Cold War relations.

By the late 1960s, the combined influences of generational change, NATO's shift from Mutually Assured Destruction to the Flexible Response doctrine, and electoral realignment in favor of Social Democrats added a further ingredient to Germany's foreign policy toolkit: the politics of détente. Initiated by Willy Brandt under a new SPD–FDP government, *Ostpolitik*, rested on Egon Bahr's 1963 formula of "change through growing closer." Treaty negotiations offered a powerful mechanism for addressing complex security needs, linking *national interests* with a positive construction of *what it meant to be German*. As Brandt declared in his October 1969 state of the union address, "the German people need peace, in the full sense of the word, with people of the Soviet Union and with the peoples of Eastern Europe. We are prepared to make an honest effort to achieve understanding, in order to overcome the consequences of the catastrophe precipitated by a criminal clique throughout Europe."[9] His vision for a new European peace order rested on a singular insight: "The key lies in Moscow."

The optimism implicit in the 1969 partisan realignment gained momentum with a proliferation of Eastern accords, commencing with the Moscow Treaty of August 12, 1970, promising a general renunciation of force. Despite painstaking wrangling on both sides, and significant US skepticism, Egon Bahr's shuttle diplomacy produced several agreements in quick succession, most importantly, the Warsaw Treaty of December 1970 and the Quadripartite Agreement on Berlin, signed in September 1971. The crowning achievement was the 1972 Basis of Relations Treaty between the two German states, allowing for permanent diplomatic missions in Bonn and East Berlin. Supplementary accords addressed commercial transit, postal and telephone services, and health service provisions, as well as tax and automobile fee waivers for visitors. Separate Berlin agreements regulated travel, visitation traffic, and "passage rights" for territorial enclaves. Bonn established full diplomatic relations with Czechoslovakia, Bulgaria, Hungary, and Romania; both states were accorded full UN membership in 1973. To avoid suspicion concerning a possible "special German path," the Federal Republic co-sponsored the Conference on Security and Cooperation in Europe (CSCE), leading to the 1975 Helsinki Accords. Efforts to establish "good neighborly relations" with the Soviet Union and its eastern minions led to Brandt's receipt of the Nobel Peace Prize in 1971.

Still committed to "the politics of negotiation," Chancellor Helmut Schmidt encountered an increasingly hostile environment as of 1979. The Soviet invasion of Afghanistan, the imposition of martial law in Poland, crackdowns on new human rights groups in Eastern Europe, and hotly contested NATO plans for theater-nuclear modernization (TNF) to counter Soviet SS-20 deployments impelled Schmidt to concentrate more on "damage limitation" than on new modes of reconciliation. *Ostpolitik* nonetheless provided a dynamic framework for superpower relations amid the ebbs and flows, despite US demands for "linkage." It also became deeply rooted in the security consciousness of German Baby Boomers, irrespective of partisan affiliation. By 1983, a proliferation of citizen initiatives opposing nuclear energy joined forces with those demanding nuclear disarmament, giving rise to the Green Party. Although the term was not used at the time, Germany increasingly came to see itself as a "civilian power" (as opposed to "checkbook diplomacy"), more intent on conflict prevention than on crisis resolution involving military means.

Schmidt's successor, Helmut Kohl, faced massive anti-nuclear protests at home, complemented by peace movements in neighboring European states. He continued détente politics, hosting the first state visit by an East German premier in 1987; he then sought the release of GDR political prisoners during his 1988 visit to Moscow. One of the amazing achievements of this era was the Intermediate-Range Nuclear Forces (INF) Treaty, signed in Washington, DC by Kremlin chief, Mikhail Gorbachev and US President Ronald Reagan on December 8, 1987. Perceived as a major victory by the peace movement, the INF obliged the United States and the Soviet Union to eliminate all nuclear and dual-capable missiles covering a range of 500 to 5,500 km. By June 1, 1991, the superpowers had destroyed a total of 2,692 missiles, coupled with intrusive on-site verification.[10]

The second mind-boggling event marking the Kohl years was the fall of the Berlin Wall on November 9, 1989, resulting in unification, with

Gorbachev's blessing, less than ten months later. Though not directly related, these two developments solidified the perception among most Germans born after the Second World War that peace could best be achieved through non-military means. The Kohl government offered substantial payments to ensure Soviet forces deployed on GDR territory a "dignified withdrawal," while channeling reconstruction contributions to USSR successor republics through bilateral and multilateral institutions. United Germany committed DM 73.6 billion in aid, DM 14 billion of which were linked to Russian troop withdrawal; it quickly signed treaties of Good Neighborliness and Cooperation with Poland, Hungary, the Czech and Slovak republics. German trade accounted for 30–35 percent of all commercial exchanges with the newly independent Central European states by 1995, a figure matching the Soviet share during the best years of the Council for Mutual Economic Assistance.[11] The FRG supported Association Agreements between the EU and democratizing CEE states; it favored both EU and NATO enlargement.

The collapse of the Iron Curtain replaced a curiously stable "balance of terror" rooted in a bipolar world order with an ever messier set of global actors less committed to traditional alliances. By the time Germans elected their first Red–Green government, most had internalized a two-pronged strategy, "security = détente + deterrence," based on the perceived effectiveness of the Eastern treaties, the Helsinki Accords, and the "velvet revolutions" that ended Soviet domination. Before the ink had dried on the 1998 coalition agreement, however, the SPD–Green cabinet faced a major foreign policy crisis in its own backyard. "Ethnic cleansing" campaigns witnessed in Bosnia and Kosovo turned the pillars of German foreign policy into mutually exclusive propositions: "never again war" versus "never again Auschwitz." A Green minister with no foreign policy experience, Joschka Fischer, became the first national leader to deploy German troops out-of-area in a NATO attack against Serbian forces. Within a decade, Bundeswehr forces would be participating in a variety of slippery slope, combat-relevant missions in the Balkans, Afghanistan, and even off the coast of Israel. Under new Defense Policy Guidelines adopted in 2003, Germany re-assigned 35,000 soldiers to serve as rapid-response forces in high-intensity operations; allocated 70,000 as stabilization forces for longer-term, low- to medium-intensity conflicts; and committed 137,500 to support units for joint operations and home duties.[12]

Although the number of troops deployed abroad has reached a new high under Merkel's leadership (3,420 as of April 2016), united Germany has tried very hard to uphold its standing as a "civilian power." As defined by Hanns W. Maull, and later Sebastian Harnisch and Franz-Josef Meiers, the main parameters of FRG foreign and security policy, known as *civilian power*, begin with the recognition of its special historical obligation to promote European integration. This is coupled with a normative approach to policy-making, stressing peace, freedom, democracy, the rule of law, justice, and human rights, balanced with national interests; it further espouses a solid commitment to multilateralism, extensive cooperation, the rule of law, and reliance on international institutions. Germany routinely seeks to "civilize" or transform international relations, favoring a "culture of restraint" over the utility of military force, but it also accepts the centrality of NATO and complementary ties to EU Common Foreign, Security and Defense Policy. Since the 1990s, it has recognized a growing responsibility to deploy Bundeswehr troops abroad, not only to meliorate humanitarian crises and prevent human rights violations but also to combat heinous forms of terrorism.

In addition to citing historical grounds, Germany couches its reluctance to apply military means in terms of its "limited financial resources."[13] As Merkel confirmed in her February 2006 speech at the Munich Security Conference:

while we can and intend to assume responsibility, in some fields we may not be able to meet everyone's expectations regarding our financial scope for defence spending ... we may not be able to do everything, but what we do, we do very efficiently. We play our role in Afghanistan with 2,500 soldiers in the ISAF mission. We play our part in Kosovo as well as in Bosnia and Herzegovina with around 3,500 soldiers. We are present on the Horn of Africa, in Sudan and in the southern Caucasus, to name only a few major regions. Now Germany participates in the mission in Rafah, which is a totally new experience, as this is a commitment to a wholly new region. We provide the largest contingent to the NATO Response Force. We are implementing the decisions taken at the Prague NATO Summit in a highly committed way in the field of strategic airlift. In other words we are making our contributions in many respects, helping many people.

We have a parliamentary army. Extending its operations to cover almost the entire world is a clear political challenge, one which requires a great deal of discussion, but we – government and opposition – have again and again jointly brought the majority of these discussions to a positive conclusion. Of course, we also want to use the synergies within the European Union, and in this connection there is greater European cooperation, for example, allowing us to increase the share of deployable troops, to name just one aspect among many.[14]

Appointed by Merkel in 2013, Ursula von der Leyen (first female defense minister) requested €130 billion in investment funds to modernize

Bundeswehr weapons systems over the next fifteen years. Now depending on a volunteer army, this suggests Germany's growing willingness to participate actively in international military campaigns, especially those directed against ISIS-style terrorism.[15]

Personal interactions between leaders had played a key role in earlier FRG efforts to reconcile with once adversarial states, beginning with the 1963 Franco-German Friendship Treaty signed by Adenauer and de Gaulle. In 1971, Chancellor Willy Brandt went swimming with Soviet leader Leonid Brezhnev near Yalta, opening the door to closer relations under *Ostpolitik*. In July 1990, Helmut Kohl and Mikhail Gorbachev were photographed wearing cardigans, symbolizing their close ties, while walking in the Caucasus during the unification negotiations. In 2001, "Vladimir" and "Gerhard" rode with their wives through snow-covered Moscow in a horse-drawn sleigh. Merkel and Putin also use first names and the informal "you" when speaking German or Russian, but their interactions are described as "cold and businesslike." Putin describes his counterpart as a "high caliber" leader and a political "heavyweight"; he reports that she "scolded" him like a school mistress during a 2009 energy dispute involving Ukraine.[16]

As Chapter 3 demonstrated, "special relationships" are characterized by a high degree of *historical intertwining, intense interactions*, and mutual *psychological resonance* between two peoples. Given the ferocity of their interactions across two world wars, followed by the GDR's forty years of Soviet subordination, German–Russian ties certainly meet the "special relationship" criteria advanced by Gardner Feldman.[17] Merkel, however, has faced "a delicate choice the Bonn Republic never had to make: a choice, or at least a trade-off," between Germany's long-standing commitment to multilateral peace-keeping and growing international pressures for military burden-sharing. She has been forced to find a new balance between "the Scylla of collective memory" and "the Charybdis of contemporary exigencies" not only in Israel but also in her efforts to shore up democratic practices beyond the Oder–Neisse border.[18] We now take a closer look at Merkel's approach to foreign policy-making, and the conditions defining her "special relationship" with Vladimir Putin.

IMMOVABLE OBJECT, UNSTOPPABLE FORCE: MERKEL, PUTIN, AND "POWER PHYSICS"

Encountering his Russian counterpart, Vladimir Putin, for the first time at the Slovenian Summit of June 2001, President George W. Bush declared:

"I looked the man in the eye. I found him to be very straightforward and trustworthy and we had a very good dialogue. I was able to get a sense of his soul. He's a man deeply committed to his country and the best interests of his country . . . I appreciate very much the frank dialogue and that's the beginning of a very constructive relationship."[19] Angela Merkel not only knows a thing or two about the Russian soul; having looked into Putin's eyes many times since 2005, she understands him better than anyone else on the international stage. Although they shared a common Cold War space prior to the fall of the Wall, they now stand on opposite sides of a re-emerging ideological divide.

Born in 1954 and raised under the shadow of Soviet hegemony, Merkel traveled as a teenager to the USSR on a language scholarship. She bought her first Beatles album in Moscow, and later returned for professional exchanges with Russian physicists. As a young adult, she hitch-hiked her way across the "fraternal socialist states" long before US Fulbright scholars were allowed to enter those countries. Her Protestant ethics and GDR experiences leave little room for double standards regarding human rights and democratic legitimacy. Born in 1952, Putin likewise understands Merkel better than the rest, given his activities as a KGB agent in Dresden, 1985–1990; only a lieutenant colonel by the time he left, his "operative skills" did position him to assume temporary control of the KGB successor, the Russian Federal Security Service, in 1998. A year later, he became acting prime minister, then acting president following Yeltsin's resignation in December 1999.[20]

In addition to sharing a love of Russian literature and a commitment to upholding historical responsibilities, both leaders grew up under the material resource constraints of a socialist command economy. Although both were political outsiders prior to 1990, each was unexpectedly catapulted into national prominence by a powerful mentor – Helmut Kohl and Boris Yeltsin, respectively – whose abuses of power they later publicly renounced. They are evenly matched in terms of personal determination; although Putin holds better cards regarding oil and gas dependency, Merkel can influence the flow of critical trade, technology, and investment. The last three factors have given civilian-power Germany the leverage needed to abandon its junior partner role, freeing it to pursue broader national and global interests.

Merkel faces fewer complaints that "she just doesn't lead" during her international appearances. One variable initially contributing to her effective triangulation of foreign policy relations amid many crises was "beginner's luck." Over time, she has developed a special decision-making skill set, albeit one that seems to derive from her socialization as a natural scientist. Having interviewed her in 2006 (only one year into her first term), Hajo Schumacher characterizes the chancellor's general approach to decision-making as "power physics" (*Machtphysik*). Extending over a ten-year period, my observations allow me to refine the "Merkel Method" of decision-making posited by Schumacher in a way that lends itself to both the domestic and foreign policy levels. Before she reacts, even in crisis situations, the chancellor looks for a clear definition of the problem and its core parameters. Although she is unlikely to have read Herbert Simon's classic work on the topic, she recognizes that all decision problems consist of "factual premises" and "value premises."[21] She attempts to discern the main actors, their motives, and interests before assessing the broader costs, benefits, and risks associated with particular solutions. Next, she considers the best level for addressing the problem, the most trustworthy actors, and a promising decision-making structure (face-to-face relations, institutional majority, or closed circle). She will not commit to a decision until she has a sense of both the short- and long-term effects associated with potential solutions, which she then uses to frame the indicators, benchmarks, and timetables that can be used for implementation.[22] Her tendency to "learn" from positive and negative experiences sometimes leads to a change in course, which brings praise and criticism from unexpected quarters; she rarely reveals how she is affected by one or the other.

Many elements of this approach were reflected in Merkel's first global performance, when she hosted the 1995 UN Climate Summit in Berlin. She learns as much as she can about the other actors, until she has registered their respective "tipping points"; she knows how to work the room but has also been known to withdraw in order to let others do the persuading. She pursued a similar course in relation to the 2007 G8 summit in Heiligendamm, and again in Brussels during her efforts to secure adoption of the 2009 Lisbon Treaty. When it comes to Russia, she is more likely to rely on France than on the United States (see below).

The Merkel Method has little in common with Putin's secretive, self-assertive approach to policy-making, driven by his strong-state inclinations, his (re)interpretation of key historical events, and his often dubious vision of national superiority. As Jennifer Yoder notes, he uses Catherine's term, *Novorossiya*, implying that the defunct Soviet Union was imperial Russia, "only under a different name"; he wants to make Russia "great again." Like Kohl's Girl, Putin initially benefited from his status as a "misunderestimated" outsider, lacking ties to new Moscow elites who secured their oligarchical power during the corrupt Yeltsin years. While the chancellor credits Putin with acting rationally with respect to his own nation, she warned President Obama in a March 2014 phone call that his Russian counterpart holds a completely different view of the world.[23] Ignoring their systemic constraints, for example, the need to secure parliamentary approval, Putin believes that Western leaders are free to operate much the way he does: bending rules or ignoring institutions (despite his law degree) to serve the interests of friends with whom he has shared earlier stages of his life.

Putin's inner circle draws heavily on acquaintances from his days in St. Petersburg; they include former KGB/FSB members, wealthy oligarchs, and bureaucratic forces (known as *siloviki* or "strong people") based in key ministries. He brought "unprecedented numbers" of men with military–security backgrounds into the political and economic sectors after his 2000 election to the presidency, accounting for 35 percent of all deputy ministers by 2003. These are men trained to respond to commands from above.[24] As the chief editor of Moscow's top radio station, Alexei Venediktov once reported: "They are really convinced that Washington decision-making works in ways very similar to Moscow decision-making. That your president can pick up the phone and call the judge [or the speaker of parliament] and give him orders."[25]

Kimberly Marten offers several vignettes attesting to Putin's questionable understanding of democracy, noting that he views all policy interactions, including foreign relations, in patron–client terms. Those who meet his expectations "will be rewarded with ongoing attention and reciprocal gifts, while those who 'offend' will be treated with disdain and shunning that far outweighs the original offense."[26] He once asked George W. Bush why he "didn't change the [US] Constitution so [he] could run again"; to his credit, Bush was "flabbergasted" by the suggestion, as well as by Putin's assumption that he had personally arranged for CBS (a TV station) to fire a critical moderator, Dan Rather. He deemed Bush weak when he supplied humanitarian aid rather than a military response to the 2008 Georgian crisis.

The Russian president later expected Obama to get a grip on the US Congress for blocking presidential initiatives at the same time he overruled his military advisors on some deployments. Citing "similarities" between their respective military lobbies and foreign ministries, "Putin seemed to lack an understanding that the secretaries of both State and Defense are political appointees serving at the president's pleasure, and that the president is Commander in Chief of a military that must follow his lead even when commanders disagree with its direction."[27]

Merkel and Putin clearly differ in their historical assessments of 1989–1990. Although she kept her regular sauna date with a friend before crossing over to "test the West" on November 9, Merkel observed twenty-five years later: "The Berlin Wall, this symbol of state abuse cast in concrete, took millions of people to the limits of what is tolerable, and all too many beyond it . . . It broke them." Conscious of her debt to the protesters who helped to make it happen, she has emerged as an outspoken defender of human rights, insisting that "the fall of the Wall has shown us that dreams can come true."[28] Putin spent that night in 1989 at the KGB offices in Dresden, located in a part of Germany known as "the valley of the clueless" because of poor Western TV reception. His primary responsibility that evening was to destroy as many secret police records as possible: "We burned so much that the oven almost exploded," he noted in a later interview.[29] When East Germans stormed the building, he called for reinforcements, but "Moscow kept silent."

Putin's five years in East Germany help to explain his ongoing attacks on the socioeconomic chaos he witnessed in Russia during "the troubles" of the 1990s. The "shock therapy" introduced in 1992 ended central planning, privatized state enterprises, liberalized prices, and eliminated many universal social services; the outcome was mass unemployment, a 20 percent inflation rate, and soaring national debt. During his first presidential term, Putin declared the collapse of the Soviet Union the "greatest geopolitical catastrophe" of the twentieth century, although he admitted that the GDR's higher living standards had attested to the deeper nature of economic failure back home: "It was clear the Union was ailing. And it had a terminal, incurable illness under the title of paralysis. A paralysis of power."[30]

The time Putin spent in the "valley of the clueless," cut off from Western and Soviet media sources radically liberalized under *glasnost* (which the GDR had banned as too democratic, e.g., *Sputnik*) meant that he experienced neither the free airing of formerly taboo topics, nor the "the enthusiasm and the lifting of spirits" later highlighted by his wife.[31] His return to Russia was marred by Yeltsin's militarized attack against the 1993 parliamentary coup plotters, then dirty, divisive election campaigns, fist-fights on the floor of the Duma, the humiliation of International Monetary Fund (IMF) conditionality in exchange for loans, and territorial losses in the Caucasus – lands that had secured imperial power under Catherine the Great. Qualifying his "catastrophe" assessment in 2010, Putin observed: "Whoever does not regret the collapse of the Soviet Union has no heart. But whoever would like to have it back in its old form has no brain."[32]

Merkel and Putin also differ significantly in their views of the state's role relative to individual rights and freedom of choice. Despite her rejection of a command economy and centralized political control, Merkel sees a legitimate role for the state in many domains, subjecting her to misunderstanding even within her own party; one example involved her insistence on tougher bank and financial market regulation after the 2008 Wall Street melt-down. Her ongoing battles with "state princes" (like Seehofer in Bavaria) might lead her now and then to envy the strong presidencies seen in France and Russia but she has clearly mastered the rough and tumble of party politics, and knows how to win. Putin, by contrast, places the state high above the needs of a pluralist society, as revealed in his 1999 Millennium Message: "For Russians, a strong state is not an anomaly to fight against. Quite the contrary, it is the source and guarantor of order, the initiator and the main driving force of any change ... Society desires the restoration of the guiding and regulating role of the state."[33] In this regard, he stands closer to Louis XIV (*l'état, c'est moi*) than to Catherine II who claimed, "I may be kindly, I am ordinarily gentle, but in my line of business I am obliged to will terribly what I will at all."

Both national leaders have managed to keep their private lives rather private, but while the chancellor as put her physical "makeover" behind her, Putin is addicted to staged photo opportunities that present him as a rugged, nature-loving macho ready for adventure, that is, as a scuba diver, a fire-fighting pilot, a motorcyclist, a big-game hunter, or a nightclub "crooner." Raised as a pastor's daughter, Merkel does not personally support gay marriage but welcomes civil partnerships and a broader understanding of *family*: "Family is there, wherever parents take responsibility for their children and children for their parents." She has allowed her multitasking minister, Ursula von der Leyen, to pursue policies that sooner reflect the GDR gender regime than conservatives' traditional "children, kitchen, church" paradigm."[34]

Since his return to the presidency in 2012, Vladimir Putin has clearly broken with the Soviet paradigm concerning gender roles, state–church relations, and other biopolitical issues. He rails against homosexuality, feminism, sexual freedom, the erosion of marriage, and declining birth rates, all of which are subsumed under the rubric of moral relativism and Western decadence; he targets the European Union (*Gayropa*), in particular.[35] The 2012 Dima Yakovlev Law outlawed "homosexual propaganda," allegedly to protect minors against gay books, movies, and activism, despite a personal appeal by Germany's gay foreign minister, Guido Westerwelle, when he visited his Moscow counterpart.

Putin used the Duma to ban further US adoptions, insisting that "the bodies of Russian children belong to the nation," even if abandoned in orphanages: many Americans had adopted "special needs" children requiring expensive medical care not available in the Motherland. Some efforts to regulate private behavior border on the absurd: one of the first laws introduced in St. Petersburg commensurate with his calls for "public hygiene" barred excessive night noise ("cat stomping"). Other statutes have targeted smoking, obscene language, and drugs, imposed age limits on mass media use, and encouraged higher birth rates. One defined "appropriate sexual relations," in an effort to stop adolescent sex. Besides efforts to bar "foreign" religions and revitalize the Orthodox Church, Putin has elevated ultra-nationalist Dmitry Rogozin to the post of deputy premier, who described his desire to expel non-Russian ethnic migrants as "ridding Moscow of the dirt."[36]

Presidential calls for public modesty are paradoxically coupled with blatantly sexist comments, not to mention photographs of Putin baring his chest on horseback or riding bear-back (literally) , suggesting his athletic qua sexual prowess. When the former Italian prime minister went on trial for sexual relations with a minor, Putin opined, "Berlusconi is standing in court because he lives with women. If he were a homosexual, no one would have touched him." When Israeli leader Mosche Katzav was accused of rape and sexual assault in 2006, Putin told Prime Minister Ehud Olmert, "Extend my greetings to your president. He fooled all of us. We envy him." Released by a girl-band called "Singing Together," a 2002 pop-song chanted, "I want a man like Putin, full of strength / I want a man like Putin, a non-drinker / I want a man like Putin that will not abuse me / I want a man like Putin that will not run away." Female admirers extolling Putin's "good husband" qualities were unfazed by his 2013 divorce from Lyudmila, much less by rumors of his affair with Alina Kabayeva, an ex-Olympic gymnast half his age; now a Duma deputy, she has two children allegedly fathered by the nation's moralist-in-chief.[37]

A former wrestler and judo expert, Putin also "bullies" those he wishes to intimidate, including a strong-willed female chancellor. Knowing her fear of dogs (she was seriously bitten twice), he presented Merkel with a black and white stuffed dog during her first Moscow visit in January 2006. A year later he unleashed his black Labrador "Kori" when she traveled to Sochi and had her reaction captured on camera; he remarked snidely, "I don't think the dog will scare you. She won't do anything bad, she likes journalists."[38] During their heated exchanges over oil and gas shut-offs in Ukraine, Putin reportedly shouted and used obscenities; he even "squeezed her arm" at the 2007 Munich Security Conference, after denouncing the pernicious effects of a "greater and greater disdain for the basic principles of international law" exhibited by "first and foremost, the United States [which] has overstepped its national borders in every way."[39] Although she remembers having her bike stolen by a Russian soldier, Merkel is the one more likely to follow Catherine's advice: "I like to praise and reward loudly, to blame quietly."

The chancellor conceives of politics as a more or less constant electrical/magnetic field, in which Russia amounts to an unstable energy field beset by "problematic tendencies." This brings us back to *power physics*: the political world, as she sees it, consists of elementary building blocks, standing in reciprocal relation to each other (*Wechselwirkungen*), that are governed by established "laws of nature" determining structures of time and place. She monitors and interprets ongoing events in terms of constantly shifting positive and negative charges in search of equilibrium, which allows her to calculate probabilities and risks. Here, too, she prefers to wait things out, to assess long-term consequences before taking action; postwar German leaders have always prided themselves on their consistency, stability, and predictability. Relying on informal networks driven by personal interests, Putin evinces little respect for laws of any sort, explaining why his foreign and economic policies (like Russia's support for Iran) often pull the state in contradictory directions. Rather than assess the bigger picture, Putin tends to talk tough, act strong, and intimidate weaker powers "while choosing battles promising a quick and easy win." Western failure to respond in kind, by flexing military muscle, is construed as a "green light to act."

Rooted in a third-century BC text by Chinese philosopher Han Feizi, the "unstoppable force paradox" used the image of a perfect spear (capable of piercing all shields) and an equally perfect shield (able to block any spear) to pose the question: *What occurs when an unstoppable force meets an immovable object?* While most scientists deny the likelihood of its real-world occurrence, Charles Moffat argues that, ultimately, the immovable object will be moved (despite an assumption of "infinite mass") because *it lacks any force holding it in place.* The only thing that can displace the immovable object is "infinite torque," which would continue to push the object regardless of its infinite mass. Without an energy anchor, the "immovable object" can be budged. I find this analogy useful for exploring German–Russian conflicts regarding the geopolitics of energy security, on the one hand, and European responses to military incursion in the Caucasus, on the other. While Putin sees himself as an unstoppable force, Merkel has assumed the role of immovable object.

CHANGE THROUGH RAPPROCHEMENT V. CHANGE THROUGH INTERDEPENDENCE: ENERGY POLICY

While European leaders across the board now recognize the stability of energy supplies as a security concern, German politicians try to separate this issue from other foreign policy disputes with Russia. Merkel's early focus on climate change (Chapter 6) led her first Grand Coalition to adopt a major Energy Turn-Around Package in 2008. Basking in high oil prices that allowed him to redirect the economy and even pay off Russia's IMF debt three years ahead of schedule, a duly re-elected Putin was exasperated by Germany's all-out campaign to develop renewable energy (RE) sources even before its post-Fukushima shift.[40] Addressing a 2010 gathering in Berlin, he declared: "I just don't understand it: you don't want gas, you don't want to develop nuclear energy any more. Do you want to heat everything with firewood?"[41]

The Soviet Union faced a unique energy dilemma for decades: controlling the world's largest known oil reserves and other costly mineral resources, it lacked the advanced technologies needed to extract them from formidable geophysical locations in Siberia. Coupled with other Cold War strengths, such as its powerful nuclear arsenal and its permanent seat on the UN Security Council, Russia enjoyed a degree of national autonomy not seen elsewhere regarding its post-1990 policy choices; it was free to follow its own development compass following the collapse of "communism."

Russian leaders' belief in the infinite nature of their energy reserves has nonetheless rendered them vulnerable to a "resource curse," as described by Terry Lynn Karl.[42] She posited in 1997 that a sudden infusion of major capital deriving from energy wealth can dramatically transform the decisions, functions, and activities of resource-rich states. Access to easy money, particularly after a sustained period of economic decline, can induce formerly cautious leaders to pursue overly ambitious, risky, or wasteful policies, characterized as *petromania*. James D. Brown argued, for instance, that Soviet authorities grew "giddy" with massive oil wealth, as world market prices jumped from US$17.50 to US$40 per barrel, between January and November, 1979. Covering 18 percent of total global production at the time and facing no real threat from resource-starved Afghanistan, Kremlin leaders nonetheless adopted a bold and incredibly costly change in strategy, risking all of their slowly accumulated gains for an ally of seemingly little value ... having carefully consumed a sizeable piece of the Afghan cake, the Soviets attempted to gulp down the rest in a single, overzealous bite. The result, rather than the hoped for quick incorporation, was prolonged, painful choking, followed by the regurgitation of all that had been previously ingested.[43]

Nine years of war resulted in an official death count of 13,833 (Western estimates put the figure at up to 75,000), costing over 5 billion rubles annually. Longer-term consequences included the strengthening of independence movements in other Soviet republics, along with the rise of warlords and a Taliban takeover of Afghanistan a few years later. Political stagnation at home, due to the octogenarian incompetence of Brezhnev and company, contributed to Gorbachev's ascension and, arguably, to the end of the USSR per se.

Vladimir Putin has fallen into the resource-curse trap on more than one occasion, beginning in 2006, when he first tried to exploit European dependence on Russian energy to discipline Ukrainian leaders trying to distance themselves from Kremlin influence. Despite recent losses in market share, Russia remains the No. 1 energy exporter, responsible for 12.7 percent of the oil, 16.7 percent of the gas, and 4.3 percent of the coal (2015 figures) produced for global consumption. Correspondingly, it supplies 35 percent of Europe's oil, 30 percent of its gas, and 26 percent of its coal imports; 80 percent of Russia's diesel products also go to Europe. Russia moreover accounts for 18 percent of the EU uranium supplies, needed to run eighteen Soviet nuclear reactors located in Bulgaria, the Czech Republic, Finland, Hungary, and Slovakia, respectively. Because reactor designs require specific kinds of fuel rods, they cannot easily be replaced, despite efforts to diversify.[44]

The post-Soviet energy sector has seen big swings in the policy pendulum over the last twenty-five years. Shock therapy, and a sudden shift from state ownership to an ill-conceived voucher system under Yeltsin rendered public assets the private property of a new class of corrupt oligarchs. Putin refers to the 1990s as a time of "troubles," which he associates with national humiliation, chaos, and insecurity. Abjuring the mass unemployment, rising debt, and IMF-imposed conditionality of that period, he has sought to restore state sovereignty without returning to a Soviet-style command economy, whose failures he observed from a distance during his five years in Dresden. As reported in 2010, his KGB activities there persuaded him that Western technologies "obtained by special means" would be "impossible to utilize" back in the USSR, which lacked the material and business infrastructures needed to incorporate them into socialist production.[45] Putin's dissertation plagiarized parts of a popular US textbook, *Strategic Planning and Public Policy*, authored by David I. Cleland and William R. King.[46] He has used his three terms as president to reassert strategic control over the energy sector by way of "network state capitalism."

Putin used heavy-handed tax evasion charges to expel Yeltsin's cronies, including raids on corporate offices by masked operatives with loaded Kalashnikovs; he manipulated trials to eliminate others posing a political challenge, such as Mikhail Khodorkovsky, now in London after ten years in prison.[47] The energy network consists of Putin loyalists dating back to his KGB and St. Petersburg days, for example, Gazprom CEO Alexei Miller and top Lukoil managers, Vagit Alekperov and Leonid Fedun (Lukoil is Russia's largest private oil player). Despite evidence that he, too, has amassed illegal wealth based on his networks, Putin declared: "It is true that I am the richest man in the whole world. I am rich. Because I collect feelings and emotions, Russia has twice granted me the greatest joy, of being able to serve it."[48]

In 2008, Merkel still had high hopes for his presidential successor, Dmitri Medvedev, who promised to modernize privatization; he did legislate greater energy efficiency, then signed decrees on renewables and recharging stations for electric vehicles. She reportedly felt duped when Putin reassumed the presidency in 2012 (extending his third term to six years) after a "managed election" devoid of real opposition. "Network capitalism" has turned Gazprom into a state-within-a-state, which the Kremlin feels free to raid regularly to finance other projects. Gazprom revenues from taxation and export duties feed the National Reserve Fund (equivalent to 5.9 percent of GDP) and the National Wealth Fund (19 percent of GDP in 2015). The problem is that significant energy revenues are creamed off the top to advance the personal interests of those who control them.

Dependent on Russia for 60–80 percent of its own fuel needs, Ukraine serves as the major "pipeline" for up to four-fifths of Gazprom's European deliveries.[49] In recent years the Ukrainian Gas Transmission System has lost its monopolistic position due to the Yamal Pipeline moving through Belarus and Poland, the Nord Stream pipeline transferring natural gas from the Baltic Sea to Greifswald, and the Blue Stream pipeline crossing through Turkey. After losing the 2005 election, Schröder became chairman of the Nord Stream operations. Former Hamburg Mayor Henning Voscherau took on the same responsibilities for South Stream in 2012. Ex-Green minister Joschka Fischer advised an energy consortium backing the Nabucco pipeline that would have bypassed Russia by delivering gas from the Caspian Sea to Austria, until its €15 billion price tag put the project on hold in 2012.[50] Merkel knows she needs to walk a fine line regarding alternative pipeline routes, co-financed by her Ministry for Economic Affairs and Energy. One country's diversification could be another's energy death knell: "Arithmetically, just one additional line of Nord Stream 2 and one of Turkish Stream might be enough to bypass Ukraine."[51]

In 2006, Ukraine's outstanding oil debt led Moscow to block all pipeline flows, affecting seventeen EU states for four days in mid-winter; Bulgaria and Slovakia experienced complete cut-offs. Russia's threat to European energy security damaged its reputation as a dependable, market-based supplier, precipitating a search for alternatives. A second shut-down in 2009 cost Russia a billion dollars in lost export revenues, at a time when a financially strapped Ukraine was paying a higher price for gas than affluent Germany. Forced to play the bad cop by way of repeated "take or pay" and "pre-pay" demands, Gazprom's obligation to fill state coffers for other projects also extracted a high price. A third cut-off was averted during the political unrest of 2014, based on "mutual restraint." Berlin coordinated trilateral negotiations, pushing Kiev to pay US$2 billion of its US$5.2 billion debt. Gazprom accepted discounted terms and agreed to "pre-pay" its transit fees for 2015.[52]

The imposition of Western sanctions in response to Putin's quick annexation of Crimea and support for separatist rebels in eastern Ukraine (see below) put several European equity swaps and commercial ventures on hold, offering a "topography of Russian oligarchs."[53] Poland and Baltic state leaders joined Merkel's call for tough sanctions, while Italy, Hungary, and Bulgaria championed Russia's "historical reliability" as an energy supplier.[54] Extended through January 2016, the sanctions targeted individuals, oil companies, and major Russian banks, affecting capitalization across the entire energy sector.[55] They came on the heels of a major European Court of Justice (ECJ) antitrust case filed by the Directorate-General for Competition, based on evidence seized in dawn raids on Gazprom operations by EU inspectors. Western sanctions have compounded Putin's other problems, including serious ruble devaluations, plunging oil prices, and declining oil demand both at home and abroad. The rise of the liquefied natural gas (LNG) trade, an unforeseen gas boom in North America, new cross-border pipelines with multidirectional interconnectors, new LNG storage facilities, suppliers and transfer hubs, as well as post-Fukushima nuclear recalibrations have shifted global demand and supply. Moscow tried to limit the damage by centralizing control over the domestic sector, utilizing state-supported subsidies and export tax exemptions, along with discretionary price cuts (or hikes) and "take-or-pay" obligations. It has, moreover, threatened to build a new gas cartel, dumped cheap gas in foreign markets, and arbitrarily switched deliveries "between established import-dependent European customers and emerging markets in Asia."[56]

Germany and Russia have become co-dependent all along the value chain. In 2014, 39 percent of Gazprom's total investments went to Germany, while 63 percent of Rosneft's European investments also landed there; the latter owns stakes in four refining companies: Gelsenkirchen, Bayern Oil, MiRO, and Schwedt.[57] One of its biggest natural gas customers, E.ON, has poured €10 billion into Russia's energy market, also supplying half of BASF Wintershall's hydrocarbon production and two-thirds of the company's reserve base. EU Energy Commissioner Günther Oettinger was a mover and shaker behind the Road Map for EU–Russia Energy Cooperation until 2050 and the Third Internal Energy Market package, among other things. Russian dominance of the global energy market is decreasing due to Germany's 2008 energy turn-around and its uploading of climate-change policies at the EU level; but Moscow's resource curse has intensified the "values versus interests" debate driving relations between a former pastor's daughter and an ex-KGB man. Brandt's *Ostpolitik* vision of integrating Russia into a Western trade-and-reconciliation orbit has given way to a new German *Frostpolitik*, drawing new territorial frontlines.[58]

SPEAKING TRUTH TO REVISIONIST POWER: MERKEL AND THE CAUCASUS CRISES

Just as the earlier financial chaos and humiliation moved Putin to reassert top-down control over major sectors of the economy, Yeltsin's disastrous management of the first Chechnya crisis motivated his hand-picked successor to reassert Russian power in the "Near Abroad." Sidelined in St. Petersburg during the fist-fighting days of the Duma, Putin rejected the *tactics* of ultra-nationalist parties under figures like Vladimir Zhirinovsky but not necessarily their foreign policy views: feeding on memories of the Great Patriotic War, opposing the "color revolutions," challenging a US-dominated world order, and reinstating the privileges of the Orthodox Church. Taking a dim view of separatist movements within his own borders, Putin declared in 1999: "We will track down the terrorists everywhere. If we find them sitting on the toilet, we will wipe them out in that location."[59] Seeking a return to Great Power status on the global stage, he used the second Chechen war as test case for renewed use of Russia's military hard power. Formerly heading the ultra-nationalist KRO-Rodina party, Deputy Prime Minister Dmitri Rogozin is now responsible for the defense industries.[60]

Like Merkel, Putin began reflecting on his nation's looming demographic deficit during his first term; in 2001, he issued a "Concept on the Demographic Development of Russia 2001–2015" and attended his first World Congress of Compatriots Living Abroad, comparable to Germany's annual Schlesien Reunion (former Second World War expellees and offspring). Unable to bully the Baltic states into granting full citizenship rights to Russians abroad, he began urging their repatriation both to shore up his declining work force and to tap into potential investment capital; only a few hundred actually returned.[61] Realizing that he could not protect Russian *citizens* outside his own boundaries, Putin's subsequent approach to Ukraine echoed another adage attributed to Catherine the Great: "I have no way to defend my borders but to extend them."

Russia's 2008 military invasion of Georgia, its 2014 annexation of Crimea, and its ongoing support for separatist rebels in eastern Ukraine are all part of a strategy to reassert control over its "historically legitimate" sphere of influence, dating back to Catherine's eighteenth-century conquests. Putin also invokes modern parallels, equating Russian efforts to "liberate" South Ossetia with US support for Kosovo's independence in 2008. His real agenda probably has more to do with his fears that mass protests against autocratic rule witnessed during the Arab Spring and various "color revolutions" could spill across the border, given his shock over the protests he encountered in relation to his 2012 "re-election."

Classified in Soviet times as an *autonomous oblast*, South Ossetia has seen several cycles of violence since 1991, in contrast to North Ossetia, which was directly integrated into the Russian Federation as an *autonomous republic*. Of its 70,000 inhabitants, 40,000 are ethnic Ossetians, the rest are Georgians.[62] Military clashes in 1991 killed 1,000 and displaced over 60,000; the 1992 Sochi Agreement created a joint peacekeeping force, comprised of 500 Russians, 500 North Ossetians and 500 Georgians. Abkhazia then declared its independence, leading to a further war that ended in 1994, after displacing another 250,000.[63]

A former architect of reform under Gorbachev, Georgian president Eduard Shevardnadze (1992–2003) initially supported civil society and media freedom. Increasing corruption, budget shortfalls and, finally, blatant electoral fraud produced mass protests labeled the Rose Revolution (November 3–23, 2003), forcing him out of office. Promising to end corruption, Shevardnadze's pro-American successor, Mikhail Saakashvili, initiated an anti-smuggling campaign in 2004, hitting the South Ossetian "backwater" especially hard. This triggered another wave of conflict, during which Georgian troops seized Russian "peace-keeping" trucks bearing missiles and other offensive weapons. Renewed corruption and reform failures re-incited protests against Saakashvili in late 2007, who responded with a violent crackdown. He then pushed for reintegration of the secessionist areas, where Russia had been supplying residents with passports and welfare benefits. Clearly overestimating his own power, Saakashvili ordered a military attack on Tskhinvali, destroying most of the break-away capital on August 7, 2008. The Kremlin responded with a massive counterattack against Gori and a military base 60 km away from Tbilisi, securing its hold on Abkhazia, South Ossetia, and a further chunk of Georgia.[64]

The new Russian president, Dmitri Medvedev declared in a *Financial Times* interview on August 27: "Only a madman could have taken such a gamble. Did [Saakashvili] believe Russia would stand idly by as he launched an all-out assault on the sleeping city of Tskhinvali, murdering hundreds of peaceful citizens, most of them Russian citizens?" Serving as prime minister, Putin told a CNN reporter, "there are grounds to suspect that some people in the United States created this conflict deliberately, in order to aggravate the situation and create a competitive advantage for one of the candidates for the US presidency," that is, John McCain, who favored a new missile defense system for Poland.[65] As EU Council president, Nicolas Sarkozy helped to broker a (non-binding) six-point peace plan, but Merkel also traveled to Sochi to deliver some "straight talk" to both Medvedev and Saakashvili. Calling for an immediate, unconditional ceasefire and a return of all military forces to their earlier positions, Merkel held both sides accountable.

Georgia had already joined the European Neighborhood Partnership (ENP) in 2004, receiving €505 million to shore up democratic reforms. Germany committed €1 million in humanitarian aid after the war, but the chancellor drew a red line regarding renewed calls for Georgian admission to NATO. Merkel had already spoken out against extending NATO membership to Georgia and Ukraine at the 2008 Bucharest summit, for which Putin was reportedly "grateful."[66] While frozen conflicts in these two states toughened US rhetoric in favor of NATO enlargement, they strengthened Merkel's resolve not to be pulled into unstable regions calling for "Article 5" alliance protection (an attack on one member counts as an attack on all). Subsequent developments in Ukraine reinforced her concerns along these lines.

With two "orange revolutions" behind it, Ukraine has also seen its share of bad governance, major political infighting, and corruption. Despite her strong human rights orientation, the chancellor kept her distance from "oil-igarch" turned prime minister, Yulia Tymoshenko, even before she was imprisoned by her ally turned rival, Viktor Yanukovych in 2011.[67] The 2004 and 2014 "revolutions" were both directed against leaders who sought to keep Ukraine in the Russian orbit. The first resulted in short-term rulers who frequently switched political alliances to secure personal power without effecting real reforms ("the worst governed country in Europe").[68] The second, known as Euromaidan, commenced on November 21, 2013, when President Yanukovych suspended preparations for a Deep and Comprehensive Free Trade Agreement with the European Union. Special police forces used batons and tear gas against the demonstrators on November 30. The protests continued until Yanukovych struck a deal with Moscow, involving Russia's purchase of US$15 billion in Ukrainian bonds and reducing its natural gas costs by a third. Ukraine's willingness to sign the EU Association Agreement, ahead of Moldova, Belarus, Armenia, Azerbaijan, and Georgia, would have destroyed Putin's plan to create a Eurasian Union by 2015. In October, Merkel met with Putin until 2 am, but reached no agreement on de-escalation. Protests intensified during December and January, as did government efforts to crackdown on them; February 20 saw the worst violence, resulting in eighty-eight deaths, when uniformed snipers fired at protestors.

The "Weimar Triangle" (Germany, France, Poland), met on February 20 in Kiev, at which point Merkel and Steinmeier emerged as the central Western actors. Long, dramatic negotiations led to a plan for new elections at the end of the year, but Yanukovych disappeared on February 21. Armed, pro-Russian groups seized public buildings in the Crimean capital on February 27: "The annexation of Crimea occurred lightning fast and out of the blue, as did the appearance of ethnic Russian and North Caucasus militia leaders and fighters in eastern Ukraine."[69] Merkel made multiple calls to Putin, who claimed that no regular Russian soldiers were engaged on the peninsula despite the presence of "little green men," wearing uniforms without identifying insignia. A first break between the two leaders occurred in early March after a very "frosty" telephone exchange in which the latter admitted that the militias active in Crimea did have direct ties to his forces; 40,000 Russian troops undertook exercises along the eastern Ukraine border. Merkel told Obama that Putin had "lost touch with reality" and was "living in another world."[70]

The chancellor convened an international contact group to discuss possible sanctions on March 6, then took a principled stance against Putin's decision to move up the referendum: "We are now experiencing in Europe, in Ukraine, a conflict about spheres of influence and territorial claims, which we got to know in the nineteenth and twentieth centuries, a conflict we thought we had overcome ... a breach of international law in Central Europe, after which we cannot ... go back to business as usual."[71] Having lobbied long and hard to sustain good relations with Moscow, Merkel led the sanctions charge to prevent Russian expansion to the southeast. On March 14, she met with the heads of major German corporations who accepted the need for sanctions, offering a united front. Organizers of the March 16 referendum claimed that 97 percent of voters had approved Crimean secession. Wasting no time, Putin signed an annexation treaty on March 18.

French elites were not so unified: Sarkozy deemed the referendum legitimate. Hollande had to be persuaded not to deliver a Mistral helicopter carrier, after leading a delegation to Moscow that had declared EU sanctions "counter-productive and harmful," though German companies were taking a bigger economic hit.[72] Merkel, in turn, canceled bilateral government consultations as well as the G8 summit scheduled for Sochi. The Council of Europe stripped Russia of parliamentary voting rights. Poland and the Baltic states moved closer to panic.

On April 7, separatists occupied state buildings in Donetsk, Luhansk, and Kharkiv, likewise calling for independence. Merkel charged Putin with violating the 1994 Budapest Memorandum on Security Assurances which had obliged Kiev to give up 2,000 strategic and 2,500 tactical nuclear weapons, in exchange for security promises; a 1997 Treaty of Friendship, Cooperation, and Partnership had allowed the Kremlin to keep its Black Sea Fleet at Sevastopol. As Putin saw it, Ukraine had secured its autonomy in exchange for agreeing to remain outside the EU and NATO camps; Western values and money had fostered poor governance, recurrent "Maidans" and political instability. Fearing regime-change contagion at home, Putin played the strongman vis-à-vis the vulnerable eastern front; he used nationalist terms suggesting that the "loss" of Ukraine had induced "phantom pains in the soul of the Russian people."[73] The goal, Marlene Laruelle argues, was not to reconstitute a divided nation but rather to punish the turncoat state "for not respecting the rules of the game."[74]

Insisting that only local and volunteer forces were militarily engaged, Putin declared: "Take a look around post-Soviet places. There are many uniforms that look just like that. Go into any of our stores, and you'll be able to buy such a uniform there." He later admitted supporting "self-defense forces." By April, the EU had extended the list of actors targeted by the sanctions, including members of the National Security Council, Secret Services, the Chechen president, the governor of Krasnodarer, two deputy defense ministers, and the deputy of the General Chief of Staff. The second breaking-point for Merkel occurred with the downing of Malaysian Airlines Flight 17 over separatist territory on July 17, 2015, claiming 298 (mostly Dutch) lives. Having called Putin over thirty times a month, she stopped communicating for a time. As of this writing, few of the 2015 Minsk Agreement terms seem to be holding.[75]

While some analysts have declared the *Ostpolitik* tradition of seeking Russian "change through rapprochement" dead, others still hope for "change through interconnection."[76] Visiting Berlin in 2010, Putin called for the formation of a "harmonious economic community stretching from Lisbon to Vladivostok."[77] He now views European Neighborhood policies, association agreements, conditionality, and "the logic of routine" as tools for transferring a "normatively unacceptable civilization against which Russia needs to undertake measures of political hygiene."[78] His post-2012 stress on *Gayropa* and Western decadence entails a counter-offensive against efforts to lead the Near Abroad countries to reject his Eurasian Union as well as his promotion of "sovereign democracy." As Dimitar Bechev observed, "while Russia cannot replace the EU as a purveyor of functional integration, the EU is in no position to effectively balance and contain Russian might with coercive means ... " Two rival narratives are at play: "Europe's story of political, economic, and institutional transformation in line with its liberal democratic credo ... and a counter narrative blending traditionalism, religious values, nostalgia for the Soviet past, and the historical myths of victimhood and resistance linking Russia to its neighbors."[79]

The Kremlin's mercantilist policies regarding energy exports are at odds with its political control of those resources, but that is not the only contradiction driving events in the Caucasus. Putin sees no parallels between Russia's campaign against "separatist terrorists" in Chechnya and European perceptions of secessionist forces in eastern Ukraine. Both are nonetheless symptomatic of his insistence that Russia be treated as "a rule-maker of equal standing ... rather than a rule-taker like the other post-communist countries on the EU's periphery."[80] Merkel reportedly shakes her head over Putin's antics but sees no point in tirades. She uses democratic reasoning but does not "moralize"; he, in turn, respects the economically powerful country she represents. Although he appears as a tough dog to the outside world, Merkel sees him as essentially fearful, his greatest angst being that "he could end like Ceaușescu." The Arab Spring, the Gezi Park rebellion, and the Maidan revolts have turned Putin's fears into a phobia, according to people in the Chancellor's Office.[81]

Germany often stood up to its own allies during *Ostpolitik* years, working hard to accept Russia as an equal partner with legitimate security needs, based on two world wars. Her GDR experiences notwithstanding, Angela Merkel was the only Western leader to grasp the real nature of the power game at stake. In December 2014, sixty foreign policy elites, including ex-chancellors Schmidt, Kohl, and Schröder, criticized Merkel for her tough sanction stance. She was nonetheless the only Western ruler (along with Steinmeier), who traveled to Moscow to mark the seventieth anniversary of Nazi capitulation – although she skipped the military parade. She accepts her nation's special historical responsibility for promoting dialogue, but a reconfigured world order requires a revised strategy for positioning Europe between Russia and the United States. That task has become much more difficult since 2012, leading us back to the "unstoppable force" paradox.

A DIFFERENT CLASH OF CIVILIZATIONS: SOFT V. HARD POWER

At first glance, the Merkel–Putin relationship reminds one of Churchill's description of Russia as "a riddle wrapped in a mystery inside an enigma." The chancellor herself has been characterized as an enigma, even though my research has persuaded me that "what you see is what you get."[82] Her values are clear, her decision-making method is consistent, and she makes a regular effort to explain her policies carefully once she has made up her mind. She supports Germany's traditional multilateralism and its culture of restraint but she also enjoys a reputation across Europe as an honest broker, to a degree not seen among her predecessors. Through it all, she has remained a fairly popular leader, facing no major rivals. The World's Most Powerful Woman thus resembles her role model, Catherine the Great, who declared: "Power without a nation's confidence is nothing."

When it comes to human rights, NGOs, and abjuring use of the military, the Chancellor often takes a harder line towards Russia than her SPD partners. In November 2012, the Bundestag reacted to Putin's raids on

German foundation offices (e.g., Konrad Adenauer Stiftung, Friedrich Ebert Stiftung) in Moscow with several draft proposals from opposing party caucuses. While the CDU/FDP version prevailed, its seventeen-point resolution read more like an exhortation to "change" than an outright condemnation of Russian practices. Germany still needs to walk a fine line between past and present, between interests and values, even if it pursues national interests more openly nowadays. As Jennifer Yoder notes, Merkel sees human rights and economic interests as two sides of a single coin that (citing the Chancellor) "should never stand in opposition to each other."[83] A growing number of "states of concern" makes it tougher to draw lines between norm-based foreign policies and active security responsibilities, however. Despite the "bad cop, good cop" differences between Merkel and Steinmeier on some issues, the CDU chancellor and her SPD foreign minister displayed a united front following Putin's annexation of Crimea.[84]

Germany has not abandoned *Ostpolitik*, but the policy contours have obviously shifted following the restoration of its national sovereignty after unification. There is still a consensus among citizens and elites that *security* requires a balance between defense and détente. *Ostpolitik* is one thread that has consistently bound East and West Germans as well. Although the GDR persistently denied its citizens freedom of expression, unlimited travel rights, and genuinely competitive elections, the living standards and social rights Merkel and her peers experienced under the Eastern Treaties of the 1970s were significantly better than the repressive Soviet practices dominating the bloc states during the 1950s and 1960s. Given their respective memories of two world wars, Putin still expects Germany to serve as a special partner, pushing its EU partners to "appreciate the Russian perspective" while helping it to meliorate "the perennial lopsidedness of its economy."[85]

The problem is that Putin views foreign policy as a relentless zero-sum game, while Merkel searches for flexible win–win options. The chancellor would rather lead the EU charge on climate change than rally troops to secure European gas supplies moving through Ukrainian pipelines from Russia. Still holding firm to its preferred model of civilian power, Germany has no choice but to accept new responsibilities for military burden-sharing. One thing is clear, however: short of an all-out invasion, which Putin himself cannot afford, no German leader is likely to place "boots on the ground" in a military engagement with Russia during my lifetime. This is a core reason for Merkel's rejection of full NATO membership for Russian neighbors that have yet to consolidate their democracies. It might have also have motivated her to appoint Ursula von der Leyen as Germany's first female defense minister, hoping that a mother of seven would be less likely to send youth into battle without an exit strategy.

Vladimir Putin has numerous reasons for presenting himself as the "unstoppable force," not the least of which is his need to keep his citizens unified despite a growing economic crisis. Russians watched as world oil prices plunged to a mere US$28 per barrel through 2015, compounded by a weaker ruble (79 to the US dollar). Although oil prices have recovered somewhat, wages had already fallen by 9 percent, adding 2 million people to the poverty rolls. Cutting off EU agricultural imports in retaliation against the sanctions has raised food prices, and bankruptcies are on the rise.[86] As the man behind Medvedev, Putin's goal with respect to the 2008 Georgia crisis, the Crimean annexation, and support for east Ukrainian rebels was to re-establish Russia as a global force as a function of *"mass x acceleration."* The downing of a Russian plane over Egypt in November 2015, along with greater involvement in Syria, has created yet another double-bind regarding ISIS terrorism, and may impel Putin to re-think his hard-power strategy: he cannot leave the "global war on terrorism" up to the United States while demanding equal status as a superpower.[87] ISIS has proven that fundamentalist insurgencies defy conventional military strategies.

Still, a growing number of confrontations between the two superpowers over the last decade makes it harder for Germany to be a partner to both. Merkel is just as concerned about US willingness to apply unilateral force without the legitimation of a UN Security Council resolution as was her former nemesis, Green Foreign Minister Joschka Fischer. But even as the World's Most Powerful Woman, the modern equivalent of Catherine the Great, Merkel would not be able to hold her ground as the proverbial "immovable object" without the necessary force and friction to anchor her in place: that is the role of NATO, combined with the collective economic power of the European Union. Merkel does not accept ex-Belgian Prime Minister Eysken's characterization of Europe as "an economic giant, a political dwarf and a military worm."[88] Germany is a loyal, committed, and financially supportive member of the transatlantic alliance. Having served as the home base for thousands of short- and intermediate-range nuclear missiles under superpower control, a virtual Ground Zero for forty years, it knows all too well that military strength is what NATO is for – but only as a last resort.

The chancellor's aversion to an historical male tendency to talk tough, rattle sabers, and draw symbolic lines in the sand brings us back to the gender dimensions of the Merkel-Putin relationship. Although the president undoubtedly admires Catherine's imperial contributions to Russian greatness and devotion to the Orthodox faith, the empress would probably be offended by his self-aggrandizing cultivation of a "macho personality cult."[89] As Stephen White and Ian McAllister observed:

Within a year of his accession, foundry workers in the Urals were casting him in bronze; not far away, weavers were making rugs with the president's face inside a golden oval. In Magnitogorsk, the overalls Putin had worn during a visit were on display in the city museum. A factory in Chelyabinsk had begun to produce a watch with a presidential image on its dial, and a local confectioner was selling a cake with the same design; a "Putin bar" had opened elsewhere in the town, selling "Vertical power" kebabs and "When Vova was little" milk-shakes. An all-female band had meanwhile "taken the airwaves by storm" with its single "Someone like Putin" (someone who, among other things, "doesn't drink" and "won't run away"). Putin's fiftieth birthday in September 2002 brought further tributes: *Argumenty i fakty* readers wanted to present their president with a samurai sword, a portable toilet "so that he can wipe out whoever he wants whenever he wants ... "[90]

Sexualized appeals are a regular part of the package: women have offered to have Putin's "love children." One group publicized a video of themselves clad in white shirts and underpants, baking him a chocolate birthday cake ("decorated with a heart") and "squirting whipped cream into their mouths." In July 2011, another set ("Putin's Army") advertised a contest called "I'll Rip [It] for Putin": the video ended with a cleavage-heavy young woman "ripping her tank top down the middle, while asking, 'What are you prepared to do for your president'?"[91] Putin's "mobilization of machismo," centering on his own personality, is part of a larger, nationalistic legitimation strategy, intended to shore up support at home despite deteriorating economic conditions.

Putin utilizes gendered images to undermine his political competitors and critics at home and abroad, as Valerie Sperling shows. In 2007, a state-sponsored youth camp, for example, featured "a large poster exhibit of three male opposition leaders, Mikhail Kasyanov, Garry Kasparov, and Eduard Limonov, portrayed their faces photoshopped onto female bodies clad in bustiers and thigh-high stockings, transforming them into a trio of most unmanly transvestite-prostitutes who had sold out Russia."[92] The "patriotic enlistment" of masculinity intensified in the wake of the Ukrainian uprisings, with the president portraying himself as a tough guy willing and able to rescue distressed Mother Russia from her Western "liberal-fascist enemies." He invoked homophobic terms to dismiss rebellions in the Caucasus, for example, starting with Georgia: "A rose revolution, next they'll come up with a light blue one" (slang for a gay male). In April 2014, a Russian TV program claimed that females who had supported Ukrainians' "fascistic" anti-Yanukovych protests were behaving badly due to sexual deprivation. The list included Dalia Grybauskaité (president of Lithuania), Victoria Nuland, (US Assistant Secretary of State), Iryna Farion (an ultra-right Ukrainian politician), Tatiana Chernovol (an activist- journalist), and Olga Bogomolets (who coordinated on-site emergency medical aid). The anti-Kremlin agitation seen among the so-called "Furies of the Maidan" was ascribed to gender pathologies ranging from lesbianism to sexual inhibition.[93]

But Putin's gender-baiting does not stop there, nor does it respect superpower boundaries. Shortly after the downing of MF17 in eastern Ukraine unleashed a new wave of sanctions, Deputy Prime Minister Rogozin tweeted a pair of photos: one side featured Putin petting a leopard on his lap, the other Barack Obama cuddling a white poodle, suggesting that Obama could only handle a small dog, compared with Putin's ability to calm a wild animal. The caption indicated, "We have different values and different allies."[94] When Hillary Clinton compared his claim of "protecting" Ukraine's Russian minority to Hitler's justification for seizing Polish and Czech lands in the 1930s, Putin responded during a French radio interview that it was "better not to argue with women ... When people push boundaries too far, it's not because they are strong but because they are weak. But maybe weakness is not the worst quality for a woman."[95]

These examples render Putin's respect for Merkel, a former GDR citizen, all the more incongruous; she is one tough woman, his effort to exploit her fear of dogs notwithstanding. According to Bernd Ulrich, the Ukrainian crisis constituted a "gender turning-point in world history." Having (reportedly) reached the limits of his own power, President Obama put a crisis precipitated by a "classic Kremlin macho" into the hands of a woman who "chose her own, female-European method of stopping Vladimir Putin: talking, talking, talking, remaining unflustered and above all [using] economic sanctions instead of tanks, missiles and bombs."[96] While I welcome the fact that men now recognize women's leadership skills in the national security domain, I doubt that gender made a difference in this case. Merkel took lethal defensive weapons for Ukraine (demanded by US hardliners) off the table not because she was a woman or a pacifist, but because she realized they would merely cause Putin to up the ante with new military aid to the separatists. Although Germany had a greater stake in Russian trade and investment than all of its EU counterparts, she led by example with strong sanctions because she knows that Putin is very vulnerable regarding the national economy. If he cannot deliver the goods to his people in the longer run, or finds himself trapped in a never-ending insurgency, his support will erode. The Afghan War cleared a path for Gorbachev, the Chechen disaster helped to topple Yeltsin. As the latter said in a 1993 speech, "You can build a throne with bayonets, but you can't sit on it for long."[97]

For Angela Merkel, negotiation is not a matter of hard or soft power; it is merely a rational approach to meliorating complex problems. It is striking that many European women have served as defense ministers since 1990, in Sweden, France, Germany, Croatia, Norway, Denmark, Slovakia, Latvia, the Czech Republic, Spain, Slovenia, Lithuania, the Netherlands, Italy, Albania, Montenegro, and even Bosnia-Herzegovina. Now eligible for combat, others are moving into power positions within the military.[98] They remain grossly underrepresented in the board rooms of global energy conglomerates and the military–industrial complex setting the parameters of "the national interest," however.

Regarding Merkel's performance in this arena, policy success can only be indirectly measured in terms of "containment." It would be unfair to expect Germany's first female chancellor to single-handedly pull a macho-authoritarian Russian ruler back into line. Some pundits characterize them as an old married couple, each able to anticipate the tricks and grudges of the other, but this type of gratuitous "gendering" ignores the historical complexity of their relationship.[99] The "special relationship" between their countries contributed to three major reconfigurations of the world order during the twentieth century alone. Having refined its *civilian power* practices since its founding in 1949, Germany united has no incentive at this point to abandon a formula that has contributed to extraordinary peace and prosperity in Europe for nearly seventy years: as much negotiation as possible, as little military involvement as necessary. Putin remains a wild-card, and will continue to seek quick victories in places where he fears no direct NATO response. He exploits memories of Russian suffering at the hands of the Germans but he also recognizes Merkel as the leader most capable of preserving her country's historical responsibility along these lines.

No matter how hot the political water becomes, Merkel has proven to be very strong. It would not hurt, however, to add another role model to her list of women who defied the odds and changed the world: Eleanor Roosevelt, the heart and mind behind the 1948 United Nations Declaration of Human Rights that motivates the chancellor on so many fronts.

NOTES

1. Mishra, *Angela Merkel – Machtworte*, p. 222.
2. Created in 1666 by Louis XIV, the French Academy did not admit its first woman, Marguerite Perey, until 1962; its first "full" member, as of 1979, was Yvonne Choquet-Bruhat. Curie's daughter Irene secured a Nobel Prize in Chemistry in 1935.
3. Kornelius, *Angela Merkel: Die Kanzlerin und ihre Welt*, p. 16.
4. NATO's double-track approach of the 1980s combined these elements, allowing for Pershing II and cruise missile deployments to counter a Soviet SS-20s build-up.
5. Mushaben, *From Post-War to Post-Wall Generations*.
6. Citing General Lord Ismay, first Secretary-General of the NATO.
7. Ekkehard Brose, "When Germany Sends Troops Abroad: The Case for a Limited Reform of the Parliamentary Participation Act," Stiftung für Wissenschaft und Politik, Berlin, September 2013.
8. Emil J. Kirchner, cited in Mushaben, *From Post-War to Post-Wall Generations*, p. 173
9. Regierungserklärung von Bundeskanzler Willy Brandt vor dem Deutschen Bundestag in Bonn am 28. Oktober 1969.
10. Mushaben, *From Post-War to Post-Wall Generations*, pp. 234–235.
11. Ibid., p. 191.
12. Franz Josef Meier, "The Security and Defense Policy of the Grand Coalition," in Marco Overhaus, Hanns W. Maull, and Sebastian Harnisch (eds.), *Foreign Policy of the Grand Coalition: Base Line and First Assessment, Foreign Policy in Dialogue*, 7/18 (2006), p. 53.
13. Sebastian Harnisch and Hanns W. Maull (eds.), *Germany as a Civilian Power? The Foreign Policy of the Berlin Republic* (Manchester University Press, 2001).
14. Munich Security conference website, downloaded June 4, 2015.
15. "Von der Leyen will 130 Milliarden Euro investieren," *Die Zeit*, January 16, 2016.
16. Ralf Neukirch and Matthias Schepp, "Chilly Peace: German–Russian Relations Enter a New Ice-Age," *Der Spiegel*, May 30, 2012.
17. Gardner Feldman, *The Special Relationship between West Germany and Israel*.
18. Meier, "Security and Defense Policy of the Grand Coalition," p. 59.
19. "Bush and Putin: Best of Friends," BBC, June 16, 2001, available at: www .news.bbc.co.uk/2/hi/europe/1392791.stm.
20. Fiona Hill and Clifford Gaddy, *Mr. Putin: Operative in the Kremlin* (Washington, DC: Brookings Institution, 2013).
21. Herbert A. Simon, *Administrative Behavior: A Study of Decision-Making Processes in Administrative Organization* (New York: Macmillan, 1947).
22. Hajo Schumacher's 2006 dissertation, "Machtphysik: Führungsstrategien der CDU-Vorsitzenden Angela Merkel im innerparteilichen Machtgeflecht, 2000–2004," University of Duisburg, supplied the foundation for *Die zwölf Gesetze der Macht. Angela Merkels Efolgsgeheimnisse*.

23. Patrick Donahue and Tino Andresen, "Merkel Eye for Russian Empress Shows Putin Ties are Complex," Bloomberg, March 4, 2014.
24. Olga Kryshtanovskaya and Stephen White, "Putin's Militocracy," *Post-Soviet Affairs*, 19(4) (2003), pp. 292, 296.
25. Kimberly Marten, "Informal Political Networks and Putin's Foreign Policy: The Examples of Iran and Syria," *Problems of Post-Communism*, 62(2) (2015), p. 74.
26. Ibid.
27. Ibid., p. 75.
28. Source for both quotes is "Merkel zum Mauerfall-Jahrestag: 'Träume können wahr werden,'" *Frankfurter Allgemeine Zeitung*, November 9, 2014.
29. Wladimir Putin, with Natalija Geworkjan and Andrei Kolesnikow, *Aus erster Hand. Gespräche mit Wladimir Putin* (Munich: Heyne, 2000).
30. Hill and Gaddy, *Mr. Putin*, p. 122.
31. Ibid., p. 124.
32. Quotes like this were summarized in a "Putin quiz" in which *Der Spiegel* asked readers to identify the real quote among three options. See Benjamin Bidder, "Quiz zum Kreml-Boss: Das hat Putin nicht wirklich gesagt, oder?" available at: www.spiegel.de/quiztool/quiztool-64350.html, last accessed June 10, 2014.
33. Cited in Hill and Gaddy, *Mr. Putin*, p. 36; further, Nikolai Petrov, Masha Lipman, and Henry E. Hale, "Overmanaged Democracy in Russia: Governance Implications of Hybrid Regimes," Carnegie Papers No. 106, February 2010.
34. Lang, "Gender Equality in post-Unification Germany."
35. Andrey Makarychev and Sergei Medvedev, "Biopolitics and Power in Putin's Russia," *Problems of Post-Communism*, 62(1) (2015): 45–54.
36. Ibid., p. 47.
37. Ibid., p. 49.
38. Bruce Hounsell, "Putin Uses Dog to Intimidate Merkel," *Foreign Policy*, June 14, 2007.
39. Kornelius, *Angela Merkel: Die Kanzlerin und ihre Welt*, p. 184.
40. Hill and Gaddy, *Mr. Putin*, p. 145.
41. Bidder, "Quiz zum Kreml-Boss."
42. Terry Lynn Karl, *The Paradox of Plenty: Oil Booms and Petro-States* (Berkeley: University of California Press, 1997).
43. James D. Brown, "Oil Fueled? The Soviet Invasion of Afghanistan," *Post-Soviet Affairs*, 29(1) (2013), p. 64.
44. Alexander Gusev and Kirsten Westphal, "Russian Energy Policies Revisited: Assessing the Impact of the Crisis in Ukraine on Russian Energy Policies and Specifying the Implications for German and EU Energy Policies," Stiftung Wissenschaft und Politik, Berlin, December 2015, pp. 8–9, 32, 44.
45. Hill and Gaddy, *Mr. Putin*, p. 156.
46. Igor Danchenko and Clifford Gaddy reached this conclusion ("The Mystery of Vladimir Putin's Dissertation," presented at the Brookings Institution, March 30, 2006), after reviewing his thesis on "Strategic Planning of the Reproduction of the Mineral Resource Base of a Region under Conditions of the Formation of Market Relations."

47. Hill and Gaddy, *Mr. Putin*, p. 149.
48. Bidder, "Quiz zum Kreml-Boss"; also, Karen Dawisha, *Putin's Kleptocracy. Who Owns Russia?* (New York: Simon & Schuster, 2014).
49. Adam N. Stulberg, "Out of Gas? Russia, Ukraine, Europe, and the Changing Geopolitics of Natural Gas," *Problems of Post-Communism*, 62(2) (2015), p. 116.
50. Frank Dohmen and Alexander Jung, "Europe's Failed Natural Gas Strategy: Gazprom Hopes to Build Second Baltic Sea Pipeline," *Der Spiegel*, May 18, 2012.
51. Gusev and Westphal, "Russian Energy Policies Revisited," p. 30.
52. Stulberg, "Out of Gas?" p. 116.
53. Gusev and Westphal, "Russian Energy Policies Revisited," p. 34.
54. Stuhlberg, "Out of Gas?," p. 120.
55. Sabine Fischer, "EU Sanktionen gegen Russland: Ziele, Wirkung und weiterer Umgang," *SWP Aktuelle*, 26 (March 2015).
56. Stuhlberg, "Out of Gas?" p. 115.
57. Gusev and Westphal, "Russian Energy Policies Revisited," pp. 16, 33.
58. Tuomas Forsberg, "From *Ostpolitik* to 'Frostpolitik'? Merkel, Putin and German Foreign Policy towards Russia," *International Affairs*, 92(1) (2016): 21–42.
59. Bidder, "Quiz zum Kreml-Boss."
60. Marlene Laruelle, "Russia as a 'Divided Nation': From Compatriots to Crimea. A Contribution to the Discussion on Nationalism and Foreign Policy," *Problems of Post-Communism*, 62(2) (2015): 88–97.
61. Ibid., p. 93.
62. Michael Merlingen and Rasa Ostrauskaité, "EU Peacebuilding in Georgia: Limits and Achievements," Working Paper No. 35, Leuven Center for Global Governance Studies, 2009.
63. Ibid., p. 6.
64. "A Chronology of the Crisis: Georgia Crisis," *IISS Strategic Comments* 14, No. 7, September 2008.
65. Both quotes stem from the IISS special issue.
66. Bush angered Merkel at the summit by going "off-script," calling for Georgian and Ukrainian NATO membership; see "NATO Allies Oppose Bush on Georgia and Ukraine," *New York Times*, April 3, 2008.
67. Joshua A. Tucker, "Enough! Electoral Fraud, Collective Action Problems, and Post-Communist Colored Revolutions," *Perspectives on Politics*, 5(3) (2007): 535–551.
68. Anders Åslund, *Ukraine: What Went Wrong and How to Fix It* (Washington, DC: Peterson Institute for International Economics, 2015).
69. Marten, "Informal Political Networks," p. 83.
70. Tony Paterson, "Ukraine Crisis: Angry Angela Merkel Questions whether Putin is 'In Touch with Reality,'" *The Telegraph*, March 3, 2014; Andreas Rinke, "Wie Putin Berlin verlor: Moskaus Annexion der Krim hat die deutsche Russland Politik verändert," *Internationale Politik*, May/June 2014, p. 38.
71. Cited by Liana Fix, "Leadership in the Ukraine Conflict: A German Moment," in Niklas Helwig (ed.), *Europe's New Political Engine: Germany's Role in the*

EU's Foreign and Security Policy (Helsinki: Finnish Institute of International Affairs, April 2016), p. 116.

72. Laure Delcour, "Dualitäten der französischen Russlandpolitik: Die Ukrainekrise als Bewährungsprobe," *DGAP Analyse*, No. 4 (March 2015), p. 5.

73. Andreas Umsland, "Berlin, Kiev, Moskau und die Röhre: Die deutsche Ostpolitik im Spannungsfeld der russisch-ukrainischen Beziehungen," *Zeitschrift für Aussen- und Sicherheitspolitik*, 6(3) (2013), p. 415.

74. Laruelle, "Russia as a 'Divided Nation'," pp. 83, 95.

75. "Ukraine Ceasefire: The 12-point Plan," BBC, February 9, 2015.

76. Sabine Fischer, "Die EU und Russland, Konflikte und Potenzial einer schwierigen Partnerschaft," *SWP-Berlin* (December 2006); Frank Walther Steinmeier, "Europa new denken," *Frankfurter Allgemeine Zeitung*, September 1, 2006.

77. Neukirch and Schepp, "Chilly Peace."

78. Andrey Makarychev, "A New European Disunity: EU–Russia Ruptures and the Crisis in the Common Neighborhood," *Problems of Post-Communism*, 62(6) (2015), p. 314.

79. Dimitar Bechev, "Understanding the Contest Between the EU and Russia in Their Shared Neighborhood," *Problems of Post-Communism*, 62(6) (2015), p. 341.

80. Ibid., p. 345.

81. Tina Hildebrandt, Michael Thumann and Bernd Ulrich, "Die Krimkrise: Wie weit geht Russland? Test the West," *Die Zeit*, March 6, 2014.

82. Catherine Mayer, "The Angela Enigma," *Time Magazine*, September 23, 2013.

83. Jennifer Yoder, "From Amity to Enmity: German–Russian Relations in the Post Cold War Period," *German Politics and Society*, 33(3) (2015), p. 52.

84. She also drew Chinese ire by inviting the Dalai Lama to the Chancellor's Office against Steinmeier's advice in September 2007. See Ulrich Speck, "Germany Plays Good Cop, Bad Cop on Ukraine," Carnegie Europe, June 25, 2014.

85. Yoder, "From Amity to Enmity," p. 55; citing Hannes Adomeit, p. 56.

86. George Friedman, "Low Oil Prices Will Make Russia More Aggressive in 2017," *Forbes Magazine*, December 27, 2016.

87. "Russia Plane Crash: 'Terror Act' Downed A321 over Egypt's Sinai," BBC, November 17, 2015.

88. Craig R. Whitney, "War in the Gulf: Europe Gulf Fighting Shatters Europeans' Fragile Unity," *New York Times*, January 25, 1991.

89. Sperling, "Putin's Macho Personality Cult."

90. Stephen White and Ian McAllister, "The Putin Phenomenon," *Journal of Communist Studies and Transition Politics*, 24(4) (2008): 604–628.

91. Sperling, "Putin's Macho Personality Cult," pp. 15, 19.

92. Ibid., p. 16.

93. Ibid., p. 19.

94. John Hall, "Kremlin Mocks Obama's Masculinity by Tweeting Picture of Him Holding a Poodle Next to Putin Petting a Leopard," *Daily Mail*, August 1, 2014.

95. Carl Schreck, "Putin Dismisses Clinton's Hitler Comparison With Sexist Jab," Radio Free Europe, June 4, 2014, available at: www.rferl.org/content/putin-dismisses-clintons-hitler-comparison-with-sexist-jab/25410658.html.

96. Bernd Ulrich, "Keine Angst vorm Fliegen," *Die Zeit*, June 16, 2016.
97. Televised speech of October 4, 1993, cited in Donald Murray, *A Democracy of Despots* (Montreal: McGill-Queens University Press, 1995), p. 8.
98. The ECJ nullified Germany's constitutional ban on women's service with a weapon in 2000 (*Tanja Kreil* v. *Bundesrepublik Deutschland*, C-285/98).
99. Kornelius, *Angela Merkel: Die Kanzlerin und ihre Welt*, p. 198.

5

Madam Non and the Euro Crisis: Shaping Economic Integration and Governance

Although Germany is the largest net contributor to European Central Bank (ECB) funds shoring up Greece, Spain, and other imperiled national economies, Angela Merkel has staunchly resisted blanket financial bailouts since 2009, to the chagrin of many EU partners. Citing Goethe, Merkel declared early on that each member state should "sweep away [the junk bonds] in front of its own door" to "render every city district clean" (*Ein jeder kehr' vor seiner Tür, und rein ist jedes Stadtquartier*).[1] While the Lehman Brothers collapse in the United States unleashed the 2008 crisis, one observer claimed that the Hypo Real Estate Holding AG (HRE) in the chancellor's own backyard constituted "the biggest black hole in Europe's financial history."[2] The HRE bank and various state banks eventually cost German taxpayers €100 billion, coupled with €90 billion from the ECB. Outvoted by Nicolas Sarkozy and other leaders pushing for Eurobonds and bailout mechanisms later on, Angela Merkel's hardline stance on austerity led to a serious break in the traditionally sacred Franco-German relationship.

The fact that most Germans supported Merkel's hang-tough position on the bailouts did not stop the pundits from mocking the chancellor for espousing the Swabian *Hausfrau* as a role model for fiscal responsibility amid the massive debt crises sweeping the continent. Known for their extraordinary thriftiness and cleanliness (e.g., the *Kehrwoche* practice), the real housewives of Baden-Württemberg probably had trouble comprehending the bank-driven financial frenzy of the last two decades.[3] As Merkel stressed in several speeches, the iconic Swabian lives within her means. Although women drive the national economy via their roles as primary consumers, household managers, wage earners, and investors,

they have been curiously absent from supranational negotiations determining the parameters of Euro stabilization packages and national austerity programs. Their very limited presence inside corporate boardrooms,
on the trading floors, and in financial regulatory institutions goes a long
way to explain why women have been so negatively affected by the global
financial crisis; the precariousness they encounter goes well beyond the
problems of high unemployment and slow growth. At issue here is the link
between descriptive and substantive representation in a supranational
context: even with a woman calling most of the shots, decisions that
may be "good for the whole" can produce disproportionately negative
consequences for specific groups. The negative externalities became the
problem of individual member states, who passed them on to women
disadvantaged from the start, exactly the situation that the 1996 adoption
of EU *gender mainstreaming* was designed to prevent.

This chapter describes a complex set of European financial breakdowns
all too simply subsumed under the *Euro crisis* label. The economic turbu-
lence afflicting the EU since 2008 arose across three distinct stages. Each
phase has elicited a different response from Chancellor Merkel, who has
had to juggle its changing parameters under diverging party-political
configurations: a Grand Coalition, 2005–2009; a conservative–liberal
government, 2009–2013; then a second Grand Coalition, 2013–2017.[4]
Although fifteen of twenty-seven EU members shared a single currency at
the outset, most national leaders responded during phase one with uncoordinated stimulus plans, bank bailouts, and industry-specific rescue programs. Very few were still in power by the time the crisis receded. The first
period had a particularly disruptive impact on the Franco-German axis,
the major driving force of European integration since the 1950s.

The second stage was marked by sovereign debt crises stretching from
Ireland to Greece by 2010. This gave rise to a "Troika," comprising the
IMF, the EU Commission, and the ECB, which quickly adopted a one-
size-fits all approach fixated on monetary policy. This era shifted the
balance of power among Community organs, allowing the Commission
to assert control over national budgets. Beyond exacerbating the debt
crisis in weak states, this stage essentially reversed two decades of institutional progress for women *within* the EU. Germany's stubborn adherence
to a "no bailout" clause over the next two years raised fears of a possible
domino effect, giving rise to a third stage: a Euro crisis that worsened
conditions in peripheral countries, though they were not the only ones
violating the "Maastricht criteria." This period rendered many temporary
budget cuts permanent in poorer states, affecting an array of social

benefits and public services essential for gender equality. In this case, the chancellor's policy choices indirectly benefited women at home while disproportionately harming their counterparts in other EU member states.

Angela Merkel's dominant role in the financial crisis has highlighted the Community's long-standing *democratic deficit* problem; Commission President Jean-Claude Juncker has done nothing to halt the erosion of co-decision powers belonging to the European Parliament, just for starters. The austerity policies promoted by non-elected Troika actors have moreover undermined national welfare and labor relations policies. While the male-dominated banking sector has returned to business as usual, women have been forced to pick up the slack for major social service cutbacks.[5] Another consequence has been the exponential *increase* in debt among the poorer states, especially in Greece, the poster child of tax evasion and state spending gone wild: in many respects, the cure turned out to be worse than the disease. The conditionalities imposed under the EU Six-Pack, the Fiscal Pact, and the European Semester process bear a suspicious resemblance to the failed structural adjustment programs (SAPs) inflicted on African and Latin American economies throughout the 1970s and 1980s.[6]

With the exception of Christine Lagarde, who replaced a disgraced Dominique Strauss-Kahn as head of the IMF in May 2011, Angela Merkel encounters mostly male faces in her dealings with the Council, the Commission, and the ECB.[7] According to *critical mass theory*, a female "n" of two would have a hard time making a difference under any circumstances.[8] The world of finance offers especially tough challenges, presuming that any woman who finds a seat at the table would "naturally" reflect on the gender consequences of her decisions. A globalized economy nonetheless produces ripple effects, extending well beyond the intended arena.

In other policy domains explored in this book, it is fairly easy to identify particular life experiences that have shaped Merkel's leadership style and performance. The factors driving her choices in this arena are more difficult to discern. Having lived under a chronically underperforming socialist command-economy for thirty-five years, Merkel ardently upholds *freedom* as a core value but she cannot escape an all-German fixation on *security*, dating back to Otto von Bismarck. In contrast to most of her GDR compatriots, she enjoyed privileged access to hard-to-access goods, thanks to care packages from Western relatives. But she also internalized an appreciation for guaranteed healthcare, paid leave policies, subsidized childcare, and state pensions. Over the last ten years she has reintroduced "Eastern" gender policies to foster work–family reconciliation.

To the chagrin of conservative hardliners, Merkel usually eschews rigid, ideological positions, another reaction to her GDR upbringing. Heading the CDU Opposition in 2003, she temporarily embraced radical neo-liberalism at her party's Leipzig conference, building on Gerhard Schröder's unpopular structural reforms known as Agenda 2010/Hartz IV. Disapproving voters quickly handed conservatives a string of state electoral defeats that led Merkel back to a softer form of *ordo-liberalism* and the *social market economy*, models credited with launching West Germany's postwar economic miracle. The steps she took at home during the first stage of the crisis did not align with the no-bailout, rule-driven approach she pursued at the European level, although she now admits that her country has profited immensely from the single currency *and* short-term Greek debt-servicing.

In fact, the austerity paradigm she tenaciously imposed on other Eurozone states contravenes Germany's own experiences with economic collapse and reconstruction across multiple historical periods. This raises the question: why did Merkel reject a growth model that had launched the economic miracle of the 1950s and 1960s (debt forgiveness), ensured social peace and industrial productivity during the 1970s and 1980s (*concerted action*), and dominated Kohl's response (massive social transfers) to industrial collapse in the Eastern Länder throughout the 1990s. For debtor states, Merkel advocated the same structural reforms that had cost her predecessor the 2005 elections; yet her domestic agenda over the last ten years has relied on diverse fiscal stimuli, including significant state subsidies for education, smart technologies, RE generation, and childcare facilities.

Merkel has leveraged various EU mandates to drive holistic reforms at home, but she insisted on a very narrow push for structural reforms to foster competitiveness in countries lacking Germany's high-value production and export capacity. One nation's massive trade surplus becomes another's negative current account balance. Dependent on tourism, shipbuilding, mineral fuels, non-mechanized agriculture and, currently, limited EU subsidies for islands overwhelmed by refugees, the Greek economy provides the most striking example. Despite her desire to avoid the moral hazard inherent in bailouts, the pressures applied to debtor countries after 2010 shifted the burden of adjustment from the center to the periphery: as wealthy investors fled to the safety of its highly ranked bonds, the FRG saved roughly €100 billion in interest costs on its public sector debt between 2010 and 2015.[9] Facing a potential €90 billion "haircut" in case of Greek default, heavily exposed German banks found themselves profiting from high interest, debt-servicing loans, letting them "largely off the hook" with improved balance sheets.[10]

A third paradox raised by Merkel's approach to the Euro crisis pertains to EU economic governance. Modeled after the German Central Bank (Deutsche Bundesbank), fixated on price stability, the ECB embraced a similar limited mandate; overruled by Kohl regarding one-to-one DM/East-Mark conversion rates in 1990, the Bundesbank was more successful in writing strict convergence criteria and a no-bailout clause into the 1991 Maastricht Treaty. Germany and France nonetheless used their dominant positions in the European Council to dumb down the "excessive deficit procedure," insisting for years on greater discretion in justifying their own repeated violations of the 3 percent deficit criterion. By 2009, most Eurozone states had broken the Stability and Growth Pact rules.

By forcing a return to *strict conditionality*, Merkel succeeded in restricting bigger bailouts demanded by France but she did so at the cost of transferring significant supervisory and resolution powers over her own banks to the ECB. Given a purported threat to the Euro's existence, she watched the ECB move beyond its very narrow price-stability mandate as it took on rating-agency functions and moved into the fiscal domain, even superseding member state budgetary authority. The chancellor's preferred crisis narrative won out against other "perfectly viable alternatives" being pursued in Anglo-Saxon countries. Germany impelled the EU to accept its rules but failed to recognize that while it got what it wanted in the short run, it "changed the reality on the ground," leading to a need for the very measures it had initially opposed.[11]

Merkel's initial response to the Wall Street melt-down of 2008 and the crisis epidemic that followed mirrors her reaction to the 1999 revelations that her mentor, Helmut Kohl, had been personally entangled in a web of illegal campaign finance donations. Like her faith in West German democracy back then, her trust in the free market system was temporarily shaken. Both evoked a *principled reaction* on Merkel's part, but I argue here that fundamental disparities among member state economies sooner required a *pragmatic approach*. This time she was forced to master a new policy domain, virtually overnight, under circumstances that left no space for her usual small-steps approach. While her earlier socialization experiences helped her to master and market critical policy reforms in the national context, they did not lend themselves to effective supranational translation. In this case, the pastor's daughter's attempt to frame the crisis as a "morality tale of 'Northern saints' and 'Southern sinners'" played well with her domestic audience but alienated the rest, giving rise to anti-EU parties in those states that will hinder integration efforts in other policy domains for years to come.[12]

This chapter commences with a description of two concepts that have shaped German monetary and fiscal policies since 1949, *ordo-liberalism* and the *social market economy*, arguing that Merkel's domestic policies continue to build on these precepts. Next, I review key events that unleashed a three-stage financial crisis, starting with the Wall Street melt-down of 2008 that had a debilitating effect on the traditional Franco-German relationship. Intransigence at the European level plays an ostensible role in Merkel's shift from social market thinking to a narrower emphasis on *fixed rules* by stage two. Here the chancellor faced the perennial problem of "bounded rationality," limiting her search for alternatives to those prescribed by monetarists in an effort to generate an intergovernmental consensus.[13] Because her own house was in order, she ignored the conditions next door, although she must have been troubled by the fact that her structural demands soon brought down a number of democratically elected governments.

Next, we examine the consequences of Troika *austerity* measures, especially in relation to women, stressing the extent to which the once gender-friendly Commission yielded to neo-liberal pressures, allowing the ECB to undermine the Community method of decision-making as well as the social dimensions of the *acquis communautaire*. I then consider whether the debt crisis might have been prevented from spinning out of control, had leaders worked harder to ensure *the balanced participation of women and men* in decision-making, that is, in national finance ministries, the ECB, and in corporate boardrooms. Paradoxically, the chancellor who invoked the self-limiting thriftiness of the Swabian housewife at the height of the crisis shifted to the theme of women's institutional empowerment in 2014, when she took the surprising step of adopting a binding 30 percent gender quota for German corporate boardrooms. Pursuing the politics of small steps, her favorite *modus operandi*, Merkel's effort to add a gender dimension to the Euro crisis amounts to a sad case of "too little, too late" on several fronts.

FROM MARSHALL PLAN TO UNIFICATION: ORDO-LIBERALISM AND THE SOCIAL MARKET ECONOMY

As seen in earlier chapters, many contemporary Germany policies have deep roots in the lessons derived from its seminal role in two world wars.

The extraordinary reparation costs arising from the Versailles Treaty contributed to a lack of democratic consolidation under the Weimar Republic; the high inflation and mass unemployment of the Great Depression years fostered support for Adolf Hitler, who promised to make Germany "great again." Dating back to this era, *ordo-liberalism* sought to define a "third way" between the unfettered, laissez-faire capitalism seen in the United States and the command-style, collectivist economy imposed by the Soviet Union. It squared the circle of a free market based on competition with a strong state capable of regulating, and thus mitigating, destructive conflicts between workers and employers, as well as between public and private interests. Commensurate with *Staatsräson* thinking, ordo-liberalism assumes that the state upholds a higher purpose than self-interested economic actors: it must therefore engage in deliberate rule-making, providing a legal, social, and ethical order that preserves liberal values vis-à-vis "greedy self-seekers" and "antagonistic class interests."[14] Ordo-liberalism posits that governments are responsible for designing and enforcing market rules that maintain price stability, balanced budgets, and fair competition across all sectors; it further holds that individuals as well as states need to assume the risks and costs of their own decisions.

Postwar Christian Democrats rejected an unfettered "free market." The party's 1947 Ahlener Program declared:

The capitalist economic system does not do justice to the state and social life-interests of the German people ... The contents and goal of new social and economic order can no longer be the striving for capitalist profits and power-mongering, but only the well-being of our people. Based on a societal order the German people should receive an economic and social constitution that suits justice and human dignity, serves the spiritual and material rebuilding of our people and secures both internal and external peace.[15]

This belief led them to adopt the *social market economy* (SME) as the logical complement to ordo-liberalism.

Serving as the first West German economics minister from 1949 to 1963, Ludwig Erhard, assisted by Alfred Müller-Armack, conceptualized the SME in response to the political oppression, economic exploitation, and physical devastation inflicted by the Nazi regime after the Great Depression. Its fundamental charge is "to protect the freedom of all market participants on both the supply and demand side, whilst also providing for a strong safety net." Construed as the foundation for an open society, it promotes "a strong social fabric" by way of full employment, solidarity, and economic stability.

Market mechanisms are supposed to ensure efficient production, stable pricing, consumer choice, and technological innovation. State regulatory powers warrant a level playing field for businesses, a positive investment climate, and the capacity of individuals to "act on their own initiative."[16]

Its second charge is to foster social participation and equal opportunity by way of "a strong welfare system ... providing social security for persons unable to provide for themselves," due to age, ill-health, or job loss. The Economics Ministry curiously notes on its website that the SME is not specifically mentioned in the constitution, but Article 20 (Basic Law) declares the Federal Republic "a democratic and social federal state"; *social* in this context is a synonym for *welfare*. The 1990 Treaty on Monetary, Economic and Social Union between the FRG and GDR moreover declared the SME the central element of a united German economic order. The problem is that governments of different partisan stripes do not apply the same yardsticks to questions of regulation and welfare; conservatives tend to emphasize rule-following behaviors and responsibility, while those left of center stress the role of social protection.

The US narrative has mythologized the extent to which American money and free-market thinking hauled Germany out of the fascist ashes with the Marshall Plan. Refusing to meet the original request for US$22 billion to aid European reconstruction and "contain" communism, Congress finally approved a US$12.4 billion package for all recipients, signed by Harry Truman on April 3, 1948, weeks before Western allies introduced the Deutsche Mark. Beneficiaries were required to use the loans to purchase goods produced in the United States; about 40 percent went to the coal industry. Albrecht Ritschl notes that this was only one component of "an enormous sovereign debt relief programme."[17] Germany's interwar borrowing binge had made it look "like Greece on steroids": by mid-1945, the Reich owed European creditors nearly 40 percent of its prewar GDP, based on distorted exchange rates; real public debt stood closer to 300 percent. All other Plan recipients "were (politely) asked to sign a waiver" in 1947, blocking *their* debt claims against Germany until it had fully repaid its Marshall loans. The US-engineered D-Mark essentially erased its domestic debt but not that of other European states with ratios approaching 200 percent of GDP. Negotiated in 1953, the London Agreement "perpetuated these arrangements, and thus waterproofed them for the days when Marshall Aid would be repaid and the European Payments Union would be dissolved."[18] German debt acquired prior to 1933 was subject to reduced interest rates, while the settlement of post-1933 debts was delayed in anticipation of eventual unification. No final repayment conference was scheduled following October 3, 1990. The current FRG position is that these debts have ceased to exist.

This scheme clearly fell outside the national ordo-liberal paradigm: the debt forgiveness extended in 1947 to a state convicted of profound crimes against humanity not only led to its rapid economic reconstruction but also ensured its reintegration into the community of European nations. NATO assumed a significant proportion of the fledgling state's defense costs, freeing capital for productive investment. Concerted action between employers and labor unions ensured a balance between wages and prices, coupled with dramatic productivity increases well into the 1970s.[19]

Chancellor Kohl later proved to be less generous than the victorious powers when it came to forgiving debt. Introducing the D-Mark into East Germany in July 1990 against the counsel of Bundesbank officials, Kohl immediately transferred DM 350 billion in "old" GDR debt to the new states and their local governments.[20] One has to question Kohl's ability to "learn from history": he also took US President Reagan to the Bitburg Cemetery but refused to name illegal campaign donors in 1999 as a matter of "honor." The debt obligations imposed on the Eastern Länder impeded their recovery by at least a decade, driving up federal debt based on the need for massive social transfers.[21] Financial subsidies averaging DM 100 billion per year consisted largely of social security payments, equivalent to 20 percent of Eastern GDP. As late as 2001, the eastern economy was still "on the brink," despite an estimated unification cost of DM 2 trillion.[22]

The Kohl government likewise did a poor job of leveling the playing field to ensure effective competition during its fire-sale of GDR industries. Countless citizens were forced out of dwellings they had inhabited for decades, after Westerners filed 2 million lawsuits "reclaiming" properties on behalf of deceased relatives, which they immediately re-sold to real-estate speculators.[23] While the range of available products increased as Western chain stores replaced state retail outlets, Easterners receiving less than 80 percent of Western wages faced higher prices at (what remained) the only grocery in town; Eastern pensions will not reach the 100 percent mark until 2020. Conservative mitigation of the human costs of structural reform were also self-serving. Economist Rüdiger Frank contends that,

The transfers didn't end up all in East Germany, they rather passed through it like a boomerang ... Now, who benefited from all that investment? It was West German companies who expanded to the east. So that was a subsidy to West German industry. Infrastructure projects, highways, roads, telecommunication networks, who did that? West German companies, because all the East German construction companies were either bankrupt or bought up by West German competitors ... another subsidy to West German industry.[24]

Under the terms his negotiators injected into the Stability and Growth Pact, Kohl's social transfers would have been labeled "crass Keynesianism." Decade-long investments in a second economic miracle would have also been banned under existing EU competition and deficit restrictions. The FRG exceeded the Maastricht debt threshold multiple times beyond the point when it might have used unification to justify its actions; its 2010 debt ratio stood at 70 percent.[25] The fiscal equalization system still redistributes tax revenues from the rich south (Bavaria, Baden-Württemberg) to poor northern states (Bremen, Berlin, Schleswig-Holstein), as well as from West to East. Other federal infusions addressing structural weaknesses amount to 5 percent of the Eastern GDP.[26] Real growth requires investment and job creation. Since 2008, state subsidies for RE have gone a long way toward reducing unemployment in rural areas like Mecklenburg-Vorpommern (Chapter 6).[27]

Despite her brief flirtation with neo-liberalism in 2003, Merkel is quite comfortable with a national economic framework combining ordo-liberalism rules with social benefit policies. Indeed, her first- and third-term experiences imply that she finds it easier to cooperate with Social Democrats than with her FDP partners who took a turbo-capitalist turn toward tax cuts and deregulation after the 2009 elections. The chancellor declared in January 2014:

The social market economy is our compass, because unlike any other economic and social order, it places people at its center. That's exactly what matters: the individual as the center of our activity ... Politics that locate not the state, not organizations, not particularistic interests but rather the individual in the middle of our dealings ... can create the basis for a good life in Germany and Europe. The sources of a good life are freedom, rule of law, political stability, economic strength and justice. The Grand Coalition government [her second] will make the sources of a good life available to all, to open the best possible chances to everyone.[28]

Having registered in 2003 that her own voters reject the gospel of capitalism unchained, Merkel realized that the structural reforms she demands of other EU states cost Schröder the chancellorship in 2005.

This makes it even harder to fathom why she would reject measures that had not only rebuilt the Western economy and consolidated its fledgling democracy in the 1950s but also secured a good life and preserved social peace when Eastern unemployment hit 25–30 percent in the 1990s.[29] What led to her fixation on a kind of ordo-liberalism that jettisoned social market principles in favor of pure austerity? What moved Merkel to abandon her initial demand that private creditors assume responsibility for their own bad judgment, in favor of a "cold-hearted," all-or-nothing demeanor vis-à-vis jobless Mediterraneans?[30] The short-term loans reluctantly extended to Greece for debt servicing have pushed that country into a deeper hole, from which no one expects it to re-emerge for at least a decade. We now turn to the onset of the European financial crisis, and the German response shaped by Merkel's first Grand Coalition through 2009.

STAGE ONE: BANKERS, BAILOUTS, AND "CRASS KEYNESIANISM"

In 1850, German immigrants Henry, Emanuel, and Mayer Lehman opened a cotton trading business in Montgomery, Alabama, naming it after themselves. Lehman Brothers flourished for over 100 years; expanding into investment banking, the company underwrote its first stock offering in 1889. Surviving the stock market crash of 1929, its directors offered creative financing packages to other companies throughout the Great Depression. The growing corporation did not undertake its first major merger until 1977, but the following decades brought multiple sales, spin-offs, and internal rivalries that probably would have left its founders spinning in their graves.

By 2000, the company's net income began to exceed US$1 billion per annum, becoming a major underwriter for mortgage-backed securities. By spring 2008, the US mortgage markets were heading for a beating, however, and the firm was accused of underreporting overextended loan problems. By September 9, its shares had plunged 45 percent; reporting nearly US$4 billion in third-quarter losses, Lehman Brothers commenced talks with the US Treasury and the Federal Reserve, hoping to arrange a sale. On September 14, both the Bank of America and Barclays had pulled their purchase offers, leading what was left of the company to file for Chapter 11 bankruptcy the next day. Its US$639 billion in assets rendered this the largest bankruptcy filing in US history.[31]

The interval between the Lehman collapse and its assault on European financial markets was brief. Analogous to the breath-taking collapse of socialist regimes in 1989, the 2008 tsunami hit capitalist financial houses and national banks with such speed and ferocity that decision-makers had nowhere to turn. What began as a subprime mortgage crisis in the United States quickly morphed into a cesspool of toxic assets, dubious credit records issued by self-interested ratings agencies, revelations of massive tax evasion, mind-boggling sovereign debts, plunging consumer confidence, and the loss of life-time savings for millions of average citizens.[32] Its rapid spread derived, in part, from the ongoing failure of even affluent Euro countries to adhere to Maastricht-mandated deficit and debt limits.

The events of 2008 exposed the dark side of financial markets, ranging from hedge funds, short-sales, and "collateralized" debt, to credit default swaps, zombie banks, and "tail-risks." These developments had their roots in the deregulation and merger-mania crazes of the Reagan and Thatcher years. *Competition* as understood by Adam Smith has been replaced with globalized *competitiveness* á la Goldman Sachs, Wall-Mart, and Amazon. The toxic "products," short-sales, and profit-mongering infecting the financial markets had become so complicated by 2008 that not even their inventors could decipher them, although the latter continued to insist on year-end bonuses running in the millions.[33]

The result was a widespread liquidity crisis and a global credit squeeze. The suspension of interbank lending hit deficit economies the hardest as loans-based-on-loans stopped trickling down to the poorer countries.[34] The Euro area saw a €200 billion drop in the market capitalization of its complex banking groups from mid-September through late November.[35] Leaders rushed to rescue overextended banks in Ireland and Spain, for example, which had actually seen surplus budgets prior to the bursting bubbles. Contrary to logic, banks deemed "too big to fail" were rendered even bigger in the sell-offs accompanying the crisis.[36]

The magnitude of the crisis led the business-friendly *Frankfurter Allgemeine Zeitung* to write:

It's the rhetoric of Sept. 11 ... But this crisis actually has much larger dimensions than the attack against the twin towers and collapse seven years ago. Why? Because, this time, the attack on all-American doctrines is not the work of some foreign enemy. It comes from within, from the depths of the system. Largely unobstructed by its own state controls, American capitalism has created its own suicide bomber whose explosives – derivatives – have had an even greater effect than the flying bombs of the jihadists. The whole world – and not just New York – has a new ground zero now – Wall Street ...

But the *Schadenfreude* derived from blaming American financiers was short-lived:

Germany will also pay a high price for the sins of the US financial system – higher even than the €320 million that the KfW [Credit Institute for Economic Reconstruction] so prematurely transferred to the bankruptcy administrators of Lehman Brothers. Even if German banks and their credit systems are spared from the chain reaction of a crash, the after-effects on this side of the Atlantic will be plenty painful: shrinking growth, higher unemployment and less room to maneuver.[37]

The crisis hit Germany with full force on October 5, 2008. The chancellor was immediately barraged with criticism for her alleged inability to respond rapidly with a "comprehensive plan" to the crisis washing across Europe. Asked how the two countries were going to tackle the financial melt-down, President Sarkozy declared, "France is working on it, Germany is thinking about it."[38] Merkel and her SPD finance minister nonetheless arranged for an immediate €50 billion bailout package for HRE Bank, despite Peer Steinbrück's subsequent characterization of the UK's massive fiscal expansion program (worth €200 billion) as "crass Keynesianism."[39] The next thing she did was to reassure voters that their savings would be federally guaranteed; the backdrop for her announcement was, ironically, a painting by Bernd Zimmer, called "After the Blast," depicting a hilly landscape after a major storm.[40] Fearing massive job losses in its export-dependent industries just as it moved out of recession, Merkel secured parliamentary approval for a €480 billion rescue package by October 17.[41] Twelve days is not a lot of time to forge a massive compromise between adversarial parties in two legislative chambers resting on diverse coalitions, compared with the centralized powers of presidential decree enjoyed by Sarkozy. That month Merkel vetoed an EU27 proposal for a €130 billion stimulus program, along with subsequent spending proposed by the rotating Council president Sarkozy, earning her the title of *Madam Non.*

FINANCIAL BLITZKRIEG AND THE FRANCO-GERMAN AXIS

Joining a long list of postwar benchmarks, 2016 marked fifty-five years of cooperation among the six founding members of European Coal and Steel Community (ECSC). To avoid "pouring the new wine of democracy into the old bottles of nationalism," the ECSC's founding fathers soon added common agricultural and nuclear policies (Euratom) to their framework for a new regional order; the result was an unprecedented period of peace and prosperity. Ratified in 1963, the Franco-German Friendship Treaty also played a quintessential role in advancing European integration. The larger context in which these two countries have cooperated and compromised in the name of Europe has changed dramatically since the fall of the Wall in 1989, however. First, the inclusion of thirteen Central East European (CEE) states since 2004 has shifted the Community's geographic center from Saint-André-le-Coq in Auvergne, France, to Westerngrund in Bavaria. It moreover disrupted the balance between "rich" and "poor" member states. A third factor chipping away at the centrality of Franco-German cooperation is the process of generational change. As an Easterner, Merkel lacked the emotional connection to France that had fostered those bilateral ties from the reign of Adenauer through Kohl. As noted earlier, shared recollections of wartime experiences have played a crucial role in shaping Germany's ties with countries like Israel and Russia since 1949. Lacking any first-hand memories, Gerhard Schröder set the stage for Merkel's increasing focus on "national interests."[42] As strained relations between Schröder and Chirac further revealed, personality also matters. Although Merkel and Sarkozy were both conservatives, they occupied parallel universes.[43] Described as "ever present and ever active, a Hyperpresident," Sarkozy was bound to irritate a female leader committed to pragmatism, small steps, and humility.[44] Systemic differences supplied another source of tension between the two states. As the head of a highly centralized, unitary polity enjoying almost unlimited budgetary powers, Sarkozy evinced no sympathy for the complexities of German federalism, much less for the extraordinarily active role of the Constitutional Court in proscribing the limits of Merkel's crisis responses.[45]

Still, the new chancellor's first state visit took her to Paris in 2005, the day after her inauguration; Nicolas Sarkozy and François Hollande, in turn, headed for Berlin within hours of their respective swearing-in ceremonies. Although neither initially evinced strong ties to the EU, Merkel and Sarkozy brought new salience to their special role in integration insofar as both wielded the EU Council gavel during their first terms in office: Germany presided from January to July 2007, France between July and December 2008. The presence of a first female chancellor inspired a new metaphor for German–French relations: the "couple Merkozy." It is worth noting that money issues often trigger domestic disputes even in happy marriages; in this case, the woman, who appears to be the primary breadwinner, has won those arguments more often than not.[46]

To join the Euro area, member states must meet five essential "convergence criteria," grounded in Article 140 of the 1991 Treaty of European Union (Table 5.1). The Maastricht convergence criteria mandated

TABLE 5.1 *Maastricht Conversion Criteria*

	Price stability	Sound public finances	Sustainable public finances	Durability of convergence	Exchange rate stability
What is measured					
How it is measured	Consumer price inflation rate	Government deficit as percent of GDP	Government debt as percent of GDP	Long-term interest rate	Deviation from a central rate
Convergence criteria	Not more than 1.5 percentage points above the rate of the three best performing member states	Reference value: not more than 3%	Reference value: not more than 60%	Not more than 2 percentage points above the rate of the three best performing member states (in terms of price stability)	Participation in ERM II for at least 2 years without severe tensions

Source: European Commission, Brussels, available at: http://ec.europa.eu/economy_finance/euro/adoption/who_can_join/index_en.htm.

concrete limits on deficits (3 percent), debt (60 percent), and inflation (1.5 percent) relative to GDP, coupled with a no-bailout rule; diverging degrees of competitiveness were not addressed prior to Euro adoption. Both countries had repeatedly violated the Maastricht convergence criteria, but only one could blame the extraordinary costs of unification. Sarkozy and Merkel introduced stimulus packages targeting specific groups and industries in the wake of the Wall Street debacle. The French National Assembly passed one law to stabilize the financial system in October 2008. Concerned about losing his country's Triple-A bond rating, Sarkozy focused on investment, offering a flagship program consisting of 1,000 projects, 75 percent of which were to be in place by 2009 to convey the impression of decisive leadership. France extended a one-time payment of €200 to each adult drawing benefits, but €1,000 to each consumer exchanging a car (ten years or older) for one meeting new CO_2 emission standards. The package foresaw a further infusion of €26 billion for 2009–2010. Sarkozy later introduced a short-term work program limited to six weeks at a time, for a maximum of 600 hours per year (equivalent to eighteen weeks).[47]

In contrast to the lame-duck response of US President Bush and the "jack-in-the-box policy" of his French counterpart, the chancellor opted for "a calm and muddling-through approach towards crisis management."[48] Merkel was perturbed by Sarkozy's effort to shift the rescue burden to the EU (and thus Germany) at the same time that he was enacting tax loopholes for millionaires and billionaires back home. She secured Bundestag and Bundesrat approval for three stimulus packages within thirteen months. Having already supplied €480 billion for bank bailouts, the Grand Coalition extended a mere €13 billion to the non-financial sector, including tax relief and a 50 percent reduction in social security contributions for employers. Adopted in November, its "Securing Jobs by Strengthening Growth Pact" also propped up small- and medium-sized companies. Merkel convened a meeting of ministers, economists, trade unionists, and employer representatives to justify a second stimulus program of €40–50 billion in January 2009, within days of having declared, "We will not take part in a senseless competition [of stimulus programs] costing billions. That is not something we intend to do."[49] Eventually passing five stabilization laws, Germany injected €70 billion into its own economy during this stage.[50]

Beyond funding infrastructure projects, the state offered an "environmental premium" of €2,500 to purchasers replacing automobiles at least nine years old. It granted wage subsidies to workers in training and extended the short-time working rule, from six to eighteen months, up to twenty-four months for 2009 (back to eighteen months by 2010). The Federal Employment Agency covered 60 percent of lost pay (67 percent for parents) owing to reduced hours. Enrollments surged between May 2008 and May 2009, rising from roughly 50,000 to 1.5 million; this saved an estimated 500,000 full-time jobs, keeping the number of jobless citizens steady at 3.5 million.[51] Alexander Riesenbichler and Kimberly Morgan hold that Germany's long-established "toolkit of flexible labor market instruments," coupled with prior wage restraint and industrial restructuring, gave its employers more room to maneuver than their European counterparts.[52] Merkel mollified fiscal conservatives with a constitutional "debt brake" (Article 109/3 BL). As of 2016, the Federal Government can only seek credits equivalent to 3.5 percent of the GDP; the Länder cannot pursue any credit financing as of 2020.

The structural reforms undertaken by her predecessor had already kicked in, leaving Merkel better positioned to address crisis conditions at home. As regional consumption declined, the FRG quickly secured new customers in China and Russia for its luxury cars and mechanical engineering products.[53] By this point, the chancellor was heading a new coalition; the FDP took charge of the economics ministry, and Wolfgang Schäuble (CDU) replaced Steinbrück (SPD) as finance minister. These developments may have shaped her belief that "German ideas" could be effectively transferred to other national contexts. Assuming that honesty was the best policy (while shifting blame to the previous government), Greek Finance Minister George Papakonstantinou admitted on October 20, 2009 that his country's debt ratio had been "miscalculated": the actual rate was not 3.6 percent but 12.8 percent of GDP. Rating agencies swiftly assigned Greek bonds "junk" status, killing its access to private capital markets. Fears of default quickly spread to Ireland, Spain, and Portugal. European neighbors increasingly urged Germany "to use its economic firepower to safeguard the Eurozone."[54]

Although the FDP pushed for "more market," the chancellor seemed to have lost her faith in its free-wielding forces by 2010. Addressing the Bundestag in May, she declared first, "Too many competition-weak members of the Eurozone have lived beyond their means and have gone the way of a debt trap ... That is the real cause of the problem." The rules, she contended, "cannot be oriented towards the weak, rather they must be oriented towards the strong. I know that is a hard message. Economically it is an absolute necessity ..." Here she ostensibly conflated the effect – countries living beyond their means – with the real cause of the problem, that is, oversized, deregulated banks engaging in irresponsible lending. She nonetheless stressed in the same government declaration:

Since the banking crisis of 2008 we have seen again how, lacking boundaries and rules, behaviors shaped solely by profit-seeking can have a destructive effect on financial markets ... The market alone – to put it frankly – will not correct these faulty developments. It is the job of politics – of parliaments and governments – to intervene and, when in doubt, to forbid [such behaviors], to render the risks surmountable.[55]

If greedy banks had not purchased toxic credit debt swaps master-minded by Wall Street, neither citizens nor governments would have been able to secure questionable loans allowing them to live far beyond their means. Unlike physics, markets do not rely on immutable laws but thrive instead on irrational behavior and risk-taking; they also depend on a subjective element: trust. Focusing on her home base, the chancellor "dithered for months with EU level support," inducing panic in the sovereign bond market that created a vicious circle: panic triggered austerity policies, which further widened bond-spread values between Germany and the debtor states, that were then used to justify demands for more austerity.[56]

By the end of stage one, the chancellor "controlled which crisis narrative would carry the day."[57] By refusing to accept bailouts until debtor countries agreed to her preferred structural reforms, however, Merkel underestimated the immediate trust issue. What began as a (containable) Greek insolvency problem morphed into a systemic crisis, as countries not previously affected plunged into debt ("the Merkel crash"), afflicting 40 percent of the Eurozone. At this point the chancellor realized, "this is our historical task; if the Euro fails, then Europe fails."[58] By that time the European financial crisis had already taken its toll on the Franco-German axis.

STAGE TWO: NORTHERN CREDITORS, SOUTHERN SCAPEGOATS, AND SOVEREIGN DEBT

If the Wall Street melt-down came as a "huge surprise," the next stage "came as an avalanche" not even anticipated by the rating agencies.[59] Germany's recovery from the unification doldrums allowed it to interpret the sovereign debt problem as the "crisis of others," separate from its real economy. Merkel was already preoccupied with an overhaul of national energy policy in the wake of Fukushima, with Putin's aggressive behavior in the Caucasus, as well as with constant wrangling among members of her own CDU/CSU–FDP government. By 2012, French debt would exceed 90 percent of GDP, unemployment would rise to 10.2 percent, and Sarkozy would lose his own job. His final months were reduced to the practice of "Merkel decides, France follows." The path from *Merkozy* to *Merkollande* was bound to be rocky.[60]

Already into her second term, the chancellor considered socialist President Hollande a novice, but he was immediately plunged into crucial decision-making over ECB powers, the European Stability Mechanism (ESM) financing, and Europeanizing banking rules. The two met near Reims on July 8, 2012, to kick-off a year-long celebration of the 1963 Friendship Treaty. Shortly thereafter they agreed to a mega-billion Euro rescue package at the Élysée Palace. France's immoveable national protectionism clashed with Germany's irresistible competitive advantage. What two French presidents deemed to be solidarity was viewed by Germans as a plot to have them pick up the bill for high Gaullist bank exposure to Mediterranean profligacy. "After repeated and bad-tempered clashes with the French president at a Brussels summit in the early hours of Friday morning," Merkel got her way: postponement of ECB banking supervision until 2014, coupled with legal provisions for a "Chinese Wall" between the ECB's supervisory and monetary powers.[61] She also won the battle to accord the Commission more power to monitor member state national budgets and fiscal policies via the European Semester.

With her own deficit under control, Merkel blocked the merger of the Franco-German EADS with British defense contractor BAE that could have jeopardized jobs in Bavaria. Berlin also refused to pay its €600 million share for the development of the new Airbus A350 wide-body jet, a liability the French had already paid.[62] Refusing to see itself as a debtor nation, France tried to refashion itself as the protector of southern European states, while Germany found allies among the creditor countries. Together they account for 48 percent of the Eurozone's combined GDP and ECB capital share (21 percent France, 27 percent FRG). Yet their role in pulling the Community out of financial quicksand was limited to "intermittent, occasional leadership when the sharp edges of opposing positions had to be softened and final compromises had to be brokered," a far cry from the innovative nature of past joint interventions.[63] Still, the collateral damage inflicted on the Franco-German relationship does not come close to the mass casualties the Euro crisis has imposed on Portugal, Italy, Ireland, Greece and Spain.[64]

The end of military dictatorship in 1974 had led Greece's newly elected leaders to engage in deficit spending to secure the trust of displaced elites by expanding public sector employment and limiting taxes on the wealthy (e.g., ship-building families). Modest welfare benefits were added to win the hearts and minds of citizens traumatized by years of civil war.[65] The decision to admit Greece to the European Community in 1981 was intended to foster democratic consolidation and economic development, a logic applied to Spain and Portugal shortly thereafter. Greek per capita income increased steadily, while registered unemployment hovered between 9 and 11 percent until 2007. Southern members were the primary beneficiaries of EU social and structural funds, enabling them to modernize production and reduce regional inequalities. EU programs had provided direct benefits to Greek women.[66] Developmental assistance shifted with the eastern enlargements of 2004–2005.

Household borrowing and consumption boomed once the Euro arrived in 2002. Though free of toxic assets, Greece saddled itself with excessive Summer Olympics (2004) costs and questionable military expenditures, while tolerating blatant tax evasion. Ironically, actors linked to Germany's military industrial complex refer to Greece as "our best customer." It spent €6 billion in 2000, and another €8.6 billion on weapons in 2008, equivalent to 3 percent of GDP (the NATO average is 1.7 percent); home to only 11 million, Greece continued to account for 15 percent of all German arms sales through 2011: it owns more tanks (mostly Leopards) than any other EU state.[67] Sovereign debt suddenly became a problem, when liquidity-stricken northern banks stopped lending to Greece in 2008.

The Troika has repeatedly blocked Greek efforts to cut defense spending, which actually falls outside its mandate. Yiannis Panagopoulos (GSEE trade union federation) reported:

After running through all the reasons why austerity wasn't working in my country I brought up the issue of defence expenditure. Was it right, I asked, that our government makes so many weapons purchases from Germany when it obviously couldn't afford such deals and was slashing wages and pensions? Merkel immediately responded: "But we never asked you to spend so much of your GDP on defence." She then mentioned the outstanding payments on submarines she said Germany had been owed for over a decade.[68]

By May 2010, violent street protests had erupted in Athens. The Troika promised €110 billion, under "very strict conditionality," solely for the purpose of debt-servicing. Fritz Scharpf claims that the extremely asymmetric nature of the bargaining between the creditor and debtor states "resembled ... an unconditional surrender."[69] All state bonds were placed under British law (not even in the Eurozone), requiring Greece to "voluntarily" surrender its national sovereignty to the lenders. As one analyst observed, "It's as if they were borrowing from a Mafia loan shark to repay an advance from their grandmother."[70]

Although the existing unemployment benefit fell well below the poverty line, the Greek government announced in April 2010 that it would reduce that budget by €500 million. In June 2011, the state placed 30,000 civil servants over 60 (100,000 by 2012) on "labor reserve," analogous to Germany's short-work approach to older Easterners after unification. Receiving 60 percent of their salary, those unable to find private sector jobs after twelve months were shifted to early (reduced) pensions; other pension cuts affected the incomes of multigenerational households. Although 22 percent earned only 83 percent of the European *average*, the IMF recommended a 15 percent wage cut for all workers and a 20 percent reduction in the *minimum* wage (€595 per month) for those under 24 – a moot point, given high youth unemployment. Public sector wages took a 25 percent hit.[71] While the poverty rate remained fairly steady between 1982 and 2008 (those depending on less than 60 percent of the *median* income), it rose to 22.9 percent in 2011, by which point the median income had declined by 12.2 percent. Another 31 percent were described as "at risk of poverty."[72]

In 2011, the standard VAT rate rose from 19 percent to 23 percent. While corporate tax rates declined from 40 percent (2000), to 24 percent (2010), to 20 percent (2012), taxable income thresholds for average citizens were lowered from €12,000 to €9,000, then to €5,000. A new property tax surcharge hit 5 million home owners; tax notices now arrive with electricity bills, and utilities are cut off in the event of non-payment, without means-testing. Contractors, professionals, and large companies find it easier to hide their earnings, costing the state an estimated €10–20 billion a year in lost revenues.[73] The Troika moreover forced the PASOK government to amend its labor law to shift national collective bargaining to firm-level negotiations; this deliberate strategy to undercut unions has been applied across the board.[74]

By July 2011, the Troika had released only €65 billion of the €110 billion promised, but the interest clock was already ticking. Further payment was postponed twice through March 2012, "due to a lack of progress." This contradicts Kevin Featherstone's documentation of a fivefold increase in reforms affecting financial management, auditing, performance evaluation, personnel, and reorganization adopted during those two years.[75] In 2011, Greek debt rose to €360 billion. The new plan was to bring it *down* to 120 percent of GDP (exceeding its pre-Troika ratio) by 2020. Greek debt has almost doubled since 2008 as a consequence of the conditionalities that were imposed in order to fix it.[76] The debt ratio stood close to 177 percent by the end of 2015. Tim Jones offers a sobering explanation as to why nothing had improved:

When the IMF, European and ECB bailouts began in 2010, €310 billion had been lent to the Greek government by reckless banks and the wider European financial sector. Since then, the "Troika" of the IMF, EU and European Central Bank have lent €252 billion to the Greek government. Of this, €34.5 billion of the bailout money was used to pay for various "sweeteners" to get the private sector to accept the 2012 debt restructuring. €48.2 billion was used to bailout Greek banks following the restructuring, which did not discriminate between Greek and foreign private lenders. €149.2 billion has been spent on paying the original debts and interest from reckless lenders. This means less than 10% of the money has reached the people of Greece.[77]

Playing again to her domestic audience, Merkel declared in spring 2011: "It is also about not being able to retire earlier in countries such as Greece, Spain, and Portugal than in Germany. Instead everyone should try a little bit to make the same efforts … we can't have a common currency where some get lots of vacation time and others very little."[78] As a cabinet member back in 1993, she should have recalled Kohl's derogatory comments on the declining work ethic among Germans themselves: "We cannot secure our future by organizing our country like a collective amusement park."[79] It is even more curious that the data-driven Merkel overlooked a few of her own policies: Germany did not raise its retirement age to 67 until 2007, lowering it again to 63 "for some" in 2014.[80]

Indeed, OECD statistics show that Germans, on average, retire earlier than their Mediterranean counterparts: in 2009, Merkel's male compatriots left work at 61.8 years of age, compared with Greek and Portuguese averages of 61.9 and 67, respectively. Prior to the crisis, Greek women retired from the *double* burden at 59.6, compared with 60.5 years among Germans; Eastern females overcompensate for lower employment rates among married Bavarian women. Their Spanish and Portuguese counterparts work three years longer. German laborers enjoy at least twenty days paid holiday per annum, or up to thirty days in "Catholic" states. Laborers in the *formal* economy get twenty-two vacation days in Portugal, twenty-one in Spain, and twenty in Greece (five more after ten years).[81]

In 2012, informal labor, devoid of paid vacation time, accounted for 24 percent of the GDP in Greece, and 19 percent in Spain and Portugal.[82]

Reportedly hurt by Greek media items featuring her with a Hitler mustache and a swastika armband, Merkel admits that the single currency has been a boon to German exports; she does not mention the direct profits her country accrues from Greek debt-servicing. Peter Simon, SPD vice-chair of the European Parliament's Committee on Economics and Finance, reported in June 2015 that Germany had already earned over €94 billion in interest on its short-term contributions (€221 billion) to the "rescue" packages.[83] It moreover benefits from a growing stream of young, skilled southern Europeans migrating for jobs. Local Spanish officials offer free German classes, to ease the welfare burden at home after bearing their higher educational costs; this spares German employers the need to raise wages for its nationals amid a skilled labor shortage. Today's brain drain will become tomorrow's lack of innovation and growth on the Iberian peninsula.

Also missing from this debate is the very expensive problem of caring for refugees; the number reaching Greek shores rose from 67,000 in 2014 to 163,000 by August 2015. When David Cameron attacked the "swarm" of 3,000 refugees hoping to enter the United Kingdom via Calais, the EU opted for a voluntary redistribution program encompassing merely 40,000 refugees (see Chapter 7).[84] Due to austerity cuts, many Greeks are unable to cover their own food, medical care, and sanitation costs; how can they pay to assist thousands of new arrivals, forced to "sleep rough" on Kos and Lesbos? No billionaires have stepped forward to buy those islands, despite the Troika's 2015 demand for "a veritable fire sale of state property." The privatization of ports, concessions, and other state holdings is expected to bring in €50 billion in five years, barely enough to pay the interest on the current Greek debt.[85]

National rescue packages introduced during stage one rapidly increased public deficits across the region. As Table 5.2 illustrates, Greece was not the only country increasing its public debt ratio during the crisis years.[86] By 2012, the *average* debt ratio among the seventeen Eurozone states exceeded 91 percent, up from 88 percent the year before. National figures range from over 100 percent in Belgium, Ireland, Greece, Italy, and Portugal, to less than 10 percent in Bulgaria and Estonia, although the latter hardly qualify as *Europe's Top Models* of fiscal accountability. Among the EU27, the ratio rose from 81.4 percent to 84.9 percent.[87] Sovereign bailouts have cost over a trillion Euros in cheap ECB loans (Long-Term Refinancing Operations). Here, too, the

TABLE 5.2 *Gross Public Debt relative to GDP, 2009–2012*

	Greece (%)	Spain (%)	Italy (%)	Portugal (%)	Germany (%)	Eurozone (%)	USA (%)
2009	129.4	53.9	116.0	83.1	74.4	79.9	90.4
2010	145.0	61.2	118.6	93.3	83.0	85.6	99.1
2011	165.3	68.5	120.1	107.8	81.2	88.0	103.5
2012	160.6	80.9	123.5	113.9	82.2	91.8	108.9

Source: European Commission: Statistical Annex of European Economy, Brussels, spring 2012, tables 78 and 79.

banks that borrowed money immediately returned 75 percent to the ECB as "insurance" instead of using it to extend domestic loans.

There was little evidence as of 2016 that the global financial system is any more sustainable now than it was before the crisis hit. More intent on penalizing than bolstering weak economies, austerity hounds ignore the fact that the need to pay high "risk premia" on short-term loans and bonds precludes training investments in youth (52 percent are jobless); this makes real growth impossible. The result has been a vicious circle of unsustainably high deficits, thwarted consolidation, violent protests, and a lot of human suffering.[88] Greece has been isolated, "bailed out ... then ring-fenced and ... firewalled," but the truth is, "Europe's debt zombies keep coming back to life in scarier forms."[89]

STAGE THREE: THE EURO CRISIS, THE TROIKA, AND THE EU
DEMOCRATIC DEFICIT

Saddled with the extraordinary costs of unification, Germany was hardly a model of fiscal prudence during the two decades preceding the 2008 Wall Street crash. National debt rose from 18.4 percent of GDP in 1959, to 41.8 percent in 1989, then to 60.3 percent by 1996; the Bundesbank ascribed DM 1.2 trillion of the DM 2.13 trillion total to unification. Public debt hit 81 percent of GDP by 2011.[90] Federal prosecutors have imposed substantial fines and CEO replacements on the Deutsche Bank, especially, for its unorthodox financial transactions, suggesting that corruption is not an innately southern phenomenon.[91]

The single currency emerged out of competing visions in response to the European malaise of the 1980s. While Commission President Jacques Delors wanted to infuse EU reforms with a real social dimension, German

Foreign Minister Hans-Dietrich Genscher hoped for political union. President François Mitterrand envisioned a monetary union that would weaken the hegemonic Bundesbank, yielding a Euro that was "a little less German and a little more French."[92] Helmut Kohl's desire to prove that Germany would remain a good European after unification led him to accept the French logic of *one market – one currency*, despite obvious gaps between the Community's hard and soft currency states.

Fearful that surrendering control of the D-Mark would endanger price stability, the *sine qua non* of ordo-liberalism, Germany wanted to ensure that "it would not have to share membership of the EMU [Economic and Monetary Union] with countries whose economic policy was, in some sense, grossly mismanaged. The budget deficit and government debt were the two best observable proxies for the somewhat hard to define notion of economic mismanagement."[93] Prior to 2008, the Maastricht criteria "had been breached many times by almost every single Eurozone member state without ever a sanction being imposed."[94]

Monetary union was expected to pressure laggard states into alleviating structural deficits and improving competitiveness, with the ECB (modeled on the Bundesbank) serving as watch-dog. Instead, the opposite occurred: the criteria comprised an "arithmetic formula, not a growth plan." Between 1999 and 2008, a uniform exchange rate and the convergence of nominal interest rates pushed Eurozone economies farther apart. As Fritz Scharpf observed,

In low-inflation Germany, real interest rates increased, domestic demand declined, unemployment escalated, and real wages fell. By contrast, real interest rates turned negative while domestic demand, employment, and nominal unit labor costs increased in Greece, Portugal, Spain, and Ireland (but not in Italy). Since the Monetary Union (EMU) had eliminated exchange-rate risks, the dramatic divergence of capital accounts was conveniently bridged by private capital flowing from surplus to deficit economies.[95]

As noted earlier, the 2009 elections replaced the Grand Coalition with a CDU/CSU–FDP government purportedly more favorable to Merkel, but concerns over an upcoming election in wealthy North Rhine-Westphalia kept her courting the domestic audience. The rhetoric shifted from "this-is-an-American-problem" to "this-is-a-Greek problem," coupled with sensationalized *Bild Zeitung* articles demanding that Greeks bail themselves out by selling off their islands. Meanwhile, the British press caricatured Merkel as a sexualized dominatrix. The CDU/CSU–FDP had a harder time getting its act together than her first Grand Coalition: Merkel preferred "small steps" to buy time, CDU Finance Minister Schäuble urged greater political union, the FDP demanded tax cuts, and the CSU resorted to anti-EU populism. Reactive crisis management became the least common denominator, although a pledge to help Greece regain access to credit markets "would have cost Germany nothing in practice, but it would have stabilized the Eurozone and laid the foundations for greater stability in the future."[96]

In this case, Merkel's tendency to let conditions ripen before deciding which way to head only exacerbated financial speculation. Scharpf noted that Germany did not agree to write-down Greek bonds "until Athens was already walking the plank"; it took a while for Merkel's experts "to realize that letting Greece go bankrupt might trigger speculative attacks on the solvency of other EMU member states whose economies had also become dependent on capital inflows – with the consequence that the Monetary Union itself might break apart on the fault line dividing surplus and deficit economies."[97] That occurrence would have threatened "the huge external-credit position which surplus economies had built up during the first decade of the Monetary Union," forcing those states to save their domestic banks again. Government officials and unions finally realized "that exports had greatly benefited from an undervalued real exchange rate, and that a collapse of the euro was likely to produce a major revaluation of nominal exchange rates and massive job losses."[98]

Merkel was increasingly at odds with Commission President José Manuel Barroso, whom she accused of supporting "Bazooka policies" in the form of Eurobonds. To restore market trust, and to prevent her own country from picking up most of the bill, Merkel insisted on IMF involvement, a sure sign that rescue credits would be tied to austerity-heavy conditionalities. The Constitutional Court ruled in September 2011 that neither the EU's temporary financial rescue plan, nor the ESM violated the Bundestag's right to adopt the budget and control its implementation. To render such guarantees compatible with the Basic Law, however, the government had to attain prior approval from the Budget Committee. The resignation of two chief economists, Axel Weber (Bundesbank) and Jürgen Stark (ECB), coupled with internal coalition disputes, led her to anticipate committee resistance. She thus "reinterpreted" the court's verdict after the November summit, submitting the ESM proposal to the Plenary Session, thereby securing Green opposition votes.[99] Now the leading lady on the EU stage, Merkel outlined her crisis management strategy in December 2011, calling for a "fiscal union," mandatory debt brakes across the Eurozone, Commission supervision of national budget plans, automatic sanctions, rejection of Eurobonds, and use of the ECB only as a lender of last resort.[100] In July 2015, sixty-five members of her own party voted against yet another Greek rescue package.

Neither the Community Method, requiring European Parliament consent, nor the Council's usual qualified majority vote (QMV) were used to set the conditions during this stage. Taking its place was "an entirely discretionary regime whose scope of delegated authority far exceeds the limits of generally allowable delegation in constitutional democracies."[101] Formerly limited to policy *initiation*, the Commission has experienced a dramatic increase in power under the Fiscal Compact, the Six-Pack, the Excessive Deficit Procedure, the ESM, and the European Semester. It now possesses "practically unlimited authority to investigate economic conditions in member states, to identify imbalances on a wide variety of indicators, to define some … as 'excessive', to recommend their correction through policy responses involving the full range of national competences, and to enforce these with severe sanctions – unless a [reversed] qualified majority of the Council should interfere."[102]

It is not surprising that ECB President Mario Draghi chose the *Wall Street Journal* to declare unilaterally in February 2012 that "the European Social Model is dead."[103] It is troubling, however, that someone who has never held electoral office believes he could do "whatever it takes" to override the democratic preferences of European voters in need of welfare services. The Fiscal Pact is a misnomer insofar as it dictates which fiscal policies and public services governments may *not* offer to stimulate their moribund economies, now that currency devaluation is no longer an option. The European Semester obliges the Commission to review national budgets *before* they are even communicated to their respective parliaments.[104]

It is one thing for Wolfgang Schäuble to accept sacrifices and conditionality rules for his own country. I concur with Scharpf, however, that there is "no normatively acceptable argument" for allowing a German minister, or chancellor, to impose discretionary orders and severe sanctions on somebody else's country without predetermined, democratic decision-making processes.[105] Former minister Yanis Varoufakis claims that Jeroen Dijsselbloem, presiding over the Euro-Group, shut him out of a meeting of EU finance ministers, with the argument that it was an "informal" session that permitted his exclusion.[106] For Greek citizens, "being ruled by the Euro group of the ECOFIN Council is not democratic self-government but the rule of foreign governments."[107] Never mind

Christine Lagarde's characterization of a duly elected Tsipras government, rejecting a take-it-or-leave it conditionality package, as little more
than children behaving badly.[108] The neo-liberal argument that public
debt alone, resulting from "too much spending" on welfare policies, has
stunted economic growth fails to explain the "30 golden years" of unprecedented prosperity that accompanied postwar social security regimes. It
also ignores the model most credited with postwar and post-Wall German
success: the social market economy.

This raises a second puzzle: this chancellor has pursued a pragmatic,
progressive approach to women's employment in her own country by
leveraging EU policies in relation to work–family reconciliation. She
even chose an iconic female figure, the Swabian housewife, to convey
the need for personal economic responsibility during the first stage of
the European crisis. She demonstrated no visible interest in upholding
broader EU gender equality mandates in relation to the austerity programs
that followed, however. What is Merkel missing when it comes to interpreting the wisdom of the Swabian housewife?

THE WISDOM OF THE SCHWÄBISCHE HAUSFRAU, REVISITED

In December 2008, Chancellor Merkel took advantage of a CDU convention in Stuttgart to frame the global financial crisis in local terms, applying
a gender metaphor:

All at once we're reading everywhere as to why the financial markets stood on
the brink of collapse, even [hearing] from people who shortly before had
recommended investments they didn't understand themselves. Actually it is all
very simple. Here in Stuttgart, in Baden-Württemberg, one would have only had to
ask a Swabian housewife. She would have given us a few short but accurate words
of wisdom, sounding like this: you can't live beyond your means for long periods.
That is the core of the crisis.[109]

The fact that Merkel stressed female logic in matters of money management shortly after the crisis commenced could be interpreted to mean that
she favors women's involvement in economic policy-making at all levels.
She has consistently included a critical mass of women in her three
cabinets, but with the exception of Lagarde, Troika negotiation sessions
were heavily male dominated. Prior to 2014, the ECB management team
consisted of twenty-one men and zero women. Heather McRobie is not
alone in questioning whether the hell-or-high water, profit-mongering,
and ruthless push for "competitiveness" witnessed over the last decade

owes itself to a peculiar type of masculinity: "Was the crisis caused by too much testosterone on Wall Street? One cannot deny the negative impact of gender inequity within the financial elite, but the predominant concern with the 'glass ceiling' for female investment bankers strikes an odd note when . . . most women are not even in the building."[110]

This did not stop *Der Spiegel* from featuring Merkel on its July 4, 2015 cover as Europe's proverbial *Trümmerfrau* with a subtitle reading, "If the Euro fails, Merkel's chancellorship fails." It is a bit curious that the entire burden for cleaning up the mess created by mostly male bankers, stock-traders, and national leaders should fall on Merkel's shoulders. But then it was the work of maniacal men like Hitler and Himmler who inflicted terrible suffering and destruction during the Second World War, leaving women behind to clean up that mess. Ranging in age from 15 to 50, the Rubble Women dug the defeated Reich out from under 400 million meters³ of rock and ash in heavily bombed German cities. Comprising two-thirds of the survivors in Berlin, 60,000 females were "recruited" to clear out and rebuild the nation, for which they received 60 cents per hour (70 cents for men), plus double monthly rations of fat, 100 grams of meat, and a half kilo of bread.[111] When they finished cleaning, they added 11 million children to the postwar population, credited with driving the Economic Miracle. The ideal of the Swabian wife as an unpaid, stay-at-home-mom with time to "work, work, work, and build a house," was tied to the restoration of traditional gender roles (*Kinder, Küche, Kirche*), made possible by a new economic boom.[112] When Merkel was mocked by reporters and bloggers for her homey 2008 analogy, Finance Minister Schäuble quickly declared that *his* mother had been a bona fide *schwäbische Hausfrau*.

Pundits intent on maligning either Merkel, southern homemakers, or both have clearly not kept up with the times. The German debate over care subsidies for "non-working" mothers, coupled with strong opposition to boardroom quotas for women, suggests that hardline conservatives and captains of industry feel more threatened by change than by crisis. Despite much empirical evidence to the contrary, they continue to insist that women prefer full-time, unpaid carework and economic dependency based on the bread-winner model. Women in their own parties, like Ursula von der Leyen, a mother of seven turned defense minister, are actually leading the charge for affordable childcare and the right to serve as political leaders, CEOs, and financial managers.[113]

Patrick Bernau, for example, published a very unflattering description of female Württembergers in the *Frankfurter Allgemeine Zeitung*, citing an old southern adage on how to test a potential Swabian bride: "If you gave her a block of cheese and she ate the rind, she was too unrefined. If she cut the whole rind off, she was wasteful. Only a girl who would carefully scrape the rind off the cheese was qualified to become a good Swabian wife."[114] Never mind the fact that her would-be Swabian husband probably did not bathe more than once a week, drank too much, and spent a lot of time hanging out in animal stalls back in the eighteenth century. Bernau did not explain why these alleged female simpletons opted for a progressive Green political makeover in 2012, replacing a state government in Baden-Württemberg that had been dominated by conservative men since 1949.

Jens Berger, author of *Stress Test Deutschland* (involving the banking crisis), moved the female icon into the twentieth century but rejected her as a role model for even a "halfway modern economy." Claiming Merkel was buying into the "cardinal mistake" of German economic thinking, he wrote: "the economic ideal of the Swabian housewife reinforces the tacky, petty bourgeois world-view that belongs to the stereotype of the classical CDU voting stratum, just like the row house with the little gnome statue spoiling the front yard."[115] Berger insists that a country full of ladies emulating those in the *Ländle* would stop the flow of money and credit dead in its tracks, bringing the economy to its knees in their refusal to purchase things they do not need:

If all members of an economy want to save and nobody wants to take on debt, then there is nobody who wants to have the money saved. They wouldn't need any more banks, there wouldn't be any savings books or accounts for allowances, or state loans and bonds, and then the Swabian housewife would be forced not to "save" her money but to "hoard" it. Let us assume that the spouse of the Swabian housewife, or at least this is what the cliché says, "works at Daimler." Suddenly there would not be any customers who would lease a Mercedes Benz or buy on credit; the number of sales would plunge and the Swabian housewife's spouse would have to be fired and spend the future drawing Hartz IV – but naturally only after the newly precarious Swabian family had first used up all of its savings.

Bernau argues along the same vein:

Very few politicians know what the life of a Swabian housewife is really like. It is very rarely luxurious ... Let's assume the state really cuts all of its expenditures. Pretty soon it will no longer buy any more service cars for its top officials. That will irritate not only the top officials who will have to drive around in older cars – but also the car makers who will sell fewer automobiles and perhaps have to let workers go. Or the state will not renovate the kindergartens: then handworkers will have fewer contracts and take on fewer apprentices. Many positions will disappear, people will not have jobs, so they will also save. Now it's the turn of small shop owners in the city where suddenly there will be no customers.

This is exactly the kind of male-dichotomous thinking that drives neo-liberal austerity policies that keep Europe's "debt zombies ... coming back to life." It also highlights the fallacy of all-or-nothing economic thinking: had the Kohl government invested generously in childcare following unification, Germany would not be facing a looming demographic crisis and a shortage of skilled workers today. The Maastricht stability criteria never mandated deficit- or debt-free balance sheets, nor did the "savers" trigger the 2008 financial crisis; the culprits were bankers greedy for short-term gain who took enormous risks on "financial products" they knew nothing about. It is not women who clip coupons and make soup out of leftovers who starve state coffers, but rather millionaires and billionaires who hide their money in secret Swiss accounts, off-shore tax-shelters, or in Commission President Juncker's home state of Luxembourg, to avoid paying their fair share of taxes.

Even after IMF chief Lagarde secured a CD listing major tax-evaders by name in 2010, national governments were slow to react. The share of wealthy Greek depositors seeking alternative havens for their money grew by 27.9 percent in May, following a 47.2 percent rise in April 2015.[116] By contrast, North Rhine-Westphalian authorities announced in April 2016 that they had already *recovered* €600 million in fines and penalties from such evaders. One could also note that corruption at Volkswagen was more likely to cause job losses among car makers than household thrift; in fact, Daimler AG reported in 2012 that its luxury car sales rose by €27 billion (9 percent), as did "unanticipated" profits, up 4.9 percent over 2011.[117]

As Scharpf, Matthijis, and others attest, there are good reasons to criticize Merkel's performance in this domain, but her use of a gendered metaphor is not one of them. Rather than imply that all people should avoid all spending all of the time, she said: "You can't live beyond your means *for long periods.*" In order for banks to engage in sound lending practices, some people have to save: that is the essence of banking. As John Maynard Keynes further determined, in times of crisis, savings are not enough; the state occasionally needs to "prime the pump" to secure the common good: that is the essence of the social market economy. Merkel's own "cash for clunkers" program provided €5 billion in subsidies to the automotive industry in 2008. Once Wall Street excesses, fraudulent bank dealings, and the need for massive bailouts made the news, CEOs like Josef Ackermann (Deutsche Bank) began to discover their own inner-*Hausfrau*, leading one female economist to question, "Why isn't Mrs. Ackermann in the board room?"[118]

Nor are Swabian housewives the austerity poster-girls of yesteryear; they are better educated, socially engaged, savvy if thrifty consumers. The Cultural Association of Swabian Housewives website offers workshops on Facebook/Internet safety for children, along with seminars on local history, health, homes, gardens, environmental and consumer protection.[119] The Memmingen chapter describes itself as "a team of entrepreneurs, alternative medicine specialists, physiotherapists, nutrition counselors, yoga instructors, English teachers, economics and finance advisors, insurance saleswomen and 'naturally also always *Hausfrauen*' and *Hausmänner*." They use credit cards sparingly (mostly while on vacation) and save prodigiously, as do their husbands, to cover a third of a home's value when they apply for mortgages – no subprime crisis in this region! Their reluctance to live wildly beyond their means does not preclude their enjoyment of "the good life."

As Julia Kollewe discovered in Gerlingen, Swabian women buy quality goods from local producers, avoiding preservatives and genetically modified organisms (GMOs) at farmers' markets. They still recycle stale bread into dumplings but they now drive Mercedes, own flat-screen TVs, and fur coats (which they sometimes wear inside out, "so as not to appear ostentatiously rich"). They offer "master housewife" training courses across an assortment of hospitals, nurseries, elder-care homes, and rehabilitation centers. They organize organic food cooperatives, lobby for schools, and invest more in their own pensions than most Germans. Gerlingen's 20,000 inhabitants control more purchasing power than any other town in Baden-Württemberg, an estimated €500 million a year; their spouses work for Bosch and Daimler, neither of which required a bailout. While they do not all qualify for "the top 1 percent," these women do share a belief that supporting families, promoting healthy consumption, investing in human capital, saving to make ends meet, and assuming personal responsibility are great for economic growth and stability.[120]

At the personal level, Merkel is also a woman who lives within her means. While many German politicians are drawn to Mallorca or Tuscany, she still visits the weekend house in the Uckermark that she acquired before becoming chancellor. When she bakes for her spouse, he complains that she "doesn't put enough crumbles" on the cake (his father was a pastry specialist). She is proud of her *Pflaumenkuchen* (plum cake) and potato soup, and even serves soup at official gatherings, including her first inauguration. She did splurge a bit for her fiftieth and sixtieth birthday celebrations, however, inviting hundreds of guests to hear top-notch scientific lectures. One of the world's most powerful leaders, she lives in a central Berlin apartment close to the Museum Island, relying on one housekeeper and a few police at the street entrance; her husband does most of the grocery shopping, but she is occasionally sighted at Ulrich HIT market, a discount store in *Stadtmitte*; she even took Chinese Prime Minister Li Keqiang there for a visit.[121] The chancellor buys long-lasting blazers – "not especially cheap but also not luxurious" – from designer Bettina Schönbach, based in Hamburg. She has never been sighted wearing Prada or carrying a Gucci handbag. Wall Street, DAX, and FTSE managers, Greek, Italian, and Irish politicians, IMF and ECB directors could all learn a lot from these women. But this still leaves us with the puzzle as to why a pragmatic politician like Merkel opted for such a hardline, principled austerity approach to the countries constituting the weakest link in a very faulty lending chain.

ASSESSING THE IMPACT OF FINANCIAL CRISES: GENDER BLIND ǂ GENDER NEUTRAL

If the terms descriptive and substantive representation are to have real-world meaning, then they must be applied at all levels where policies are formulated. Given the supranational nature of the Euro, we also have to assess the impact of Merkel's hard-won policies regulating its use beyond her own boundaries. One further needs to consider potential EU rules that might have restricted the chancellor's policy options. I argue here that, rather than limit her choices, EU mandates should have *expanded* her room for maneuver; instead, she yielded to domestic electoral pressures and an uncharacteristic focus on a few key variables at the expense of the larger "energy field."

The European Community's obligation to ensure equal pay for equal work dates back to Article 119 of the Treaty of Rome, ratified in 1957. By the late 1990s, gender equality in all of its facets had been declared "a core EU value," reinforced by its inclusion in the Amsterdam Treaty, the Lisbon Treaty, and the Charter of Fundamental Rights. Its primary law status obliges key Community organs, that is, the Commission, the Council, and the European Parliament, to actively *promote* equality between the sexes.[122]

Angela Merkel was just finishing her term as Minister for Women and Family in 1994, when Belgian feminist Sabine de Bethune issued the first report on female participation in the Community's own institutions. The unflattering portrait compiled by the "Women in Decision-making Network" she coordinated led the Commission to create the European Women's Lobby which pushed, in turn, for the adoption of gender mainstreaming (GM) in 1996. Anchored in the *acquis*, GM helped a new generation of EU equality experts to prove that few public policies are as gender neutral as traditional decision-makers like to claim. GM addresses both the descriptive and substantive dimensions of representation. It aims to secure the "balanced participation of women and men" at every stage of the policy-making process across all sectors, as well as ensuring (at a minimum) that neither group is disproportionately affected in negative ways. EU officials must call upon specially trained experts to conduct a formal "gender impact assessment" utilizing sex-disaggregated data before they adopt *any* program requiring Community funding. The GM mandate likewise applies to all member states. It is the Commission's responsibility to undertake potential equality interventions, for example, in relation to the EU budget.[123]

Presiding over the Commission from 2004 to 2014, José Manuel Barroso resolutely ignored his duty to uphold the gender *acquis* throughout the Euro crisis; his successor, Jean-Claude Juncker, has performed no better. In fact, Juncker served for nineteen years as Luxembourg's prime minister, rendering him partly responsible for systematic efforts to render his country a safe harbor for corporate tax evaders, as revealed in the "Lux-Leaks" scandal.[124] The chancellor supported the appointment of both Commission presidents, only to be disappointed by their respective lack of resoluteness regarding both the Euro crisis and the 2016 Brexit vote.[125]

First, Barroso used the distraction created by the financial crisis to dismantle gender equality "machinery" that had been specifically designed to foster gender consciousness and equality initiatives at the top. Women accounted for only 33 percent of the Commissioners during his two terms. In 2010, when gender perspectives might have prevented increasingly precarious conditions for women, Barroso eliminated the High Group of Commissioners on Gender Equality created in 1995.[126] Although the Europe 2020 strategy calls for raising female labor market participation to 75 percent, he transferred the Gender Equality Unit from its very effective historical base in the Directorate-General of Employment to the weaker Directorate-General of Justice. The share of funds specifically allocated for gender equality initiatives declined from 0.20 percent of the EU budget in 1999 to 0.03 percent in 2012.[127] As former EU insiders Agnès Hubert and Maria Stratigaki report, major monitoring tools introduced during the crisis, like the Annual Growth Survey and European Semester, hardly mention women. The EU Pact for Gender Equality (2011–2020) exhorts member states to use their National Reform Plans (NRPs) to incorporate targeted policies, especially regarding Employment Guidelines, and "to make appropriate use of agreed gender equality indicators developed within the Joint Assessment Framework ..."[128] Yet the Commission rarely includes such measures in its Country Specific Recommendations.[129]

One woman joined five men on the ECB Executive Board in 2014; as of this writing, its Governing Council consists of two females and twenty-three males. Given the dearth of women at the Troika table, it is even more troubling that gender-watchdog organs at lower levels have faced draconian cuts or elimination, contravening an EU obligation to *establish* member state equality agencies.[130] In 2011, Spain abolished its Ministry for Equality (created in 2008), along with related regional monitoring and service institutions. Established in 2007 to meet gender *acquis* requirements, Romania's National Agency for Equal Opportunities ceased operations in 2009. Ireland cut the Equality Authority's budget by 40 percent (from €5.5 to €3.3 million), then shut down the Women's Health Council and Crisis Pregnancy Agency.

Contemporary austerity programs also violate the EU's equal pay imperative dating back to 1957, reinforced by ECJ case law. The average EU pay gap stood at 16 percent in 2011, exceeding 21 percent even in wealthy Germany. Mediterranean states dominate the crisis headlines, but Latvia's minimum statutory salary for teachers (80 percent female) dropped to €6,000 per year, a 30 percent cut since 2008; short-term workers in Portugal now receive €4 per hour, €2 less than in 2011.[131] Cuts in "needless state spending" on social services have re-privatized care, contravening other EU mandates. The Gender Equality Pact calls for *increases* in affordable childcare through 2020, but Greek and Portuguese cuts shut down public kindergartens. Italy reduced full-time primary classes and after-school care, crucial for solo parents; even Dutch authorities reduced tax benefits for childcare users. In 2010, 28 percent of women's "inactivity" was attributed to a lack of care services, highlighting another paradox: "First, women are pushed out of the workforce at the same time as the mother is exalted as a key 'community' figure in conservative discourse. Then, state provisions are rolled back, resulting in women facing gender-specific challenges even as they do precisely what conservatism is demanding of them: being a mother."[132]

Introduced in 2010, the European Semester (ES) expands the Commission's power to "recommend" macro-economic allocations to member states commensurate with Europe 2020 targets. Governments are supposed to apply Community priorities in designing their NRPs, based on feedback from regional and local authorities, social partners, and stakeholders; women's organizations are rarely included. The Commission evaluates national budgetary plans submitted in April, then issues Country-Specific Recommendations (CSRs) in May–June. The European Council formally endorses the CSRs by June–July, which member states use to draft their next budgets in the autumn. Beyond a lack of political will, there is no logical reason to exclude gender-specific data from the ES process, for example, increases in unpaid work, elimination of public sector jobs, lower wages, cutbacks in child- and elder-care services. This is exactly what gender mainstreaming requires. Instead, the Commission has used its ES powers to strike national budget lines that serve these ends. This makes no sense.[133]

It is also hard to reconcile with the EU's own push, initiated by Commissioner Viviane Redding in 2012, to adopt a 40 percent quota to increase women's presence on "non-executive" boards in publicly listed companies.[134] The Commission stressed three reasons for this initiative, citing evidence of improved company performance; a need to "mirror the market" while improving corporate governance and ethics; and making better use of a "neglected" talent pool in response to demographic changes.[135] A 2007 Catalyst study found that Fortune 500 companies with female board members saw an 83 percent higher return on equity, 73 percent more in sales, and a 112 percent rise in invested capital. McKinsey & Co. found a 41 percent higher return on equity for companies with the largest share of female board members.[136] Accounting for 80 percent of daily household purchasing, women are essential contributors to stability and growth. The Commission is clearly not practicing what it preaches with respect to the balanced participation of women and men in its own economic decision-making.

Despite Merkel's authoritative role in Euro crisis deliberations, German financial institutions are no more gender balanced than the Commission. SPD Chancellor Schröder opposed efforts by his own cabinet members to mainstream gender.[137] Neither Merkel's 2005 Grand Coalition nor her 2009 conservative–liberal government pushed for more than "voluntary efforts" among corporations. CDU Labor

Minister Ursula von der Leyen was vehemently opposed by Women's Minister Kristine Schröder, and the chancellor, when she first tried to introduce a mandatory quota: women held only 3.2 percent of the board seats in Germany's 200 largest publicly traded companies, 2.2 percent among the top 100 at the time.[138] Once the Euro crisis had crested, Merkel nonetheless overrode opponents back home, introducing a three-pillar 30 percent quote for women in corporate and public service management, effective 2016.[139] Better late than never?

CONCLUSION: LOOKING FOR BALANCE BETWEEN MARKET AND COMMUNITY

As Bezya Tekin observes, "crisis periods accelerate identity (re)negotiations, forcing political communities to reconsider themselves ... and bring change in self-perceptions, as well as norms and institutions."[140] Despite her preference for data-driven policies and holistic approaches to problems back home, the World's Most Powerful Woman has remained singularly fixated on structural remedies that have disproportionately hurt females beyond German borders. Her penchant for "following the rules" has not included a host of EU hard- and soft-law provisions that would have required a mixed strategy ensuring that low-paid women, dependent on state pensions, for example, were protected from cuts. While some critics argue that the single currency was a "premature birth" or a "miscarriage" from the start, the bigger problem rests with an ideologically driven notion of *growth*, rooted in the so-called Washington Consensus.[141] Instead of concentrating on job creation, human capital investments, and redistributive taxation, neo-liberals obsess over shareholder value, short-term profits, and cutting "the costs" of human labor. Their insistence that governments eliminate "wasteful" welfare expenditures ignores the fact these programs were installed after the Great Depression for the very purpose of sustaining consumption across major crisis periods.

Triggered by Wall Street excesses, financial deregulation, globalized borrowing, and the rise of banks "too big to fail," the Euro crisis has undermined many Community policies and processes that secured peace and prosperity for sixty years. Generational change, diverging experiences with migration, Eastern enlargements, and the rise of spoiler parties using the European Parliament as a soapbox for domestic discontent have also chipped away at national leaders' ability to keep their eyes on the integration prize. The Franco-German friendship worked best when it was guided by shared historical memories and a value commitment to "peace at any price." Given the size of their respective economies, cooperation between the two is a necessary but no longer sufficient guarantor of an effective, forward-looking Community. Although they still function as first-responders in times of crisis, the EU's two founding members now represent a geographical divide: France identifies itself as part of a North–South linchpin pushing solidarity; Germany wants to bridge East–West "competitiveness" gaps by way of structural reform.

During the first stage of the financial crisis, Chancellor Merkel blamed "irresponsible bankers for what they had unleashed into the world."[142] She sought tougher regulation of financial institutions, coupled with a transaction tax on risky trades. By 2011, Volker Kauder had declared, too optimistically, "Now all of a sudden, Europe is speaking German ... not as a language, but in its acceptance of the instruments for which Angela Merkel has fought so hard, and with success at the end."[143] As the crisis unfolded, it became clear that Europe not only had a deficit/debt problem but also deeper governance problems. Merkel came to prefer a "stability union" resting on a common approach to financial policy, fiscal policy, and economic policy, along with greater "democratic authority."[144] The paradox is that she has advanced the first three by undercutting the fourth. Her interest in reshaping the European Council as a "second chamber" underestimated the European Parliament's long struggle to democratize the EU by enhancing its own co-decision powers.

The Lisbon Treaty, credited to Merkel, aimed to enhance parliamentary powers at both levels.[145] The Troika, however, has pushed aside the EU's only directly elected body and uses the European Semester to supersede the democratically legitimated appropriations of national legislatures. The monetarist approach to saving the Euro deliberately "bypassed the Community Method in favor of asymmetric bargaining between creditor and debtor states. When those emergency measures, adopted in disregard of the Maastricht rules, were followed by institutional reforms, the new euro regime even abandoned the pretense of relying on political consensus in the Council."[146] The Troika has stripped Eurozone states of long-established mechanisms of parliamentary control, revealing "the unprecedented power of unaccountable international financial institutions, banks and agencies to shape the dynamics of government bond markets across the globe, and therefore, the trajectories of national and regional political economies."[147]

The Euro crisis moreover attests to the limits of monetary policy, which allows a restricted circle of non-elected experts to pursue macro-economic stability in response to short-term imbalances. The aim of fiscal policy, by contrast, is to guarantee the *long-term* well-being of all citizens who are supposed to debate and decide their respective merits at regular intervals. Voter outrage over policies inflicted by non-democratic elites "high above and far away" since 2009 has injected Euroskeptical and even Europhobic parties into "the participatory heart" of the Community, challenging the integration project per se. Should the Troika's socially-blind austerity policies plunge the Community into a broader existential crisis, we should hope, along with Scharpf, "that the response will not again be about saving the euro. It should be about saving Europe."[148]

Irish Times reporter Derek Scally claimed that the logic behind Merkel's approach "is not far from Margaret Thatcher's legendary put-down of socialism: eventually you run out of other people's money."[149] The chancellor personally rejects comparisons with Thatcher, and her policies in other domains invalidate the analogy. She is a long way from dismantling the German social security state, and clearly prefers ordo-liberalism to the erratic financial Darwinism of Fleet Street. Scally also contends her "method" consists primarily of reverse-engineering:

Dr. Merkel claims, somewhat disingenuously but not entirely incorrectly, that she has been calling for growth measures since January [2012]. The point is this: what the lady wants is what she thinks she can get – and, then, usually on her terms. If what she thinks she can get shifts – for instance, a change in Europe's political wind – she simply alters course and claims she always wanted that, while keeping her eye on a long-term path.

He nonetheless concluded, "In any other situation, with anyone other than Dr. Merkel, that would be considered good negotiation."

Bloomberg correspondents Alan Crawford and Tony Czuczka also accuse her of offering "a steady series of speeches that shift and hone her position as events evolve," instead of one highly-orchestrated, dramatic statement driving a vision for Europe.[150] After thirty-five years of GDR life, imposing a single, "highly orchestrated" vision on 510 million Europeans is the last thing Merkel would want to do. Mariam Lau, by contrast, describes the chancellor as perhaps "Germany's last *real* conservative ... who is very stingy about spending the money of other people, as if it were a part of herself ... managers, whose miscalculations cost countless workplaces but whose bonuses remain untouched; a complete decoupling of accomplishment from profit-mongering, all that is frivolous to a fiscally political conservative."[151]

Pursuing small steps until she can figure out which way a crisis is heading is nothing new for Merkel. Having read Kondratieff while on a mid-crisis vacation, she has a deep appreciation for cycles, thus her long-term goal is to crisis-proof the Eurozone through "rules" that preclude the need for future bailouts bankrolled by Berlin. The problem in this case is that financial ups and downs are not subject to immutable laws that would allow a physicist to recalibrate her methodology based on predictable reactions to positive and negative particle shifts. Nor are financial markets driven by rational actors, no matter how often economists repeat this claim.

Markets are about trust, consumer confidence, and other elements of human psychology that can easily be manipulated by media histrionics. Stockmarket gurus once spent weeks parsing Allan Greenspan's 1996 reference to their own "irrational exuberance."[152] This is one place where waiting for the dust to settle on the main variables did not work for Merkel: analysts now admit that an early bailout for Greece's 2008 insolvency problem, coupled with demands that private creditors pay the price for *their* speculative losses, could have stopped that country from tail-spinning into an ever deeper crisis. Merkel's statements shoring up citizen trust at home fueled fears across global financial markets, waiting for her to "lead." The turning point came in 2012: declaring that he would "do whatever it takes to save the euro ... and believe me, it will be enough," Mario Draghi transcended the ECB's very "narrow reading of its price stability mandate" with two rounds of long-term refinancing operations; he did not solve the bigger problem but he did calm the market long enough for political leaders to consider other options.

There is no single answer as to why, in this case, the chancellor committed early on to a particular course and then refused to deviate as it became clear that the cure was exacerbating the disease. I can only point to four situational factors that complicated her decision-making processes. The first centers on the multi-level nature of the crisis; a second was the speed with which it unfolded; a third element involved a partisan shift in the composition of her government; coupled with, fourth, a heavy dose of economic crisis fatigue tied to the extraordinary costs of unification. Nor should we forget that by 2011 she was busy putting her physicist skills to work, enacting a major energy turn-around after the Fukushima Daiichi melt-down.

German insistence on price stability is rooted in negative national experiences stretching from the Weimar Republic to the Great Depression, ending in the Nazi regime.[153] Merkel had little exposure to inflationary concerns during her thirty-five years under a socialist command-economy; she also lacked her predecessors' personal attachments to France and the European Community. She looked first to Germany's "national interest" or, as seen in her relations with Russia and Israel, to "national responsibility." Some of her earlier moves, for example, her 2003 Leipzig speech, her choice of Paul Kirchhof as finance minister right before the 2005 elections, and an ill-fated attempt to have ex-Bundesbank president Hans Tietmeyer chair her national advisory council suggest that economics was not her strong suit.[154] Only three years into her first term in 2008, she found it hard to resist the "no bailout" orthodoxy of her own stability hawks. By the time she discovered her inner-European ("if the Euro fails, then Europe fails"), the Merkozy relationship was also on the rocks, forcing her to go it alone as the head of the EU's strongest economy.

Second, the speed with which the banking crisis hit undercut her usual practice of mastering the details and waiting for patterns to emerge before making a decision. In contrast to earlier Wall Street fiascos (1929, 1987), this one was magnified by the instantaneous power of the Internet, which globalized the impact of collapsing financial institutions literally over night. There were no familiar data for Merkel to assess at the outset, given the murky, financial transactions and toxic assets that triggered the collapse; she could not look into the books until her own banks came begging for help. She spent long nights mastering those instruments, and equally long nights hammering out short-term compromises with other EU leaders through 2010, based on Germany's traditional aversion to monetary instability.

Another problem was that Merkel did not realize that conservatives and social democrats followed ordo-liberalism using different measures and means. Kohl relied heavily on "savings packages," while Schröder injected "a serious dose of ordo-liberal, market-enhancing competition," by matching structural reforms with active labor market policies. Electoral politics moreover redefined the decision-making context: stage one of the crisis coincided with Merkel's first Grand Coalition, when both the finance and labor portfolios were held by SPD ministers who supported fiscal stimuli at home. Stage two was dominated by a conservative–liberal government, with two FDP economics ministers and (Kohl ally) Wolfgang Schäuble running the finance ministry; he continued in that post during Merkel's second Grand Coalition, taking a hard line on austerity and balanced budgets.

Perhaps Merkel also embraced austerity conditions that her own citizens would have rejected to circumvent the internal party resistance she had faced during her first term: CDU/CSU hardliners had characterized their first female chancellor as a "secret leftist," due to her economic caution. Signs of weakness at home would have undermined her ability to stay the course with regard to structural reforms at the EU level. This makes it all the more ironic that she was forced to rely on Social Democrats and opposition Greens to secure Bundestag approval for the hard-driving conditionality of subsequent rescue packages – which those two parties should have rejected had they been true to their own ideological roots. By stage three, tough SPD reforms imposed by Schröder were pulling Germany out of a recession exacerbated by big unification debts that had been incurred by conservative Kohl. Merkel's constituents had no stomach for another decade of "solidarity taxes."

It might be a stretch to attribute Merkel's tendency to reduce the debt problems of weaker states to "moral hazards" necessitating iron-clad rules to her upbringing as a pastor's daughter. Framing the crisis as a tale of "Northern saints" and "Southern sinners" nonetheless allowed her to apply familiar values – free will, individual responsibility, modesty, and living within one's means – to a complex web of bad behaviors at many levels. Another outcome was her realization, better late than never, that integrating and unifying the region "was, is and remains the most consistent, the greatest and the most promising idea that Europe has ever seen. It is the legacy of the political generation that preceded us. It is the task of our political generation today to protect this legacy and to make this century the century of Europe."[155]

Her respect for the Swabian housewife notwithstanding, Merkel has drawn at least one very significant gender conclusion from the financial mess she was forced to clean up: the need to increase women's presence across corporate, banking, and financial management boards. That is only the tip of the proverbial iceberg: the EU needs to follow its own rules mandating the balanced participation of women and men in all facets of its own decision-making. As Stanford economist, Paul Romer, stressed at a 2004 venture-capitalist meeting: "A crisis is a terrible thing to waste."[156]

NOTES

1. Sarkozy's open-mike comment of October 4, 2008 was more graphic: "You know what she said to me? "*Chacun sa merde!*" ("To each his own shit!"), cited in Carlo Bastasin, *Saving Europe: Anatomy of a Dream* (Washington, DC: Brookings Institution, 2015), p. 1.

2. Bastasin, *Saving Europe*, p. 17; "Europe sees Three Bank Bailouts in Two Days," *Der Spiegel*, September 29, 2008.

3. I experienced *Kehrwoche* in 1983–1984: rotating weekly, each household in my Stuttgart apartment complex was required to sweep the entrance hall and stairs for the whole building.

4. Kurt Hübner, "German Crisis Management and Leadership: From Ignorance to Procrastination to Action," *Asia Europe Journal*, 9(2) (2012): 159–177; also, Waltraud Schelkle, "A Tale of Two Crises: The Euro Area in 2008/09 and in 2010," *European Political Science*, 10 (2011): 375–383.

5. Jill Rubery and M. Karamessini (eds.), *Women and Austerity: The Economic Crisis and the Future for Gender Equality* (Abingdon: Routledge, 2013).

6. Chelsea Brown, "Democracy's Friend or Foe? The Effects of Recent IMF Conditional Lending in Latin America," *International Political Science Review*, 30(4) (2009): 431–457.

7. The IMF's first female director assumed her post after Strauss-Kahn was charged with rape and engaging with prostitutes at official functions.

8. Mushaben, "The Politics of Critical Acts"; see further Dahlerup, "The Story of the Theory of Critical Mass."

9. Geraldine Dany, Reint E. Gropp, Helge Littke, and Gregor von Schweinitz, *Germany's Benefit from the Greek Crisis* (Halle: Leibniz Institut für Wirtschaftsforschung, August 10, 2015), available at: www.iwh-halle.de/d/pu blik/iwhonline/io_2015-07.pdf.

10. Matthias Matthijs, "Powerful Rules Governing the Euro: The Perverse Logic of German Ideas," *Journal of European Public Policy*, 23(3) (2016), p. 377.

11. Ibid., p. 388.

12. Ibid., p. 376.

13. Simon, *Administrative Behavior*.

14. Werner Bonefeld, "Freedom and the Strong State: On German Ordoliberalism," *New Political Economy*, 17(5) (2012): 633–656.

15. Cited in Lau, *Die Letzte Volkspartei*, p. 20.

16. All quotes stem from the Economics Ministry website at: www.bmwi.de/EN/Topics/Economy/social-market-economy.html.

17. Albrecht Ritschl, "Germany, Greece and the Marshall Plan," *Economist*, June 15, 2012.

18. Ibid.

19. Andrei Markovits, *The Politics of the West German Trade Unions: Strategies of Class and Interest Representation in Growth and Crisis* (Cambridge University Press, 1986).

20. "Finanzen: 'Da fällt die Guillotine,'" *Der Spiegel*, August 7, 1995, pp. 40–43.

21. Stefan Berg, Steffen Winter, and Andreas Wassermann, "Germany's Eastern Burden: The Price of a Failed Reunification," *Der Spiegel*, September 5, 2005.

22. Wolfgang Thierse, cited in Christoph Dieckmann, "Ostdeutschland steht auf der Kippe: Identitätskrise, mehr Arbeitslose, wirtschaftliche Abkoppelung," *Die Zeit*, January 14, 2001.
23. Daniela Dahn, *Wir bleiben hier oder Wem gehört der Osten: Vom Kampf um Häuser und Wohnungen in den neuen Bundesländern* (Berlin: Rowohlt, 1994).
24. Cited in John Pfeffer, "The Costs of German Reunification," *Huffington Post*, November 12, 2014.
25. "Verstoß gegen EU-Defizitgrenze: Rückfalltäter Deutschland," *Süddeutsche Zeitung*, May 17, 2010.
26. Wolfgang Streek and Lea Elsässer, "Monetary Disunion: the Domestic Politics of Euroland," Max Planck Institute for the Study of Societies 14/17, Cologne, 2014, p. 17, available at: www.mpifg.de/pu/mpifg_dp/dp14-17 .pdf.
27. "Cost of Unification/Made in Germany: Fall of the Wall, 25th Anniversary," Deutsche Welle report, November 5, 2014, available at: www.youtube.com/ watch?v=A4v3zeDKjNM.
28. Regierungserklärung von Bundeskanzlerin Merkel, 29. January 2014, available at: www.bundesregierung.de/Content/DE/Regierungserklaerung/2014/ 2014-01-29-bt-merkel.html.
29. Konstantin von Hammerstein and Rene Pfister, "A Cold Heart For Europe: Merkel's Dispassionate Approach to the Euro Crisis," *Der Spiegel*, December 12, 2012.
30. Hubert Zimmermann, "No Country for the Market: The Regulation of Finance in Germany after the Crisis," *German Politics*, 21(4) (2012): 484–501.
31. Josh Fineman and Yalman Onaran, "Lehman Brothers' Corporate History and Chronology: Timeline," *Bloomberg News*, September 15, 2008.
32. Angelo Mozilo of Countrywide Financial coined the term "toxic" in reference to worthless mortgage products. On April 17, 2006, he expressed shock at his own company's "80/20" loans: "In all my years in the business I have never seen a more toxic product."
33. Andrew Ross Sorkin, "Five Years after TARP, Misgivings on Bonuses," *New York Times*, August 26, 2013.
34. William A. Allen and Richhild Moessner, "The Liquidity Consequences of the Euro Area Sovereign Debt Crisis," Bank for International Settlements (BIS) Working Paper No. 390, October 2012.
35. Huw Macartney, *The Debt Crisis and European Democratic Legitimacy* (Basingstoke: Palgrave, 2013), p. 27.
36. By 2013, the four largest US banks (JP Morgan Chase & Co., Bank of America Corp., Citigroup Inc., Wells Fargo & Co.) were roughly US$2 trillion bigger than prior to the 2008 bailouts. See Cheyenne Hopkins, "Too-Big-to-Fail Bill Seen as Fix for Dodd–Frank Act's Flaws," *Washington Post*, April 24, 2013.
37. Cited in "The World from Berlin: Germany will Pay a High Price for US Sins," *Spiegel-International*, September 26, 2008; "Europe Sees Three Bank Bailouts in Two Days," *Spiegel-International*, September 29, 2008.

38. Markus Feldenkirchen, with Dirk Kurbjuweit, Alexander Neubacher et al., "Madam No," *Spiegel International,* December 1, 2008.
39. Cited by Hübner, "German Crisis Management," p. 162.
40. Margaret Heckel, *So regiert die Kanzlerin. Eine Reportage* (Munich: Piper, 2009), p. 65.
41. Mishra, *Angela Merkel – Machtworte,* p. 51.
42. Wittlinger, *German National Identity in the Twenty-first Century.*
43. Ralf Neukirch, Mathieu von Rohr, Michael Sauga et al., "Parallel Universes in Paris and Berlin: Is the Franco-German Axis Kaput?" *Der Spiegel,* October 22, 2012.
44. John Gaffney, "Leadership and Style in the French Fifth Republic: Nicolas Sarkozy's Presidency in Historical and Cultural Perspective," *French Politics,* 10(4) (2012), p. 349.
45. Ben Clift and Magnus Ryner, "Joined at the Hip, but Pulling Apart? Franco-German Relations, the Eurozone Crisis and the Politics of Austerity," *French Politics,* 12(2) (2014): 136–163.
46. In 2014, Merkel's annual salary was €327,700, compared with €202,180 for Hollande.
47. Waltraud Schelkle, "Policymaking in Hard Times: French and German Responses to Economic Crisis in the Euro Area," in N. Bermeo and J. Pontusson (eds.), *Coping with Crisis: Government Reactions to the Great Recession* (New York: Russell Sage, 2012), pp. 130–160; see also Peter A. Hall, "The Economics and Politics of the Euro Crisis," *German Politics,* 21(4) (2012): 355–371.
48. Hübner, "German Crisis Management," p. 163.
49. Ibid., p. 164.
50. Schelkle, "Policymaking in Hard Times."
51. Ibid.
52. Alexander Riesenbichler and Kimberly J. Morgan, "From 'Sick Man' to 'Miracle': Explaining the Robustness of the German Labor Market During and After the Financial Crisis 2008–2009," *Politics & Society,* 40(4) (2012): 549–579.
53. Merkel visited China seven times in seven years, convening joint meetings with PRC cabinet members. Markus Deggerich, Ralf Neukirch, and Wieland Wagner, "Merkel in China: Berlin's Cozy New Relationship with Beijing," *Der Spiegel,* August 29, 2012.
54. Hübner, "German Crisis Management," p. 165.
55. Deutscher Bundestag, 17. Wahlperiode, 42. Sitzung, May 19, 2010, pp. 4128–4129.
56. Matthijs, "Powerful Rules," pp. 377, 386.
57. Ibid., p. 376.
58. Deutscher Bundestag, May 19, 2010, pp. 4128–4129.
59. Hübner, "German Crisis Management," p. 160.
60. Wolfram Hilz, "Getriebewechsel im europäischen Motor: von Merkozy zu Merkollande?" *Aus Politik- und Zeitgeschichte,* December 19, 2012.
61. Bruno Waterfield, "Merkel Wins Major Victory over Hollande," *The Telegraph,* October 19, 2012; see also, Joachim Schild, "Mission

Impossible? The Potential for Franco-German Leadership in the Enlarged EU," *Journal of Common Market Studies*, 48 (2010): 1367–1390.

62. Neukirch et al., "Parallel Universes."
63. Schild, "Mission Impossible?" p. 23.
64. These are the so-called PIGS of southern Europe. While not originally included, Ireland has found its way into the group (hence PIIGS, also known as GIIPS), although northern banks profiting from risky lending are the ones meriting derogatory labels.
65. Maria Petmesidou, "Statism, Social Policy and the Middle Classes in Greece," *Journal of European Social Policy*, 1(1) (1991): 31–48; Luis Ayala, "Social Needs, Inequality and the Welfare State in Spain: Trends and Prospects," *Journal of European Social Policy*, 4(3) (1994): 159–179.
66. Sarantis E. G. Lolos, "The Effect of EU Structural Funds on Regional Growth: Assessing the Evidence from Greece, 1990–2005," *Economic Change and Restructuring* (Wiesbaden: Springer, 2009); see further, Maria Stratigaki, "Gendering the Social Policy Agenda: Anti-discrimination, Social Inclusion and Social Protection," in Gabriele Abels and Joyce Marie Mushaben (eds.), *Gendering the European Union: New Approaches to Old Democratic Deficits* (Basingstoke: Palgrave Macmillan, 2012), pp. 169–170.
67. Hauke Friederichs, "Unser bester Kunde," *Die Zeit*, July 30, 2013.
68. "German Hypocrisy over Greek Military Spending has its Critics up in Arms," *The Guardian*, April 19, 2012.
69. Fritz W. Scharpf, "After the Crash: A Perspective on Multilevel European Democracy," MPIFG Discussion Paper, Max Planck Institute, Cologne, 2014, p. 6.
70. Cited in Theodoros Papadopoulos and Antonios Roumpakis, "The Greek Welfare State in the Age of Austerity: Anti-social Policy and the Politico-economic Crisis," *Social Policy Review*, 24 (2012), p. 206.
71. Despite a decline to 42.5 percent, better paid retirees enjoy higher replacement rates; those subject to part-time, interrupted, or precarious employment collect 30 percent of their former pay, although the retirement age is now the same for women and men. Full pensions are granted only to persons who have worked for forty or more years. Employer contributions were cut by up to 25 percent; the state imposed a 3–7 percent "solidarity" tax on pensions over €1,400 a month. See Papadopoulos and Roumpakis, "The Greek Welfare State," pp. 213–215.
72. Theodore Mitrakos, *Inequality, Poverty and Social Welfare in Greece: Distributional Effects of Austerity*, No. 174, Bank of Greece, Athens, February 2014, pp. 9–10.
73. "Greece Struggles to Address its Tax Evasion Problem," *The Guardian*, February 24, 2015.
74. Christoph Hermann, "Crisis, Structural Reform and the Dismantling of the European Social Model(s)," *Economic and Industrial Democracy*, 36 (2014): 1–18; Klaus Busch, Christoph Hermann, Karl Hinrichs, and Thorsten Schulten, "Euro Crisis, Austerity Policy and the European Social Model: How Crisis Policies in Southern Europe Threaten the EU's Social Dimension," Friedrich Ebert Stiftung, Berlin, February 2013; Christoph

Degryse, Maria Jepsen, and Philippe Pochet, "The Euro Crisis and its Impact on National and European Social Policies," Working Paper No. 2013.05, European Trade Union Institute.

75. Kevin Featherstone, "External Conditionality and the Debt Crisis: The 'Troika' and Public Administration Reform in Greece," *Journal of European Public Policy*, 22(3) (2015), pp. 302 ff.

76. Papadopoulos and Roumpakis, "The Greek Welfare State," p. 207.

77. Tim Jones, "Six Key Points about Greek Debt and the Forthcoming Election," Jubilee Debt Campaign, January 2015. Under the SAPs of the 1980s, Latin America borrowed $272.9 billion, of which $170.5 billion was used to repay interest; $22.9 billion remained as northern bank reserves; $56.6 billion was sent abroad, leaving only $22.9 billion for national use. See Sue Branford and Bernardo Kucinski, *The Debt Squads: The US, the Banks and Latin America* (London: Zed Books, 1988), p. 47.

78. "German Chancellor on the Offensive: Merkel Blasts Greece over Retirement Age, Vacation," *Der Spiegel*, May 18, 2011.

79. Helmut Kohl, Regierungserklärung in der 182. Sitzung des Deutschen Bundestags zur Zukunftssicherung des Standorts Deutschland, October 21, 1993.

80. "Older German Workers Jump at Chance to Retire at 63," National Public Radio, August 13, 2014.

81. Valentine Pop, "Merkel under Fire for 'Lazy Greeks' Comment," *EU Observer*, May 19, 2011.

82. See at: http://ec.europa.eu/europe2020/pdf/themes/07_shadow_economy.pdf.

83. Simon cited this figure in remarks to a student group from the University of Tübingen who visited Brussels in June 2015.

84. "Calais Crisis: Cameron Condemned for 'Dehumanising' Description of Migrants," *The Guardian*, July 30, 2015.

85. Busch et al., "Euro Crisis, Austerity Policy and the European Social Model," pp. 20–22.

86. Sebastian Royo, "How Did the Spanish Financial System Survive the First Stage of the Global Crisis?" *Governance* (2012): 1–26; and Arne Heise, "Governance Without Government or: The Euro Crisis and What Went Wrong with European Economic Governance," University of Hamburg, August 2012.

87. Eurostat, 150-2012, October 24, 2012.

88. Elena Becatoros and Derek Gatopoulos, "Greece Austerity Bill Triggers Riots, Political Revolt," Associated Press, July 17, 2015.

89. Mark Blythe and Matthias Matthijs, "The World Waits for Germany: Berlin is Moving to Solve Europe's Crisis, but not Fast Enough," *Foreign Affairs* (June 8, 2012), p. 3.

90. Deutsche Bundesbank, Monthly Report, March 1997, available at: www.indexmundi.com/germany/public_debt.html.

91. Katharina Slodczyk, "Wegen Libor-Skandal: 2,5 Milliarden-Dollar-Strafe für Deutsche Bank," *Handelsblatt*, April 23, 2014.

92. Streek and Elsässer, "Monetary Disunion," p. 7.

93. A. Alesina and R. Perotti, "The European Union: A Politically Incorrect View," NBER Working Paper No. 10342, 2004, p. 13.

94. Heise, "Governance Without Government," p. 6.

95. Scharpf, "After the Crash," p. 5.

96. Jones, cited in Hübner, "German Crisis Management," p. 166.

97. Fritz W. Scharpf, "No Exit from the Euro-Rescuing Trap?" MPIFG Discussion Paper 14/4, Max Planck Institute, Cologne, 2014, p. 8.

98. Ibid.

99. "Axel Weber tritt Ende April zurück," *Schwäbisches Tageblatt*, February 12, 2011; "EZB-Chefvolkswirt Jürgen Stark tritt zurück," *Die Zeit*, September 9, 2011.

100. Asked about her grand scheme, Merkel responded: "I really believe that it is reasonable and promising for us to work our way out of the crisis step by step, because the one overarching solution doesn't exist. But, of course, you can only take these steps if you have an idea of the direction you are taking." See "Angela Merkel on Europe: 'We Are All in the Same Boat'," *Der Spiegel*, June 2, 2013.

101. Scharpf, "After the Crash," p. 7.

102. Ibid.

103. Brian Blackstone, Matthew Karnitsching, and Robert Thomson, "Europe's Banker Talks Tough: Draghi Says Continent's Social Model is 'Gone,' Won't Backtrack on Austerity," *Wall Street Journal*, February 24, 2012. For contrast, see Jens Bastian, "Defining a Growth Strategy for Greece: Wishful Thinking or a Realistic Prospect?" Friedrich Ebert Stiftung, Bonn, October 2015.

104. Introduced in 2010, the European Semester involves an "annual cycle of economic policy guidance and surveillance"; key actors are economic and finance ministers.

105. Scharpf, "No Exit," p. 3.

106. "Ich wurde als gefährlicher Dummkopf dargestellt," *Zeit Magazine*, July 30, 2015.

107. Scharpf, "After the Crash," p. 10.

108. "Greek Crisis Summit Called after Talks Fail and Bank Fears Grow – As It Happened," *The Guardian*, June 19, 2015.

109. Mishra, *Angela Merkel – Machtworte*, pp. 55–56.

110. Heather McRobie, "When 'Austerity' Sounds like 'Backlash': Gender and the Economic Crisis," New Left Project 14, September 2012, available at: www.newleftproject.org/index.php/site/article_comments/when_austerity_sounds_like_backlash_gender_and_the_economic_crisis; see also Alison Konrad, Vicki Kramer, and Sumru Erkut, "The Impact of Three or More Women on Corporate Boards," *Organizational Dynamics*, 37 (2008): 145–164.

111. Susanne Lachenicht, "Mythos Trümmerfrau? Trümmerräumung in Heilbronn (1944 –1950)," *Heilbronnica*, 2, Beiträge zur Stadtgeschichte, Stadtarchiv Heilbronn, 2003, pp. 319–360.

112. Swabian women were immortalized in a poem titled, *"Schaffe, schaffe, Häusle baue,"* see at: www.historisches-wuerttemberg.de/kultur/kompon/s onstige/haeusle.htm.
113. In summer 2012, women from the Hans Seidel Stiftung in Munich and CSU women in Nuremberg applauded wildly when I supported quotas during a guest lecture sponsored by the US State Department.
114. Patrick Bernau, "Die schwäbische Hausfrau," *Frankfurter Allgemeine Zeitung*, May 16, 2010.
115. Jens Berger, "Die schwäbische Hausfrau als Kardinalfehler deutschen Denkens," February 13, 2012 (excerpt from *STRESSTEST Deutschland*); "Vom Überleben in der Krise: Staat ist keine schwäbische Hausfrau," *Die Tageszeitung*, November 16, 2012.
116. Kerin Hope, "Anxious Greeks Pull Money from Banks Amid Fears of Capital Controls," *Financial Times*, June 10, 2015.
117. Dorothee Tschampa, "Daimler Profit Unexpectedly Rises on Mercedes-Benz Demand," *Bloomberg News*, April 27, 2012.
118. Frau Ackermann is Finnish. See Rolf Obertreis, "Josef Ackermann: Lob der schwäbischen Hausfrau," *Der Tagesspiegel*, May 28, 2010; Vytene Stasaityte, "Auf der Suche nach Frau Ackermann," *Stern Magazin*, May 30, 2010.
119. See at: www.swabianhousewife.com/netzwerk.
120. Julia Kollewe, "Angela Merkel's Austerity Poster Girl, the Thrifty Swabian Housewife," *The Guardian*, September 17, 2012.
121. "Angela Merkel und Chinas Premier Li kaufen ein: Hier ist der Kunde Kanzler," *Der Tagesspiegel*, October 12, 2014.
122. Gabriele Abels and Joyce Marie Mushaben (eds.), *Gendering the European Union: New Approaches to Old Democratic Deficits* (Basingstoke: Palgrave Macmillan, 2012).
123. Several director-generals introduced *gender budgeting* in 1998, tracking revenues, expenditures, and outcomes to determine who benefits. See Diane Elson, "Gender Mainstreaming and Gender Budgeting," European Commission/DG Education, Brussels, March 4, 2003.
124. James Crisp, "Grumpy Juncker: 'Call it EUleaks, not Luxleaks!'" *Eur-Activ*, September 17, 2015.
125. Nikolaj Nielsen, "Berlin wants Juncker to Resign as EU Commission Chief," see at: https://euobserver.com/institutional/134177.
126. In 2005, the new president spent two weeks on the yacht of Greek shipping magnate, Spiro Latsis, a month before the Commission approved €10 million in state aid for his shipping company. "Barroso Defends Link to Shipping Tycoon," *The Guardian*, April 20, 2005.
127. Agnès Hubert and Maria Stratigaki, "Assessing 20 years of Gender Mainstreaming in the EU: Rebirth from the Ashes?" *Femina Politica*, 2 (2016): 21–36. Also, European Gender Institute equality index, available at: http://eige.europa.eu/rdc/eige-publications/gender-equality-index-2015-measuring-gender-equality-european-union-2005-2012-report.
128. Elomäki, *The Price of Austerity*, pp. 7–8.

129. European Women's Lobby, "Gender-Blind Austerity Measures to Undermine Recovery," June 28, 2012; Cécile Gréboval (ed.), *Ticking Clocks: Alternative 2012 Country-specific Recommendations to Strengthen Women's Rights and Gender Equality in the EUROPE 2020 STRATEGY* (Brussels: European Women's Lobby, 2012).

130. After two days of interrogation, French officials decided not to charge Lagarde with a €280 million embezzlement scam; she pays no taxes on her annual IMF salary of $467,940, plus $83,760 in "allowances," according to Angelique Chrisafisin, *The Guardian*, May 25, 2013.

131. Eurostat 2013; Elomäki, *The Price of Austerity*, pp. 7, 11.

132. McRobie, "When 'Austerity' Sounds like 'Backlash'"; Elomäki, *The Price of Austerity*, pp. 8–9.

133. European Women's Lobby, "Gender-Blind Austerity Measures."

134. European Commission, "Impact Assessment on the Cost and Benefits of Improving the Gender Balance in the Boards of Companies Listed on Stock Exchanges," COM (2010) 614 final/SWD (2012) 349 final, Brussels, November 14, 2012.

135. European Commission, "Women on Board" Factsheets, Nos. 1–4, Brussels.

136. R. Bernadi et al., "Does Female Representation on Boards of Directors Associate with the 'Most Ethical Companies' List?" *Corporate Reputation Review*, 12 (2009): 270–280; Claude Francoeur, Réal Labelle, and Bernard Sinclair-Desgagne, "Gender Diversity in Corporate Governance and Top Management," *Journal of Business Ethics*, 81 (2008): 83–95.

137. Only the Red–Green ministries headed by women adopted gender mainstreaming between 1998 and 2005; Mushaben, "Girl Power, Gender Mainstreaming and Critical Mass."

138. Susanne Beyer and Claudia Vogt, "Women and Power: Why Germany Needs a Gender Quota," *Der Spiegel*, February 4, 2011; Yasmin El-Shaarif and Stefan Kaiser, "Kampf der Ministerinnen: Drei Frauen, drei Quoten," *Der Spiegel*, March 5, 2012; "The Business World has Simply Stood Still," *Der Spiegel*, February 4, 2011.

139. "Merkel Rejects Quotas for Women," *Der Spiegel*, February 3, 2011; Antje Sirleschtov, "Frauenquote beschlossen: 30 Prozent Frauen in Aufsichtsräte," *Der Tagesspiegel*, March 6, 2015.

140. Beyza Ç. Tekin, "Rethinking the Post-National EU in Times of Austerity and Crisis," *Mediterranean Politics*, 19(1) (2014), p. 25.

141. In 1998 candidate Schröder characterized the introduction of a single currency without a fiscal union as a "sickly premature birth," which was then misquoted by Foreign Minister Kinkel as a "miscarriage." See *Süddeutsche Zeitung*, March 28, 1998.

142. For details, see Heckel, *So regiert die Kanzlerin*, p. 68.

143. Alan Crawford and Tony Czuczka, *Angela Merkel: A Chancellorship Forged in Crisis* (New York: Bloomberg Press, 2013), p. 86.

144. Kornelius, *Angela Merkel. Die Kanzlerin und ihre Welt*, pp. 264–265.

145. Gabriele Abels and Annegret Eppler (eds.), *Subnational Parliaments in the EU Multi-level Parliamentary System: Taking Stock of the Post-Lisbon Era* (Innsbruck: Studienverlag, 2015).

146. Scharpf, "After the Crash," p. 13.
147. Papadopoulos and Roumpakis, "The Greek Welfare State," p. 203; also, Ben Crum, "Saving the Euro at the Cost of Democracy?" *Journal of Common Market Studies*, 51(4) (2013): 614–630.
148. Scharpf, "After the Crash," p. 15.
149. Derek Scally, "Merkel Wants Us in Touch with Our Inner German Housewife," *Irish Times*, June 2, 2012.
150. Crawford and Czuczka, *A Chancellorship Forged in Crisis*, pp. 101 ff.
151. Lau, *Die letzte Volkspartei*, p. 204.
152. The Federal Reserve Chair's speech at the American Enterprise Institute on December 5, 1996 is available at: www.federalreserve.gov/boarddocs/spee ches/1996/19961205.htm
153. Rainer Hillebrand, "Germany and its Eurozone Crisis Policy: The Impact of the Country's Ordo-Liberal Heritage," *German Politics & Society*, 33(1/2) (2015): 6–24.
154. Kirchhof advocated a flat-rate tax of 25 percent; Merkel's announcement slashed the CDU's twenty-one-point lead over the SPD to seven points; see further Severin Weiland, "Eklat um Ex-Bundesbanker Tietmeyer: Merkel-Alleingang verprellt SPD," *Der Spiegel*, October 15, 2008.
155. Deutscher Bundestag, May 19, 2010, p. 4131.
156. Cited in Jack Rosenthal, "A Terrible Thing to Waste," *New York Times*, July 31, 2009.

PART III

"METHOD MERKEL" AND THE PUSH FOR DOMESTIC REFORMS

In this section we explore Angela Merkel's efforts to negotiate reforms between the supranational and national levels, as well as between the federal and state levels regarding RE, migration, and asylum policies. These domains attest to a fundamental transformation of both the context and content of domestic policy-making since Merkel first became chancellor in 2005. They also reflect a deeper modernization of societal relations as a function of generational change. The aim is to assess the relative influence of personal socialization factors as well as the impact of different coalition factors on the chancellor's political style and decision-making powers.

As a professional physicist and former environmental minister, it is not surprising that Merkel would assume a leading role with respect to climate-change policies at both the national and supranational levels. Her speeches contain many references to *sustainability* as a multifaceted concept, hence my focus on RE and "green growth." At the outset of this project, I hypothesized that despite her natural science qualifications, this chancellor was likely to encounter serious resistance to her energy proposals, given the powers exercised by conservative "state princes" and the formidable influence of the automotive industry. Her active support for nuclear energy during her first Grand Coalition (2005–2009) encountered the ire of SPD leaders, while her push for dramatic reductions in greenhouse gas (GHG) emissions provoked resistance at the Länder level. The Fukushima melt-down of 2011 dramatically shifted the paradigm, however, allowing the chancellor not only to hijack long espoused Red–Green positions but also to rein in recalcitrant state leaders, sensitive to voter *Angst* involving all things nuclear.

According to climate-change experts, rising sea levels, massive droughts, and other extreme weather patterns are giving rise to a new type of refugee crisis, as desperately poor people flee to "higher ground." It is hard to imagine Europe opening its doors to new waves of foreigners, given its miserable treatment of the millions who have already crossed the Mediterranean from Africa and the Middle East since 2012, hoping to escape a wide array of ethno-religious wars and failed economies. Having long refused to accept itself as a "land of immigration," Germany now ranks second only to the United States in terms of the number of foreigners it welcomes each year. Cognizant that a looming demographic deficit could bring national growth and prosperity to a grinding halt by 2030, Chancellor Merkel began leveraging a series of migration reforms to expand the FRG's skilled labor pool well before she defied all odds and opened her country to more than a million refugees in 2015. The resurgence of "Fortress Europe" thinking across the EU member states and the rise of right-wing populist groups nonetheless complicates her efforts to address the day-to-day problems of new arrivals where "belonging" really counts: cities are the places where integration ultimately succeeds or fails.

6

Fukushima, mon Amour: Merkel and the (Supra) National Energy Turn-Around

Regularly commuting between Berlin and Leipzig during East German times, Angela Merkel would have had significant first-hand exposure to the devastating ecological consequences of coal mining and chemical production stretching from Zeitz to Dessau via Bitterfeld. Hailing from a country that had actively prosecuted its citizens for sharing "state secrets" on deteriorating health conditions in heavily afflicted areas, she nonetheless had a lot of catching up to do when Helmut Kohl named her Minister of the Environment, Nature Conservation and Reactor Safety in 1994.[1] Although Merkel was a rare political commodity, an Eastern female physicist, her ministry was stripped of many core responsibilities and resources once she was appointed; they were turned over to a more reliable Western man, Jürgen Rüttgers who was in charge of Education, Science, Research and Technology. Lacking previous exposure to Western social movements, Merkel was immediately confronted with waves of sometimes violent anti-nuclear protests, followed by an embarrassing nuclear waste transport scandal that peaked in 1998.[2] This portfolio nonetheless provided the young minister with her first opportunity to occupy the world stage as an effective mediator, hosting 869 delegates from 170 countries at the first UN Climate Summit in Berlin in April 1995.[3] The chancellor has characterized that experience in countless interviews as the highpoint of her eight years in the Kohl cabinet.

Leading her first Grand Coalition as of 2005, Merkel's mediation skills drove her to center stage once more in 2007. This time she acted in her capacity as the rotating EU Council President and as Chair of the G8 summit meeting that convened in the North Sea resort town of Heiligendamm, where she acquired the honorary title of "Climate

Chancellor." Sooner driven by data than ideology, Merkel was credited with compelling even US President George W. Bush to accept the reality of global warming. Finally able to put her physicist training to good use, Merkel moved her own party to co-adopt an Energy Turn-Around plan with the SPD in 2008. Her support for greenhouse gas (GHG) reductions and RE technologies included the use of nuclear power, a major source of ongoing conflict between the conservative and social-democratic coalition partners.

Following the formation of a new CDU/CSU–FDP coalition in 2009, Angela Merkel set out to reverse a Red–Green government decision of 2000 to cap the life-span of all German nuclear plants, as well as to bar construction of new ones. The Fukushima Daiichi melt-down of March 2011 precipitated a 180-degree policy turn-around, however. Merkel immediately ordered a shut-down of seven reactors for safety reviews; another problematic plant (Krümmel) was taken off line permanently. Shortly thereafter, the chancellor convened an Ethics Commission for Secure Energy Provision to review national policies. By May her government announced that six more sites would cease operations by 2021, and the three newest facilities would go off-line by 2022.

Since 2011, Germany has witnessed an exponential increase in its research, development, consumption, and export of renewable technologies, recent conflicts over RE subsidies, carbon storage, and grid issues notwithstanding. Having already surpassed EU clean energy and CO_2 reduction targets set for 2020, it has a vested interest in ensuring that other member states follow suit. Neither GHG emissions nor climate change recognize national boundaries in their effects. German efforts and investments will have been in vain if its neighbors fail to adhere to existing regulatory requirements, much less to accelerate plans for their own energy turn-arounds, given the monumental increases in fossil fuel consumption expected to occur in China, India, and Brazil over the next decade. As seen in earlier chapters, the new chancellor became very adept at leveraging EU policies for the purpose of overcoming conservative opposition to long overdue domestic reforms, including those in the energy field.

European integration is not merely a top-down process, however. While EU organs play a key role in downloading shared community values and binding operational concepts (e.g., *freedom of movement*), the integration process affords many opportunities beyond uncoordinated diffusion for uploading benchmarks, indicators, and mechanisms developed and tested within progressive member states.[4] *Downloading* consists of all top-down measures applied by the

Commission – ranging from moral suasion, pilot projects, and supplemental funding to "shaming and blaming," negative sanctions, and binding court verdicts – to foster transposition and implementation in each member state. I define *uploading* as deliberate efforts made by individual member states to have their national policies, indicators, and implementation strategies adopted as the "community norm" when such practices are seen (above all, by the Commission) to be more rigorous, advanced, or inclusive than those applied in other member states.[5] In a federal system like Germany, the Commission's reliance on directives (mandating *supranational ends* but not the *national means* of implementation) can often lead to a re-loading of policies at lower levels. *Re-loading* entails efforts by member states, or subaltern governments to challenge, reinterpret, delay, or otherwise circumvent the application of existing EU requirements. Goal displacement and/or unanticipated consequences may trigger further Community action, giving rise to a catalog of "best practices" over time. To achieve her goals in relation to environmental sustainability, reducing GHG emissions, and promoting an industrial revolution based on renewable energy sources, the chancellor has been forced to engage in a three-level game.

During her first term as head of government, Merkel's lack of familiarity with the byzantine world of global banking and finance forced her to rely on internal and external monetary experts, leading her to harden her position on austerity even after conditions took a turn for the worse. Midway into her second term, she was eminently more qualified, and more confident, when it came to directing a European response to the Japanese nuclear disaster of 2011. Familiar with both the devastating effects of Chernobyl and the GDR's callous disregard for chemical and coal-mining run-offs, Merkel the physicist was finally in her element. Scientific expertise was not the only factor in her decision to end German reliance on atomic energy, however. Her learning experience in this case, dating back to her years as Environmental Minister, involved coming to terms with Westerners' deep-seated distrust of the nuclear industry.

This chapter begins by reviewing German attitudes and activism pertaining to environmental issues over several decades, especially in relation to nuclear energy. Next, I summarize national energy policies initiated in the 1980s that provided Germany with "comparative advantages," which made it possible for Merkel not only to mandate a complete nuclear shutdown but also to accelerate a national energy turn-around. Her concerns regarding climate change, rooted in the 1990s, positioned her as a "mover and shaker" in this field years ahead of most national leaders.

I then describe German reactions to the Fukushima Daiichi melt-down and the proliferation of laws that shaped the parameters of Merkel's *Einstieg in den Ausstieg* ("entry into the exit") on the nuclear energy front. Their implementation ultimately depends on the predilec-tions of sixteen states, however, including a few surprising "forerun-ners." I further consider the extent to which Germany's accelerated energy strategy is driving Europe's pursuit of competitive, low-carbon economies. Having exceeded multiple EU emissions and sustainability goals (*Europe 20–20–20*) ahead of schedule, Germany is well positioned at both the supranational and national levels to define best practices for other member states, provided it can persuade Central East European nations, worried about Russia, that pooling sovereignty in the energy domain is a win–win proposition. I conclude with reflections on criti-cisms of FRG policies prior to Fukushima, and the special conditions that enabled Merkel to reconfigure yet another policy domain in Germany.

ENVIRONMENTALISM AS A NATIONAL VIRTUE IN GERMANY

German environmental activism over the last fifty years stands in stark contrast to Rachel Carson's notion of "a silent spring."[6] The old Federal Republic witnessed countless summer protest camps, hot autumns, and winters of discontent, occasionally ending in violent clashes between citizens and the state. Ironically, these mobilizations played a key role in transforming Germany from a country historically steeped in authoritar-ian, top-down rule to one dedicated to fact-checking counter-experts, professionalized citizen initiatives, a very influential Green party and "contentious democracy."

A sentimental, metaphysical love of nature and devotion to environ-mental conservation has deep historical roots in the German psyche: romanticized notions of *Heimat* (homeland), the *Wandervogel* move-ment, and other ecological conceptualizations predating National Socialism regularly captured the imagination of Germans across the poli-tical spectrum. The re-arming of Germany in 1957, and the secret deploy-ment of atomic weapons led Defense Minister Franz Josef Strauss (CSU) to raid the offices of *Der Spiegel* in 1962. Its editor, Rolf Augstein, was arrested on suspicion of treason for releasing the details. Spontaneous mass demonstrations followed, ultimately securing juridical guarantees for freedom of the press regarding "nuclear" issues, although the official files were not declassified until 2012.[7]

Just as the physical devastation of two world wars began to recede from public memory, the two parts of the nation divided came to recognize themselves as constituents of a new "community of destiny," owing to their shared status as a potential nuclear battlefield throughout the Cold War.[8] Ironically, it was the much-loved US president, John F. Kennedy, who initiated the NATO shift from a defense strategy known as *Mutually Assured Destruction* to *Nuclear Utilization Theory* (i.e., from MAD to NUT) under the *flexible response* doctrine. By the 1980s, most Germans would come to realize that America's flexible response and the deployment of short-range, *use-'em-or-lose-'em* Pershing II missiles on their soil meant that their country could potentially be destroyed in the name of being "defended."[9]

Mass demonstrations of the late 1960s led to a New Left monopolization of environmental themes following the formidable "extra-parliamentary opposition" (APO) movement, while right-wing ecologists continued to operate on the margins.[10] Initial protests were rooted in the anti-rearmament campaigns and Easter marches of the 1950s, which merged with new forces opposing military emergency laws (*Notstandsgesetze*), the Vietnam War, and Third World dictatorships (e.g., the Shah of Iran). The turn to nuclear energy in the 1970s added a third dimension, accompanied by dramatic site occupations, "green" camps, blockades against nuclear waste transports, reprocessing and storage (Gorleben). Whyl (Upper Rhine) witnessed a nine-month occupation in 1975, while mass rallies in Brokdorf drew over 50,000 in 1981.[11] Reinforced by comparable movements in neighboring countries, German mobilization against Pershing II and Cruise missile deployments resulted in movement professionalization, with demonstrations attracting over 500,000 on a single day in Bonn in October 1984.[12] A new generation of science- and media-savvy counter-experts, operating out of non-governmental research institutes, highlighted links between nuclear waste reprocessing and the production of weapons-grade plutonium.[13] Indeed, the 1986 Chernobyl catastrophe, dispersing massive amounts of radiation throughout Europe, provided the empirical confirmation they needed to turn a majority of German voters into nuclear skeptics, if not active protesters per se.[14]

The political coming-of-age of an FRG Baby Boom, blessed with expanded higher educational opportunities and access to new communications technologies, contributed significantly to the shift from *APO* to *IPO*, that is, from *extra-parliamentary* to *institutionalized political opposition.*[15] Life-cycle effects saw millions of student protesters moving beyond intermittent acts of "fundamental opposition," into thousands of local citizen initiatives devoted to *eco-pax* causes. Despite their stark differences, leftist fundamentalists (*Fundis*) merged with political realists (*Realos*) to form a Green party based on four pillars: ecological preservation, gender equality, non-violence, and grassroots democracy. Their long march through the institutions began in local city councils, proceeded through state governments, and culminated in the 1998 election of the first Red–Green coalition, headed by ex-SDS activist Gerhard Schröder; six cabinet members were also veterans of the '68 movement.[16] Between 1998 and 2005, the Greens did more to advance their ecological goals than their gender equality aims, establishing a proactive pattern that continued through the Grand Coalition of 2005–2009.

Prior to the first nuclear mishap at Three Mile Island in the United States, German protestors had created an "alternative community college" at Whyl to educate citizens on nuclear issues and renewable energy sources. Founded in 1977, the *Öko-Institut* in Freiburg/Breisgau published the first book invoking an "energy turn-around" in 1980.[17] By the time Merkel became chancellor, it employed over 165 scientists, economists, lawyers, and communications experts in Freiburg, Darmstadt, and Berlin, overseeing 350 projects per year. Germany's countless ecological research institutes, public and private, give it an expertise advantage over most EU states. It enjoys an extraordinary degree of elite consensus, even among industrialists, concerning the need for climate-change indicators, RE expansion, and national technology promotion abroad. As the new environmental minister noted herself in 1996, "One cannot combat the problem of the ozone hole by referring to the unemployment statistics."[18] By the time the 2011 earthquake fractured the foundations of Japan's globalized economy, Germany was well ahead of its European neighbors regarding a commitment to green technologies and climate-change mitigation.

OPERATION HEAD START: GERMAN ENERGY POLICY, 1935–2010

Like the German attachment to nature, the state's involvement in the energy sector has deep historical roots. Dating back to 1935, the Energy Economy Law adopted by the Nazi regime recognized energy sources as part of a natural monopoly. Unlike other states, Hitler's government allowed private utilities to dominate a region based on "mutual demarcation treaties and exclusive supply agreements" with municipal administrations, a practice that continued after 1945.[19] Seven major electricity companies became responsible for rebuilding and managing the high-voltage electricity grid, shutting out effective competition until their number was reduced to four in the early 1990s. West Germany joined five other states in creating Euratom in 1957, to foster peaceful uses of atomic energy. It passed its first Nuclear Energy Act in 1959, leading to the construction of thirty-two commercial reactors between 1962 and 1989; the nuclear share of energy generation rose to a peak of 30.7 percent in 1999, falling below 23 percent by 2010.[20]

Germany's energy import dependence (70 percent) had already pushed it to hunt for new domestic supplies after the 1973 oil embargo, when unemployment crossed the 1 million threshold for the first time since the Great Depression. An emerging environmental movement posed significant legal challenges to the coal and nuclear industries once the Greens entered the Bundestag in 1983. Controlling 80 percent of all electricity production, the Big Seven raised prices, using wind-fall profits to expand their holdings in the natural resource and nuclear arenas, "securing a vertical integration of fuel, generation, distribution, and commercialization" of the entire energy sector.[21] Over time ministers, state secretaries, and utility managers benefited from the proverbial revolving-door leading in and out of the Federal Economics Ministry. Though hardly comparable to the "lavish subsidies" routinely accorded the coal and nuclear sectors, R&D funds for alternative energy sources rose from DM 20 million to DM 300 million by 1982 under Helmut Schmidt (SPD). His successor, Helmut Kohl (CDU) cut the R&D budget by almost 50 percent, just as environmental and anti-nuclear protests were reaching their peak. The *Süddeutsche Zeitung* later revealed that Kohl had pressured scientists into approving Gorleben as a permanent nuclear waste storage site.[22]

Europe-wide concerns over acid rain and early signs of global warming nonetheless precipitated two Bundestag Commissions of Inquiry focusing on climate and the environment in 1980 and 1986, respectively, both of which called for sharp reductions in national and industrial CO_2 emissions. Focusing on coal as the major CO_2 emitter, electricity consumers filed suit against a long-standing "penny subsidy" (*Kohlenpfennig*) to the domestic coal industry; each hard-coal workplace relied on a "sales-aid" subsidy amounting to €70,000 per year.[23] Black coal production shrank from the 150 million tons produced by 607,000 miners in 1957, to 25.6 million tons mined by 35,000 as of 2005, leading to mass unemployment in the

Saarland and *Ruhrpott*. In 2007, the Grand Coalition agreed to close the eight remaining mines by 2018, a plan revised after Fukushima.[24]

The late 1980s saw a failed attempt to require utility companies to purchase electricity directly from renewable energy sources at a fixed price under the *feed-in tariff* model (FITM). A second bill passed in October 1990 was supported by all parliamentary caucuses, the Länder governments, the Environmental and Research ministries; it was, however, strongly opposed by the Economics Ministry, viewed as a "natural enemy."[25] Busy reconfiguring the energy domain in the eastern states, utility company managers did little to mobilize against this Electricity Feed-In Law (*Stromeinspeisegesetz*). Although limited in scope, it "ignited a boom" in the wind energy field, increasing capacity nearly sixtyfold by 1995, based on the mandatory inclusion of privately produced supplies into larger, conglomerate networks. It stimulated decentralized energy generation among countless small- and medium-size producers, even in the economically depressed East.[26] The Environmental Ministry published studies affirming the benefits and viability of RE sources. Former opponents like the German Engineering Association and recalcitrant labor unions joined the bandwagon. Despite increasing profits and stakeholders, the Economics Ministry successfully reasserted control over the 1997 Energy Reform Law, bolstered by neo-liberalizing pressures at the EU level.

The 1998 election of a Red–Green government swung the pendulum back toward rapid development, providing substantial support for the weaker photovoltaic sector. A new Renewable Energies Law in 1999 raised the RE target to a 12.5 percent share of the electricity market by 2010, 20 percent by 2020, and 50 percent by 2050. CDU Opposition leader Merkel warned that Germany's competitive export industries would suffer under projected energy cost hikes. The Greens' strong showing in the 2002 elections gained their environmental minister a seat at the "energy summit" table, however, admitting Minister Jürgen Trittin "into the last bastion of oligarchic policy-making in that sector."[27] By the time she campaigned for the chancellorship in 2005, Merkel had come to recognize RE as an incredible "export and job engine" that was beginning to outpace the pharmaceutical and chemical industries, securing its further advance.

THE GREENING OF ANGELA MERKEL

In June 1953, East German workers in the chemical industry in Saxony mobilized quickly and vehemently against SED efforts to raise production norms dramatically during a period still characterized by material scarcity. Appropriately named, the Bitterfeld (Bitter Field) region now stands as a metaphor for decades of unmitigated pollution, toxic dumping, and deteriorating public health (widespread bronchial diseases, stunted bone growth among children); it was matched only by the environmental degradation witnessed in mining areas. By the mid-1980s, SED officials had literally strip-mined over 130 hamlets and towns out of existence, producing a "moon landscape" saturated with poisonous cesspools and chemical cocktails.[28]

The 1953 uprising rendered East German officials highly suspicious of any and all types of independent citizen mobilization. Eventually, the very groups it tried so hard to repress, the peace and ecology movements, created a foundation for the non-violent protests that brought down the geriatric regime in 1989.[29] Socialist leaders initially tolerated local tree-planting projects and bicycle "demonstrations" in the 1970s, but the proliferation of underground newsletters, environmental libraries (often supported by Westerners), and the fusion of human rights, peace, and ecology groups that found shelter in Lutheran churches (Wittenberg, Berlin, Leipzig) triggered Stasi raids and youth arrests in the 1980s.[30] Many environmentalists characterized the massive shut-down of GDR industries after unification as one of Germany's most radical environmental achievements.

The socialist state adopted its first Nature Protection Law in 1954 and embedded "ecological protection" into its 1968 constitution, establishing a Ministry for Environmental and Water Preservation fourteen years prior to its Western counterpart. Joining the UN in 1973, the GDR had a hard time reconciling its obsession with material production, state security, and fraternal Soviet relations with new international pressures to combat the pollution, deforestation, soil contamination, and health consequences linked to chemical fertilizers, uranium mining, and industrial accidents: in 1970 alone, its factories registered 1,584 fires, 117 explosions, and 728 other disasters.[31] Its brown-coal dependency, rising after the 1973 OPEC price hikes, generated twice the sulfuric acid emissions seen in the West, consumed by a population only one-fourth the size of the FRG. It created a Society for Nature and the Environment in 1980, but its own scientists and medical personnel were barred from releasing data and raising public consciousness. In 1982 and 1985, the Council of Ministers issued two resolutions outlawing the "Collection and Evaluation ... of Information over the Condition of the Natural Environment in the GDR." Efforts to do so cost many their jobs or even time in prison, including nuclear critics like physicist Sebastien Pflugbeil. Although parts of the GDR experienced radiation waves that rendered produce unfit for consumption, its own citizens had to rely on West TV and radio for news regarding the Chernobyl nuclear melt-down of 1986.

Approved in 1956, the first GDR nuclear power plant at Rheinsberg commenced operations in 1966. Utilizing a Soviet pressurized-water reactor design, it extracted cooling water from the Nehmitzsee, which it discharged into another nearby lake, Stechlinsee. Scheduled to go off-line in 1992, it was shut down in 1990 due to safety problems. A larger, Soviet-model plant employing over 10,000 workers in Greifswald (Mecklenburg-Vorpommern) became the site of two major accidents, both the product of human error. In 1975, an electrician short-circuited the wiring of a pump to show his apprentice how to bridge electrical circuits; the resulting fire destroyed the control lines of five of six main coolant pumps. In late November 1989, three of six cooling water pumps were switched off for a test, triggering a near melt-down when ten fuel elements were damaged. It, too, was shut-down immediately after unification. Construction of the Stendal station (Sachsen-Anhalt) began in 1983; this Moscow design utilized a new steel cell composite technique that would have rendered it the largest nuclear power generator in united Germany, but the plant was never completed. Its two standing cooling towers were demolished in 1994 and 1999.[32]

Despite the close ties between local peace, ecology, and church groups, the pastor's daughter who studied physics kept her distance from dissident politics, although she joined in church activities after moving to Berlin, mostly at the Gethsemane parish. Her apartment on Schönhauser Allee was only a few blocks away from the Zionskirche, a hotbed of eco-activism and Stasi raids. She also attended talks and peace services at Rainer Eppelmann's Samaritan Church to show that she "was against the GDR" but nothing more, despite the Lutheran postulate, "preserve creation."[33] The one GDR experience that she did take with her into the Western environmental ministry was a deep commitment to recycling. She also cleared the streets of cars lacking catalytic converters, opposed UK plans to sink the *Brent Spar* oil platform in the North Sea, and pushed the auto industry to reduce average fuel consumption to 5 liters per 100 km.

Slow to unfold, the conservative turn against nuclear energy completed by Merkel in 2011 had its roots in the 1986 Chernobyl disaster. Beyond bailing out farmers whose crops were ruined by massive radiation clouds reaching all the way to Portugal, Environmental Minister Klaus Töpfer had watched a chemical explosion at the Swiss Sandoz Corporation reverse two years of clean-up efforts along the scenic River Rhine.

Before he lost his job over his increasingly proactive stance, Merkel's ministerial predecessor opined, "What I learned from Chernobyl is how dependent we are on the security precautions of other nations ... We environmental politicians have been the first to experience what globalization means."[34]

Replacing him at the cabinet table in 1994, the former Women's Minister was not enthusiastic about her new post, despite her success in mastering the details "at lightning speed." Her toughest ministerial battles occurred in this domain, including the only time in her career she dissolved into tears following a cabinet vote against one of her proposals; she later claimed that the surprise this triggered helped her to win the second round two days later.[35] She faced bitter internal resistance to her efforts to incorporate the phrase "social-ecological market economy" in the CDU's 1994 party platform, to mandate catalytic converters, and summer speed limits to reduce smog and ozone levels below the EU minimum. Kohl's coalition partners in the Bavarian CSU branded her a leftist and "a traitor to the fatherland."[36]

As environmental minister, Merkel likewise bore responsibility between 1995 and 1998 for castor-transport scandals involving long-term leaks, state failure to monitor plant safety, and years of corporate lies.[37] Having visited Chernobyl in 1996, she learned the hard way that her own nuclear plants were grossly under-insured for damage likely to ensue from a worst-case scenario. Since 1977, the federal government has invested over €1.6 billion in the *Salzstock* repository near Gorleben, already plagued with contaminated ground water. Remedying the leakages and final-storage problems tied to the first nuclear-waste transport (Le Hague to Gorleben) has cost the state over €3 billion.[38]

The chancellor's positive working relationship with Finance Minister Peer Steinbrück (SPD) and Foreign Minister Frank-Walter Steinmeier (SPD) shored up her popularity for most of the first Grand Coalition. She reinforced her position at home vis-à-vis CDU/CSU hardliners by courting leaders at the European and international levels, including the new French president, Nicolas Sarkozy. January 2007 marked the onset of the German Consilium Presidency, and its year-long leadership of the G8.[39] Only the second woman to preside over the EU Council of Ministers and the G8 after Margaret Thatcher, Merkel proved to be an effective mediator at the Heiligendamm summit of June 6–8, 2007. She invited Brazil, India, China, and South Africa to participate in a subsequent G8 meeting in Potsdam, focusing on climate change and biodiversity, on March 15–17, to smooth the path to the 2009 UN Climate meeting in Copenhagen. Instead, the United States and the BASIC (Brazil, South Africa, India, China) countries hammered out a secret deal, sidelining the ambitious EU; for the more ecological states, Copenhagen was a bust. Merkel had extracted a vague promise from Bush at Heiligendamm to cut US carbon emissions in half and limit its global warming to 2°C by 2050; once back home, he refused to support a Kyoto follow-up agreement.[40]

Under the newly instituted "troika" system linking the previous and subsequent EU Council presidencies, Germany also participated in dossier negotiations over bio-diversity, GMOs, mercury, titanium dioxide waste, water politics, and soil protection (although Länder leaders strongly opposed federal action on the latter). The FRG pursued tough negotiations over the adoption of Europe 20–20–20, playing a forerunner role by raising its own GHG reduction target to 21 percent for 2012 and 40 percent by 2020, in exchange for aggregate EU targets of 8 percent and 30 percent, respectively.[41] Gabriel was less successful in his efforts to "upload" a New Deal featuring an *ecological industrial policy* at an informal Council session in Essen. Germany then turned to securing the parameters of the Lisbon Treaty, which introduced a new energy chapter (Chapter XXI).[42]

Despite differences over nuclear energy, Merkel found more common ground with her SPD environmental minister, Sigmar Gabriel, than with CSU economics minister, Michael Glos. Increasing concerns over climate change as a security issue strengthened the position of Gabriel and Steinmeier. The Grand Coalition adopted an *Integrated Energy and Climate Program* in August 2007 (fourteen measures), followed by a smaller package in 2008. Although reportedly annoyed with the automobile industry's failure to honor a voluntary agreement on CO_2 emissions, Merkel thwarted Commission wishes by making her own deal with Sarkozy to ease restrictions during the Portuguese presidency in late 2007.

The return to a normal CDU/CSU–FDP coalition in 2009 saw a dramatic slow-down. The chancellor reversed the Red–Green decision of 2000 to cap the life-span of all nuclear plants (responsible for 23 percent of energy generation) and to bar construction of new ones (Figure 6.1). The Fukushima Daiichi melt-down of March 2011 precipitated a paradigm shift, however: Japan's nuclear power industry argued after the fact that a catastrophe of this magnitude had been "simply" unforeseeable.[43] Germany's geographic location includes very few earthquake faults, and it is unlikely to face a killer tsunami along its northern coast. Merkel's sudden decision to uphold the Red–Green withdrawal from nuclear energy stemmed from her recognition of the potential for

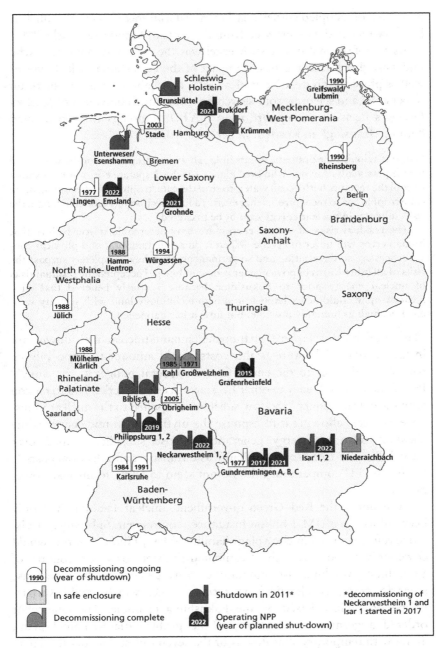

FIGURE 6.1 Nuclear Reactors in Germany, pre-Fukushima, 2011
Source: Based on a map by Clean Energy Wire using data by the Federal Office for the Safety of Nuclear Waste Management (BfE). Redrawn with kind permission.

human error, coupled with her earlier ministerial encounter with a nuclear industry repeatedly exonerated from the costs of "unforeseen risks."[44]

As a professional physicist, Merkel was the only national leader who understood the data and future impact of the Fukushima melt-downs as well as physicist-premier Naoto Kan. Her rapid about-face was the result of personal and scientific soul-searching – the moral equivalent of Joschka Fischer's decision to support 1999 NATO bombings to stop Serbian "ethnic cleansing" in Kosovo. In her own words:

Without a doubt, the dramatic events in Japan were a deep blow for the world and for me personally. Anyone who even glanced at the desperate effort in Fukushima to cool the reactors with ocean water, to stop the catastrophe from becoming more catastrophic has to recognize . . . that even in a high-technology land like Japan, the risks inherent in nuclear energy cannot be mastered . . .

The residual risks of atomic energy are only acceptable if you believe that human error will never intervene. When it does, the temporal and physical consequences are so devastating and so permanent, that they completely surpass the risks of all other forms of power generation combined. I accepted the residual risks of nuclear energy prior to Fukushima because I utterly believed that such a catastrophe could never happen in a high-technology land with security standards as high as humanly possible. But now it has happened.[45]

The total bill for Japan's earthquake/tsunami/nuclear melt-down, not including potential future health costs, could amount to €300 billion, roughly equivalent to the entire German federal budget at the time.[46] Preaching fiscal solvency to other EU states in crisis, Merkel had to reckon with the extraordinary "shadow subsidies" supplied to the nuclear industry each year, allowing it to espouse the myth that atomic energy is the cheapest form of energy generation. Those subsidies totaled over €203 billion up to 2010, excluding waste transport and disposal costs.[47] Curiously, EU competition rules do not seem to apply to nuclear power plants.

Even under the Red–Green government, nuclear facilities had only been subject to a DM 1 billion insurance requirement. Subsequent legislative reforms raised nuclear plant liability to €2.5 billion, but this would cover only 1/100–1/1000th of estimated disaster costs in a country of 81 million. Anything else, amounting to 99 percent of the worst-case scenario costs, is classified as *residual risk*, which could surpass €500–600 billion, based on the Fukushima example. The chancellor ordered a permanent shutdown of the problematic Krümmel plant, along with temporary shut-downs of the seven oldest reactors for safety reviews. On March 22, she appointed an expert Ethics Commission to reassess national policies, co-chaired by former minister Klaus Töpfer and German Science Foundation president, Matthias Kleiner. Its seventeen members (fourteen men, three women) deliberated until June 15. Despite the highly complex subject matter, it broadcast its hearings on public television. Defining the energy turn-around "as the clearest example of a knowledge-based transformation process of our time," the experts concluded that a nuclear exit within a decade was both feasible and necessary, based on Germany's "courage for innovation, confidence in its own strength and with a binding process of monitoring and steering."[48]

Merkel had already declared in May that six plants would cease operations by 2021, followed by the three newest facilities in 2022. Bavaria's thirty-three-year-old Grafenrheinfeld plant near Schweinfurth was the first to go off-line permanently on June 27, 2015, seven months earlier than planned, reportedly to save E.ON €80 million in fuel taxes.[49] State leader Seehofer has refused to consider a nuclear waste storage site within his own borders, although Bavaria drew almost 66 percent of its power from nuclear generation (2007 figures).[50]

GERMAN RESPONSES TO FUKUSHIMA

On March 11, 2011, the global public bore direct witness to one of the most devastating earthquakes in Japanese history. Only the Hoei earthquake of 1707 (290,000 deaths) and the 1896 Meiji-Sanriku quake with its 30-meter high tsunami (27,000 deaths) produced higher short-term fatality rates; 55 percent were over 65.[51] The Great Eastern-Japan earthquake of 2011 resulted in 22,500 deaths and destroyed 220,00 buildings. The projected infrastructure, agricultural, and fisheries costs will run upwards of €150 billion.[52]

Having registered twenty-three smaller quakes over the previous two days, seismologists expected the next one to hit between 6.8 and 8.1 on the Richter scale; they never anticipated a 9.0 event. The epicenter lay 370 km outside of Tokyo, near the Miyagi coast; in less than 3 minutes, a terrestrial plate some 400–500 kilometers long and 200 kilometers wide broke away and shifted 25 kilometers below the Earth's surface. The island of Honshu slid 4 meters to the east; within 15 minutes the first tsunami waves, 10–30 meters high, hit communities 130 kilometers away from the epicenter. Authorities reported 11,000 missing by May 11; the number rose to 15,413 by June.[53]

But this was only stage one of the Japanese catastrophe. The tsunami knocked out all fail-safe systems for the coastal Fukushima Daiichi nuclear plant, setting off a chain of nuclear melt-downs, a real case of "critical mass." Although three active reactors (out of six) might have survived the quake alone, the 14-m water-wave that followed caused the ground (10 m below sea-level) to subside further, rendering the 5.7-m protective wall too low.[54] Why, one wonders, would engineers put the emergency back-up system in the basement of a power plant on coastal soil that had been "reclaimed" from the sea? Low-level diesel generators flooded, demolishing pumps and wiping out cooling systems; this triggered hydrogen explosions and core melt-downs at temperatures reaching 3000°C. TEPCO managers had no emergency plan to counter the massive release of radioactive material beyond setting up a twitter account and appointing a press-speaker five days into the crisis.

It took over 29,000 engineers, fire department units, construction workers, and nuclear experts from the United States and France several months to start quantifying the damage, including levels of radiation exposure, oceanic contamination, and soil liquefaction.[55] By July, a new water decontamination system was processing 43 tons of highly radio-active water *per hour* for recycled "cooling." Over 110 tons of radio-toxic water remained in the power plant basement. By late September, many brave workers managed to install a steel-polyester "protective covering" for blocks 1, 3 and 4. Prime Minister Naoto Kan understood the long-term melt-down consequences better than most, having studied physics at the Tokyo Institute of Technology. He sacrificed his own political career to force a zig-zagging remedial response from nuclear industry bosses.[56]

TEPCO's top managers (one of whom immediately went on leave) argued that they "simply could not have anticipated" a catastrophe of this magnitude, and therein lies the key to understanding Merkel's dramatic turn-around on Germany's nuclear energy future. Given its geographic location, her country's exposure to tectonic shifting is rare, although it has seen a few major quakes over the centuries; it is also unlikely to witness a killer tsunami along the North Sea coast. Merkel's response to Fukushima rather derived from her grasp of human error, the hyper-reaction of the German public, and the state's standard practice of limiting nuclear industry liability for "unforeseen risks." Designating nuclear energy as "too risky to fail," Peter Hennicke and Paul Welfens make the case that "the residual risk [*Restrisiko*] is actually the main risk [*Hauptrisiko*]."[57] Their calculations show that a major nuclear disaster in either France or Germany would result in a "massive destabilization of

public finances, the collapse of the *Euro* bailout fund, and overall destabilization of the EU economies."[58]

The German reaction *in* Japan was far from rational; the domestic
response was even worse in terms of media hyperbole and public hysteria.
As Europe's strongest nuclear power proponent, French President
Sarkozy sent a team of top nuclear experts for "moral reinforcement,"
and a major shipment of boron reactor-coolant. Germany sent forty-three
technical relief experts and three detection dogs to Minamisanriku
for a day and a half (shorter than any other search group), along with
a 58-meter-tall robotic cement pump (nicknamed "the Giraffe") to spray
water on Block 4.[59] Air France offered one-way tickets to Europe at
economy-class prices; Lufthansa immediately ended its service to Tokyo.
Ignoring advice from its own Expert Commission on Radiation, the FRG
immediately relocated all embassy personnel from Tokyo to Osaka (who
stayed away longer than other foreign diplomats) and shut down its
school in Tokyo-Yokohama, about to celebrate the 150th anniversary of
German–Japanese relations. BMW, Bosch, and Volkswagen relocated
their employees, giving them the option to return home, although VW
did contribute €2.5 million for relief costs. Members of the Bavarian State
Opera canceled their fall 2011 Asian tour, while citizens back home
stopped eating at Sushi restaurants, though the fish consumed there did
not come from Japan.

German media, including *Bild, Spiegel,* and the *Frankfurter Allgemeine
Zeitung,* wallowed in horror images; headlines referred to the *Super-GAU*
("greatest presumable accident"), "Tokyo in Death-Angst," "the Dance
of Death at the Reactor," and "Japan's Atomic Inferno," declaring "Japan
is done for." Kan's efforts to limit panic-provoking information flows
triggered German comparisons with the "*Führer's* bunker at the end of
World War II." Aerial attempts to assess the damage became *Kamikaze-
Flyers,* while clean-up crews became "scrap-reactor death-candidates."[60]
One press photograph showed the corpses of "catastrophe victims" without revealing that all were tsunami fatalities (few foreign correspondents
reported directly from Tokyo). The Japanese Ambassador in Berlin
pleaded for calm.[61] Max Planck Institute director, Gerd Gigerenzer,
observed:

The Germans reacted quite differently than the rest of the world. Much more
nervous … We are really more afraid of radiation than other things, and make
much less ado about the earthquake victims. The Fukushima incident will
experience the same fate as its predecessors, the financial crisis, swine flu and
the E-hec (ethyl-hydroxy-ethylcellulose) contamination. These topics have a few

minutes of currency, then they are quickly forgotten. We hardly learn anything from them, except that they make us very upset for a short period of time.[62]

He was proved wrong on that last point. A subject that had never been at the top of the conservative agenda became Merkel's *cause célèbre*. The Christian parties' occasional utterances about a moral obligation to "preserve creation" turned into a discourse over energy efficiency and technological innovation geared toward secure, sustainable, competitive, and affordable power generation. Despite ongoing conflicts over fracking and "clean coal," Fukushima led to an unprecedented all-party consensus regarding environmental positions that had been deemed too radically "green" through the 1970s, 1980s, and 1990s. Within four weeks, parliamentarians had pulled together to approve over 700 pages of new laws, following a cabinet resolution of June 6; Länder officials even agreed to fast-tracking procedures. Although a tradition of state steering in the energy field has granted Germany a forerunner role at the EU level, it offers no guarantee of compliance among the sixteen states. We now consider the legislative parameters of its post-Fukushima energy turn-around.

FULL SPEED AHEAD, MOSTLY: GERMAN ENERGY POLICY, 2011–2015

Although the first Grand Coalition had committed Germany to significant emission reductions and renewable energy cultivation in 2008, Fukushima rendered the plan's "fundamental architecture" obsolete.[63] Nuclear plants had been expected to keep energy costs low long enough to render REs ready for prime time. Still, Germany's twenty-year head-start vis-à-vis other EU states had already begun to pay off: by 2006, Germany had raked in over €56 billion for its green technology exports, and cut its own energy import bill by €20 billion; other green-led markets account for €1 trillion in annual volume. By 2008, it had surpassed the EU 2020 target (20 percent) by eliminating 110 million tons of CO_2, reducing its GHG emissions by 26.4 percent. It had created 1.8 million jobs across the environmental protection arena, and hoped to add another 500,000 workplaces by 2020.[64]

Commensurate with Merkel's mediation at Heiligendamm, the Grand Coalition embraced an *Integrated Energy and Climate Program*, along with an *International Climate Initiative* in December 2007. Proceeds from carbon-emission certificate sales supplied revenue for pilot programs. The Ministry for the Environment, Nature Conservation and

Nuclear Safety issued "Ten Principles for a Sustainable Energy Supply" in 2008. They centered on: (1) ensuring supply security; (2) boosting the economy; (3) expanding renewable energies; (4) phasing-out nuclear power; (5) utilizing (clean) coal efficiently; (6) building future power grids; (7) consuming electricity efficiently; (8) reducing the fossil heat requirement; (9) cutting traffic emissions; and (10) acting globally, by sharing clean technologies with other nations.[65]

Prior to the Fukushima disaster, Grand Coalition partners had likewise agreed on an *Energy Policy Road Map: New Thinking – New Energy* that established goals, benchmarks, and timetables, in some cases moving beyond regulations under negotiation at the EU level. By 2020, it aimed to: (a) cut GHG emissions to 40 percent below 1990 levels; (b) double national "efficiency" by increasing energy productivity by 3 percent annually; (c) raise RE usage to 18 percent of primary energy production (50 percent by 2050); and (d) enhance RE reliance from 15 percent of gross power consumption to 30 percent. It foresaw a thermal energy increase from 7 to 14 percent, and fossil fuel replacement (70 percent imported) with bio-fuels, to reduce GHG emissions another 7 percent. It also hoped to raise Combined Heat & Power (CHP) generation to 25 percent by 2020.

The Road Map likewise enjoyed broad support under the 2009 conservative–liberal coalition, but hefty internal coalition conflicts impeded progress. Fukushima forced the government to become more proactive. Announcing her nuclear exit decision, Merkel accelerated the charge of a climate-friendlier light brigade with a forty-year Energy Package.[66] Between June 30 and July 8, 2011, the Bundestag adopted eight implementation laws.[67]

Box 6.1

Post-Fukushima Energy Legislation and Amendments, June–July 2011
(1)13th Law Amending the Nuclear Energy Act repealed the 2009 extension of nuclear power plant operations. The "lights out" plan will be completed by 2022.

(2) Law on the Legal Framework for Promoting Electricity Generation and Renewable Energies (2012) targets cost efficiency, market and system integration, and transparency; it extended system bonuses for wind energy installations through 2014, using flexible premiums to foster electricity storage for high demand periods.

Box 6.1: Cont

(3) 1st Law on Maritime-related Improvements seeks to accelerate approval processes by "bundling" permissions for off-shore wind turbine installations, instead of treating them as individual projects, often thwarted by delays.

(4) Law on Measures for Accelerating Network Expansion for Electricity Generation and Transfer foresees the construction of smarter grids and networks, especially in high-intensity regions.

(5) Law on New Regulations for Energy-Economic Requirements foresees coordination among all transfer and storage networks, and includes the government in a comprehensive "needs planning" structure.

(6) Amendments to the Law establishing a Special Energy and Climate Fund collect returns on all emission certificates sales (formerly limited to profits exceeding €900 million).

The CDU/CSU–FDP government embraced binding targets for expanding RE sources to 18 percent of total power consumption, rising to 60 percent by 2050. It supported an RE share of 80 percent for electricity (then at 10.3 percent), reducing energy consumption for transport 40 percent, and doubling CHP use to 25 percent by 2050.[68] The proliferation of lucrative, decentralized market niches for CHP generators and other *ecopreneurs* led some Länder to turn away from dominant energy providers like Bewag, GASAG, and Vattenfall. In Berlin, for example, citizens campaigned in 2012 for a re-municipalization (de-privatization) of electricity provision.[69] State officials opposed building-rehab measures as an infringement on their competencies (since they were likely to bear the costs).

While the 2011 shut-down of seven nuclear facilities did not trigger major shortfalls, other problems ensued. Lawmakers had expected fuel taxes paid by nuclear operators to generate €1.4 billion for RE R&D between 2011 and 2016. Shut-downs ended payments to the Climate Fund, cutting investment revenues in half; officials had trouble filling the gap as the price of CO_2 certificates dropped. The states used the 2009 constitutional "debt-brake" as their excuse for not replacing the lost tax revenues.[70]

The feed-in tariff system led to a mushrooming of regional energy cooperatives. Their numbers rose from 66 in 2001 to 736 by 2012; 31 percent were privately owned, 13 percent by banks or funds, and 11 percent by local farmers, with the Big Four energy companies controlling merely 5 percent.[71] Covering the needs of 160,000 households, cooperative investments rose from €792 million in 2011 to €1.2 billion in 2013.[72] The conservative–liberal coalition approved a 30 percent cut in solar subsidies in 2012, however, resulting in job losses and bankruptcies in a sector facing new Chinese competitors. It continued granting carbon emission and feed-in surcharge *exemptions* for the most energy-intensive industries (aluminum, steel).[73]

Merkel drew on recommendations from the National Academy of Science Leopoldina, the German Academy for Technical Sciences (ACATECH), the Union of German Academies of Science, and the Council for Sustainable Development.[74] She moreover initiated an international peer-review process, whose first report was titled *Sustainability Made in Germany – We Know You Can Do It* (2009). Five male and two female evaluators from Sweden, Finland, the United Kingdom, the Netherlands, India, Canada, and the United States criticized coordination problems between federal and state governments, adding new indicators in its 2013 report. In 2014, Gabriel's restructured super-ministry (Economics and Energy) issued its second "energy turn-around and monitoring" report.[75]

Allowing for experimentation in some areas, federalism raises complex competency questions at all levels.[76] While officials support "the most thrifty, rational, socially- and environmentally sustainable, resource-saving, low-risk and macro-economically priceworthy production and utilization of energy possible," they differ in their interpretations of Articles 72 and 74 BL. Conflict-ridden issues include spatial planning, construction requirements, and infrastructural adaptation.[77]

The energy turn-around also raises burden-sharing and financial equalization questions. Major cities consume more energy but have less "space" for meeting their own needs (Berlin generates only 3 percent, Hamburg 15 percent).[78] Local authorities bear the brunt of citizen complaints over noise pollution from "monster masts" (wind turbines), bad biomass odors, and potential health risks from electromagnetic waves. They object to landscape changes tied to energy and carbon storage, transport, and high-tension grids benefiting users in other states.[79] Some regions enjoy cumulative advantages, while others face price inelasticity. Bavaria's enormous solar capacity renders it a net recipient of EEG support (€1.23 billion); North Rhine-Westphalia has big needs but low capacity, forcing it to pay €1.85 billion; Sachsen-Anhalt has substantial wind-power potential but has to buy expensive turbines from steel-

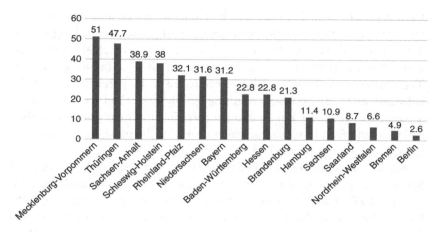

FIGURE 6.2 State Rankings: Electricity Generation from Renewable Energy Sources, 2012 (in percent).
Source: adapted from Dieckmann et al., *Vergleich der Bundesländer*, p. 51.

producing North Rhine-Westphalia; Baden-Württemberg receives €35 million to utilize wind energy for high-value industrial production; bucolic Mecklenburg-Vorpommern collects €162 million, consuming only a fraction of the power it generates.[80] Besides refusing to store its share of nuclear waste, Bavaria has resisted a federal plan to expand power lines through its territory – for its own use!

As Figures 6.2 and 6.3 illustrate, the post Fukushima turn-around has fostered RE growth and innovation across even the poorest Eastern states. Brandenburg and Thüringen have displayed the most effort, proportionate to their size and economic strength.[81] In July 2016, lawmakers revised the Renewable Energy Law, introducing a paradigm shift; rather than rely on guaranteed federal subsidies, producers will have to engage in "market competition" as of 2017 for fewer grants, which will exclude small private energy generators in the name of "cost effectiveness." The law is expected to lead to the formation of local energy cooperatives.

Last but not least, the post-Fukushima shut-downs have done little to eliminate federal conflicts over permanent nuclear waste storage. Baden-Württemberg's first Green premier, Winfried Kretschmann, broke the "southern front" stalemate in 2013 by allowing federal authorities to explore his state for a potential new site. Initiated by Green MP Sylvia Kotting-Uhl, six women representing all parties carved out the *Lex Asse* in February 2013 to accelerate the removal of radioactive waste from the unstable Schachtanlage Asse II site. Technical problems have

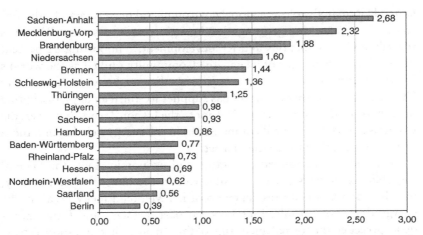

FIGURE 6.3 Workers Directly and Indirectly Involved in RE Generation, 2013 (in percent).
Source: Dieckmann et al., *Vergleich der Bundesländer*, p. 85.

yet to be resolved, but all documentation is available online in the hope of securing public trust in the process. As of 2013, no agreement had been reached regarding operator compensation and responsibility for decommissioning costs. Giving up on Gorleben, a joint Bund–Länder commission issued specified *search criteria* for final storage in its last report of July 2016.[82]

Well before the earth began to rumble in Japan, Germany's accelerated push for alternative and renewable fuels had become a goose laying golden eggs, contributing to a jobs and export boom. After the ECJ rejected a legal challenge to Germany's path-breaking feed-in-tariff mechanism in 1998, seventeen member states and over thirty non-EU countries rushed to adopt it.[83] Merkel's loss of faith in a distant country admired for its rigorous scientific standards and technological proficiency until 2011 strengthened her belief that Germany could and should master a major paradigm shift in the energy sector. Not surprisingly, her second Grand Coalition has continued to "upload" components of its turn-around model to the EU level.

"LOCATION, LOCATION, LOCATION": UPLOADING NATIONAL PRIORITIES AND PRACTICES

Having established her eco-diplomacy credentials at the 1995 UN Climate Summit in Berlin, Merkel used her 2007 term as EU Council President to expand Germany's role as a global environmental player. Her "leadiator" stance on climate-change mitigation brought new intensity to EU efforts regarding CO_2 reductions and RE development.[84] Importing 82 percent of its oil and 57 percent of its gas, the Community ranked as the world's largest energy importer. The 2009 price dispute between Russia and Ukraine led the former to cut off gas supplies for thirteen days, disrupting life across southeastern Europe.[85] Prior to the Lisbon Treaty, however, the Commission lacked formal competencies in the energy field beyond those needed to complete the single market.[86]

Given its founding-member status and economic clout, the Federal Republic has always played a visible role in the European Community, but the 2007 Council presidency accorded Merkel a lucky break in the energy domain. Consultations between past, present, and future presidents preceded the formal anchoring of this "troika" in the Lisbon Treaty, giving Germany a chance to influence EU policies during the Finnish and Portuguese rotations as well. Green Papers and Commission Communications issued in 2005–2006 helped to counter Länder resistance to policy centralization. In 2010, the EU was still a long way from achieving the RE target of 12 percent it had set in 1997. Its Renewable Energy Road Map, released in January 2007, supplied a convenient launching-pad for Merkel initiatives.[87]

Lacking sufficient expertise in new domains, the Commission has a long history of drawing on 300 standing committees tied to EU organs (*comitology*). It moreover relies on input from 1,000 specialized groups (with 30,000 advisors), incorporated into an online "expert group register" since 2005.[88] National specialists thus have many venues for behind-the-scenes participation in EU deliberations. The Second European Climate Change Program, for example, sought advice from stakeholders representing industry, academia, NGOs, and member-state authorities, focusing on agriculture, waste, transport, R&D, industry, energy supply, and flexibility mechanisms. Germany and Denmark made detailed presentations to the Meeting of Member States' Energy Economic Analysts in May 2011, to show how their national plans incorporated the 2050 Energy Road Map.[89]

While commissioners, directorate-general staff, and European parliamentarians swear to uphold supranational interests, they clearly bring their domestic know-how and mobilizational experience to bear in formulating EU initiatives. Germany influences EU policy by sharing data and technical knowledge as one of eleven countries on the Member State Energy and Development Experts Group, and as one of fourteen authorities on the Expert Group on Energy Labelling. In 2014, it supplied one of four professors guiding the Expert Group on Climate Policy for International Maritime Transport. It accounted for two of the nine research institutes involved in the modeling of GHG emissions in transport models, and held two of sixteen academic seats on the Science and Technology Advisory Council, for example. Powerful national ministries also loan civil servants to Brussels for up to three years, where significant mutual learning processes occur. One interview partner noted that Germans are the fastest to adopt a "European mindset" in relation to climate-change activities. There are exceptions, of course: pro-market Energy Commissioner, Günther Oettinger (CDU), is often at odds with his Green and SPD compatriots in the Directorate-General for the Environment or in the European Parliament's largest standing committee (Environment), where Germans occupied ten of the seventy-one seats in 2015.[90]

Documenting the exact points at which Merkel or her ministers redirected the course of EU energy and environmental policies would require a battery of interviews in Brussels beyond the scope of this analysis. Given the extended negotiations preceding *co-decision*, it is also impossible to connect six months of presidential input with concrete legislative outputs. Process-tracing offers at least indirect evidence of successful German uploading relative to longer-term EU climate change and RE goals. Directive 2003/87/EC, for example, established a detailed trading scheme for GHG emissions, but the EU "toolbox" of supportive financial instruments was not significantly expanded until 2008, with troika support. Directives and regulations issued in 2009 would have been at least two years in the making. Merkel undoubtedly pushed for a shift from voluntary approaches to binding indicators, benchmarks, and timetables, given her adoption of these mechanisms at home. During Germany's Council presidency, member state leaders accepted a set of collective targets known as Europe 20–20–20, requiring twenty-seven national action plans and yearly "tracking" of their progress.

In spring 2007, presiding Germans initiated talks on a treaty to replace the ill-fated Constitution of Europe, rejected in French and Dutch referenda. Merkel was personally credited with securing Lisbon Treaty ratification in 2009, according energy a new legal foundation (Title XXI) at "the heart of European activity." A further Road Map (2011) accelerated the Community push for a highly competitive, low-carbon economy by 2050, based on the formula, *renewables = job creation + sustainability*. Adopted in 2014, the *Europe 2030 Plan: Climate and Energy Goals for a Competitive, Secure and Low-carbon EU Economy* combined multi-faceted market instruments, R&D funding, innovation policies, and technology transfers commensurate with German policies of the last decade. It calls for citizen participation and political transparency to counter perceived EU democratic deficits, while upholding the *subsidiarity principle*. The latter could prove tricky, insofar as it allows national parliaments to object to Community measures that might "better" be left to regional or domestic policy-makers within the multi-level governance structure.

Using 1990 as a baseline, Europe 2030 raises projected GHG reductions to 40 percent, rising to 80 percent by 2050, using domestic measures alone. The EU pledged a 40 percent reduction during the 2015 global negotiations in Paris. Sectors covered by its Emissions Trading System (ETS) are to decrease their emissions by 43 percent; this will be achieved by altering the cap by 2.2 percent annually, to be shared equitably among the member states. Binding for the EU (but not individual members), RE use is to increase to 27 percent; as the Union's largest CO_2 emitter, the FRG raised its own quota to secure agreement. The 2030 framework foresees ETS reform based on a *market stability reserve*, aiming to eliminate "surpluses," enhance market integration, diversify supplies, and develop indigenous sources. All measures will be "informed by" a comparative report on energy prices and costs, assessing the key drivers and rising price differentials (e.g., cheap US gas) vis-à-vis its main trading partners.

CONCLUSION: PROMISE V. PERFORMANCE

As noted earlier, the criteria needed to assess "successful leadership" vary from one policy domain to another. Analyzing German environmental performance prior to the Fukushima disaster (1990–2010), Roger Karapin challenged its overall effectiveness.[91] Disaggregating ecological outcomes in eleven areas, he attributed its greatest success to the unanticipated consequences of unification rather than to deliberate state action: "Remarkably, by 2004, 86 percent of Germany's decline in energy-related CO_2 emissions had taken place in the eastern states," home to only a fifth of the population, accounting for 7 percent of GDP, and less than 30 percent of total CO_2 emissions in 1990.[92] He credits its second largest net reduction to increasing RE use, stimulated by feed-in tariff policies rolled back during Merkel's second term. He deemed voluntary industrial agreements, eco-tax reform, and emissions trading "flawed and relatively ineffective" (only 7 percent of emission reductions). Household energy performance certificates have also fallen short.[93] More troubling, perhaps, is the fact that the "greener" energy becomes, the more citizens use it, for example, on air conditioning, vacation travel, iPhones, and expensive barista-quality coffee machines.

Although some of Karapin's findings still hold, others have been overtaken by circumstances. The massive shut-down of environmentally toxic GDR industries produced equally disastrous unemployment levels in the East, which the shift to REs and green technology has begun to remedy. Given Merkel's personal role in stimulating global climate-change action, I also take issue with his claim that "party competition matters much more than who is in government, and green parties matter much more than do social democratic, Christian democratic or other types of parties."[94] In this case, the individual leader has mattered a great deal across two Grand Coalitions and a conservative–liberal government. While parties have tinkered with the mechanisms, the chancellor has consistently raised the sustainability bar. Merkel not only made climate change a personal priority; she also possesses the scientific-technical expertise, and a grasp of new IT gadgets, needed to see it through. Fukushima allowed her to bridge the biggest eco-policy gap between the major parties, and gave her the leverage necessary to compel adversaries like the Environmental and Economics ministries, to work together. Her courageous nuclear exit moreover moved France and Japan to turn to REs for 20 percent of their power needs.[95]

Despite its EU "leadiator" role, Germany occasionally places national economic interests above the climate goals it seeks to impose on others.[96] Merkel has been accused of zig-zagging, foot-dragging, back-tracking, or even reversing course along the road to a new energy future.[97] The FRG case nonetheless proves that countries can make money and create millions of jobs by pursuing a rigorous renewable energy agenda. It has pulled together some unlikely partners, for example, British Petroleum, Royal Dutch Shell Group, and the Austrian mineral–oil consortium OMV, to generate top-down leverage, boosted from below by strong citizen support for climate-friendly policies. These pincers enable Germany to exercise leadership in "a dynamic process of competitive multi-level reinforcement among different EU political poles."[98]

At first glance, adapting to climate change appears to be a gender-neutral endeavor. Given a looming shortage of highly skilled workers, the FRG clearly needs to recruit many more women into the Science, Technology, Engineering, and Math (STEM) fields (MINT in German, for Math, Computing, Natural Sciences, Technology). In 2008, women comprised fewer than 15 percent of all new mathematics and science students, and only 8 percent in engineering. As the Euro crisis chapter showed, globalization increasingly requires us to look beyond national borders in assessing the gender impact of decisions pursued by extraordinarily influential leaders. A 2001 EU study described not only the different ways in which environmental degradation hurts women, but also the diverging ways in which they define causes, relief needs, and possible solutions.[99]

A further body of evidence suggests that women are the disproportionate victims of climate-related natural disasters. During a 1970 Bangladesh cyclone, the ratio of female to male deaths was 14:1; gender-sensitive World Bank programs lowered the ratio to 5:1 during the 2007 cyclone.[100] Women were three times more likely to die during the 2004 Asian tsunami, while 56 percent of the 2011 Japanese fatalities were over 65, the majority of whom were women.[101] Assessing the impact of 4,605 catastrophes in 141 countries from 1981 to 2001, Eric Neumayer and Thomas Plümpe concluded: "The feminists got it right. Natural disasters are a tragedy in their own right but in countries with existing gender discrimination women are the worst hit ... policy makers, international and humanitarian organizations must develop better policies to address the special needs of women in the wake of large-scale natural disasters."[102]

Merkel encountered a perfect storm with respect to united Germany's ecological needs: she was singularly qualified to grasp the rapidly advancing problems of global warming and human error in nuclear energy management. As an East German, she had witnessed not only state suppression of environmental data, but also systemic economic collapse under leaders who feared innovation as a threat to their power. As a physicist, Merkel was uniquely positioned to grasp the magnitude of the Fukushima melt-down and could calculate the damage likely to result from a future German *Super-Gau* (worst-case scenario). As a politician in a democratic society, she quickly learned that mass protests and public opinion matter.

Halfway into her second term, Chancellor Merkel had amassed a substantial amount of confidence and credibility by the time the Great Eastern Japan earthquake hit. Regularly accused of waiting out crucial political decisions, her ability to rapidly deduce which way the political wind was blowing turned out to be a useful skill, for example, for positioning turbine farms. Rather than hanging on to old industries, she embraced GHG reductions and renewable energy as potential contributors to a jobs and export boom. Her can-do attitude in this domain was reinforced by strong public support for eco-friendly, non-nuclear energy alternatives predating her arrival on the national stage. Her quick mastery of key historical lessons shaping not only this domain, but also Western relations with Israel, Russia, and Europe have endowed her with the kind of stamina and power I associate with the Energizer Bunny who "just keeps going and going and going," no matter what new crisis she encounters.

By 2012 Angela Merkel had really earned her title as the World's Most Powerful Woman, and a principled one at that. Her third term as chancellor would find her invoking a can-do spirit not only in relation to policies her compatriots wanted; she would also use it to reverse their fundamental beliefs about what it meant to be German in the face of an extraordinary global refugee crisis.

NOTES

1. Peter Wensierski, "Wir haben Angst um unsere Kinder," *Der Spiegel*, July 8, 1985 (Part I), July 15, 1985 (Part II), July 22, 1985 (Part III).
2. Rede der Bundesministerin für Umwelt, Naturschutz und Reaktorsicherheit, Frau Dr. Angela Merkel, zur Debatte zur Sicherheit von Castor-Transporten am 27. Mai 1998 im Deutschen Bundestag.
3. Wolfgang Rüdig, "Negotiating the 'Berlin Mandate': Reflections on the First 'Conference of the Parties' to the UN Framework Convention on Climate Change," *Environmental Politics*, 4(3) (1995): 481–487. See also United Nations Framework Convention on Climate Change, Report of the Conference of the Parties on its First Session, Berlin, March 28–April 7, 1995.
4. Per-Olof Busch and Helge Jörgens, "The International Sources of Policy Convergence: Explaining the Spread of Environmental Policy Innovations," *Journal of European Public Policy*, 12(5) (2005): 860–884.
5. Admitted in 1995, Sweden, especially Commissioner Margot Wallström, pushed the EU to adopt gender mainstreaming, work–family reconciliation and other gender-sensitive policies.
6. Rachel Carson, *Silent Spring* (New York: Houghton Mifflin, 1962).
7. "50 Jahre Spiegel-Affäre: Wie der Staat das Recht beugte," *Der Spiegel*, September 17, 2012.
8. Joyce Marie Mushaben, "Peace and the National Question: A Study of the Development of an 'Association of Responsibility' between the two Germanys," *Coexistence: A Review of East–West and Development Issues*, 24 (1987): 245–270.
9. Mushaben, "Cycles of Peace Protest in West Germany."
10. Jonathan Olsen, *Nature and Nationalism: Right-Wing Ecology and the Politics of Identity in Contemporary Germany* (New York: St. Martin's Press, 1999).
11. Joyce Marie Mushaben, "Innocence Lost: Environmental Images and Political Experiences among the West German Greens," *New Political*

Science, 14 (1986): 39–66; Joachim Radkau, Aufstieg und Krise der deutschen Atomwirtschaft, 1945–1975 (Hamburg: Rowohlt, 1983).

12. Joyce Marie Mushaben, "Grassroots and Gewaltfreie Aktionen: A Study of Mass Mobilization Strategies in the West German Peace Movement," Journal of Peace Research, 23(2) (1986): 141–154.

13. Alexander Roßnagel, Bedroht die Kernenergie unsere Freiheit (Munich: C. H. Beck, 1983).

14. Soviet reactors were designed to allow for easier spent-fuel extraction for this purpose.

15. Joyce Marie Mushaben, "Reflections on the Institutionalization of Protest: The Case of the West German Peace Movements," Alternatives: Journal of World Policy, 11(4) (1984): 519–539.

16. They included Joschka Fischer, Herta Däubler-Gmelin, Heidi Wieczorek-Zeul, Otto Schily, and Ursula Schmidt.

17. Energiewende: Wachstum und Wohlstand ohne Erdöl und Uran (Frankfurt: Fischer, 1980); also, Joseph Huber, Die verlorene Unschuld der Ökologie (Frankfurt: Fischer, 1982).

18. Patrick Schwarz (ed.), Angela Merkel, die Unerwartete – wie Deutschlands erste Kanzlerin mit der Zeit geht (Hamburg: Edel, 2011), p. 22.

19. Christoph H. Stefes, "Bypassing Germany's Reformstau: The Remarkable Rise of Renewable Energy," German Politics, 19(2) (2010), p. 151; see also Volker Lauber and Lutz Mez, "Three Decades of Renewable Electricity Policies in Germany," Energy and Environment, 15(4) (2004): 599–623.

20. Gerd Winter "The Rise and Fall of Nuclear Energy Use in Germany: Processes, Explanations and the Role of Law," Journal of Environmental Law, 25(1) (2013), p. 96.

21. Stefes, "Bypassing Germany's Reformstau," p. 152.

22. "Kohls Minister schönen Gutachten," Süddeutsche Zeitung, September 8, 2009.

23. Damian Ludewig, "Die Energiewende finanzieren und beschleunigen durch den Abbau umweltschädlicher Subventionen," 4. Jahrbuch nachhaltiger Energie (Marburg: Metropolis, 2014), pp. 357–376.

24. "End of an Industrial Era: Germany to Close its Coal Mines," Der Spiegel, January 30, 2007.

25. Rüdiger K. W. Würzel, "Environmental, Climate and Energy Policies: Path-Dependent Incrementalism or Quantum Leap?" German Politics, 19(3/4) (2010), p. 465.

26. Stefes, "Bypassing Germany's Reformstau," p. 156.

27. Ibid., p. 159.

28. Peter Wensierski, Von oben nach unten wächst gar nichts: Umweltzerstörung und Protest in der DDR (Frankfurt: Fischer, 1986).

29. Ehrhart Neubert, Geschichte der Opposition in der DDR, 1949–1989 (Berlin: Links, 1997); Detlef Pollack, Politischer Protest. Politisch alternative Gruppen in der DDR (Opladen: Leske & Budrich, 2000).

30. Peter Wensierksi and Wolfgang Buscher (eds.), Beton ist Beton: Zivilisationskritik aus der DDR (Hattingen: Scandica, 1981); Mushaben, "Swords to Plowshares."

31. Michael Zschiesche, "Explosionen in Bitterfeld," *Horch and Guck*, 76 (1988): 63–67.

32. "Atompolitik in der ehemaligen DDR," see: http://de.atomkraftwerkeplag.wikia.com/wiki/Atompolitik_in_der_ehemaligen_DDR.

33. Resing, *Angela Merkel*, pp. 52–54.

34. Lau, *Die Letzte Volkspartei*, p. 88; Angela Merkel (ed.), *Der Preis des Überlebens – Gedanken und Gespräche über zukünftige Aufgaben der Umweltpolitik* (Stuttgart: Deutsche Verlags-Anstalt, 1997).

35. Lau, *Die Letzte Volkspartei*, p. 90; Müller-Vogg, *Angela Merkel*, p. 96.

36. Müller-Vogg, *Angela Merkel*, p. 97.

37. Ibid., pp. 98 ff; Rede der Bundesministerin für Umwelt, Naturschutz und Reaktorensicherheit, Frau Dr. Angela Merkel, zur Debatte zur Sicherheit von Castor-Transporten am 27. Mai 1998 im Deutschen Bundestag.

38. Rudolf Hickel, "Externe Kosten: Atomstrom ist nicht noch bezahlbar," University of Bremen, April 4, 2011; Katrina Umpfenbach and Stephan Sina, "Analysis of the German Federal Government's National Renewable Energy Action Plan," Heinrich Böll Stiftung, Berlin, October 2010; see also Sascha Adamek, *Die Atomlüge: Getäuscht, vertuscht, verschwiegen: Wie Politiker und Konzerne die Gefahren der Atomkraft herunterspielen* (Munich: Heyne, 2011), pp. 169–171.

39. To avoid dominating budgetary proceedings, Germany "traded places" with Finland, assuming the presidency in 2007, rather than in 2006.

40. Regierungserklärung von Bundeskanzlerin Angela Merkel zum G-8 Weltwirtschaftsgipfel vom 6. bis 8. Juni 2007 in Heiligendamm.

41. Würzel, "Environmental, Climate and Energy Policies," pp. 467–468.

42. Jan Frederick Braun, "EU Energy Policy under the Treaty of Lisbon Rules: Between a New Policy and Business as Usual," European Policy Institute Working Paper No. 31, February 2011.

43. Japan had already experienced nuclear plant crises dating back over twenty years. See Reinhard Zöllner, *Japan, Fukushima und Wir. Zelebranten einer nuklearen Erdbebenkatastrophe* (Munich: Judicium 2011); see further Florian Coulmas and Judith Stalpers, *Fukushima. Vom Erdbeben zur atomaren Katastrophe* (Munich: Beck'sche Reihe, 2011).

44. Robert Gast, "Chronik des Versagens," *Die Zeit*, March 1, 2012.

45. See Merkel's Regierungserklärung zur Energiepolitik, *"Der Weg zur Energie der Zukunft,"* Deutscher Bundestag, June 9, 2011.

46. Ibid., p. 171.

47. Adamek, *Die Atomlüge*, p. 174; Vlado Vivoda, "Japan's Energy Security Predicament post-Fukushima," *Energy Policy*, 46 (2012): 135–143; see further Uwe Nestle, "Does the Use of Nuclear Power Lead to Lower Electricity Prices? An Analysis of the Debate in Germany with an International Perspective," *Energy Policy*, 41 (2012): 152–160. Assigning a 20 percent market share to nuclear energy, Peter Hennicke and Paul Welfens calculate that hidden subsidies, including the uninsured damages and recovery costs that will ultimately fall to taxpayers, which add up to €12,500 per household. See their study, *Energiewende nach Fukushima – Deutscher Sonderweg oder weltweites Vorbild?* (Munich: Oekom, 2012).

48. Klaus Töpfer (ed.), *Deutsche Energiewende: Eine Gemeinschaftswerk für die Zukunft* (Berlin: Ethik Kommission Sichere Energieversorgung: 2011); Klaus Töpfer and Ranga Yogeshwar, *Unsere Zukunft. Ein Gespräch über die Welt nach Fukushima* (Munich: C. H. Beck, 2011), p. 8.

49. "E.on nimmt AKW Grafenrheinfeld früher vom Netz," *Der Spiegel*, March 28, 2014.

50. Markus Wacket and Michael Nienaber, "German Government Clashes with Bavaria over Nuclear Storage Site Plan," *Reuters*, June 19, 2015. Brokdorf (Schleswig-Holstein), Philippsburg (Baden-Württemberg), Biblis (Hesse), and Isar (Bavaria) were scheduled to receive twenty-six containers of German waste, reprocessed and stored at La Hague (France) and Sellafield (United Kingdom).

51. Coulmas and Stalpers, *Fukushima*, pp. 28, 113.

52. Zöllner, *Japan, Fukushima und Wir*, p. 18.

53. Coulmas and Stalpers, *Fukushima*, pp. 23–25.

54. Ibid., pp. 51 ff.

55. Kayla Strauss, "Land Policies in Tokyo: Implications of the 2011 Tohoku Disaster," Honor's thesis, University of Missouri-St. Louis, December 31, 2011.

56. Since 1976, 70 percent of personal contributions to the LDP came from top TEPCO executives; TEPCO employed 19,000, and enriched 900,000 shareholders. By late March 2011, it was reporting €10.6 billion in losses. Coulmas and Stalpers, *Fukushima*, pp. 79–82.

57. Hennicke and Welfens, *Energiewende nach Fukushima*, pp. 10, 38–41.

58. Ibid., p. 15.

59. Zöllner, *Japan, Fukushima und Wir*, p. 34; Coulmas and Stalpers, *Fukushima*, pp. 118–119.

60. Regarding erroneous German reports, see Zöllner, *Japan, Fukushima und Wir*, pp. 147–154 ff.

61. Coulmas and Stalpers, *Fukushima*, p. 128.

62. Ibid., pp. 130–132.

63. Christian Huß, "Durch Fukushima zum neuen Konsens? Die Umweltpolitik von 2009–2013," in Reimut Zöhlnhofer and Thomas Saalfeld (eds.), *Politik im Schatten der Krise. Eine Bilanz der Regierung Merkel, 2009–2013* (Berlin: Springer, 2014), p. 528.

64. Data stem from the Agentur für Erneuerbare Energien.

65. Miranda A. Schreurs, "German Perspectives on Ecological Modernization, Technology Transfer and Intellectual Property Rights in the Case of Climate Change," American Institute for Contemporary German Studies, Policy Report No. 45. Washington DC, 2010, pp. 61–77.

66. "Chancellor Merkel Presents Germany's 40 Year Energy Plan, Calling it a 'Revolution' in Energy Supply and Efficiency," German Information Center, January 11, 2010.

67. Hennicke and Welfens, *Energiewende nach Fukushima*, pp. 36–38.

68. Bundesministerium für Umwelt, January 2009, pp. 10, 12.

69. Jochen Monstadt, "Urban Governance and the Transition of Energy Systems: Institutional Change and Shifting Energy and Climate Policies in Berlin,"

International Journal of Urban and Regional Research, 31(2) (June 2007): 326–343.

70. Huß, "Durch Fukushima zum neuen Konsens?," p. 527.
71. Miranda Schreurs and Sibyl Steuwer, "Der Koordinierungsbedarf zwischen Bund und Ländern bei der Umsetzung der Energiewende aus politikwissenschaftlicher Sicht," in Thorsten Müller and Hartmut Kahl (eds.), *Energiewende im Föderalismus* (Baden-Baden: Nomos, 2015), p. 59.
72. Jan Hildebrand, "Dezentralität und Bürgerbeteiligung – Die Energiewende im Föderalismus aus Sicht der Akzeptanzforschung," in Thorsten Müller and Hartmut Kahl (eds.), *Energiewende im Föderalismus* (Baden-Baden: Nomos, 2015), p. 136.
73. Gerritt Wiesmann, "Germany to Cut Subsidies for Solar Power," *Financial Times*, February 22, 2012.
74. Leopoldina, Acatech and Union of the German Academies of the Sciences, *Die Energiewende europäisch integriert: Neue Gestaltungsmöglichkeiten für die gemeinsame Energie- und Klimapolitik* (Berlin: March 2015).
75. *Zweiter Monitoring Bericht: "Energie der Zukunft,"* available at: www .bmwi.de/BMWi/Redaktion/PDF/Publikationen/zweiter-monitoring-bericht-energie-der-zukunft,property=pdf,bereich=bmwi2012,sprache=de,rwb=true .pdf.
76. Martin Wickel, "Klimaschutz auf Länderebene," in Thorsten Müller and Hartmut Kahl (eds.), *Energiewende im Föderalismus* (Baden-Baden: Nomos, 2015), pp. 187–202.
77. Franz Reimer, "Die Energiewende und die Kompetenzordnung des Grundgesetzes," in Thorsten Müller and Hartmut Kahl (eds.), Energiewende im Föderalismus (Baden-Baden: Nomos, 2015), p. 91.
78. Schreurs and Steuwer, "Der Koordinierungsbedarf ...," p. 59.
79. Hildebrand, "Dezentralität und Bürgerbeteiligung," p. 132.
80. Gawel and Korte, "Regionale Verteilungswirkungen und Finanzierungsverantwortung," p. 155.
81. Jochen Dieckmann, Antje Vogel-Sper, Jörg Mayer et al., *Vergleich der Bundesländer: Best Practice für den Ausbau Erneuerbarer Energien – Indikatoren und Ranking* (Berlin and Stuttgart: Federal Ministry for Economics and Energy, 2014).
82. Winter, "The Rise and Fall of Nuclear Energy Use."
83. ECJ, *PreussenElektra AG* v. *Schleswag AG*, Case ECJ C-379/98, March 13, 2001.
84. Karin Bäckstrand and Ole Elgström, "The EU's Role in Climate Change Negotiations: From Leader to 'Leadiator'," *Journal of European Public Policy*, 20(10) (2013): 1369–1386.
85. Simon Pirani, Jonathan Stern, and Katja Yafimava, "The Russo-Ukrainian Gas Dispute of January 2009: A Comprehensive Assessment," Oxford Institute for Energy Studies, February 2009.
86. Braun, "EU Energy Policy under the Treaty of Lisbon Rules."
87. *Green Paper on a European Strategy for Sustainable, Competitive and Secure Energy*, COM(2006) 105 final; *Green Paper on Market-based Instruments for Environment and Related Policy Purposes*, COM(2007) 140 final;

Renewable Energies in the 21st Century: Building a More Sustainable Future, COM(2006) 848; and *Towards a European Strategic Energy Technology Plan,* COM(2006) 847 final.

88. Rules for Commission Expert Groups (2010) 7649 final, SEC (2010) 1360 final; and Guidelines on the Collection and Use of Expertise by the Commission, COM (2002) 713.

89. ENER.Ai, Minutes of the Meeting, Brussels, August 30, 2011.

90. Oettinger's problematic Filbinger eulogy (Chapter 3) and his support for the Stuttgart 21 project caused him to lose his Minister-President post in 2011.

91. Roger Karapin, "Climate Policy Outcomes in Germany: Environmental Performance and Environmental Damage in Eleven Policy Areas," *German Politics & Society,* 30(3) (2012): 1–34. See also Felix Ekardt, "Die rechtliche Energiewende seit 2011 – ein klima-, naturschutz- und landnutzungsbezogener Erfolg?" in Bundesministerium für Umwelt, Naturschutz und Reaktorensicherheit, 4. *Jahrbuch nachhaltiger Ökonomie: Die Energiewende als gesellschaftlicher Transformationsprozess,* Marburg, 2014, pp. 255 ff; and Alexander Bürgin, "National Binding Renewable Energy Targets for 2020, but not for 2030: Why the European Commission Developed from a Supporter to a Brakeman," *Journal of European Public Policy,* 22(5) (2015): 690–707.

92. Karapin, "Climate Policy Outcomes," p. 17.

93. Herman Amecke, "The Impact of Energy Performance Certificates: A Survey of German Home Owners," *Energy Policy,* 46 (2012): 4–14.

94. Karapin, "Climate Policy Outcomes," p. 25.

95. Joern Huenteler, Tobias S. Schmidt, and Norichika Kanie, "Japan's Post-Fukushima Challenge: Implications from the German Experience on Renewable Energy Policy," *Energy Policy,* 45 (2012): 6–11; David Jolly and Stanley Reed, "French Nuclear Model Falters," *New York Times,* May 7, 2015.

96. Duncan Liefferink and Mikael Skou Andersen, "Strategies of the 'Green' Member States in EU Environmental Policy Making," *Journal of European Public Policy,* 5(2) (1998): 254–270.

97. "Der Weg zur Energie der Zukunft," Regierungserklärung von Bundeskanzlerin Dr. Angela Merkel zur Energiepolitik, Deutscher Bundestag, Berlin, June 9, 2011; Erik Gawl and Bernd Hansjürgens, "Projekt 'Energiewende': Schneckentempo und Zickzackkurs statt klare Konzepte für die Systemtransformation?" *ZBW: Leibniz-Informationszentrum Wirtschaft,* 5 (2013): 283–288, doi 10.1007/s10273-013-1525-1.

98. Miranda A. Schreurs and Yves Tiberghien, "Multi-Level Reinforcement: Explaining European Union Leadership in Climate Change Mitigation," *Global Environmental Politics,* 7(4) (2007), p. 27.

99. Irmgard Schulz, Diana Hummel, Claudia Empacher et al., "Research on Gender, the Environment and Sustainable Development: Studies on Gender Impact Assessment of the Programmes of the 5th Framework Program for Research, Technological Development and Demonstration," Institut für sozial-ökologische Forschung, Frankfurt, 2001.

100. World Bank, "Improving Women's Odds in Disasters," Washington, DC, December 12, 2013.
101. Brigitte Leoni, "Japan Quake took Toll on Women and Elderly," reporting for the UN Office for Disaster Risk Reduction, March 12, 2012.
102. Eric Neumayer and Thomas Plümper, "The Gendered Nature of Natural Disasters: The Impact of Catastrophic Events on the Gender Gap in Life Expectancy, 1981–2002,"*Annals of the Association of American Geographers*, 97 (2007): 551–566.

7

Germany as a Land of Immigration: Citizenship, Refugees, and the Welcoming Culture

Coinciding with the new millennium, a major paradigm shift in migration and citizenship policies pursued by Germany's first female chancellor represents the culmination of many forces unleashed by unification. Neither Merkel's personal experiences prior to 1989, her cabinet responsibilities for Women, Youth and Family, nor, later, for the Environment and Nuclear Safety, prepared her for an advocacy role concerning the integration of foreigners and their descendants. Raised in the GDR, she had not been directly exposed to millions of guestworkers recruited by Western industries as of the late 1950s. Although the GDR did employ 190,000 temporary laborers from "fraternal socialist states" like Vietnam and Mozambique through the 1970s and 1980s, that regime's main effort to replace a missing generation after two world wars focused instead on bringing its own women into the paid labor force.[1] Merkel's approach to migration has nonetheless done more to advance the legal rights and day-to-day opportunities of foreigners and their offspring than all of her predecessors' reforms dating back to 1949. In this chapter we explore several factors that led this newly minted conservative chancellor, a policy outsider with no prior experience in this domain, to embrace a contentious Red–Green citizenship reform, along with a sweeping set of integration initiatives subject to "implementation monitoring."

Born in the West, socialized in the East, and catapulted onto the national stage by way of unification, Angela Merkel jokingly refers to herself as a person with migration background.[2] She entered the political scene just as the Federal Republic found itself overwhelmed by GDR *resettlers*, co-ethnic *repatriates*, and unprecedented waves of *refugees* fleeing war in Yugoslavia shortly after unification. Between 1991 and 2006, a total of 15.1 million aliens entered the country while 10.9 million departed, for a net increase of 4.2 million.[3] Excluding foreign students, seasonal workers, and EU nationals, Germany took in over 1.1 million repatriates, nearly 40,000 Jewish refugees, and 872,049 asylum seekers between 1991 and 1995.[4] The response of the Kohl government was to restrict very narrow channels for legal migration even further.

From the guestworker era to the fall of the Wall, FRG politicians had erroneously referred to "failed integration" among resident aliens as *the foreigner problem*. My earlier work on immigration revealed that it was really a *German problem*, rooted in party-driven polemics, legal codes, and notions of citizenship that had not kept pace with social realities. Unification proved that FRG adherence to citizenship rooted in *jus sanguinis* contradicted many of the country's own societal needs. Economic competitiveness and the solvency of its pension system are intricately connected to the availability of skilled labor. For decades, economic marginalization and social intolerance toward foreigners was the result of a lack of positive identity among federal republicans themselves: how could one expect Turkish residents to assimilate, given citizens' reluctance to specify the contours of their own *German-ness*? Chapter 2 revealed that neither second-class citizenship perceptions among Easterners nor the "leading culture" debate among conservatives provided clear guidelines for a country historically trapped between too much and too little "national identity."[5]

As seen earlier, Merkel's quick mastery of EU processes has accorded her unprecedented influence over policy-framing at both the national and supranational level. Her earlier experiences as an Easterner, as a physicist-turned-politician, and even as a pastor's daughter once again came together in special ways, allowing her to promote a new understanding of *what it means to be German* in an age of rapid globalization. Building on relevant EU directives and implementation monitoring, Merkel has adopted a holistic approach to integration in the hope of overcoming the FRG's imminent shortage of high-tech laborers. Just as importantly, the chancellor's principled stance on the refugee crisis illustrates the extent to which she now embraces the EU as a *value community*, to a degree not witnessed in her earlier crisis responses.

Given the weak economic position of other member states, she had few grounds to fear that her stance on austerity policies or her push for sustainable energy policies would encounter resistance among her own voters. This time it is different. Merkel's decision to open Germany to a million victims of war and oppression from outside Europe could cost her the chancellorship when she runs for a fourth term in September 2017. In 2016, a volatile, right-wing populist party, Alternative for Germany (AfD), secured double-digit outcomes in four state elections; despite declining support, it could still surpass the 5 percent threshold needed to enter the Bundestag in September 2017. This time Merkel has staked out a moral claim, standing her ground irrespective of the potential political consequences: this is the pastor's daughter at her best, conditioned by thirty-five years in a country that imprisoned human rights activists and denied its own people the right to "exit."

This chapter commences with three "meta-factors" that contributed to a paradigm shift in German citizenship and immigration laws after unification. We then consider the trajectory of FRG migration laws prior to 1998, followed by a summary of EU efforts to harmonize conflicting citizenship, visa, and asylum regimes, in order to ensure *freedom of movement for people, goods, services and capital.* Next, we examine Merkel's use of migration-related "summits" to cultivate new stake-holders for her National Integration Plan, creating a foundation for youth inclusion and ethno-religious tolerance; we also explore the legal complications stemming from hardliners' rejection of dual citizenship under the 1999 reform. Thereafter, we turn to Germany's surprising response to a massive influx of Syrian refugees and Mediterranean boat-people in 2015, amid calls for a new *Fortress Europe* among neighboring states. I conclude with reflections on *intersectionality*, both in relation to Merkel's personal engagement with this topic and as it pertains to Germany's future as a "land of integration." Initially the losers of unification, more than 7 million persons of migrant descent are beginning to benefit from proactive policies fostering their education, employment, and citizenship rights, recent electoral setbacks at the Länder level notwithstanding.

GEOGRAPHY, GENERATIONS, AND GERMAN CITIZENSHIP, 1900–2005

Positing the nation as an organic community, German statutes dating back to the 1913 Reich Nationality and Citizenship Law trapped millions of human faces behind exclusionary masks of foreignness between 1949 and 1989.[6] Declaring itself the legitimate successor to the Third Reich, the fledgling Western state continued the tradition of *jus sanguinis* ("law of blood"), defining citizenship according to parental lineage. It did so to sustain ties between the peoples of the divided nation as well as to protect co-ethnic groups scattered throughout historically German territories in Eastern Europe. The Brandt Government used this framing to supply financial aid in exchange for minority protection and exit options for diasporic Germans in Poland, Romania, and Hungary, for example. By 1990, geographical reconfiguration, generational change, and globalization processes had rendered exclusively ethno-national citizenship detrimental to its broader interests. The conservative mantra, *Germany is not a land of integration*, coupled with the mythical claim that guestworkers would "some day" return to their countries of origin, resulted in contradictory Foreigner Laws that made citizenship unattainable for millions.

By the time the Wall fell, Germany was already home to 7.3 million foreigners accounting for 9 percent of the population (Table 7.1). Nearly 2 million under 18 were aliens in name only: accounting for 13 percent of live births, they comprised 30–40 percent of the elementary school enrollments in cities like Frankfurt and Berlin. Even after fifteen years of obligatory residence, fewer than 450,000 had successfully naturalized, due to burdensome rules and fees. "Dependents" comprising a single family often held different legal status, involving diverging naturalization rules.[7] Prior to 1990, applicants who met all formal requirements could still be rejected at the discretion of bureaucrats as "not in the best interest of German culture." Further discretionary criteria imposed by Land or local authorities produced enfranchisement gaps from one state to another, as well as from one urban district to the next. Berlin's naturalization rate was four times that of Bavaria, for instance, though neither exceeded 5 percent.

The Kohl years, 1991–1993, were marked by an unprecedented wave of xenophobic attacks, overlapping with the influx of thousands of refugees.[8] Though not the *cause* of ultra-nationalist violence, unification served as a *catalyst* for anti-foreigner hostility (*Ausländerfeindlichkeit*), especially among young, disadvantaged males. The first year of unity saw 1,483 physical attacks against purported aliens, ranging from gang assaults in subways to fire-bombings of temporary asylum quarters. Another 2,368 violent incidents were reported in 1991; although politicians blamed youth violence on child-rearing practices under a "socialist dictatorship," three-fourths of the arson attacks took place on Western soil. The Office of Constitutional Protection registered another 54 percent increase in 1992, resulting in seventeen deaths (nine in the West, eight in the East). Tensions eased in 1993, triggering 1,814 acts of violence, with eight fatalities.[9] Attacks occurred in towns stretching

TABLE 7.1 *Legal Classification of Migration Groups, 1991–2013*

Year	Internal EU migration	Family unification	Late resettlers (including family dependants)	Jewish "refugees"	Asylum applicants	Seasonal workers and assistants	Labor migrants according to §§18–21 AufenthG	Foreign students (1st year)
1991	128,142	–	221,995	–	256,112	128,688	–	–
1992	120,445	–	230,565	–	438,191	212,442	–	–
1993	117,115	–	218,888	16,597	322,599	181,037	–	26,149
1994	139,382	–	222,591	8,811	127,210	137,819	–	27,922
1995	175,977	–	217,898	15,184	127,937	176,590	–	28,223
1996	171,804	–	177,751	15,959	116,367	197,924	–	29,391
1997	150,583	–	134,419	19,437	104,353	205,866	–	31,123
1998	135,908	62,992	103,080	17,788	98,644	207,927	–	34,760
1999	135,268	70,750	104,916	18,205	95,113	230,347	–	39,905
2000	130,683	75,888	95,615	16,538	78,564	263,805	–	45,652
2001	120,590	82,838	98,484	16,711	88,278	286,940	–	53,183
2002	110,610	85,305	91,416	19,262	71,124	307,182	–	58,480
2003	98,709	76,077	72,885	15,442	50,563	318,549	–	60,113
2004	266,355	65,935	59,093	11,208	35,607	333,690	–	58,287
2005	286,047	53,213	35,522	5,968	28,914	329,789	18,415	55,773
2006	289,235	50,300	7,747	1,079	21,029	303,429	30,188	53,554
2007	343,851	42,219	5,792	2,502	19,164	299,657	29,803	53,759
2008	335,914	39,717	4,362	1,436	22,085	285,217	30,601	58,350
2009	348,909	42,756	3,360	1,088	27,649	294,828	26,386	60,910
2010	398,451	40,210	2,350	1,015	41,332	293,711	29,768	66,413
2011	532,395	40,975	2,148	986	45,741	207,695	38,083	72,886
2012	623,407	40,843	1,820	458	64,539	3,593	38,745	79,537
2013	707,771	44,311	2,427	246	109,580	–	33,648	86,170

Source: Data drawn from *Migrationsbericht 2014*, Bundesamt für Migration und Flüchtlinge, Berlin, p. 37.

from Aalen (Westphalia) to Zwickau (Saxony). Sensational cases in Hoyerswerda (1991), Rostock-Lichtenhagen (1992), Mölln (1992), and Solingen (1993) led to right-wing, copy-cat actions in other cities. No other European state witnessed comparable levels of xenophobic violence back then, despite the rise of radical-populist, anti-migration parties in Great Britain, France, Belgium, the Netherlands, and Denmark. This would change by 2010.

The first major break with *jus sanguinis* involved geography: forty years of physical division had undermined the "organic" community codified in the 1949 Preamble to the Basic Law. The Wall's collapse refuted many myths regarding a shared ethno-national identity among 16 million Eastern and 63 million Western Germans. Reinstatement of a common external border did not automatically bridge their antithetical views of Nazi history, guaranteed employment, and women's rights. Declaring the Oder–Neisse border permanent, the Two plus Four Agreement opened the door to countless "late repatriates" fleeing instability in Russia. Westerners perceived them as even more foreign than GDR residents; most would lose the ability to reactivate their citizenship under the 1993 Asylum Compromise.[10]

A second break overlapping with unification was generational in nature. The '68ers comprising the first Red–Green coalition (1998–2005) had been shaped by fifty years of democratic socialization, educational opportunity, and a new human rights culture. Pluralistic in orientation, they adopted the first law expanding the parameters of national belonging. Accepting Germany as a land of immigration, they extended a limited form of *jus soli* citizenship to children of migrant origin born after 1990, at least until they turned 23 (see below). Rejecting the idea that citizenship should be granted only after a long process of *self-integration*, reformers saw it as a vehicle for cultivating constitutional values and a shared sense of community among youth. Employers welcomed this and related reforms as a first step in countering a looming demographic deficit.

A third factor leading Germany to break with *jus sanguinis*, "the competition for best brains," was driven by globalization debates over residency and benefit rights for imported high-tech workers. The Maastricht Treaty unwittingly established four distinct status categories – *legal, political, economic,* and *social citizenship* – subject to diverging local, national, and supranational regulations no longer rooted in a single legal framework, the core components of EU citizenship, "rights, duties, participation and identity ... have become disjointed," as Gerard Delanty observed.[11] The addition of twelve new member states in 2004–2005 raised new concerns regarding unlimited east–west labor migration.

The culmination of these three breaks with the past was the 1999 Citizenship and Naturalization Law (*Staatsangehörigkeitsgesetz*), adopted by the first SPD–Green government. Despite countless laws and amendments regulating their behavior once foreigners were *in the country*, Germany had no provisions allowing people to *enter* its territory on a permanent basis, beyond family reunification, asylum rights, and international treaty obligations. The push for change began with Chancellor Schröder's call for a "Green Card" at the 1998 CBIT convention; equivalent to a temporary US H-1B visa, it was supposed to provide employers with a flexible, non-bureaucratic process for recruiting high-tech workers. In fact, small- and medium-size enterprises had to jump through many hoops to prove no Germans were available; big corporations found other channels. Considered a flop, the program was discontinued in 2004: despite a quota of 20,000, only 14,876 visas were issued in three years, over half to eastern Europeans.[12]

Legal provisions from 1913 to 1990 had moreover created two sets of naturalization rules, labeled entitlement (*Anspruch*) and administrative discretion (*Ermessen*), respectively. *Entitlement* encompassed eleven categories, covering those who met formal residency and self-maintenance requirements, as well as persons entitled to constitutional protection (due to war, persecution, or statelessness). This ostensible "right" to citizenship was subject to secondary criteria (i.e., living conditions, employment status, support for dependents, and even grammatical prowess) that could delay the process for years. The *discretionary* framework drew on nine categories, affecting foreign spouses, family unification, German relatives, and children of civil servants or diplomats living abroad. Implemented in 2000, the Citizenship Law applied to third-generation "migrants" but denied most the option of dual nationality. Invoking procedural grounds, the Constitutional Court rejected its rational counterpart, a bona fide immigration law (*Einwanderungsgesetz*), in 2002, but a weaker version (*Zuwanderungsgesetz*) finally passed in 2004.[13] The latter covered new forms of labor migration, residency rules, and integration measures but fell far short of the open, permanent migration systems seen across the Atlantic.

By the time Merkel became chancellor in 2005, politicians were already pushing for revisions, purportedly in response to EU mandates. Amendments to the 2004 Act promulgated by her Grand Coalition in 2007 secured a right-to-remain for refugees and "tolerated" asylum seekers whose claims had been denied. It lowered the income requirement for high-skilled laborers or potential investors (from €1 million to €500,000) but imposed welfare sanctions against those who failed to enroll in mandatory integration courses. Exempting visa-free states, it limited spousal entry to persons over 18 with a basic knowledge of German (the ECJ nullified that language rule in 2014). Would-be citizens had to pass a language test and take a naturalization oath built on constitutional norms.[14] States developed their own citizenship tests, some of which were later challenged as anti-Islamic in nature. At present, 7.4 million residents hold foreign passports, out of 16.3 million (20 percent) with a migration background.[15]

Economists and migration experts issued Cassandra-calls, predicting imminent labor shortages as early as 2000.[16] Life expectancy had risen dramatically, but Western fertility rates plunged from an average of 2.5 births in the 1960s to 1.3 births per woman by the late 1990s. Social programs enabling GDR women to combine work and family led 90 percent to become mothers prior to unification, compared with only 60 percent in the old states; Eastern fertility rates fell from 1.94 in the 1980s, to 0.77 in 1994. Whereas women aged 30–49 accounted for only 16 percent of all first births in 1960, the figure hit 50 percent in 2004. "Foreign" women display similar patterns (1.69); in 2004, only 26 percent of those mothers were Turkish, in contrast to 45 percent in 1990.[17] The combined effects of low fertility, high life expectancy, and female labor market participation make it clear that few mothers, daughters, or sisters will be around to care for aging Baby Boomers. By 2001, 22 percent of Germans were older than 60; by 2035, half will be over 50. The shift to a volunteer army has moreover eliminated a pool of conscientious objectors performing alternative service in hospitals and nursing homes.

Demographers estimate that if Germany restricts foreign entries to 100,000 per year, its population will shrink from 81.9 to 69 million by 2050; a third will be over 65. An annual admission rate of 200,000 would lower the decline to 74 million, half of whom would still be over 50.[18] These figures drove Angela Merkel to declare somewhat optimistically, "Germany can become a great immigration country" at a CDU Migration Conference in October 2014.[19]

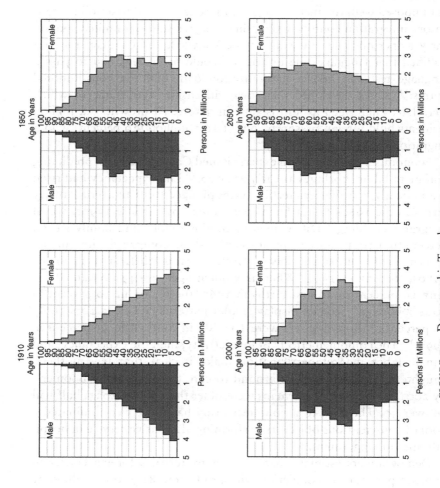

FIGURE 7.1 Demographic Trends, 1910, 1950, 2000, and 2050

Source: Adapted from Statistisches Bundesamt (ed.), *Bevölkerung Deutschlands bis 2050*, 11. koordinierte Bevölkerungsvorausberechnung.

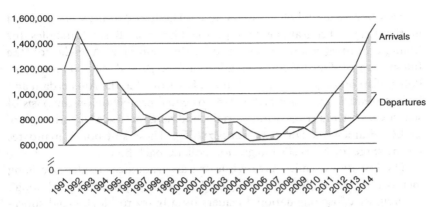

FIGURE 7.2 Arrivals and Departures across German Borders, 1991–2014
Source: Migrationsbericht des Bundesamtes für Migration und Flüchtlinge im Auftrag der Bundesregierung, BAMF, Berlin, 2014, p. 13.

LEVERAGING EUROPE AND LIVING DIVERSITY

To assess Madam Chancellor's ability to set a proactive course for the ship of state concerning migration, we first need to review key EU developments that accorded her influence over policy-framing at both levels. Once again, Merkel was in the right place at the right time, both as the national leader with the largest stake in effective "migration management," and as the EU Council President open to placing these issues on the supranational agenda during the first half of 2007.

The parameters for common migration and asylum policies were laid at the European Council meeting in Tampere, Finland, in October 1999. Recognizing the need for *social cohesion* among member states, the Council introduced "an arsenal of instruments" to cover family reunification, secure status for permanent alien residents, and common conditions of entry for paid- or self-employment. National leaders agreed to grant third-country nationals *equal protection* regarding social security, devise common rules for student admissions, set minimum standards for receiving asylum seekers, and to recognize the qualifications of non-EU nationals meriting international protection. Given its low naturalization rates and rigid job certification rules, Germany was a prime target. Like Merkel, the Commission views employment as a crucial vehicle for integrating foreign residents.

In 2000, the Commission embraced *civic citizenship*, to phase in more rights for long-term migrants; the Council declared non-discrimination "a cornerstone of the whole construction." The foundations were outlined in the Hague Programme (2004), the Common Basic Principles for Immigrant Integration Policy (2005), the Common Agenda for the Integration of Third-Country Nationals (2005), and the Commission's Policy Plan on Legal Migration (2005). Embedded in the Amsterdam and Lisbon treaties, *civic citizenship* extends equal protection on the basis of sex, sexual orientation, national origin, and religion (Race Directive 2000/43/EC, Framework Directive 2000/78/EC). These soft-policy mandates set the stage for Merkel's integration policies back home.

The last two decades have witnessed a paradoxical tendency among member states holding the rotating EU Council presidency: although sovereignty-conscious national leaders usually try to block rapid supra-nationalization, many began using their time at the helm to *advance* integration after 2000. Presidential agendas and "conclusions" foster new EU priorities, bearing the imprint of the state temporarily in charge. The German presidency chaired by Merkel (January–June 2007) was no exception. In addition to pushing EU members into a proactive response to global warming and climate change, Germany threw its weight behind a Community approach to immigration, visa, and asylum issues. The Amsterdam Treaty made immigration a supranational responsibility; the other two areas required intergovernmental agreement. One can thus view the strong emphasis on social inclusion, cohesion, and the need to "promote unity in diversity" as priorities personally supported by the chancellor.

The conclusions issued at the end of the German rotation built on earlier EU initiatives: national leaders deemed integration "a pivotal element of the comprehensive European migration policy," stressing the "opportunities, benefits and challenges of migration in a pluralistic Europe."[20] Sections 14–35 (Freedom, Security and Justice) called for:

- enlarging the Schengen area and eliminating internal controls (including land, sea, and air borders) among member states;
- supporting Commission efforts to develop a comprehensive European migration policy complementing national policies;
- fostering cooperation with third countries to manage migration flows and combat illegal entry with a Global Approach to Migration vis-à-vis Africa, the Mediterranean, eastern and south-eastern states;
- endorsing mobility partnerships, circular migration, and pilot mobility partnerships;

- recognizing migration's role in alleviating skill shortages, fostering employment growth, adjustment, productivity, competitiveness, and public finances; and
- devising proposals enabling third-country nationals to fill high-skill positions based on a single application procedure, with a common set of rights defining their residency status.

Interior Minister Wolfgang Schäuble, the force behind the 1999 Hessian petition against dual nationality, led the charge against the darker side of free movement, presumably with the chancellor's support:

- adopting measures to eliminate undeclared work and illegal employment, through dissuasive sanctions against employers;
- strengthening integrated border management (European Border Surveillance System) and mitigating pressures facing specific member states;
- operationalizing a Common European Asylum System by 2010;
- forging new visa and "return" agreements with Ukraine, Moldova, Albania, and the Balkan states;
- combating organized crime and enhancing document security with biometric means; and
- using future councils to "find solutions" to jurisdictional problems involving matrimonial and maintenance obligations.

In May 2007, Merkel presided over an informal meeting of EU integration ministers in Potsdam. This forum inspired North Rhine-Westphalia and Schleswig-Holstein to organize a national conference of Land-level integration ministers in Hannover (January 2008), as part of the Minister-Presidents Conference. It now functions as a federal body coordinating very different state approaches to the National Integration Plan. This is a clear example of Merkel wearing her EU hat to foster parallel initiatives she can support wearing her national hat. She was personally credited with securing the adoption of the Lisbon Treaty in 2009, following the French and Dutch rejection of the EU Constitution. Her next big move would involve leveraging local action plans to bring state leaders in line.

SCIENTIST AT WORK: INTEGRATION AND IMPLEMENTATION MONITORING

As a physicist, Chancellor Merkel prefers data-driven policy formulation. Following vehement debates over a German *Leitkultur* and protests against "Muslim integration" questionnaires (testing views on nudity and homosexuality), Schäuble noted in April 2006 that "there were many very well integrated foreigners in Germany ... above all the Italians." Statistics at the time revealed that Italian children were actually doing worse in school than Turkish, Russian, or Yugoslav offspring.[21]

For a chancellor fearing a dearth of skilled labor, statistics offered by the Federal Agency for Migration are very sobering: while 36 percent of children with a migration background are 3 to 5 years old, only 17 percent (35 percent among Germans) are enrolled in childcare facilities, essential for early language training. This partly explains the gap in subsequent educational achievement: as of 2013, more than twice as many (27.5 percent) were in dead-end middle schools (*Hauptschulen*): 11 percent of migrant offspring (13.3 percent boys, 9.7 percent girls) left school with no certification (5.4 percent among nationals). Only 24.5 percent attended schools leading to university; 11.5 percent entered the tertiary level, 41 percent of whom dropped out before completing a bachelor's degree. The fact that 28 percent of German students also fail to graduate suggests bigger problems in a system desperate for high-tech workers. More females complete schooling at all levels, only to evince higher unemployment rates later on (14.4 percent for migrant offspring, 6.2 percent among Germans).[22]

Problems in urban schools led cities with large migrant concentrations, such as Stuttgart, Berlin, and Frankfurt, to adopt local integration strategies well before unification. Many joined EU networks exchanging "best practices," for example, Cities for Local Integration Policy (CLIP). As Youth Minister, Merkel was exposed to a wide assortment of integration projects in the nation's capital, introduced during the 1980s by veteran foreigners' commissioner Barbara John (CDU); the annual *Carnival of Cultures* parading from Neukölln/Kreuzberg to Stadtmitte each spring attracts over 4,000 participants. In June 2006, reigning mayor Klaus Wowereit convened the city's first Integration Summit, inviting representatives of ethnic associations, youth agencies, and migration experts. Less than a month later, on July 14, Merkel personally convened the first National Integration Summit, involving eighty-six participants.

Like "Nixon going to China," it took a CDU chancellor to render migrant integration palatable to conservative hardliners beyond the urban context. The EU Council presidency allowed Merkel to leverage supranational decisions vis-à-vis national lawmakers, with the support of four previous SPD ministers who joined the Grand Coalition. Merkel was the first to accord cabinet status to federal integration commissioner,

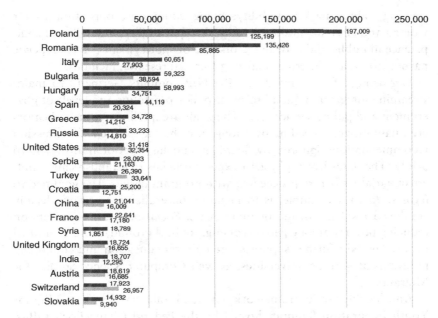

FIGURE 7.3 Migration to and from Germany, based on Country of Origin, 2013
Source: Statistisches Bundesamt and BAMF.

Maria Böhmer, who quickly became an active partner.[23] Like Merkel, this childless daughter of Catholic vintners had pursued the "hardest conceivable study" for a woman in the late 1960s: nuclear physics, mathematics, and political science. Böhmer thus shared Merkel's proclivity for setting quantifiable goals and concrete timetables for implementation.

The second national summit hosted by Merkel and Böhmer took place in July 2007, by which point the cabinet had approved 150 new measures, committing €750 million through 2011. Although three leading Turkish associations boycotted the session to protest restrictive amendments to the migration law, the chancellor presented a National Integration Plan (NIP), declaring its implementation a "central task for all society." In contrast to the Independent Commission appointed by Schröder in 2001 (two women, one foreigner among twenty-one members), the NIP drew on six expert task forces, deliberating ten core themes with input from federal, state, and local authorities, ethnic associations, and other stakeholders. The NIP relies on "self-obligation," reflective of EU social dialogues and the open method of coordination (OMC).[24] Key themes include: integration courses; language acquisition; education and vocational training, labor market mobility; living conditions, opportunities for women and girls; integration as a local responsibility; intercultural competence in public and private sectors; use of sports; media diversity; civic participation; and internationalizing German research facilities.

Consisting of 400 initiatives, the NIP commits Germany to mainstreaming integration "in all relevant policy portfolios and levels of government and public services . . ." The goals are qualitative, the indicators are quantitative, exceeding by a long shot the Independent Commission recommendations ignored by Schröder and his interior minister, Otto Schily. The data-driven physicist expects officials to establish cause-and-effect variables before proceeding with program design. The goal tied to *legal status*, for example, is to facilitate naturalizations among legally employed residents of ten or more years. *Social integration* centers on reducing poverty among persons of migrant background, using quantified ratios. The NIP further supports intercultural education and counseling programs at various universities, as well Computer Science Studies for Migrants.

Another dynamic framework emerged out of the first Migrant Youth Integration Summit, hosted by the Federal Chancellor's Office in May 2007. Roughly two-thirds of urban elementary school pupils stem from migrant families, yet 40 percent miss out on vocational apprenticeships. Eighty youth, together with media and ethnic association representatives, discussed concrete proposals in workshops focusing on language, education, local integration, and cultural diversity under the lead question: *How should our society look in 2030?* They presented their conclusions directly to the chancellor, who welcomed them back in May 2008. These adolescents likewise pursue projects involving benchmarks and deadlines.

Convened in November 2008, the Third Integration Summit drew 367 participants, where the first NIP progress report highlighted language training, labor market integration, and female occupational opportunity. Although education is subject to Länder regulation, Merkel made it a national priority under the rubric *Bildungsrepublik Deutschland*. During another integration dialogue in June 2008, she declared "the vocational educational situation . . . especially close to our hearts," welcoming cooperative efforts by Commissioner Böhmer and Science Minister Annette Schavan.[25] Attended by 120 delegates, the Fourth Integration Summit (2010) called for an action plan to render NIP goals "binding." The Fifth Summit, attracting 120 representatives, introduced the National Action Integration Plan (400+ pages) in January 2012, compiled on the basis of eleven "dialogue fora." New agreements centered on recognizing foreign occupational qualifications, civil service recruitment of ethnic youth, and intercultural healthcare provision. The Sixth Integration Summit of May 2013 drew 120 delegates focusing on labor market integration and steps toward a "genuine welcoming and recognition culture."

Conceptualizing integration as a multidimensional societal process, Merkel's promotion of local, state, and national dialogues at home mirrors EU multi-level governance. She rejected the idea of a single Migrants' Council (*Ausländerbeirat*), used at local levels for over twenty years. Although elected, these were token bodies, offering little access to policy-makers. She prefers migrant councils with *rotating memberships*, depending upon the expertise required; the EU also relies on functionally differentiated councils to deliberate new actions in specific policy fields (environment, labor, etc.).[26]

Cognizant of best practices tested and refined at the supranational level, Merkel urges stakeholders to draw on metropolitan and communal experiences. Federal officials sought advice from Berlin commissioner Günther Piening's staff in developing quantitative indicators for "implementation monitoring," for example (June 2008 interview). Data collection has improved dramatically. Government entities have dropped the term "foreigners," using "integration" in their names instead. The Federal Agency for Migration and Refugees (BAMF) began issuing annual reports in 2005, compiled by a full-time research staff. Its work is complemented by clearing houses, hotlines, and local migration councils. The German Bishops' Council created its own Migration Commission, as did the Expert Council of German Foundations. Merkel's stress on inclusiveness, transparency, and self-accountability means that integration failures can no longer be randomly attributed to ethnic groups. She expects Germans to adapt to new demographic realities, notwithstanding her gratuitous comments about the "failure of multiculturalism" at the 2010 CDU Young Union conference.[27]

Amid growing concern over home-grown terrorism after the 2005 Madrid bombing, Schäuble convened a German Islam Conference (GIC) in September 2006, shortly after Merkel's first summit. Declaring that it was "not designed to be a 'dialogue of the elite' but rather an effort to involve Muslim residents in the negotiation process," he then hand-picked fifteen plenary and working group participants. Despite his proclaimed interest in "appropriately reflecting their diversity," the invited associations represented a mere 15–20 percent of German Muslim communities; Berlin alone is home to ninety denominational "mosque tendencies." Because most do not join a religious organization, persons espousing "secular Islam" from the business, academic, and cultural sectors were not included. In fact, two vehement Islam critics, Nekla Kelek and Seyran Ates, were surprised to find themselves assigned seats on the "Muslim" side of the table.[28]

The second conference was not much better. Though urged to include at least one *hijab* wearer, Schäuble re-invited the same discussants back to the capital in May 2007. Its non-representative character led the four largest Islamic organizations to form their own Coordinating Council of Muslims in Germany (KRM) in April 2007, embracing Sunnis and Shiites but not Alevis or Ahmadiyya followers.[29] The GIC established working groups to draft recommendations involving, first, the German social system and value consensus (e.g., on gender equality, youth self-determination, cultural diversity, secularization); a second addressed religious issues and the Constitution (separation of church and state, religious symbols, mosque construction, Islamic instruction in public schools, sex education, imam training, university programs on Islamic Studies). A third considered media and the private sector as bridge-builders (youth employment, public/private hiring practices, overcoming stereotypes); security and "religious" radicalization were also discussed.

In contrast to Berlin's Islamic Forum, which meets several times a year with local mosque representatives, the national Islam Conference had produced few substantive results by the time of its final session in 2009. According to Stuttgart integration commissioner, Gari Pavkovic (interview, June 2009), it ended "as if there were no need for ongoing social dialogue." Interior Minister Thomas de Maizière announced his intention to "reorganize" the GIC as a forum for state dialogue in 2014.[30]

Although the FRG is home to over 140 religions and world-view communities, Federal-President Christian Wulff still caused a stir when he declared on the twentieth anniversary of unification that "Islam belongs to Germany." The chancellor has reiterated this line on multiple occasions, despite the rise of Salafism, the problem of migrant offspring leaving to fight for ISIS, and PEGIDA protests against an alleged Sharia takeover of Germany. At a minimum, the Islam Conference has induced leaders at the top to include Islam in the definition of German self-identity. "Sustainable integration" follows the motto *Unity as the Goal, Diversity in the Approaches*, analogous to the EU rubric, "unity in diversity."

At the 2014 Integration Summit, one bold young participant raised the question, "When will integration be achieved?" Merkel responded: "Tja, when just as many young people with migration backgrounds have finished school, can take their places at the university, and receive the same technical training degrees as those who have lived in Germany for hundreds of years. Then we will be done, and we won't need to worry about it any more."[31] The Federal Republic still has a lot of work to do in reinventing itself as a welcoming culture, but legislative reforms adopted since 2005 certainly add up to a "great leap forward."

FROM LEADING CULTURE TO WELCOMING CULTURE: THE "OPTION REQUIREMENT"

Favoring a multicultural approach to migrant incorporation, sociologist Bassam Tibi introduced the idea of a European *Leitkutur* (leading culture) in 1998.[32] *Die Zeit* editor Theo Sommer referred to a German "guiding culture" in a subsequent article dealing with the Muslim headscarf debate ("it's the head that counts, not the scarf"); he called for an integration approach that accepted different cultures but rooted them in shared democratic values. Writing for *Die Welt* in October 2000, CDU caucus chief Friedrich Merz reversed the meaning of *Leitkultur*: rejecting "multiculturalism" in favor of compulsory assimilation, he called for strict limits on immigration. Brandenburg hardliner Jörg Schönbohm, also hoping to block migration, urged a Berlin radio station to change its name from Radio Multikulti to Radio Black-Red-Gold (colors of the German flag). The term's original proponents protested its misuse, arising out of opposition to the SPD–Green Citizenship Law.

Changes in the 1990 Foreigners' Law liberalized entitlement rules, triggering a surge in citizenship applications after unification; xenophobic violence moved younger cohorts, especially, to seek legal protection via naturalization. The fact that post-Soviet repatriates oblivious to the German way of life could acquire immediate citizenship highlighted the second-class status assigned to non-national youth born and/or educated in Germany. In Berlin alone, naturalizations increased by 23.5 percent, from 9,903 (1994) to 12,228 (1995); passports granted on an *entitlement* basis rose to 73 percent, while *discretionary* cases fell to 27 percent; almost half were Turkish.[33] National figures rose from 68,526 in 1989 and 101,377 in 1990, to a high of 313,606 in 1995, falling to 248,206 by 1999. Turkish women out-naturalized men by 14 percent between 1994 and 1999. Länder disparities persist, with smaller states evincing higher rates than bigger, wealthier ones; major processing backlogs sometimes distort the numbers.[34] After complaining for decades that thousands

TABLE 7.2 *German Naturalizations, 1990–2010*

Year	Foreign population (thousands)	Number of naturalizations (thousands)	Naturalization quota (%)
1990	5,582,400	101,400	1.82
1995	7,342,800	313,600	4.27
2000	7,267,600	186,700	2.57
2001	7,318,300	178,100	2.43
2002	7,348,000	154,500	2.1
2003	7,341,800	140,700	1.92
2004	7,288,000	127,200	1.74
2005	7,289,100	117,200	1.61
2006	7,255,900	124,600	1.72
2007	7,255,400	113,000	1.56
2008	7,185,900	94,500	1.3
2009	7,130,900	96,100	1.34
2010	7,198,900	101,600	1.41

Source: BAMF and Statistisches Bundesamt.

refused to go home, federal officials began to worry that too few long-term denizens were applying for naturalization! Complicated bureaucratic procedures and high costs notwithstanding, the real stumbling block for most was the need to renounce their ethno-national citizenship. Dual citizenship is an important transitional tool for integration in a globalizing economy.

By the time the 1999 Citizenship Law kicked in, a third generation had come of age: individuals aged 18 and older who had lived there for eight years and attended German schools for six years acquired an independent right to citizenship. The limited *jus soli* (birthplace) option embedded in the 2000 reform applied retroactively to children born after 1990. There was a catch, however: these applicants had to decide by age 18–23 whether to keep their German passports or follow parental lineage. Dual citizenship was granted only in "exceptional cases," including EU nationals and persons whose countries refused to release them, like Iran. About half nonetheless managed to keep both; the overwhelming majority of those denied dual status were Turks.

Between 2000 and 2010, 440,000 children born in Germany qualified for *jus soli*, another 49,000 (born 1990–1999) were accepted retroactively. The first contingent (3,309) reached the crucial decision point in 2008, rising each year. Of the 3,316 subject to the option decision in 2013,

TABLE 7.3 *Naturalizations, Countries of Origin, and Dual Nationality, 2014*

Original nationality	Total	Retaining original citizenship		With loss of original citizenship	
		No.	%	No.	%
Total	108,420	58,146	53.6	50,274	46.4
Europe	64,391	32,974	51.2	31,417	48.8
EU states	26,541	26,000	98	541	2
Poland	5,932	5,928	99.9	4	0.1
Romania	2,566	2,515	98	51	2
Other Europeans	37,850	6,974	18.4	30,876	81.6
Russia	2,744	666	24.3	2,078	75.7
Serbia	2,223	805	36.2	1,418	63.8
Turkey	22,463	3,830	17.1	18,633	82.9
Ukraine	3,142	664	21.1	2,478	78.9
Africa	11,169	6,333	56.7	4,836	43.3
Morocco	2,689	2,682	99.7	7	0.3
America	4,645	3,737	80.5	908	19.5
Asia	26,525	14,987	56.5	11,538	43.5
Iraq	3,173	2,493	78.6	680	21.4
Iran	2,546	2,546	100	–	–
Australia and Oceania	125	112	89.6	13	10.4
Cross Continent, stateless/without specification	1,565	3	0.2	1,562	99.8

Source: Federal Agency for Migration and Refugees.

248 "lost" their German citizenship. Perhaps their own lack of children explains why lawmakers display so little understanding as to how teenagers behave. Few adolescents subject to the law comprehended the complex process: 34 percent of those polled thought that *not* responding to an official letter, written in bureaucratic techno-speak and requiring multiple forms of documentation, would hold no legal consequences. Rather than seek advice from state counselors, the WhatsApp generation gets bad information via the Internet, oblivious to how long it takes to procure official papers from Serbian, Ukrainian, Russian, Iranian, or Turkish embassies. The average process takes fourteen months; they were also put off by the cost (around €500). Intimidated by a decision with life-long consequences, over 50 percent of youth found it unjust that *they* had to choose. Once stripped of this citizenship, youth born and educated in Germany have to run the regular naturalization gamut.[35]

TABLE 7.4 *Number of Youth Eligible for the* Jus Soli *"Option"*

Birth year	Youth retroactively eligible (§ 40 StAG)	Year of decision
1990	3,316	2008
1991	3,807	2009
1992	4,059	2010
1993	4,157	2011
1994	4,487	2012
1995	4,734	2013
1996	5,343	2014
1997	5,892	2015
1998	6,348	2016
1999	6,787	2017
Total 1990–1999	49,187	
2001	38,600	2019
2002	37,568	2020
2003	36,819	2021
2004	36,863	2022
2005	40,156	2023
2006	39,089	2024
2007	35,666	2025
2008	30,336	2026
Total 2000–2008	336,541	
Option decision required birth year 1990–2008	385,541	

Source: Pro Asyl, "Die Optionspflicht im Staatsangehörigkeitsrecht: Daten und Fakten," Berlin, August 23, 2010, p. 2.

SPD pressure during Merkel's second Grand Coalition led to legislative revisions to spare rising numbers of ethnic youth from falling through the cracks. As of December 2014, children born in Germany no longer have to choose. Lawmakers largely eliminated the "option" rule, though some conditions still apply: adolescents who have lived in Germany for eight years before turning 21, attended school for six years, or completed occupational certification no longer have to renounce half of their identities. Some limitations may not be EU-compliant, however: the eight-year residency requirement could deny freedom of movement to parents who want to pursue employment in another member state, for example. Nor does it reinstate the individuals who previously had to give up their German citizenship.

Despite these limitations, Germany has witnessed a paradigm shift in citizenship and migration policies since the fall of the Wall. Demographic factors have played a crucial role in this process but they do not explain another profound shift, one that involves changing public attitudes toward persons fleeing war and oppression, especially now that the generation exposed to wartime hunger, devastation, and expulsion is dying out. In August 2014, Chancellor Merkel received a gold plaque from the Association for Deportees (*Bund der Vertriebenen*) for establishing a national day (June 20) to recall their suffering in the 1940s. She has faced heavy criticism from others for supporting a Documentation Center for Flight, Expulsion and Reconciliation.[36] As of December 2016, the building chosen for the center (Deutschlandhaus in Berlin) was still undergoing renovations. Merkel's commitment to human rights derives not only from the lack of freedom she witnessed as an Easterner but also from her recognition that a powerful, united Germany must now assume greater responsibility on the global stage, as Europe faces another extraordinary wave of refugees and asylum seekers.

THE PARADIGM SHIFT: "ASYLUM KNOWS NO UPPER LIMITS"

Most reforms leading to the welcoming culture were introduced after the migration waves of the 1990s had already dramatically declined. By 2008, the number of new applications had dropped to 28,018.[37] The question here is whether these reforms have taken sufficient root in German political culture to block politicians who might demand a return to a more restrictive framework. To understand how much is at stake, we need to return to the "receiving conditions" that awaited potential refugees prior to 1998.

Although the Iron Curtain restricted their flight prior to 1989, persons fleeing communism were more likely than other victims of oppression to secure formal asylum status under the Basic Law. Because gender-specific forms of persecution like forced marriage, rape, or female genital mutilation were not classified as "political," the fate of women and children depended completely on the status of male applicants. Trafficked women, or those who fled abusive spouses after their arrival, were subject to deportation. As Table 7.5 indicates, the numbers granted bona fide asylum status fell very short of Article 16's generous promise: *Persons persecuted on political grounds enjoy the right to asylum.* Neither the low

TABLE 7.5 *Political Asylum Seekers, 1980–1992*

Year	No. of applications	Cases decided	Cases approved	Approved cases (%)
1980	107,818	106,757	12,783	11.97
1981	49,391	110,717	8,531	7.71
1982	37,423	90,853	6,209	6.83
1983	19,737	36,702	5,032	13.71
1984	35,278	24,724	6,566	26.56
1985	73,532	38,504	11,224	29.15
1986	99,650	55,555	8,853	15.94
1987	57,379	87,539	8,231	9.40
1988	103,076	88,530	7,621	8.61
1989	121,318	120,610	5,991	4.97
1990	193,063	148,842	6,518	4.38
1991	256,112	168,023	11,597	6.90
1992	430,191	216,356	9,189	4.25
Total	1,592,268	1,293,712	108,345	8.37

Source: The Week in Germany, January 12, 1993, German Information Center, New York, p. 2.

recognition rates nor the harsh reception conditions imposed by Unity Chancellor Kohl did much to deter thousands of would-be applicants through the 1990s. On the surface, the 1993 Asylum Compromise helped to reduce the flow but did nothing to ensure that a larger share of those admitted would enjoy the full benefits of Article 16 recognition (Table 7.6).

Prior to 1980, breadwinners with pending asylum applications received temporary work permits, helping them to support themselves; by 1987, all but those from Eastern Europe encountered a five-year work ban; this, in turn, fueled public resentment over foreigners "coming to exploit the welfare system." Applicants were required to live at designated sites, even if family or friends were willing to sponsor them elsewhere. Newcomers were placed in hostels, school gymnasiums, and even containers, denying them contact with locals.[38] Nearly two-thirds were of prime working age, between 18 and 50. Conditions worsened over time: buildings already inadequate for families had their kitchens removed to prevent them from cooking. Reduced cash allocations were replaced with benefits-in-kind, healthcare access declined, and applicants allowed to work under very exceptional circumstances could not be paid more than the equivalent of €1.05 per hour.[39] The plan to stem the asylum flow by creating

TABLE 7.6 *Asylum Decisions, based on "Non-Deportable" Regulations, 1986–2003*

Year	Total applications	Recognized under §16GG		Guaranteed non-deportation		Barriers to deportation		Rejected cases		Formal decisions	
		No.	%	No.	%	No.	%	No.	%	No.	%
1986	55,555	8,853	15.9	–	–	–	–	31,955	57.5	14,747	26.5
1987	87,539	8,231	9.4	–	–	–	–	62,000	70.8	17,308	19.8
1988	88,530	7,621	8.6	–	–	–	–	62,983	71.1	17,926	20.3
1989	120,610	5,991	4.97	–	–	–	–	89,866	74.5	24,753	20.5
1990	148,842	6,518	4.38	–	–	–	–	16,268	78.1	26,056	17.5
1991	168,023	11,597	6.9	–	–	–	–	128,820	76.7	27,606	16.4
1992	216,356	9,189	4.25	–	–	–	–	163,637	75.6	43,530	20.1
1993	513,561	16,369	3.19	–	–	–	–	347,991	67.8	149,174	29.1
1994	352,572	25,578	7.25	–	–	–	–	238,386	67.6	78,622	22.3
1995	209,188	18,100	9.04	5,368	2.68	3,631	1.81	117,939	58.9	58,781	29.4
1996	194,451	14,389	7.4	9,611	4.94	2,082	1.07	126,652	65.1	43,799	22.5
1997	170,801	8,443	4.94	9,779	5.73	2,768	1.62	101,886	59.7	50,693	29.7
1998	147,391	5,883	3.99	5,437	3.69	2,573	1.72	91,700	62.2	44,371	30.1
1999	135,504	4,114	3.04	6,147	4.54	2,100	1.55	80,231	59.2	42,912	31.7
2000	105,502	3,128	2.96	8,138	7.88	1,597	1.52	61,840	58.6	30,619	29
2001	107,193	5,716	5.33	17,003	15.86	3,383	3.16	55,402	51.7	25,689	24
2002	130,128	2,379	1.83	4,130	3.17	1,598	1.23	78,845	60.6	43,176	33.2
2003	93,885	1,534	1.63	1,602	1.71	1,567	1.67	63,002	67.1	26,180	27.9

Source: MARIS, commissioned by the Federal Office for Refugee Recognition, BAMF, 2004.

conditions so awful that no one would come backfired completely, due partly to the lack of a real immigration system. A task force established by Interior Minister Schäuble reported in 1985 that rather than reduce the number of applications, the labor ban had only lengthened the processing period, increased illegal employment, welfare costs, and crime rates.

The fall of the Wall and war in Yugoslavia coincided with a tightening of the 1985 Schengen regulations (known as Dublin I), but the surge continued, rising from 193,063 applications in 1990 to 438,191 in 1993. Had they departed prior to 1989, they could have tried playing the "communism" card, although many Croatians had come to Germany as guestworkers. The constitutional guarantee of political asylum was rolled back just at the time they needed it most. The number of applications fell to 322,599 in 1994 and 166,951 by 1995, until "ethnic cleansing" campaigns against Bosnians (1995) and Kosovars (1999) forced the gate back open, due to Germany's international "temporary protection" obligations.[40] The number granted full Article 16 status (ensuring work permits and permanent residency) never surpassed 10 percent. Many were "tolerated," meaning that they could not be deported back to combat zones under international conventions. The latter were forced to renew their status every six months, making it very hard to secure legal employment and social benefits. Women whose husbands had been massacred encountered especially difficult conditions, as did their children.[41]

The hundreds of thousands who fled to Germany through the 1990s impelled the government to develop a national distribution system known as the *Königsteiner Key* (Figure 7.4), based on tax revenues and population size, rendering large cities primary recipients. Despite its wealth and size, Bavaria has been particularly reluctant to carry its share of the refugee burden. In 1996, it led the charge to deport Bosnians, after unilaterally declaring that homeland conditions were once again safe; Kosovars faced a comparable fate when the conflict reignited in 1999. By 2001, 85,500 had been repatriated, including 7,400 against their will.[42] Ironically, Bavarian hardliners are at least partly responsible for many reforms adopted prior to 2015 that have helped Merkel to turn Germany into a "culture of welcoming and recognition."

As early as 2005, Bavarians like Edmund Stoiber and Michael Glos had tried to downplay Merkel's constitutional "guideline powers." Having lost the battle over citizenship reform, conservative hardliners subsequently insisted that all persons granted formal asylum under the Red–Green government be "re-tested," without probable cause. Of the 13,633 cases reviewed, 5 percent lost their protected status, but only

Nordrhein-Westfalen	NW	21.20 %
Bayern	BY	15.30 %
Baden-Württemberg	BW	13.00 %
Niedersachsen	NI	9.40 %
Hessen	HE	7.30 %
Sachsen	SN	5.10 %
Berlin	BE	5.00 %
Rheinland-Pfalz	RP	4.80 %
Schleswig-Holstein	SH	3.40 %
Brandenburg	BB	3.10 %
Sachsen-Anhalt	ST	2.90 %
Thüringen	TH	2.70 %
Hamburg	HH	2.50 %
Mecklenburg-Vorpommern	MV	2.00 %
Saarland	SL	1.20 %
Bremen	HB	0.94 %

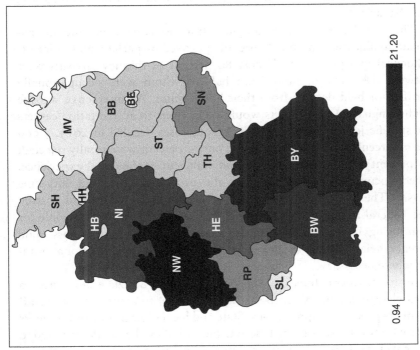

0.94   21.20

FIGURE 7.4 Königsteiner Key: Refugee Redistribution among the Länder

Source: Statistisches Bundesamt and BAMF.

37 percent of those denials held up in court; the courts reversed 13 percent of other purportedly "bad decisions," including 32 percent of the Syrian rejections.[43] In 2007, when Merkel issued the NIP, Bavarian Interior Minister Hans-Peter Friedrich issued a state ban against counseling, language courses, or job training "that would serve their integration into German society."[44] By 2016 he would be demanding Merkel's resignation via twitter.[45]

The Constitutional Court fired the first shot supporting reforms in 2012, declaring that asylum benefits, set in 1993, were too low to ensure "human dignity." The monthly stipend of €224 was raised to €374, equivalent to the level accorded welfare and Hartz IV recipients, which the Court had also forced lawmakers to raise in 2010 and 2011. At least €130 must be supplied in cash rather than in vouchers or food packages, to secure "self-dignity and a degree of participation in societal, cultural and political life."[46] Scandals in the southern state, involving forty-eight attempted suicides, photographs of refugees forced to sleep outside, and a hunger strike in 2013, drew national attention to "model conditions in poor Bremen, chaotic conditions in rich Bavaria."[47]

The next element of the paradigm shift focused on recognizing occupational qualifications attained abroad, approved by parliament (under EU influence) in April 2012. Almost 80 percent of the new arrivals were between 18 and 49, more than half of whom were occupationally certified or held degrees from their home states. An interactive website (eight languages) now directs would-be laborers to accreditation centers for specific job categories. Of the 13,344 cases decided in 2013, 9,969 (74.7 percent) were fully accredited, only 4 percent were totally rejected; 30 percent in the health field lacked sufficient professional experience. Once documentation is complete, the process takes about fifty-nine days.[48] The top sending countries are Poland, Romania, and Russia. The Federal Institute for Vocational Education (BIBB) is responsible for monitoring outcomes. Beyond standardizing procedures across state bureaucracies, officials are drawing in businesses to offer additional training where necessary.

In 2015, federal Interior Minister Thomas de Maizière announced a third change, adding 2,000 posts (up from 650) to assist the 2,800 staff members processing applications. State and local officials fought for weeks over who was most burdened, despite the €1 billion the Länder received to cover new expenses. Reducing the processing period to three months cut care costs among groups unlikely to qualify. In practice, this means expediting Balkan rejections and Syrian approvals, pushing more difficult cases back in the queue (e.g., Pakistanis: 17.6 months; Afghanis: 16.5 months).[49]

Last but not least, Merkel called upon all government agencies to promote a "welcoming culture" that recognizes difference as enrichment, to render Germany more attractive to foreign workers as part of a deliberate demographic strategy. The BAMF established a Round Table on the Receiving Society, with representatives from nineteen federal agencies; one task force focuses on *welcoming practices*, a second on *intercultural opening through political education*.[50] First convened in 2012, it follows a template already used at lower levels (e.g., in Cologne, Düsseldorf). It issued guidelines for "welcoming packages" and created a multilingual phone App to supply information on housing, job sites, healthcare, the school system, integration courses, and counseling centers. Local authorities have established hotlines to anti-discrimination offices, providing interactive maps and links to www.make-it-in-Germany.de. Partners are helping to professionalize ethnic associations as communication channels as well.

The Round Table model was first used in East Germany between the Wall's collapse and the March 1990 elections to foster civil society participation.[51] Berlin and other cities have created Round Tables on Refugee Care to develop policies sensitive to group-specific needs, for example, healthcare. "Optimizing administration" for the welcoming culture, their most important charge is to re-socialize public servants who deal with new arrivals. The "Welcoming Bureaucracies" project includes courses and workshops, helping civil servants formerly intent on keeping foreigners out to become more "customer friendly." My own experiences at Berlin's Foreigners Registration Office in 2013 – arriving the first day at 7 am, the next day at 6 am, and finally securing a *waiting number* by arriving at 5 am on the third day – stands in sharp contrast to my 10-minute wait, a booklet of sightseeing vouchers, and a very friendly "Frau Weiß" who asked lots of questions about my book project in Tübingen in April 2015.

"WE CAN DO THIS": MERKEL'S RESPONSE TO THE REFUGEE CRISIS

The global financial crisis, the Arab Springs gone bad, and ethno-religious warfare have triggered new waves of refugees across Europe since 2009. The number of first-time asylum applications across the EU hit 425,000 in 2001, falling to 200,000 in 2006: it topped 435,450 in 2013 and peaked again at 625,000 in 2014, encompassing citizens from 144 countries.

Kosovars, Syrians, and Afghanis headed the list.[52] In spring 2015, the EU revised several components of the Common European Asylum System (CEAS) to ensure that new arrivals would be "treated equally in an open and fair system – wherever they apply": these included the Asylum Procedures Directive, the Reception Conditions Directive, the Qualification Directive, the Dublin Regulation and the EURODAC regulation. It also established emergency response mechanisms to replace the Italian *Mare Nostrum* search-and-rescue operations: the Council agreed to relocate 40,000 who had landed in Greece and Italy. As of this writing, only five EU countries offer small resettlement programs; others abide by the Union's Temporary Protection Directive. Merkel was the first to call for "more solidarity" in the form of distribution quotas among participating EU states, despite mounting resistance from Hungary, the United Kingdom, and Poland. Already staggering under EU austerity demands, Greece and Italy face youth unemployment rates ranging from 41 percent to 52 percent.[53] In mid-2015, France, Austria, and Switzerland tightened border controls to block refugees trying to leave the Mediterranean states.

By May 2014, migration to Germany had reached its highest level in twenty years; over 1,226,000 have entered since 2013. The categories include new laborers who enjoy freedom of movement as EU nationals, granted in 2011–2012. The largest contingent hails from Poland (189,000), coupled with Bulgarians, Romanians, and Croatians (430,000), accounting for less than 6 percent of all foreigners.[54] Despite the "welfare fraud" and "poverty migrant" images invoked by CSU Minister-President Horst Seehofer and ex-Interior Minister Hans-Peter Friedrich, Bavarian companies were happy to find 91,000 new workers: 27 percent of the Bulgarians and Romanians hold academic degrees, while 10 percent have MINT backgrounds.[55] Indeed, 70 percent pay into social insurance funds from which they are unlikely to benefit. The Center for European Economic Research reported in 2012 that each foreign laborer pays €3,300 more to the state than she or he receives, adding up to €22 billion among 6.6 million workers.[56]

The millions who have survived perilous boat trips across the Mediterranean since 2011 pose very different integration challenges. The number filing for asylum in EU states rose from 279,000 in 2012, to 374,000 in 2013, to 562,000 in 2014. On April 19, 2015, 800 perished in the worst refugee shipwreck on record; in just four months, 1,780 died at sea, in contrast to ninety-six the previous year. Over 85 percent of the 68,000 who made it to Greek shores by June had set out from Syria, Afghanistan, Iraq, and Somalia. The 67,500 who landed in Italy came from Eritrea, Nigeria, Somalia, and Syria. Yet only 5,115 and 28,500, respectively, sought asylum in those two countries (Greece and Italy); 43 percent filed in Germany or Sweden, despite the Schengen requirement that they apply in the land of "first arrival." Asylum applications in Germany rose from 18,278 in 2008, to 169,166 in 2014; by May 2015, the number had increased another 129 percent.[57] The FRG registered 171,797 first-time applications January–June 2015, compared with 202, 834 (total) in 2014.[58]

Despite its size and wealth, Germany was not the biggest per capita recipient in 2015; its 2,510 applicants per million citizens ran a distant second to Sweden's 8,415. The FRG does have the dubious distinction of hosting the greatest number of *undecided cases*. Balkan nationals know that they can work illegally for months because processing takes so long. Albania (20.5 percent) and Kosovo (21.6 percent) stood among the top ten sending states in May–June 2015, although 99 percent have been rejected. Syria took second place, albeit as the group most likely to succeed (98–99 percent). Of the 128,918 cases decided in 2014, 35,386 were granted refuge, although only 10,239 (3.4 percent) faced a hearing. Of the 93,816 cases decided between January and April 2015, 34.7 percent were accorded protection (under diverging legal terms). Because international conventions bar their return to combat zones, rejected applicants with "tolerated status" face permanent precariousness.

By January 2016, the number of unaccompanied minors arriving in Germany exceeded 60,000; asylum applications in that group rose from 763 in 2008 to 4,399 in 2014, of whom 1,008 were under 16.[59] Another 7,500 arrived during the first half of 2015, leading cities like Hamburg and Munich to bear the brunt of traumatized, disoriented youth. In July 2015, policy-makers agreed to include those up to 18 in special programs and to distribute them among smaller communities with reserve capacity: the sooner the better, one could argue.

Sitting in Berlin as the 2015 crisis unfolded, I observed many of the chancellor's media appearances in real time; this leads me to argue that four images surfacing in July and August put a human face on asylum, triggering Merkel's dramatic change of heart as she watched other states shutting their borders. When she met 14-year-old Reem Sahwil in Rostock on July 16, she hesitated – stating literally, *wir schaffen das nicht* – indicating that Germany could not take in everyone from Palestinian refugee camps, much less from Africa. Her moment of truth arose when seventy-one refugees were found asphyxiated in a sealed truck close to the Austrian border on August 27, followed on August 30 by photographs of

3-year-old Aylan Kurdia washed up on a beach in Bodrum, Turkey, and the picture of an amputee on crutches in Budapest, setting out on a 170-km trek along the autobahn to Austria with the chancellor's portrait hanging around his neck. While Hungary shut down its trains and erected razor wire fences to seal its borders against thousands in transit, she temporarily suspended the Dublin requirements and declared that Germany would accept unlimited numbers arriving via the Balkan route. Involving dramatic late-night discussions among members of her inner circle, her decision was vehemently opposed by the federal police chief, Dieter Romann. Seehofer, on vacation, did not answer his phone when Merkel called him at 11.30 pm to notify him of what was to come.[60]

On August 31, the chancellor declared at her annual summer press conference, "we can do this," citing Germany's "orderly conditions," its economic strength, developed civil society, and demographic needs. Referencing unification, she stressed her country's capacity for "flexibility" in tough times and its constitutional imperative, declaring "asylum knows no upper limits."[61] She would stress in September, "We were quick to save the banks, we can act immediately to help communities save human beings."[62] Over 20,000 arrived on a single weekend. While leaders like Hollande, Erdoğan, and Cameron merely claimed to be "deeply moved" by these images, Prime Minister Justin Trudeau hopped on a plane two months later to accompany 25,000 Syrians to Canada.

Responsible for accommodation, meals, and medical treatment, state and communal officials appealed for help; adopted in November, the first Asylum Package doubled the federal contribution to €2 billion. In 2016, her government started paying €670 per month for each registered individual, pending a final decision. Anticipating 800,000 per year and a five-month processing period, the Länder received a €2.68 billion advance payment. Allocating €500 million to build additional social housing and 150,000 new reception places, federal authorities temporarily suspended certain construction and renewable energy requirements, and took charge of refugee redistribution. Cash payments were replaced with in-kind benefits at the receiving centers, but skilled laborers likely to be approved could seek temporary jobs after three months to expedite their integration. States issued health cards to new arrivals for immediate treatment, to be reimbursed later. Facing a 99 percent rejection rate, Albania, Kosovo, and Montenegro joined Serbia, Macedonia, and Bosnia-Herzegovina on the list of safe states.[63]

Failing to take in his refugee quota, Bavaria's Seehofer began issuing ultimatums and playing the populist card, despite an incredible outpouring of citizen engagement with the refugees, channeled through 14,000 volunteer centers by late 2015. Merkel had spoken out against hate speech and anti-migration protests, even after being called "a cunt, a traitor and a whore" when she visited a refugee facility in Heidenau, Saxony on August 26, *before* her dramatic decision to open the borders. "If we now have to start excusing ourselves for showing a friendly face in emergency situations," she declared, "then this is no longer my country."[64] By December 2015, the backlog of applications had reached 350,000.[65] The mood shifted dramatically in the wake of over 500 reported sexual assaults by "North African-looking men" in Cologne, Hamburg, and other cities on New Year's Eve 2016.[66]

After three months of internal coalition wrangling, the Bundestag adopted a second Asylum Package in January, rolling back several welcoming measures: persons from "safe" countries are placed in special centers for fast-track processing (three weeks) usually ending in rejection. Those who do not submit to "voluntary" deportation receive reduced maintenance benefits. The rest must stay in their first-admission accommodations for six months (formerly three), receiving more benefits-in-kind; they receive cash supplements only one month at a time. Free movement rules have been tightened as well. Refugees cannot leave the districts in which their Foreigner Registration Office is located, even to visit relatives in neighboring counties; if caught outside, they lose benefits and their proceedings are terminated. Persons granted subsidiary protection only become eligible for family unification after two years. Exceptions involve family members held in refugee camps in Turkey, Jordan, and Lebanon, admitted under quotas subject to EU regulation.

The second package deliberately excluded an agreement between Family Minister Manuela Schwesig (SPD) and Interior Minister de Maizière (CDU) extending special protection to women and unaccompanied minors. Only very serious illnesses warrant a right to stay, even if treatment is not generally available back home.[67] With multiple operations already behind her, wheelchair-bound Reem Sahwil was granted permanent residence. The second legislative package reduces "pocket money" benefits (€143) by charging applicants €10 per month to cover language instruction for which some groups (Afghanis) are not even eligible.[68] It is unclear whether these changes conform to EU requirements, much less to the 2012 High Court ruling requiring lawmakers to ensure refugees adequate means (€130 at the time) "to participate in social, cultural and political life."[69] Human Rights Commissioner Christoph Strässer (SPD) resigned in protest the week the bill passed.

Representing a case of "three steps forward, one step back," a 2016 Integration Law contained mostly symbolic sanctions. The problem is not that refugees are refusing to take language and integration courses, but rather that there are not enough teachers to accommodate the demand.

Merkel's decision to open Germany to 1.2 million refugees has thus far not only inspired an unprecedented volunteer movement, but also an ugly backlash. The Alternative for Germany (AfD) got its start as an anti-Euro party; its founder, Bernd Lucke, was forced out in July 2015 when Easterner Frauke Petry pushed the AfD to the far-right. Its double-digit victories in March 2016 in Rhineland-Pfalz (11.7 percent), Baden-Württemberg (14.9 percent), and Sachsen-Anhalt (24 percent) were offset by the 68.8 percent who upheld Grand Coalition policies in the first state, and gave Greens an all-time high of 30.5 percent in the second. The AfD split again in Baden-Württemberg when Petry refused to renounce two openly pro-Nazi delegates in state assemblies. Occupying opposite ends of the ideological spectrum, AfD and Die Linke are both competing for Eastern protesters.

In September 2016, voters dealt the chancellor another blow in Mecklenburg-Vorpommern, her state base, where the AfD secured 20.8 percent, with a 61 percent turnout rate. One would think that after four decades of "godless communism," Easterners would still be eager to participate in the democratic process. Having lost 300,000 younger, better educated residents since unification, the rural state of 1.6 million took in only 2 percent of the refugees (24,000) in 2015, a third of whom soon departed. As seen earlier, "Meck-Pom" received substantial financial transfers after unification and has benefited handsomely from Merkel's energy turn-around. Indeed, the refugee flow has slowed significantly nationwide: roughly 223,000 had entered by late summer 2016, only a third of the 2015 total, due in part to an EU deal with Turkey. Recep Tayyip Erdoğan's radical crackdown against thousands of putative coup supporters (July 2016) has already triggered a new asylum wave consisting of Turkish academics, according to one staff member at the Alexander von Humboldt Foundation.

The antics of obstreperous Bavarian politicians pose a bigger electoral challenge. Seehofer's ongoing "attacks on Merkel" (Schäuble's term) have ironically "turned the sister parties [CDU/CSU] into distant relatives."[70] While opposition Greens and FDP members support Merkel's migration policies, hardliners are trying to have their cake and eat it too. Seehofer has to accept Union policies for the CSU to hang on to its special power base at the national level. He must nonetheless pursue "fundamental opposition" to rally his populist base back home, dominated by old Catholic men. Women in Bavaria support many of Merkel's other modernizing efforts, for example, rights to day-care and quotas for corporate boards. Younger citizens are generally more tolerant, and want to be seen as "good Germans." Necessary, proactive integration policies are already in place. They just need time to work. Compared with the restrictions, rejection rates, and hostile attitudes witnessed prior to unification, Germany has become a welcoming culture "in word and deed" under Merkel's leadership.

CONCLUSION: MIGRATION POLICIES WITH A HUMAN FACE

Like any thinking person familiar with German history, I worry about the rise of xenophobic populist parties, but I have seen anti-immigrant parties like the *Republikaner* and the German People's Union (DVU) come and go since 1990. More disturbing is the fact that intolerant parties currently control national governments in Hungary, Denmark, and Poland, member states the Juncker Commission has failed to sanction for violating the EU *acquis*. Merkel has little patience for east European leaders who profited immensely from Community solidarity after the collapse of socialism but dismiss their responsibilities under CEAS.

EU constructs like *civic citizenship* and *social inclusion* supplied a foundation for new forms of cooperation, well before millions of refugees set out on perilous trips across the Mediterranean. They lent legitimacy to Merkel's efforts to enact reforms not only in popular domains like environmental protection but also in the integration field. Paradoxically, the chancellor has demonstrated her strongest leadership abilities in the very arena that triggered the most vociferous opposition within her own party. Taking advantage of paradigmatic reforms secured by a Red–Green government, she leveraged Grand Coalition support with mounting business worries over skilled labor shortages. She overcame hardliner resistance by pulling together public and private networks of self-monitoring business, ethnic, religious, and educational stakeholders. Although many integration initiatives impinge on state sovereignty, she circumvented Länder resistance by drawing on reform models already tested in metropolitan areas with ever larger migrant concentrations.

As CDU opposition leader prior to 2005, she would have encountered major resistance to the dramatic changes she introduced after 2007. Wolfgang Schäuble was the brain behind the CDU petition campaign against dual-citizenship during the 1999 Hessian elections. Her predecessor Gerhard Schröder initially limited his efforts to countering skilled labor shortages by way of the "Green Card" program for foreign high-tech workers. The new Citizenship Law arose under pressure from his Green coalition partners, but even then Schröder allowed SPD Interior Minister Otto Schily to side with conservatives in rejecting dual nationality. Claiming it was not his intention "to weaken the German chancellor or her government," state leader Seehofer overstepped his bounds by meeting with right-wing populist Victor Orban on March 4, 2015, who had declared "one [asylum seeker] is already too much for us." On April 19, 2015, ex-Chancellor Helmut Kohl received the Hungarian premier ("my friend") at his home, insisting that "Europe cannot become a new home for millions of people in need around the world." His new wife added that, regarding assistance for Greece, Kohl "had never wanted Europe at any price."[71] Still, on August 25, the chancellor "did something for which many European heads of government and many conservatives will never forgive her: she did the obvious. She acted in the spirit of Europe. She did not call for emergency defense but emergency relief; not protection of the real order but protection for real people."[72]

During Merkel's first Grand Coalition, Schäuble relied on a particularistic approach to a problem he defined as *Islam in Germany*, instead of addressing his compatriots' refusal to recognize Islam as the nation's third largest religion. Its twenty-year refusal to offer Islam in regular denominational/ethics instruction in schools exacerbated the marginalization of migrant youth; poorly educated and unemployed, alienated males searched for belonging in radicalized mosque communities instead. When the radical Islamic Federation (with ties to the Egyptian Brotherhood) won the first court battle to offer instruction in Berlin schools, integration veteran Barbara John (CDU) described it as "the result of our own failure to come up with a different solution earlier."[73]

Raised as a pastor's daughter in a godless state, Merkel sees religious pluralism and freedom of belief as a core component of democratic identity. She recognizes a national responsibility for persecuted peoples, and accepts Islam as "part of Germany." She has never publicly rejected *hijab* wearing in state service, leading critics to post photo shopped images of her wearing a headscarf.[74] In 2015, the Constitutional Court invalidated state laws that automatically exclude women with headscarves from teaching in public schools.[75]

The "power physicist" holds that her academic training obliges her to survey an energy field for new configurations, recognize long-term "waves," and formulate the right questions before conducting experiments. Migration is a tool for meliorating demographic deficits, local integration is a "societal science" worthy of emulation. Multiple integration summits have supplied a clear picture of positive and negative particles, the constants and waves comprising the national field. "Self-obligation" has morphed into disaggregated data sets, binding guidelines, best practices, action plans, implementation monitoring, and annual reporting requirements. "Sustainable integration" is her antidote to rising health and pension costs tied to Baby Boomer retirements; Germany has to utilize the brain power inherent in youth of migrant descent, male and female.

Existing refugee and asylum policies are far from gender-sensitive; cities, at best, no longer relocate pregnant women until three months after childbirth. Oldenburg and Bielefeld report critical midwife shortages; many women have been assaulted in transit.[76] Back in 2008, Education Minister Annette Shavan introduced a National Pact for Women in MINT occupations, pulling together 200 partners and mentors. Women account for less than 17 percent of German engineers; the number studying in these fields rose 57 percent between 2008 and 2012. Initiatives like "MINTalent" deem young women of migrant descent a "hot commodity."[77] The benefits accruing to women in this policy domain stand in stark contrast to the disadvantages they have witnessed as a result of the chancellor's particularistic approach – austerity and structural reform *über alles* – in the Euro crisis arena.

This is not to argue that Merkel deserves all the credit for the breathtaking paradigm shift in German citizenship and migration policies, or that she will be able to overcome all forces of anti-foreigner resistance. She landed in the eye of the perfect storm, given the geographic, generational, and globalization dynamics that coincided with German unification. She found a majority of her compatriots ready, willing, and able to embrace a new identity based on democratic pluralism. As she stressed in her August 31 press conference: "Let me say simply: Germany is a strong country. The motive that we need to fix these things is: we have accomplished so much – we can do this! We can do it, and when things get in the way, we'll work to overcome them." She continued:

In spite of everything, our country is still a good country. It is in good shape. The oft praised civil society is a reality for us, and it makes me proud and thankful to see how countless people in Germany have reacted to the refugees' arrival. The numbers who are there for the refugees today ... helpers, the numbers who accompany strangers through cities and offices or even take them into their homes surpass the harassers and xenophobes many times over ...

She also thanked "the wonderful media reporting about them in recent days. I will make an exception and allow myself to encourage them to keep it up; for they give our many good citizens the chance to see themselves, offering role models and examples which gives us courage."[78]

Angela Merkel realizes that the proof of any good policy lies in its effective implementation. CDU integration specialist Cemile Giousouf noted after the party's 2004 Immigration Conference, "if an eastern woman can serve as Chancellor 25 years after the Wall fell, then it could also happen in another 25 years that a politician with Moroccan or Turkish roots will lead Germany."[79] Merkel pulled off the first miracle only fifteen years into unity. Add to that her integration policies of the last ten years, and Giousouf's scenario not only sounds possible but also probable. She led her new country to break with four decades of ideologically charged CDU/CSU rhetoric insisting that Germany never was, is, or should become "a land of immigration," much less one of integration. It is now both.

NOTES

1. Scherzer, *Die Fremden*; Runge, *Ausland DDR*; Eva Kolinsky and Hildegard Maria Nickel, *Reinventing Gender: Women in Eastern Germany since Unification* (London: Frank Cass, 2003).
2. Lau, *Die Letzte Volkspartei*, p. 8.
3. Mirijam Beutke and Patrick Kotzur, "Faktensammlung Diskriminierung," Programm Integration und Bildung, Bertelsmann Stiftung, Berlin, January 12, 2015.
4. "Late repatriates," totaling 3.2 million by 2011, could reclaim *jus sanguinis* citizenship, even if their ancestors had left a century earlier. Joyce Marie Mushaben, *The Changing Faces of Citizenship: Integration and Mobilization among Minorities in Germany* (Providence, RI: Berghahn Books, 2008), pp. 32 ff.
5. For details, see Mushaben, *From Post-War to Post-Wall Generations*.
6. Bade and Oltmer, *Aussiedler*.
7. Women were especially vulnerable. Joyce Marie Mushaben, "Up the Down Staircase: Redefining Gender Identities through Ethnic Employment in Germany," *Journal of Ethnic and Migration Studies*, 35(8) (2009): 1249–1274.
8. Joyce Marie Mushaben, "A Crisis of Culture: Social Isolation and Integration among Turkish Guestworkers in the German Federal Republic," in Ilyan Basgoz and Norman Furniss (eds.), *Turkish Workers in Europe: A Multidisciplinary Study* (Bloomington, IN: Indiana University Press, 1985), pp. 125–150.
9. My earlier work criticized Edmund Stoiber's inflammatory declaration that a "flashflood" of immigrants would produce a multinational society on German soil of mixed, inferior races (*durchmischt und durchrasst*).

10. Susanne Worbs, Antonia Scholz, and Stefanie Blicke, *Die Optionsregelung im Staatsangehörigkeitsrecht aus der Sicht von Betroffenen* (Berlin: Bundesamt für Migration & Flüchtlinge, 2012).

11. Gerard Delanty, "Models of Citizenship: Defining European Identity and Citizenship," *Citizenship Studies*, 1(3) (1997): 285–303.

12. Holger Kold, "How Successful was the Green Card?" January 1, 2005, available at: www.bpb.de/gesellschaft/migration/kurzdossiers/58181/success.

13. "Eklat im Bundesrat: Union wirft Wowereit Verfassungsbruch vor," *Berliner Zeitung*, March 23/24, 2002; Werner Kolhoff, "Urteilsverkündung," *Berliner Zeitung*, June 21, 2002.

14. Eric Leise, "Germany to Regularize 'Tolerated' Asylum Seekers," *Migration Information Source*, April 5, 2007.

15. *10. Bericht der Beauftragten der Bundesregierung für Migration, Flüchtlinge und Integration über die Lage der Ausländerinnen und Ausländer in Deutschland*, October 2014. Here I cite the press summary of the 400 +-page report, p. 4.

16. Ralf E. Ulrich, "Die zukünftige Bevölkerungsstruktur Deutschlands nach Staatsanghörigkeit, Geburtsort und ethnischer Herkunft: Modellrechnung bis 2050," Gutachten für die Unabhängige Kommission "Zuwanderung," Berlin and Windhoek, April 2001.

17. BAMF Migrationsbericht 2013, *Bevölkerungsentwicklung* (Berlin: 2015), pp. 45–46.

18. Peter Schimany, "Migration und demographischer Wandel," BAMF, Forschungsbericht 5, 2008; Beutke and Kotzur, "Faktensammlung Diskriminierung."

19. "Merkel: Deutschland kann tolles Integrationsland werden," *Frankfurter Allgemeine Zeitung*, October 22, 2015.

20. For the German Conclusions, see: www.eu2007.de/de.

21. Mushaben, *Changing Faces of Citizenship*, p. 201.

22. BAMF, *Migrationsbericht* 2014, pp. 18–19.

23. Like Merkel, Böhmer entered the Bundestag in 1990, having served as Rheinland-Pfalz's equal opportunity commissioner (1982–1990), in addition to party executive posts. She presided over the CDU Women's Union in 2001, following Rita Süssmuth, who chaired the Independent Commission on Immigration. Böhmer first learned about the Integration Summit through the media, suggesting that Merkel was the instigator. Lau, *Die Letzte Volkspartei*, p. 147.

24. The OMC's intergovernmental framework nudges member states toward common goals in specific domains; it establishes common measuring instruments (disaggregated statistics, indicators, guidelines), draws up national action plans and benchmarks, using peer pressure among participating states, all of which is monitored by the Commission.

25. Merkel Speech online, June 4, 2008, available at: www.bundesregierung.de/Content/Rede/2008/06/2008/06-04-merkel-integration.

26. The European Council consists of heads of government; the General Affairs Council includes the latter and foreign ministers. Only "responsible" ministers attend the nine substantive councils.

27. *Reuters*, see: www.reuters.com/article/idUSTRE69F1K320101016, October 16, 2010.
28. Personal interview with a GIC participant, 2009.
29. They include the *Zentralrat der Muslime in Deutschland* (ZMD), the *Türkisch-Islamischen Union der Anstalt für Religion* (DİTİB), the *Islamrat für die Bundesrepublik Deutschland* (IRD), and the *Verband der Islamischen Kulturzentren* (VIKZ).
30. See *Zugewandert – Angekommen? Chancen der Vielfalt*, October 2014: Die Rede von Thomas de Maizière bei #cduvielfalt.
31. Merkel speech, December 1, 2014.
32. Bassam Tibi, *Europa ohne Identität, Die Krise der multikulturellen Gesellschaft* (Munich: Bertelsmann, 1998).
33. Tables available at: www.statistik-berlin.de/pms/2a1/1996/96-08-23b.html.
34. Mushaben, *The Changing Faces of Citizenship*, ch. 1.
35. Christian Babka von Gostomski, "The Naturalisation Behaviour of Foreigners in Germany, and Findings Concerning *Optionspflichtige*," Bundesamt für Migration & Flüchtlinge, Berlin, 2011; see also Worbs, Scholz and Blicke, *Die Optionsregelung*.
36. "Die Kanzlerin der Vertriebenen," *Politik im Spiegel*, August 29, 2014.
37. BAMF, *Aktuelle Zahlen zu Asyl*, June 2015, p. 3.
38. "Flüchtlinge in Deutschland: Leben in Containern," Deutschlandfunk, 11. October 2014.
39. Dietrich Thränhardt, *Die Arbeitsmigration von Flüchtlingen in Deutschland: Humanität, Effektivität, Selbstbestimmung* (Munich: Bertelsmann, May 2015), p. 13.
40. See: www.bamf.de/SharedDocs/Anlagen/DE/Publikationen/Broschueren/das-deutsche-asylverfahren.pdf?__blob=publicationFile; and www.bamf.de/SharedDocs/Anlagen/DE/Publikationen/Migrationsberichte/migrationsbericht-2010.pdf?__blob=publicationFile.
41. Anne Radmacher (ed.), *"Ich bete jeden Tag, bitte laß uns bleiben": 14 Porträts asylsuchender Frauen aus aller Welt* (Munich: Goldmann, 1993).
42. *Migrationsbericht der Ausländerbeauftragten 2001* (Berlin), p. 50.
43. Thränhardt, *Die Arbeitsmigration*, p. 20.
44. Richtlinie für die Förderung der sozialen Beratung und Betreuung von Leistungsberechtigten nach dem Asylbewerberleistungsgesetz und von Ausländerinnen und Ausländern in staatlichen Unterkünften (AsylSozBR), January 5, 2007, amended 2010 (AllMBl: 3).
45. "Ex-Minister Friedrich legt Merkel Parteiaustritt nahe," *Der Spiegel*, March 18, 2016.
46. "Asylbewerber müssen ab sofort mehr Geld bekommen," *Der Spiegel*, July 18, 2012.
47. Thränhardt, *Die Arbeitsmigration*, p. 15.
48. *Bericht zum Anerkennungsgesetz 2015*, pp. 16, 83.
49. Lenz Jacobsen, "Der Umbau beginnt," *Die Zeit*, May 8, 2015.
50. BAMF, *Runder Tisch Aufnahmegesellschaft*, Berlin, 2013.
51. Joyce Marie Mushaben, "Die Lehrjahre sind vorbei! Re-Forming Democratic Interest Groups in Eastern Germany," *Democratization*, 8(4) (2001): 95–133.

52. Eurostat news release, March 2015.
53. "Merkel warnt vor erheblichen Spannungen in der EU," *Frankfurter Allgemeine Zeitung*, June 25, 2015.
54. "Zuwanderung auf höchstem Stand seit 20 Jahren," *Die Welt*, May 22, 2014.
55. "Seehofer verteidigt Stimmungsmache gegen Zuwanderer," *Der Spiegel*, January 1, 2012; Benjamin Knaack and Gregor Peter Schmitz, "Kabinett beschließt Maßnahmenpaket gegen 'Armutsmigration,'" *Der Spiegel*, August 27, 2014; "Deutschland profitiert vom Akademiker-Ansturm," *Der Spiegel*, January 20, 2012; Vera Kämper, "Fachkräfte in Bayern: Die Zuwanderungsprofiteure," *Der Spiegel*, January 17, 2014; "Deutschland profitiert von Zuwanderung aus Osteuropa," *Der Spiegel*, December 27, 2013.
56. David Böcking, "Ausländer bringen Deutschland Milliarden," *Der Spiegel*, November 27, 2014.
57. BAMF *Aktuelle Zahlen zu Asyl*, May 2015, p. 17.
58. UN Human Rights Commission, "The Sea Route to Europe: Mediterranean Passage in the Age of Refugees," pp. 3, 11; Sachverständigenrat deutscher Stiftungen für Integration und Migration, "Krise der europäischen Asylpolitik: Kollektive Aufnahmeverfahren mit fairen Quoten einrichten," SVR- Forschungsbereich, 2015-1.
59. Benjamin Schulz und Ansgar Siemens, "Minderjährige Flüchtlinge: Jung, allein, traumatisiert," *Der Spiegel*, April 15, 2015.
60. "The Makings of Merkel's Decision to Accept Refugees," *Der Spiegel International*, August 24, 2016.
61. Sommer-Pressekonferenz der Kanzlerin zu aktuellen Themen, August 31, 2015, available at: www.youtube.com/watch?v=5eXc5Sc_rnY; Tina Hildebrandt and Bernd Ulrich, "Angela Merkel: Im Auge des Orkans," *Die Zeit*, September 20, 2015.
62. Press conference, September 7, 2015, available at: www.bundesregierung.de/Content/DE/Mitschrift/Pressekonferenzen/2015/09/2015-09-07-merkel-gabriel.html.
63. "Flüchtlingskrise: Kabinett beschließt neues Asylgesetz," *Der Spiegel*, September 29, 2015.
64. Hildebrandt and Ulrich, "Im Auge des Orkans."
65. Florian Gathmann and Kevin Hagen, "Was jetzt gilt – und was noch kommt," *Der Spiegel*, January 12, 2015.
66. Joyce Marie Mushaben, "The Sad Truth Highlighted by Germany Assaults," CNN, January 12, 2016, available at: www.cnn.com/2016/01/11/opinions/mushaben-cologne-attacks.
67. "Flüchtlingskrise: Was steht im Asylpaket II?," *Frankfurter Allgemeine Zeitung*, January 29, 2016.
68. Katharina Schüler, "Asylpaket II: Viel Härte, wenig Wirkung," *Die Zeit*, February 25, 2016.
69. "Entscheidung des Bundesverfassungsgerichts: Asylbewerber müssen ab sofort mehr Geld bekommen," *Der Spiegel*, July 18, 2012.
70. "Merkel lehnt Gabriels Forderung nach Solipakt für Deutsche ab," *Der Spiegel*, February 26, 2016.

71. "Refugee Policy Focus of Seehofer, Orban Meeting," *Deutsche Welle*, March 4, 2015; "Lösung der Flüchtlingskrise liegt nicht in Europa," *Der Tagesspiegel*, April 17, 2015; "Helmut Kohl wollte Europa nie um jeden Preis," *Der Tagesspiegel*, August 21, 2015.

72. Thomas Assheuer, "Flüchtlingskrise: Unsere Willkommenskultur," *Die Zeit*, November 1, 2015.

73. Joyce Marie Mushaben, "Educating for Citizenship: Re-assessing the Role of Islamic Instruction in German Schools," *Politics & Religion*, 3 (2010), p. 16.

74. She has visited Berlin schools with many headscarf-wearers. See Peter Müller, "Merkel beim Schulbesuch: Da kommt ein Mädchen mit kurzem Rock, da gucken die Kerle alle," *Der Spiegel*, May 12, 2015.

75. "Ein pauschales Kopftuchverbot für Lehrkräfte in öffentlichen Schulen ist mit der Verfassung nicht vereinbar," press release issued by the Constitutional Court, No. 14/2015, March 13, 2015.

76. Alison Gerard and Sharon Pickering, "Gender, Securitization and Transit: Refugee Women and the Journey to the EU," *Journal of Refugee Studies*, 27(3) (2013): 338–359.

77. Bundesministerium für Wissenschaft und Forschung, "Der VDI sucht Frauen mit Migrationshintergrund," December 5, 2012.

78. Summer press conference, August 31, 2015.

79. Daniela Vates, "CDU: Spaghettifresser und Zonenwachtel," *Frankfurter Rundschau*, October 22, 2014.

8

"Misunderestimating" the World's Most Powerful Woman, or Why Gender Still Matters

> A leader takes people where they want to go. A great leader takes people where they don't necessarily want to go but ought to be.
>
> Rosalynn Carter

In 2016, a series of German state elections ended with double-digit gains for the right-wing populist party, the Alternative for Germany (AfD). Journalists and critics across the board immediately pounced on the idea that their first woman chancellor would not survive the 2017 national elections. Their ranks included many who had predicted shortly after her first inauguration in 2005 that the Grand Coalition was doomed to fail, that her subsequent conservative–liberal government was (continuously) on the brink after 2009, and that, after being elected for the third time in 2013, she would probably retire ten months later when she turned 60, because she would be worn out.[1] No such suggestion was made regarding Helmut Kohl when he commenced his fourth term at age 66.

Second only to leaders confronting the Great Depression and the Second World War, Angela Merkel has mastered an extraordinary array of European crises, all packed into a single decade. To borrow a metaphor, she has been "surrounded by the Four Horsemen of the Apocalypse: War haunts Ukraine, Death harvests refugees in the Mediterranean, Famine brings economic hardship to Greece, and Pestilence is busy spreading scepticism from Britain."[2] Shortly after the Brexit vote and Germany's first home-grown terrorist attacks since the Baader-Meinhof era (1970s), she admitted in July 2016, "there are some evenings when I am very glad to go to bed ... I am not under-overloaded."[3] Although I am not a betting woman, my money is still on the crisis-tested chancellor.

Since the 1970s, scholars have generated a plethora of organizational studies, laboratory experiments, and surveys hoping to determine whether or not women and men "lead differently." Because males have dominated the public domain for centuries, it is understandable that citizens everywhere have a tendency to view leadership as something inherently male. Unfortunately, most conflate the ways in which men *behave* with what really *works* when it comes to policy change. Mega-studies conducted by industrial psychologists and business scholars infer that empirically tested differences are rarely statistically significant.[4] Gender variations tend to disappear when men and women occupy the same positions and manage concrete tasks; this allows researchers to control for differences rooted in specific societal contexts, institutional imperatives, or situational factors. As Alice H. Eagly and Mary C. Johannesen-Schmidt stress, however, "small differences, when repeated over individuals and occasions, can produce large consequences."[5]

We need not dwell for long on the stereotypical traits and behaviors ascribed to each sex across national boundaries, usually assessed by way of formal "inventories" and scales.[6] Women are generally characterized as community-minded, cooperative, demure, emotional, gentle, helpful, kind, nurturing, participatory, quiet, relationship-oriented, risk-averse, sensitive, subordinate, supportive, sympathetic, and warm – although few of these traits applied to the first "Iron Lady," Margaret Thatcher. Men are purportedly ambitious, aggressive, assertive, competitive, controlling, daring, dominant, forceful, independent, loud, rational, rule-oriented, and self-confident – adjectives that did describe Merkel's predecessor, Gerhard Schröder. Focusing on *personal traits* impels researchers to confuse style with substance, however. "Projecting gravitas" is a far cry from being able to marshal controversial policies through complex legislative processes, no matter how essential they may be to the national interest.[7] While the last two decades have given rise to a growing feminist-theoretical complex, quantitative studies assessing quotas and diverging modes of *representation* rarely draw on detailed treatments of women's real-world performance as leaders across multiple terms in office, the purpose of this study.

Historically rooted stereotypes still shape the ways in which voters and pundits *perceive* and *judge* women lucky enough to secure powerful positions; they generate their own realities, wedging female leaders between the proverbial rock of expectations and the hard place of institutional imperatives. Through the early 1990s, women who conformed to ascribed gender profiles, for example, by looking "feminine," were judged incapable of meeting the rigors of high political office. How could a caring mother participate in parliamentary debates lasting until 2 am, or fly off to a three-day global summit with no time to wash her hair? Germany's Green *Feminat* of the 1980s proved that an all-woman party executive could complete its tasks during normal working hours; no one asked why men needed longer to get the job done. As Merkel's early years in power demonstrated, women sometimes benefit from "misunderestimation": they can actually appear *more* effective in cases where traditional elites or voters did not expect much from them in the first place.[8]

Although she rejects the feminist label, Angela Merkel has lent new credence to the equality mantra of 1960s: *the personal is the political.* Her path to power was unconventional, yet "Kohl's Girl" proved to be a very fast learner; by 2015, she ranked ninth among the world's best paid political leaders and had secured her standing as its "Most Powerful Woman" ten times over.[9] Her Protestant and GDR upbringing through the 1950s and 1960s, her activities as a natural scientist in the 1970s and 1980s, and her political re-education in an alpha-male party arena following unification have all contributed to her success. Drawing on the intersectionality theme, Angela Merkel's atypical socialization experiences have rendered her a *particular kind of national leader* exercising *special types of executive power* in pursuit of *selective political norms*, enabling her to introduce *new policy priorities.*[10]

Like most chemical reactions, the effect of personal experiences on Merkel's performance has been cumulative rather than additive, but one can still discern instances in which one socialization factor prevails over others. Whereas her east-to-west re-acculturation exerts influence over *policy substance*, her upbringing as a pastor's daughter in a "godless" state drives her strong commitment to human rights and freedom-of-movement *norms*. Gender factors, combined with her post-GDR antipathy toward confrontational, ideological positions factor into her *leadership style*, while the physicist is clearly at work in matters of *program design* and *evaluation*. Detailed case studies help us to sort out how different dimensions and degrees of women's *representation* play out across various policy domains. Gender matters, but one of the primary lessons of comparative public policy analysis is that "context" is crucial.

In an earlier study analyzing the chancellor's first two coalition experiences through 2013, I revisited the role of "hard" and "soft" powers traditionally ascribed to male and female leaders by comparing the management styles exhibited by Kurt Georg Kiesinger and Angela Merkel. Both had directed a Grand Coalition as well as a majority coalition government. I attributed significant overlaps in their respective modes of GC operation to the exceptional party-political constraints, that is, the need to reconcile normally adversarial CDU/CSU and SPD orientations. To the extent that gender mattered, it was the forceful minister-president from Baden-Württemberg who had to abandon "hard" tactics to manage the strong personalities from opposing parties comprising his cabinet.[11] Serving as chancellor from 1966 to 1969, Kiesinger adopted "soft" leadership skills, combining mediating, listening, working groups, and informal management techniques.[12] Merkel drew on similar skills during her first term but was ironically viewed as less effective in managing her second government, based on a traditional albeit unruly conservative–liberal majority, starting in 2009. The voters presented an ostensibly relieved Merkel with a second Grand Coalition in 2013.[13] Analyzing differences in the behavior of two leaders – one male, one female – under diverging partisan configurations allowed me to highlight the importance of institutional factors, such as the specific nature of the coalition, the shift from a "bipolar" two-and-a-half party system in the 1960s to a fluctuating, multi-party system after 1990, and the EU's increasing influence over national decision-making. These factors also pre-shaped Merkel's opportunities for advancing women's descriptive and substantive representation across different policy domains; the advent of new parties allowed her to draw on "opposition" Green support at the national level, for instance, while also depriving her of consistent coalition allies at the Länder level.[14] New EU mandates provided additional leverage for many of her reforms.

This chapter begins with a treatment of two leadership models that help to explain why the "Merkel Method" may have worked better in some domains than others. While she was criticized early on for not meeting the expectations of the male-normed "transactional" model, I argue that her preferred "transformational" style proved largely effective over time, not only because her reforms took Germany in a direction citizens usually wanted to go, but also because it is what the circumstances required. A key question is whether the globalized, post-unification context will oblige all future chancellors to adopt core elements of this model, irrespective of their sex or socialization.

Next, I summarize Merkel's most noteworthy policy achievements to date, contending that there is no single set of indicators that can be used to judge her "successful" or not. Different levels of government require diverging consensus, compromise, and concession mechanisms; one must also weigh the cost of short-term victories against potential long-term gains. Merkel usually focuses on the latter, making her a rare commodity among elected politicians. It is also hard to suppress one's own values in assessing a leader's performance. In my judgment, her greatest *empirical* accomplishments to date involve the national energy turn-around and her proactive migration/integration policies. In *normative* terms, I find Madam Chancellor's principled stance on the refugee crisis more courageous than her personalized commitment to Israel's security.

Finally, I address the question: does gender still matter with regard to perceptions and patterns of women's leadership? In what respects has Merkel lived up to feminist-theoretical expectations regarding the advance of women's descriptive, substantive, and transformative representation? Has her staying power across three terms chipped away at gender stereotypes at the highest levels of government? Has the first female chancellor rendered the executive branch more representative in numerical terms? Have her policies served the substantive needs of women and minorities in ways not witnessed in the past, even if her motives are not explicitly "feminist?" Have her actions helped to fundamentally redefine women's and men's proper place in public and private life, as well as Germany's place in the world? As far as her own citizens are concerned, I would answer in response to all of these questions: yes, she certainly has, although women beyond her borders have sometimes experienced less positive outcomes. In becoming a very powerful Madam Chancellor, Angela Merkel has subjected the nation united to many long overdue makeovers in ways that will make her a very tough act to follow. We now turn to lessons that might be derived from her evolving leadership style.

GENDER AND STYLE: TRANSFORMATIONAL V. TRANSACTIONAL LEADERSHIP

While Americans are rather casual about labeling someone a "real leader," Germans are hesitant to stress qualities inhering in a single person; they avoid the word *Führer* for obvious historical reasons, and even the term *Führung* is rarely used in day-to-day politics. Warren Bennis and Burt Nanus equate the ephemeral nature of leadership with "the Abominable Snowman, whose footprints are everywhere but who is nowhere to be seen," but even that metaphor implies something essentially white and male.[15] German sociologist Max Weber delineated three sources of legitimate rule, labeled charismatic, traditional, and legal *authority*. FRG politicians tend to talk more about power (*Macht*), competencies, and party goals than about their personal agendas. By definition, parliaments utilizing proportional representation require greater cooperation, compromise, and sharing the credit for positive outcomes than winner-take-all systems.

Rooted in US business administration and organizational psychology studies, the contemporary literature offers two ideal types that conveniently align leadership with traits and behaviors typically ascribed to men and women. Both seem to concentrate more on *style* than on *outcomes*. The male-normed version, *transactional leadership*, foresees a leader who commands behavioral compliance from employees. It carries strong Weberian overtones (popularized by Robert Dahl), assuming that it is "A's job to make B do what s/he would not ordinarily do." This model stresses (presumably) consistent performance standards, designated assignments, and task-specific goals, fixated on worker compliance and task completion; the effective manager depends "quite heavily on organizational rewards and punishments to influence employee performance."[16] The general style, "command and control," relies on hierarchical structures, organizational loyalty, narrowly delineated objectives, and clear lines of authority, suggesting accountability. Business studies suggest that male managers pay close attention to employees' mistakes but evince little concern for personal circumstances or workplace conditions (e.g., sexual harassment) that might hinder their effective performance. Scholars also ascribe a hands-off approach ("long periods" of non-engagement) to such leaders, at least until a crisis requires a form of heroic, personalized decision-making.

German chancellors occasionally respond to major conflicts by declaring an issue a *Chef-Sache*, a serious matter for the boss. Gerhard Schröder, for instance, cultivated his image as the *Basta!* ("That's it!") chancellor, conveying at least the appearance of exercising "ultimate control over the decision-making process."[17] Further behaviors that fall under this model include the *personalization of politics*, that is, presenting oneself as the embodiment of change, as well as *efforts to centralize power* by expanding the day-to-day reach of the Chancellor's Executive Office (BKA). Some rely on "secret" or closed-circle governing, while others offer incentives, special deals, or trade-offs to key actors in order to secure compliance. Such leaders are often imbued with charisma and vision, but as SPD Chancellor Helmut Schmidt once famously declared, a politician "who has visions should go see a doctor."

Generically, if not genetically ascribed to women, *transformational leadership* "occurs when the leader stimulates the interest among colleagues and followers to view their work from a new perspective."[18] According to contemporary scholars, the transformational leader "generates an awareness of the mission or vision of the organization, and develops colleagues and followers to higher levels of ability and potential ... to look beyond their own interests towards interests that will benefit the group."[19] Instead of drawing clear lines between superiors and subordinates, this leader cultivates stakeholders by displaying empathy and fostering a participatory environment to garner trust and respect. Commands are replaced by teamwork and "plain speaking"; control yields to partnership; and authority defined in terms of rungs on a power-ladder matters less than shared principles, pragmatism, and participation. For the record: community expert Mary Parker Follett developed a model along these lines in the early 1900s, long before US business schools discovered Total Quality Management techniques. Leadership, she wrote, "is not defined by the exercise of power but by the capacity to increase the sense of power among those led. The most essential work of the leader is to create more leaders."[20]

Emotional intelligence is another quintessential trait linked to this model, that is, "the ability to monitor one's own and others' feelings ... and to use this information to guide one's own thinking and actions."[21] Far from touchy-feely, emotional intelligence rests on self-control, self-confidence, the ability to handle conflict, and tolerance for stress.[22] Merkel has often stated publicly how "hard" certain decisions have been for her personally, empathizing with her constituents; although she has learned to use "spin," she still draws on quotidian metaphors, like the Swabian housewife, to forge connections with average citizens. In a rapidly changing global environment, "IQ and technical skills are probably baseline requirements for executive roles, but without emotional intelligence the best-trained manager won't make a great leader."[23] Recent studies suggest that even in the corporate world, executive boards that include women are better at managing change, which simultaneously renders them more profitable.[24] Her exposure to the global banking crisis and various Volkswagen scandals undoubtedly helped her to turn the corner in calling for more women as financial and business decision-makers.

Katje Glaesner attributes Merkel's success to additional soft skills that fit this model, starting with a tendency to listen and to communicate in terms easily understood by the public; using trust and discretion to generate an atmosphere of respect, loyalty, and team spirit; openly admitting lessons learned; and conveying long-term goals anchored in a positive image of society.[25] Parker Follett would add the ability to "integrate" ostensibly conflicting interests (win–win) by getting to the roots of a problem, which one can best do by including more stakeholders affected by the policy in question. A final set of qualities – drive, ambition, and "bite," added to persistence and energy – suggests an alpha personality rarely ascribed to women, although all of these elements define Merkel's character; she gets by on less than five hours of sleep but claims that she retanks "like a camel" during quieter stages.[26] The chancellor's ability to keep her private life private has been nothing short of phenomenal; the weekend house in the Uckermark is her refuge. Merkel's effectiveness in juggling shifting domestic coalitions and multi-level governance demands while hammering away at five major crises in the space of ten years renders it a moot question as to whether these are quintessentially feminine traits or modern "quality management" skills.

Based on her calm demeanor, emotional intelligence, clear communication skills, cultivation of stakeholders, reliance on expert working groups, and principled responses to highly controversial issues, I would classify Angela Merkel as the political embodiment of a transformational leader. Having followed her activities for more than two decades, I offer my own definition of what is often referred to as the "Merkel Method" (see Box 8.1), building on the insights of journalists granted the rare privilege of conducting in-depth interviews with her at various stages of her political career.[27]

Box 8.1: The "Merkel Method": Fifteen Steps to Becoming Madam Chancellor

(1) Nothing succeeds like success, but remember that politics does not have to be particularly attractive or awe-inspiring in order to be successful. Eventually they will stop talking about your hair.

(2) Avoid rigid, ideological thinking at any cost: the politics of *small, pragmatic steps* is often more successful than grand promises and sweeping reforms.

(3) The two greatest virtues a politician can possess are *self-discipline* and the ability to *keep quiet*, especially when all of your rivals are busy "making statements."

(4) You need to remain resolute, apply tactical skills, display a lot of patience, and take advantage of lucky breaks in order to overcome a party full of egos (Remember: you are surrounded by "enemies, arch-enemies, and party-friends").

Box 8.1: Cont

(5) Always wait until you see the data before you decide on a solution, and do not be afraid to change your course when the data start pointing in a different direction. Trial and error is the only way that the human race has actually advanced.

(6) As any natural scientist would do, run through the entire experiment in your head before you commit to a major decision. Consider your antagonists as particles operating in a constant energy field in which positively and negatively charged elements can change or combine with something else in an instant.

(7) As a woman operating in a man's world, nonetheless learn to observe the constants, the patterns, the strengths and weaknesses driving male behavior. They will not do the same regarding your behavior, which will make it easier for you to keep a step ahead and to outmaneuver them.

(8) Minimize your risks by studying the issue, doing the math and lining up the probabilities but realize that you always need to anticipate unintended consequences and long-term effects.

(9) Make a plan, understand the legislative calendar and stick to it. Recognize that the "rainbow" coalitions dominating the Bundesrat (black–yellow, red–green, black–red, red–red, green–black, etc.) are likely to change with the next state elections.

(10) Sometimes you need to walk a tightrope, but it helps to have a network of supportive women behind (or below) you.

(11) Build bridges and create new stakeholders when you cannot secure the support of the old ones; accept the fact that it may take all night. You can power-nap on your Lufthansa version of "Air Force One."

(12) Have the free-spirited soul of a pirate but never take more than your share of the booty or credit. Recognize that going where others fear to tread may force you to walk an occasional electoral gang-plank, but thanking others will foster loyalty.

(13) When times are tough and/or voters feel down and out, reinvoke the German *Economic Miracle* narrative – better yet, the *Rubble Woman* ethos – for inspiration and justification. By now most people do not remember who Ludwig Erhard was anyway. To add a regional touch, remind them of their mothers, for example, hardworking *schwäbische Hausfrauen*.

(14) Guard your private feelings and personal life very carefully and only use them as reserves in difficult times, also known as the go-home-and-bake-*Pflaumenkuchen* (plum cake) strategy.

(15) Having people constantly *Mis-underestimate* you is the best way to ensure that you will win. Think "tortoise and the hare," David and Goliath, and the "little engine that could." The Great Leap Forward was an absolute disaster; small steps have helped you to reach the top.

RECONFIGURING THE BERLIN REPUBLIC:
MERKEL'S POLICY LEGACIES

Exploring the nature of "scientific revolutions," Thomas S. Kuhn wrote in 1962: "Almost always the men who achieve these fundamental inventions of a new paradigm have been either very young or very new to the field whose paradigm they change . . . obviously these are the men who, being little committed by prior practice to the traditional rules of normal science, are particularly likely to see that those rules no longer define a playable game and to conceive another set that can replace them."[28] Only eight years old when Kuhn's work was published, Angela Kasner had little cause to reflect on gender biases in the sciences, nor could she have imagined that forty years later she would personally embody his profound understanding of *paradigm change* at many different levels. Following her career as a rare female physicist conducting quantum chemistry experiments, she entered national politics as a complete outsider in 1990. As a result, she lacked the vocabulary, knowledge, and confidence normally acquired via the "oxen tour," as well as the contacts and loyal constituents tied to a strong state base. Her youth and newcomer status compelled her to draw on personal life-lessons acquired in the GDR to find her way in a very different governance game. Her courageous break with Helmut Kohl in 1999 over a campaign finance scandal nonetheless opened the door to a political cultural revolution across united Germany.

In Part I we assessed Merkel's contributions to the Berlin Republic at the *meta-historical level,* based on her effectiveness in fostering a positive national identity among *Ossis* (Easterners) and *Wessis* (Westerners), coupled with her ability to strengthen Germany's special relationship with Israel in the face of generational change. It is impossible to measure success or failure with regard to collective identity and historical responsibility; the best indicator I could find to assess Merkel's performance at this level centers on *reconciliation.* Was she able to transcend dialectical differences shaping deeply rooted interpretations of German history, and has she provided an affirmative framework that can survive generational change?

Privy to the blessing of postwar birth, Merkel recognized better than the "old men" criticized by Antje Vollmer that citizens need to identify positively with their country not only to master the past, but also in order to share responsibility in facing future challenges. In these cases she led by example: "I like living here . . . I have confidence in this country, and I am a part of its shared history – with all of its pains and its good sides."[29]

Openly admitting that she, too, had struggled with conflicting views of the *Shoah*, over getting along with the SED regime and finding new meaning in 1968 made it easier for other Germans to break with the ideological thinking that had framed these events prior to 1989. East–West differences will persist, of course, but they will be no more antagonistic than those between northern and southern, urban and rural regions. Merkel moreover built bridges between the two populations by grafting new policies onto old roots, building on Western environmentalism and Eastern childcare guarantees, for example. Despite their diverging human rights experiences, she has encouraged both sides to embrace migration and asylum rights by reminding them of the peaceful miracle of unification.

Four decades of special relations between the Federal Republic and Israel supplied the new chancellor with a ready-made framework on the official front, but even here she drew on her personal experiences to redirect an historically over-determined relationship. She "completed the circle" of reconciliation by bringing Poland and other countries victimized by the Nazis into youth exchanges with Israel, while expanding Germany's human rights agenda to include Palestinians.[30] Like her erstwhile Green nemesis, Joschka Fischer, the Protestant CDU chancellor not only recognized the permanent nature of her country's moral responsibility to Israel; both also broke a post-war taboo by openly criticizing Israel and insisting that Germany can no longer use its past to avoid military force when it comes to defending human rights. Generational dynamics have nonetheless contributed to changes in these arenas in contradictory ways. When it comes to synthesizing East–West identities, generational change works as a facilitator. Upholding the special German–Israeli relationship will become a lot harder, however, with the passing of cohorts (parents, grandparents) whose personal Second World War memories led to reconciliation across many sectors after the 1960s.

Identity formation is, by definition, a subjective process embedded in social constructions; it therefore makes sense that Merkel would draw on personal experiences in repositioning herself between antithetical GDR and FRG interpretations of German history. Raised as a pastor's daughter in an atheist state, she was cast as a clueless Easterner into the world of know-it-all Western politicians, rendering her a double outsider; that status forced her to make up and play by her own rules. She laid the foundation for a united German identity still rooted in collective responsibility for the past, no matter how complicated right-wing populist parties (harking back to a not-so-golden past) are making her life as of this writing.[31] She built on Fischer's efforts to anchor responses to the

Israeli–Palestinian conflict in broader EU partnerships, rendering them more sustainable. To the outside world, Germany has become a "normal" country; the chancellor's performance at this level qualifies as a success.

Viewed as an effective mediator at the *international level* during her first term, Merkel's foreign policy skills have been sorely tested by the external crises dominating her second and third terms, explored in Part II. While old and new EU member states willingly deferred to her management of Russian aggression in Georgia and Ukraine, they were seriously divided over German austerity demands during the height of the Euro crisis. Coinciding with her first Grand Coalition, the banking crisis elicited a stimulus response back home; constrained by a new conservative–liberal coalition as of 2009, Merkel jettisoned that approach at the EU level. Domestic elites remained more or less united behind their leader through both crises, in large part because she drew on established national templates grounded in ordo-liberal price stability, *Ostpolitik* and civilian power. The indicator I use to evaluate her performance in these two cases centers on *containment*. Did Merkel manage to "save the Euro" and block Russian advances in ways that ensure longer-term stability on both fronts?

The Law of Unanticipated Consequences produced many positive "spill-overs" for European integration through the 1990s. The shared memories of two devastating world wars informed the willingness of first six, then nine, twelve and, eventually, fifteen Western leaders to engage in gradual processes of completion, deepening, and enlargement. The rapid inclusion of twelve new Eastern members between 2004 and 2005 upset the balance between rich and poor states, however. Electoral volatility, globalization, and generational change have increasingly led CEE leaders to view the EU in instrumental terms, fracturing the value consensus cultivated by its founding states. Merkel quickly internalized the traditional FRG commitment to transatlanticism, multilateralism, and détente but like her SPD predecessor, she finds it easier to assert national interests, as well as to assume new defense responsibilities beyond regional borders. Her second term strengthened her appreciation for EU values, despite her calls for German-style structural reforms. While Poland and the Baltic states approve of her hard talk vis-à-vis Putin, they evince little tolerance for her tough love regarding their own budgetary and refugee policies.

I would rate the chancellor's performance regarding the Euro crisis as mixed: saving the Euro has extracted a heavy cost in relation to the historical Franco-German friendship and the rise of virulent Euroskeptic parties. While the AfD arose in opposition to the common currency, it has morphed into a rather misogynist, anti-migration party that has chipped away at the popularity and legitimacy Merkel enjoyed at home through 2015.[32] Although most Germans supported her handling of Putin, AfD elements (including unabashed neo-Nazis) are courting Russian autocrats, a mere twenty-five years after Easterners escaped the choke-hold of Soviet subordination. Given their low turn-out during the last two national elections, it is hard to understand their anger at being "ignored" by political elites; they enjoy clean environments, generous pensions, travel rights, freedom of expression and assembly, and significant TV-time, all sorely lacking in Putin's Russia. Merkel was generally successful in containing Russian aggression in the trans-Caucasus, and brokered new cooperation over energy security and the so-called "war on terrorism." Her ability to achieve more in these domains has been limited by external dynamics and uncontrollable actors in other countries.

The *level of Bund–Länder relations* should provide a national leader with her best chance of realizing her goals, based on clearly defined boundaries, her familiarity with decision-making processes, institutional norms, and regular interactions with key players. While Angela Merkel will probably be remembered most for her quick response to the 2011 Fukushima disaster and her dramatic decision to "suspend Dublin" in 2015, her engagement with energy and migration issues began well before those two crises hit. Her early years in the Kohl cabinet coincided with an unprecedented wave of xenophobic violence, the consequence of four decades of anti-integration policies. She later confronted massive waves of sometimes violent protest, only to discover that demonstrators were right about the leaky nuclear waste transports. Unlike Marie Curie, Merkel did not confine herself to the quiet complacency of a laboratory; still, she has expanded the world of scientific opportunity for women through her political application of power physics.

A chancellor opting for a transformational leadership style is more likely to produce results that are, well, transformational; thus, the best indicator as to whether or not she proved successful in these two domains boils down to *fundamental policy change*. Have Merkel's reforms produced a lasting paradigm shift, and, if so, are her energy and migration policies sufficiently rooted in German political culture to ensure their continuation once she leaves office? Although her refugee policies have encountered stiffer resistance than her turn-around on nuclear energy, I conclude that both of these data-driven "revolutions" will survive, facilitated again by processes of generational change.

Japan's nuclear disaster presented Merkel the physicist with the perfect storm: she understood the science behind climate change, recognized public distrust of the nuclear industry, foresaw Russian threats to European energy security, and anticipated the comparative export advantages awaiting Germany in the green technologies arena. Her development of new stakeholders through earlier feed-in-tariff subsidies, coupled with the energy frameworks adopted by the EU and her first Grand Coalition precluded serious Länder resistance. Incentives may change, and strong interest groups could slow implementation, but the paradigm shift is real. Here it is easy to measure the results in terms of legal mandates, GHG reductions, and increasing RE use in energy generation, testifying to Merkel's effective leadership in this domain.

Hard facts regarding refugee "integration" are more difficult to come by, largely because learning a language, securing jobs, and internalizing community values can take years. The main problem (as of this writing) is a general asylum application backlog, along with a shortage of teachers for the mandated orientation courses. The number entering Germany has dropped significantly, from 1.1 million in 2015 to 223,000 by mid-2016; applications are now being processed at record speeds, for example, 57,000 in August 2016, three times more than the monthly figure in 2015. Corporations, economists, and demographers all back the chancellor: among 132 enterprises polled in July 2016, 73 percent had already accepted refugees as apprentices.[33] Though most are better off now than during the first post-unity decade, the fact that some Easterners still fall between the cracks owes more to Schröder's Hartz IV reforms than to Merkel's refugee policy. Social media exchanges fostering perceptions of relative deprivation are not supported by the data. The same voters who reject migrants today will need these trainable youth to finance their pensions through 2050. Partisan de-alignment since the late 1980s, added to the proliferation of new parties since 1990, have accorded the AfD disproportionate electoral influence, leading to complicated coalitions.

Responding to critical CDU losses in five state elections, the chancellor reaffirmed her principled stance on the refugees at a September 2016 press conference. Providing protection for over a million people in need was not something Germany could master "overnight." Had she able to turn back the clock "by many, many years," the chancellor mused, she "would have better prepared [herself], the federal government and participating stakeholders" at all levels to address such a crisis. Signaling another break with the failures of the Kohl era, she continued:

We weren't exactly world champs in matters of integration ... which is why we have to over-exert ourselves now, myself included ... To the people who fear being overrun by foreigners, I can only reply: Germany will not be shaken to its foundation ... If these people specifically want us to exclude people of Muslim faith, that runs against our constitution, our obligations under international law and the ethical foundation of our party ... I feel absolutely certain that we will come out of this complicated stage better than when we entered it.[34]

Angela Merkel entered national politics with a faith in dialogue and democratic processes that had been lost among traditional politicians. Her political experiences since the 1990s have made her more cautious about articulating her policies but they have not tempered her belief in Germany's ability to overcome formidable challenges. She now reinforces "facts of the case" arguments with substantive references to EU, international, and FRG constitutional law.

As a female Easterner, she owed her jobs in the Kohl cabinet to an informal CDU "diversity" requirement.[35] It is also worth recalling that her first two portfolios covered areas subject to fierce conservative resistance: women's rights and environmental protection. Operating in a post-unity climate fraught with deep societal divisions, Merkel had to quickly position herself between warring fronts that pitted feminists against patriarchs, Westerners against Easterners, industrial barons against citizen initiatives, all topped off with neo-Nazis battling leftist anarchists in the streets of Berlin. As a non-feminist heading the Women's Ministry and as a pro-nuclear energy advocate in the Environmental Ministry, she learned a great deal about conflict management. Her first term was marked by expanding circles of stakeholders, including specialized work groups that forged interparty agreements on federalism reform, corporate taxes, healthcare reforms, and anti-terrorism measures.[36] Her willingness to accept conflict as a regular feature of pluralist democracy mirrors the early wisdom of Parker Follett:

What people often mean by getting rid of conflict is getting rid of diversity, and it is of the utmost importance that these not be considered the same. We may wish to abolish conflict, but we cannot get rid of diversity. We must face life as it is and understand that diversity is its most essential feature ... Fear of difference is fear of life itself. It is possible to conceive conflict as not necessarily a wasteful outbreak of incompatibilities, but a normal process by which socially valuable differences register themselves for enrichment of all concerned.[37]

Merkel's management of the refugee issue qualifies her, in my judgment, as a very effective, moral leader and paradigm-shifter, even if the 2017 national elections could render her an unlucky politician.

THE GENDER CARD: "TO PLAY OR NOT TO PLAY, THAT IS THE QUESTION"

Although she was not the first woman to seek the Democratic presidential nomination in US history, Pat Schroeder was intensely scrutinized as such throughout the 1987 primaries by the male-dominated media. Asked point blank by one reporter, "Are you running as a woman?" the veteran Congressional representative from Colorado replied: "Do I have a choice?"[38] During Merkel's first run for the chancellorship, her SPD rival's fourth wife, Doris Schröder-Köpf, insisted that the childless CDU candidate would be incapable of producing good family policies. Ironically, her internal party critics referred to her as *Mutti-Merkel* (Mommy Merkel).[39] Over the next two terms that disparaging label ironically morphed into an accolade at home and abroad, especially after the chancellor opened Germany to hundreds of thousands of refugees in summer 2015.

As I argued in Chapter 1, it takes time to "become" a leader; as an Eastern female Merkel had to run a particularly challenging gauntlet at a pace unmatched by her Western male peers. As a natural scientist she drew quick lessons from "trial-and-error" events; as a pastor's daughter fond of humility, she outmaneuvered over-confident male rivals through patience and "silence." But she also faced initial resistance from Western females, as she stressed in 1993: "Naturally I notice that it's not easy for many women in my own caucus who are older than I to accept my approach to women's policies. Many have toiled and struggled for 10, 15 years, and suddenly German unification comes along, and I'm sitting in the Women's Minister armchair."[40] Bolstered by ten Most Powerful Woman designations, the chancellor who avoided gender issues during her first two campaigns now admits to having been disadvantaged as a female politician. Initially opposed to quotas, she recognizes that individual determination alone cannot abolish exclusionary, institutionalized norms. Merkel learned first-hand how sex interacts with religion, class, and national origin, shaping an individual's *access to power*; just as importantly, her personal experience with intersectionality has shaped her *use of power*.

Women nowadays have an easier time rising to power in times of crisis, despite a deeply embedded assumption that major political–economic breakdowns usually require a charismatic, male hero to swoop in, declare something a *Chef-Sache*, and save the day. Claudia Keller attributes this to women's capacity for instilling trust.[41] She notes that women from left to right, Angela Merkel, Hannelore Kraft, Malu Dreyer, and Julia Klockner, to name a few, all stepped in when established party leaders disappeared into the vortex of scandal or defeat. Former Constitutional Court justice Christine Hohmann-Dennhardt, already credited with cleaning up a mess at Daimler, was recently named Volkswagen's first executive responsible for "integrity and law." The UK's Theresa May also falls into this category, despite her personal opposition to Brexit.

While displaced CDU-gatekeepers imagined Merkel filling a temporary leadership void in 2005, her second run for national office in 2009 featured a larger-than-life campaign poster of a smiling chancellor with the simple motto, "We have the strength." By then the "we" included several ambitious women brought into her cabinet also intent on modernizing the CDU, like Ursula von der Leyen, Annette Schavan, Maria Böhmer, and assistant Beate Baumann. *Descriptive representation* concentrates on women's physical presence in government, measured largely in numerical terms; sex-based stereotypes start to wither away once they reach critical mass, roughly 30 percent.[42] Party-based quotas of the 1980s had helped women to cross that line in the Bundestag before Merkel took charge, but their numbers have risen from 26.2 percent of the seats at the end of Kohl's reign, to 32.5 percent during the Red–Green years, to 37.1 percent by June 2015.

Resistant to binding quotas, the CDU finally adopted a weaker "quorum" rule in 1996, specifying that one of every three party offices and ballot-list spots be filled by a woman. The CSU reserves 40 percent of the seats on internal party executive boards at regional and national levels but ignores the pipeline problem at lower levels. As Louise Davidson-Schmich shows, these mechanisms produce an "elevator effect," at best: women who overcome significant barriers rooted in local and regional party cultures quickly move into higher party offices. Having been identified, trained, and recruited for elective office by gatekeepers pressured to meet their quotas, these women secure prominent ballot slots, making them more likely to win than their self-selected male counterparts. This does not resolve the problem of low female membership rates, limiting the size of the pool: women account for less than 26 percent of CDU members. The parties railing the loudest against Merkel's policies evince the smallest female membership bases, that is, the AfD (15 percent) and the CSU (20 percent).[43]

Often confined to legislative bodies, descriptive representation data tell us little about the women behind the scenes. Collectively derided as Girls' Camp, Merkel's inner circle includes powerful female media moguls as well as discrete, reform-oriented men. Her ability to shore up descriptive representation at the executive level is limited by civil service regulations, in stark contrast to the 5,000+ *political* appointments a US president can use, in theory, to reshape federal departments and agencies. Nor can the chancellor directly influence Constitutional Court nominations, subject to election by parliamentarians and other designated officials. While only five females have led Länder governments to date, women now occupy powerful roles at the national level, even if their numbers have been fairly constant since the Red–Green years. One obvious example is Ursula von der Leyen's appointment as Germany's first female defense minister. Women comprise nearly 50 percent of the Federal Chancellor's Office staff, half of whom were under 40 in 2008. Of the nineteen (out of 450) aides who gave birth during Schröder's last thirty-five months in office, few returned to work. There were forty-nine FCO births during Merkel's first thirty-two months, most of whom resumed their posts under improved family leave options enacted in 2007 under a childless CDU chief; they included Hildegard Müller, the first State Secretary to return to this post since 1949.[44] The pool of those eligible for high administrative office has expanded accordingly. Merkel has even introduced a "Girls' Day" meeting with young women at the Chancellery.[45]

Increasing women's numerical strength is ultimately a function of "all things being equal," which they usually are not, obliging us to consider Merkel policies that can help level the societal playing field. Justified or not, female politicians are expected to do a better job serving women's needs and interests, while male leaders presumably make policies benefiting everyone. *Substantive representation* pertains to women's ability to reshape legislated policies, based on the presumption that they are "natural" experts in health, education, welfare, and family matters. Is it fair to expect Merkel to be more gender-sensitive to policy consequences than her predecessors just because of her sex? My earlier policy studies have persuaded me that "better policies for women" are usually better policies for everyone. While Merkel avoided gender themes during her first two campaigns, she declared in May 2013 that real equality will be achieved only when both men and women change their roles and behaviors.[46]

While GDR policies sought to reconcile work and family obligations for women, they did nothing to redefine the gender division of labor, the focus of Western feminists. Drawing lessons from both sides, this chancellor has done more to advance gender equality in united Germany than all of her predecessors combined. Effectively leveraging EU mandates, she has impelled lawmakers to guarantee infant- and childcare along with paternal leave, to adopt corporate quotas, and to fund special programs for women in the MINT/STEM fields. Her reasons are mixed, focusing on equality as well as on the looming demographic deficit. In 2015, birth rates reached the highest levels in thirty years, following a financial crisis decline.[47] Merkel's modernized family policies, expanded occupational opportunities, and cracks in the corporate glass ceiling add up to a great, substantive leap forward for German women – and men.

Finally, we turn to *transformative representation*: to what extent has this chancellor used her life experiences and political power to open up *new spaces* for women and men, as well as to carve out a new place for Germany in the world? Has she redefined not only the meaning of power but also average citizens' understanding of who has a right to exercise it? I would argue that this chancellor has broken the mold regarding outdated leadership models in another sense: beyond serving as a role model for young women attracted to politics, Merkel's "intercultural opening" policies of the last decade have created new windows of opportunity for parliamentarians and administrators of migrant descent. Just as importantly, she has given Germans the right to identify emotionally with their own nation. She observed in 1993, "we Germans have a very cramped relationship to the question, whether we are allowed to love our homeland. Especially in the old federal states (sic). It does not help us to advance, to act as if we have no connection to our country and don't even trust ourselves enough to say that we feel at home here."[48]

While effective leadership is hard to quantify, it is possible to count critical policy changes in terms of laws passed, action programs initiated, investments made, etc. My study of Merkel's contribution to Germany's post-unity transformation has been limited to six policy domains over a span of twelve years; a treatment of many other issues she has been forced to tackle since 2005 would require another volume. The list includes but is not limited to religious freedom, family and educational policies; active labor market strategies; R&D promotion; health and pension policies; taxation issues, anti-terrorism concerns and federalism reform. Merkel's frequent trips to China and her leading role in many EU debates have elevated Germany's standing on the world stage, giving her once-divided nation greater leverage in global affairs than it enjoyed as a "rump-state" during the Cold War era; the next step could include securing a permanent seat on the UN Security Council. One could argue further that the UK Brexit vote and the challenges posed by Le Pen voters in France have enhanced Germany's partner status vis-à-vis the United States, possible complications arising from an unsympathetic Trump administration notwithstanding.

Obviously, Merkel's story cannot be divorced from the first twenty-five years of German unification. Her first three decades "in the waiting room" of the GDR fueled a faith in democracy that has been tempered by time and experience, but in contrast to Kohl and Schröder, she was better prepared – as an outsider – to identify critical "punctuation" points that made it both possible and necessary for her to break with postwar path-dependencies. Globalization and generational change have also played key roles in her efforts to establish a new equilibrium. In a speech appropriately titled "Germany can do more," the not-yet-chancellor declared at the 2003 Leipzig party conference:

If, after calculating, deliberating and weighing [the options], one comes to the solid conclusion that there is no alternative, then it is the duty of honest and sincere politics (sic) to tell the people that it is better to enter unfamiliar territory if it will lead them to the goal than to avoid crossing new territory at the cost of not being able to reach the final destination ... Courage is not an end in itself. But courage is also necessary.[49]

ANGELA MERKEL'S NATIONAL LEGACY: WIR SCHAFFEN DAS!

Since the 1980s, the European Union has come to embrace a system of decision-making committed to a "pooling of sovereignty." By the late 1990s, the EU had replaced a conventional, male-normed mode of decision-making, "power over," with a distinctive mode of supranational authority better described as "power with."[50] Command and control mechanisms preferred by transactional leaders are useless in the face of complex, border-transcending problems like climate change, migration, and terrorism. The fact that Germany has been ruled by two Grand Coalitions across three election cycles suggests that voters themselves prefer a different approach to power. As Parker Follett noted, "it is possible to develop a conception of power with, a jointly developed power, a coactive power, not a coercive power ... Genuine power can only be grown, otherwise it will slip from every arbitrary hand that tries to grasp it."[51]

But old paradigms die hard, as Kuhn observed, especially in the minds of those who have benefited from them in the past. Because Merkel did not engage in typical, transactional behaviors during her first term, she was regularly accused of "just not leading." Critiquing her first four years, Axel Murswieck declared, "Merkel has the strength of will and the ambition but no vision and therefore no charisma; she cannot be characterized as the great leader of change."[52] Helmut Kohl's claim to great leadership owed largely to the mind-boggling fall of the Berlin Wall. Enjoying majorities in the Bundestag and Bundesrat through the 1980s, his record had been plagued by policy-paralysis (*Reformstau*). Unification provided a unique opportunity to jettison old paradigms, but CDU/CSU hardliners ignored the need for radical changes in the male-breadwinner models underlying taxation, childcare, welfare, pension, and even migration policies, preferring to bask in the glory of having triumphed over socialist East Germany.

Definitions of charisma and vision are themselves rooted in gendered expectations linked to the transactional model. A "charismatic" speaker named Adolf Hitler used command and control to pursue a genocidal vision known as the Final Solution, but that hardly rendered him a great leader. At issue is whether the criteria used to assess Merkel's leadership have "been all too heavily imprinted with the image of deep male voices and muscle-flexing staging."[53] She reflected in 1991, "my ambition consists of wanting to master a given task in a rational way, and that led to a relatively rapid rise that sooner frightened me. It was certainly not my goal, to secure one office after another ... I don't just plunge into an adventure without reflecting on the sense or [without] deliberating the risks."[54] She added later, "my principle is not 'Basta' but rather ... reflect, consult and then decide." It is hard to explain how someone lacking charisma could have chalked up such unprecedented popularity ratings throughout her first term, leading observers like myself to realize that the CDU's key campaign promise in 2009 consisted of "more Merkel." A more serious problem for the chancellor, clearly a policy innovator, is not that she lacks vision, passion, or the will to lead, but rather that male hardliners and malcontents oppose the *direction* in which she is taking them, fearing that they will lose their privileged positions. One of Angela Merkel's greatest contributions to the Berlin Republic since 2005 has been her successful modernization of the CDU itself.

Murswieck was right in one respect: at the end of her first term in 2009, "Experiment Merkel" came to an end, subjecting "Merkel the Chancellor" to a very tough leadership test based on several crises of global proportions.[55] Qualitative leadership investigations like this one are the academic equivalent of "shooting at a moving target." External environments, institutional dynamics, and policy contexts are subject to constant change, as the 2008 financial melt-down, the

2010 Euro crisis, the 2011 Fukushima disaster, the 2014 Crimean annexation, and the 2015 refugee crisis made clear. Building on nearly three decades of process-tracing observations, I have attempted to establish links between specific institutional requirements, shifting internal and external contexts, and a specific leader's socialization experiences. Taken together, I hope that these factors will open the door to further qualitative assessments of the transformative potential of female politicians, based on what Brigitte Geissel labels a "multiple orientations" approach.[56]

I am still proud to be a feminist scholar, following the argument that Dale Spender offered the year I became an Assistant Professor:

Feminism has fought no wars. It has killed no opponents. It has set up no concentration camps, starved no enemies, practiced no cruelties. Its battles have been for education, for the vote, for better working conditions, for safety in the streets, for child care, for social welfare, for rape crisis centers, for women's refuges, reforms in the law. If someone says, "oh, I'm not a feminist," I ask, "Why? What's your problem?"[57]

My detailed study of Angela Merkel across three terms has nonetheless taught me that a woman leader need not openly and regularly declare herself a feminist in order to "make a difference." More important than the political label we attach to ourselves is the ability to think holistically and long term, while upholding a Weberian "ethic of responsibility."

After completing two ministerial terms in 1998, the new CDU General-Secretary indicated that she "would someday like to find the right time to exit politics. That is a lot harder than I used to imagine it. But I don't want to be a half-dead wreck ... after a phase of being bored I would come up with something else to do." She added, "there are women who have left politics from one day to the next. It's probably easier for them than men, because during their time as politicians they have stayed better connected to the practical side of life. They don't have as much angst."[58] It is not my place to speculate on whether or not Angela Merkel will complete a fourth term as chancellor; there are no signs that she found the last one "boring," however.

Accepting the CDU chancellor nomination for the first time in May 2005, Angela Merkel declared: "It's not about parties, it's not about careers, about He or I, He or She, or however it's being formulated these days. It is about something else. We want to serve Germany. I want to serve Germany. Germany can do this, and together we can do this."[59] This pragmatic can-do spirit was sorely lacking in both the Federal Republic and the GDR by the time the Wall fell in 1989. Since unification,

Angela Merkel has spent most of her political career trying to persuade her compatriots to embrace this simple motto: *Wir schaffen das* – We can do this. She has proven that she can lead at many levels, and to their credit millions of German have followed her into a stronger, more tolerant, gender equitable, and ecologically sustainable Berlin Republic. She has also shown that one woman leader can make a tremendous difference.

NOTES

1. Kornelius, *Angela Merkel: Die Kanzlerin und ihre Welt*; "Konservative K-Frage: 'FAZ' spekuliert über Merkels Karriere-Ende," *Der Spiegel*, October 13, 2010.

2. Tim Oliver and Michael John Williams, "Special Relationships in Flux: Brexit and the Future of the US–EU and US–UK Relationships," *International Affairs*, 92(3) (2016), p. 552.

3. Angela Merkel's summer press conference, July 29, 2016.

4. See Rosabeth Moss Kantor, *Men and Women of the Corporation* (New York: Basic Books, 1977); Alice H. Eagly and Linda L. Carli, "The Female Leadership Advantage: An Evaluation of the Evidence," *The Leadership Quarterly*, 14 (2003): 807–834; Sally A. Carless, "Gender Differences in Transformational Leadership: An Examination of Superior, Leader and Subordinate Perspectives," *Sex Roles*, 39(11/12) (1998): 887–902; Thomas W. Kent, Carrie A. Blair, Howard F. Rudd, and Ulrich Schuele, "Gender Differences and Transformational Leadership Behavior: Do Both German Men and Women Lead in the Same Way?" *International Journal of Leadership Studies*, 6(1) (2010): 52–66; and Paul L. Koopman, Deanne N. Den Hartog, Edvard Konrad et al., "National Culture and Leadership Profiles in Europe: Some Results from the GLOBE Study," *European Journal of Work and Organizational Psychology*, 8(4) (1999): 503–520.

5. Alice H. Eagly and Mary C. Johannesen-Schmidt, "The Leadership Styles of Women and Men," *Journal of Social Issues*, 57(4) (2001), p. 795.

6. Examples include the Multifactor Leadership Questionnaire, the Leadership Behavior Inventory, the Global Transformational Leadership Scale, the Positive Organizational Behavior Model, and the Ethical Leadership Scale.

7. Patricia Schroeder, "And Please Call Me Ms. President," *New York Times*, February 22, 1999, p. A17.

8. Men are often judged successful even when they perform poorly: Wall Street firms continued to pay out multimillion dollar bonuses after the 2008 meltdown, "to keep the best people" who had brought down the system in the first place!

9. Thomas C. Frohlich, "20 Highest-Paid World Leaders," *Wall Street Journal*, March 18, 2016.

10. Davidson-Schmich, "Gender, Intersectionality, and the Executive Branch."

11. Mushaben, "The Best of Times, the Worst of Times"; Jonathan Olsen, "Leadership and Inter-party Relations in Grand Coalitions: Comparing Angela Merkel and Kurt Georg Kiesinger," *German Politics*, 20(3) (2011):

342–359; and Karlheinz Niclauß, "Kiesinger und Merkel in der Großen Koalition," *Aus Politik und Zeitgeschichte*, B-16 (2008): 3–11.

12. For historical accounts, see Reinhard Schmoeckel and Bruno Kaiser, *Die vergessene Regierung. Die Große Koalition 1966 bis 1969 und ihre langfristigen Wirkungen* (Bonn: Bouvier, 1991); Joachim Samuel Eichhorn, *Durch alle Klippen hindurch zum Erfolg: Die Regierungspraxis der ersten Großen Koalition, 1966–1969* (Munich: Oldenbourg, 2009); and Niclauß, "Kiesinger und Merkel in der Großen Koalition."

13. Merkel did not include positive references to the FDP during the 2013 campaign, indicating that she did not want to continue that coalition configuration.

14. Oskar Niedermayer (ed.), *Die Parteien nach der Bundestagswahl 2009* (Wiesbaden: Springer, 2011).

15. Warren Bennis and Burt Nanus, *Leaders: Strategies for Taking Charge* (New York: HarperCollins, 1997), p. 19.

16. James Burns (1978), cited in Barbara Mandell and Shilpa Pherwani, "Relationship between Emotional Intelligence and Transformational Leadership Style: A Gender Comparison," *Journal of Business and Psychology*, 3 (2003), p. 390.

17. Karl-Rudolf Korte, "Solutions for the Decision Dilemma: Political Styles of German Chancellors," *German Politics*, 9(1) (2000), pp. 12–13.

18. Burns, cited in Mandell and Pherwani, "Relationship between Emotional Intelligence and Transformational Leadership Style," p. 390.

19. Ibid.

20. Mary Parker Follett, *Creative Experience* (New York: Longmans, Green, 1930), pp. 300–301.

21. Mandell and Pherwani, "Relationship between Emotional Intelligence and Transformational Leadership Style," p. 388.

22. Salovey and Mayer, 1990, cited in Mandell and Pherwani, Ibid., p. 390.

23. Mandell and Pherwani, Ibid., p. 398.

24. "Companies With More Women Board Directors Experience Higher Financial Performance," available at: www.catalyst.org/media/companies-more-women-board-directors-experience-higher-financial-performance-according-latest.

25. Katje Glaesner, "Angela Merkel – mit 'Soft Skills' zum Erfolg?" *Aus Politik und Zeitgeschichte*, 50 (2009): 28–34; see also Barbara Schaeffer-Hegel, Helga Foster, and Helga Lutoschat (eds.), *Frauen und Macht: Zum Wandel der politischen Kultur durch die Präsenz von Frauen in Führungspositionen* (Pfaffenweiler: Pfaffenweiler Press, 1995).

26. *Brigitte Talk* interview, May 3, 2013, available at: www.brigitte.de/aktuell/brigitte-live/brigitte-live–angela-merkel–der-brigitte-talk-im-video-1069491 0.html.

27. Among the more inspiring were others cited throughout this work: Roll, *Die Erste*; Schumacher, *Zwölf Gesetze der Macht*; Müller-Vogg, *Angela Merkel*; and Lau, *Die Letzte Volkspartei*.

28. Thomas S. Kuhn, *The Structure of Scientific Revolutions* (University of Chicago Press, 1962), pp. 89–90.

29. Kornelius, *Angela Merkel: Die Kanzlerin und ihre Welt*, pp. 95–96.
30. Gardner Feldman, *Germany's Foreign Policy of Reconciliation*.
31. Willy Brandt, another exception, caused a sensation when he fell to his knees at the Warsaw Ghetto memorial site in December 1970.
32. Frank Decker, "The 'Alternative for Germany': Factors Behind its Emergence and Profile of a New Right-wing Populist Party," *German Politics*, 34(2) (2016): 1–16.
33. See the report, "Wir Zusammen: Flüchtlinge erfolgreich integrieren," Ralph und Judith Dommermuth Stiftung, Düsseldorf, 2016, p. 24.
34. Merkel's comments at the September 19, 2016 press conference in Berlin can be viewed at: www.youtube.com/watch?v=hbUWP7iyhac.
35. Koelbl, *Spuren der Macht*, p. 53; Sarah Wiliarty, *The CDU and the Politics of Gender in Germany: Bringing Women to the Party* (Cambridge University Press, 2010).
36. Eva Krick, "Regieren mit Gipfeln – Expertengremien der großen Koalition," *Zeitschrift für Politikwissenschaft*, 20(2) (2010): 233–265; Bukow and Seemann, *Die Große Koalition*; Egle and Zohlnhöfer, *Die zweite Große Koalition*.
37. Parker Follett, *Creative Experience*, pp. 300–301.
38. "And Please Call Me Ms. President," *New York Times*, February 22, 1999.
39. She does have two grown step-sons. Dirk Kurbjuweit, "Angela the Great or Just 'Mom' – Merkel's Dream of a Place in the History Books," *Der Spiegel*, November 3, 2009.
40. Koelbl, *Spuren der Macht*, p. 52.
41. Claudia Keller, "Die Männer schaffen das nicht alleine," *Die Zeit*, December 20, 2015.
42. Drude Dahlerup, "From a Small to a Large Minority: Women in Scandinavian Politics," *Scandinavian Political Studies*, 11(4) (1988): 275–298; Mushaben, "The Politics of Critical Acts."
43. Davidson Schmich, *Gender Quotas and Democratic Participation*, pp. 14–15.
44. Monika Dunkel, "Babyboom: Kreißsaal Kanzleramt," *Stern Magazin*, June 23, 2008.
45. Claudia Michalski, "Pink Painting ist das neue Green Washing," *Die Zeit*, October 23, 2015.
46. She did this during an hour-long interview sponsored by a women's magazine; see *Brigitte Talk*, available at: www.youtube.com/watch?v=9v-1W58s4e8, posted on May 18, 2013.
47. Saskia Nothofer and Sascha Venohr, "Deutschlands neue Kinder," *Die Zeit*, October 19, 2016.
48. Koelbl, *Spuren der Macht*, p. 53.
49. Cited in Mishra, *Angela Merkel – Machtworte*, p. 130.
50. Abels and Mushaben, *Gendering the European Union*.
51. E. M. Fox and L. Urwick (eds.), *Dynamic Administration. The Collected Papers of Mary Parker Follett* (London: Pitman, 1940), p. 72.
52. Axel Murswieck, "Angela Merkel als Regierungschefin und als Kanzler-Kandidatin," *Aus Politik und Zeitgeschichte*, B-51 (2009), p. 29.
53. Glaesner, "Soft Skills," p. 21.

54. Koelbl, *Spuren der Macht*, p. 47.
55. Murswieck, "Angela Merkel als Regierungschefin und als Kanzler-Kandidatin," p. 32.
56. Brigitte Geissel, "Innovative Potenziale von Politikerinnen," *Aus Politik und Zeitgeschichte* B31.32 (2000): 24–29.
57. Dale Spender, *Man Made Language* (1980), cited at: www.goodreads.com/author/quotes/83682.Dale_Spender.
58. Koelbl, *Spuren der Macht*, p. 61.
59. Müller-Vogg, *Angela Merkel*, p. 259.

Bibliography

Abels, Gabriele. "Das 'Geschlechterdemokratiedefizit' der EU. Politische Repräsentation und Geschlecht im europäischen Mehrebenensystem," in Eva Kreisky, Sabine Lang, and Birgit Sauer (eds.), *EU. Geschlecht. Staat* (Vienna: WUV, 2001), pp. 185–202.

Abels, Gabriele. "90 Jahre Frauenwahlrecht: Zum Wandel von Geschlechterver-hältnissen in der deutschen Politik," in Gabriele Abels (ed.), *Deutschland im Jubiläumsjahr 2009: Blick zurück nach vorn* (Baden-Baden: Nomos, 2011), pp. 197–219.

Abels, Gabriele and Annegret Eppler (eds.). *Subnational Parliaments in the EU Multi-level Parliamentary System: Taking Stock of the Post-Lisbon Era* (Innsbruck: Studienverlag, 2015).

Abels, Gabriele and Joyce Marie Mushaben (eds.). *Gendering the European Union: New Approaches to Old Democratic Deficits* (Basingstoke: Palgrave Macmillan, 2012).

Adamek, Sascha. *Die Atomlüge: Getäuscht, vertuscht, verschwiegen: Wie Politiker und Konzerne die Gefahren der Atomkraft herunterspielen* (Munich: Heyne, 2011).

Adorno, Theodor W. "What does Coming to Terms with the Past Mean?" in Geoffrey Hartman (ed.), *Bitburg in Moral and Political Perspective* (Bloomington, IN: Indiana University Press, 1986), pp. 114–129.

Ahbe, Thomas. "Die Konstruktion der Ostdeutschen. Diskursive Spannungen, Stereotype und Identitäten seit 1989," *Aus Politik und Zeitgeschichte* 41/42 (2004): 12–22.

Ahrend, Martin (ed.). *Mein Leben, Teil Zwei* (Cologne: Kiepenheur & Witsch, 1989).

Allen, William A. and Richhild Moessner. "The Liquidity Consequences of the Euro Area Sovereign Debt Crisis," Bank for International Settlements (BIS) Working Paper No. 390, Basel, October 2012.

Amecke, Herman. "The Impact of Energy Performance Certificates: A Survey of German Home Owners," *Energy Policy*, 46 (2012): 4–14.

Annesley, Claire and Francesca Gains. "The Core Executive: Gender, Power, and Change," *Political Studies*, 58 (2010): 909–929.

Åslund, Anders. *Ukraine: What Went Wrong and How to Fix It* (Washington, DC: Peterson Institute for International Economics, 2015).

Asseburg, Muriel. "50 Jahre deutsch–israelische diplomatische Beziehungen," *SWP-Aktuell 40* (Berlin: Stiftung Wissenschaft und Politik, 2015).

Asseburg, Muriel and Jan Busse. "Deutschlands Politik gegenüber Israel," in Thomas Jäger, Alexander Höse, and Kai Oppermann (eds.), *Deutsche Außenpolitik, Sicherheit, Wohlfahrt, Institutionen, Normen* (Wiesbaden: Verlag für Sozialwissenschaften, 2011), pp. 693–716.

Ayala, Luis. "Social Needs, Inequality and the Welfare State in Spain: Trends and Prospects," *Journal of European Social Policy*, 4(3) (1994): 159–179.

Babka von Gostomski, Christian. "The Naturalisation Behaviour of Foreigners in Germany, and Findings Concerning *Optionspflichtige*," Bundesamt für Migration & Flüchtlinge, Berlin, 2011.

Bade, Klaus J. and Jochen Oltmer (eds.). *Aussiedler: Deutsche Einwanderer aus Osteuropa* (Osnabrück: Universitätsverlag Rasch, 1999).

Bäckstrand, Karin and Ole Elgström. "The EU's Role in Climate Change Negotiations: From Leader to 'Leadiator'," *Journal of European Public Policy*, 20(10) (2013): 1369–1386.

Bahr, Egon. *Was wird aus den Deutschen? Fragen und Antworten* (Reinbeck: Rowohlt, 1982).

Bahro, Rudolf. *Die Alternative: Zur Kritik des real existierenden Sozialismus* (Cologne: Europäische Verlagsanstalt, 1977).

Barack, Mitchell, Sharon Pardo, and Lars Hänsel. "Measuring the Attitudes of Israelis towards the European Union and its Member States," Konrad Adenauer Stiftung and KEEVOON, Berlin and London, 2009.

Bartos, Helene. "Israeli–German Relations in the Years 2000–2006: A Special Relationship Revisited," Master's thesis, University of Oxford, 2007.

Bastasin, Carlo. *Saving Europe: Anatomy of a Dream* (Washington, DC: Brookings Institution, 2015).

Bastian, Jens. "Defining a Growth Strategy for Greece: Wishful Thinking or a Realistic Prospect?" Friedrich Ebert Stiftung, Bonn, October 2015.

Beauftragte der Bundesregierung für Migration, Flüchtlinge und Integration, "10. Bericht über die Lage der Ausländerinnen und Ausländer in Deutschland." Berlin, October 2014.

Bechev, Dimitar. "Understanding the Contest Between the EU and Russia in Their Shared Neighborhood," *Problems of Post-Communism*, 62(6) (2015): 340–349.

Beckett, Clare. *Thatcher* (London: Haus, 2006).

Ben Natan, Asher and Niels Hansen(eds.). *Israel und Deutschland: Dorniger Weg zur Partnerschaft – Die Botschafter berichten über vier jahrzehnte diplomatischer Beziehungen, 1965–2005* (Cologne: Bohlau, 2005).

Bennis, Warren and Burt Nanus. *Leaders: Strategies for Taking Charge* (New York: HarperCollins, 1997).

Berglar, Peter von, Hans Filbinger et al., *Deutsche Identität heute* (Weikersheim: Hase & Koehler, 1983).

Bernadi, R. et al. "Does Female Representation on Boards of Directors Associate with the 'Most Ethical Companies' List?" *Corporate Reputation Review*, 12 (2009): 270–280.

Beutke, Mirijam and Patrick Kotzur. "Faktensammlung Diskriminierung," Programm Integration und Bildung, Bertelsmann Stiftung, Berlin, January 12, 2015.

Beyer, Heiko and Ulf Liebe. "Antisemitismus heute. Zur Messung aktueller Erscheinungsformen von Judenfeindlichkeit mithilfe des faktoriellen Surveys," *Zeitschrift für Soziologie*, 42(3) (2013): 186–200.

Blythe, Mark and Matthias Matthijs. "The World Waits for Germany: Berlin is Moving to Solve Europe's Crisis, but not Fast Enough," *Foreign Affairs*, June 8, 2012.

Bolgherini, Silvia and Florian Grotz (eds.). *Germany after the Grand Coalition: Governance and Politics in a Turbulent Environment* (Basingstoke: Palgrave Macmillan, 2010).

Bonefeld, Werner. "Freedom and the Strong State: On German Ordoliberalism," *New Political Economy*, 17(5) (2012): 633–656.

Borchard, Michael and Hans Maria Heyn. "Das Heilige Land und die Deutschen," Konrad Adenauer Stiftung, Jerusalem and Ramallah, 2015.

Bortfeldt, Heinrich. "United yet Separate: A View from the East," in Konrad H. Jarausch (ed.), *United Germany: Debating Processes and Prospects* (New York: Berghahn, 2013), pp. 44–63.

Boysen, Jacqueline. *Angela Merkel* (Munich: Ullstein, 2001).

Branford, Sue and Bernardo Kucinski. *The Debt Squads: The US, the Banks and Latin America* (London: Zed Books, 1988).

Braun, Jan Frederick. "EU Energy Policy under the Treaty of Lisbon Rules: Between a New Policy and Business as Usual," European Policy Institute Working Paper No. 31, Brussels, February 2011.

Bredow, Wilfried von. *Deutschland – Ein Provisorium?* (Berlin: W. J. Siedler, 1985).

Brose, Ekkehard. "When Germany Sends Troops Abroad: The Case for a Limited Reform of the Parliamentary Participation Act," Stiftung für Wissenschaft und Politik, Berlin, September 2013.

Brown, Chelsea. "Democracy's Friend or Foe? The Effects of Recent IMF Conditional Lending in Latin America," *International Political Science Review*, 30(4) (2009): 431–457.

Brown, James D. "Oil Fueled? The Soviet Invasion of Afghanistan," *Post-Soviet Affairs*, 29(1) (2013): 56–94.

Brückner, Peter. *Versuch, uns und anderen die Bundesrepublik zu erklären* (Berlin: Klaus Wagenbach, 1984).

Bukow, Sebastian and Wenke Seemann (eds.). *Die Große Koalition: Regierung – Politik – Parteien 2005–2009* (Wiesbaden: Verlag für Sozialwissenschaften, 2010).

Bürgin, Alexander. "National Binding Renewable Energy Targets for 2020, but Not for 2030: Why the European Commission Developed from a Supporter to a Brakeman," *Journal of European Public Policy*, 22(5) (2015): 690–707.

Busch, Klaus, Christoph Hermann, Karl Hinrichs, and Thorsten Schulten. "Euro Crisis, Austerity Policy and the European Social Model: How Crisis Policies in Southern Europe Threaten the EU's Social Dimension," Friedrich Ebert Stiftung, Berlin, February 2013.

Busch, Per-Olof and Helge Jörgens. "The International Sources of Policy Convergence: Explaining the Spread of Environmental Policy Innovations," *Journal of European Public Policy*, 12(5) (2005): 860–884.

Busse, Jan. "Zwischen historischer Verantwortung und Zweistaatenlösung: Die Nahostpolitik der Bundesregierung unter Kanzlerin Merkel," *SWP-Studie*, 8 (March 2009).

Carless, Sally A. "Gender Differences in Transformational Leadership: An Examination of Superior, Leader and Subordinate Perspectives," *Sex Roles*, 39(11/12) (1998): 887–902.

Carroll, Susan J. "Reflections on Gender and Hillary Clinton's Presidential Campaign: The Good, the Bad, and the Misogynic," *Politics & Gender*, 5(1) (2009): 1–20.

Carson, Rachel. *Silent Spring* (New York: Houghton Mifflin, 1962).

Clemens, Clay. "From the Outside In: Angela Merkel as Opposition Leader, 2000–2005," *German Politics & Society*, 24(3) (2006): 1–19.

Clift, Ben and Magnus Ryner. "Joined at the Hip, but Pulling Apart? Franco-German Relations, the Eurozone Crisis and the Politics of Austerity," *French Politics*, 12(2) (2014): 136–163.

Cohen, Matthew S. and Charles D. Freilich. "Breakdown and Possible Restart: Turkish–Israeli Relations under the AKP," *Israel Journal of Foreign Affairs*, 8(1) (2014): 39–55.

Coulmas, Florian and Judith Stalpers. *Fukushima. Vom Erdbeben zur atomaren Katastrophe* (Munich: Beck'sche Reihe, 2011).

Craig, Gordon A. *The Germans* (New York: Putnam, 1982).

Crawford, Alan and Tony Czuczka. *Angela Merkel: A Chancellorship Forged in Crisis* (New York: Bloomberg, 2013).

Crum, Ben. "Saving the Euro at the Cost of Democracy?" *Journal of Common Market Studies*, 51(4) (2013): 614–630.

Daiber, Nathalie and Richard Skippin. *Die Merkel Strategie* (Munich: Carl Hanser, 2006).

Dahlerup, Drude. "From a Small to a Large Minority: Women in Scandinavian Politics," *Scandinavian Political Studies*, 11(4) (1988): 275–298.

"The Story of the Theory of Critical Mass," *Politics & Gender*, 2(4) (2006): 511–522.

Dahn, Daniela. *Wir bleiben hier oder Wem gehört der Osten: Vom Kampf um Häuser und Wohnungen in den neuen Bundesländern* (Berlin: Rowohlt, 1994).

Dany, Geraldine, Reint E. Gropp, Helge Littke, and Gregor von Schweinitz. *Germany's Benefit from the Greek Crisis* (Halle: Leibniz Institut für Wirtschaftsforschung, 2015).

Dausend, Peter and Elisabeth Niejahr. *Operation Röschen: Das System von der Leyen* (Frankfurt: Campus, 2015).

Davidson-Schmich, Louise. "Gender, Intersectionality, and the Executive Branch: The Case of Angela Merkel," *German Politics*, 20(3) (2011): 325–341.

Gender Quotas and Democratic Participation: Recruiting Candidates for Elective Offices in Germany (Ann Arbor, MI: University of Michigan Press, 2016).

Dawisha, Karen. *Putin's Kleptocracy. Who Owns Russia?* (New York: Simon & Schuster, 2014).

Decker, Frank. "The 'Alternative for Germany': Factors Behind its Emergence and Profile of a New Right-wing Populist Party," *German Politics*, 34(2) (2016): 1–16.

Decker, Frank and Volker Best. "Looking for Mr. Right? A Comparative Analysis of Parties' 'Coalition Statements' Prior to the Federal Elections of 2005 and 2009," *German Politics*, 19(2) (2010): 164–182.

Delanty, Gerard. "Models of Citizenship: Defining European Identity and Citizenship," *Citizenship Studies*, 1(3) (1997): 285–303.

Delcour, Laure. "Dualitäten der französischen Russlandpolitik: Die Ukrainekrise als Bewährungsprobe," *DGAP Analyse*, 4 (2015).

Del Sarto, Raffaella. "Plus ça change … ? Israel, the EU and the Union for the Mediterranean," *Mediterranean Politics*, 16(1) (2011): 117–153.

Demmer Ulrike and Daniel Goffart. *Kanzlerin der Reserve: Der Aufstieg der Ursula von der Leyen* (Berlin: Berlin Verlag, 2015).

Detraz, Nicole. "Environmental Security and Gender: Necessary Shifts in an Evolving Debate," *Security Studies*, 18 (2009): 345–369.

Deutscher Bundestag, "Die Zukunft Ostdeutschlands," Fragestunde zum Thema Aufbau Ost vom 8. Februar 2001.

Dieckmann, Jochen, Antje Vogel-Sper, Jörg Mayer et al., *Vergleich der Bundesländer: Best Practice für den Ausbau Erneuerbarer Energien – Indikatoren und Ranking* (Berlin and Stuttgart: Federal Ministry for Economics and Energy, 2014).

Diner, Dan (ed.). *Ist der Nationalsozialismus Geschichte? Zu Historisierung und Historikerstreit* (Frankfurt: Fischer, 1987).

Dolling, Irene, with Daphne Hahn and Sylka Scholz. "Biomacht – Biopolitik," *Potsdamer Studien zur Frauen- und Geschlechterforschung* 2 (1998).

Dorn, Thea, Jana Hensel, and Thomas Brussig (eds.), *Sind wir ein Volk? 25 Jahre nach dem Mauerfall* (Freiburg: Herder, 2015).

Dülcke, Dana and Sascha K. Futh. "Die 'Mutter der Nation' gegen den 'Panzerkandidaten': Geschlechterbilder in der Berichterstattung der Printmedien zum Bundestagswahlkampf 2013," in Christine Holtz-Bacha (ed.), *Die Massenmedien im Wahlkampf. Die Bundestagswahl 2013* (Wiesbaden: Springer, 2015), pp. 249–273.

Duncan, Liefferink and Mikael Skou Andersen. "Strategies of the 'Green' Member States in EU Environmental Policy Making," *Journal of European Public Policy*, 5(2) (1998): 254–270.

Dyson, Kenneth and Thomas Saalfeld, "Actors, Structures and Strategies: Policy Continuity and Change under the German Grand Coalition (2005–09)," *German Politics* 19, No. 3–4 (2010): 269–282.

Eagly, Alice H. and Linda L. Carli. "The Female Leadership Advantage: An Evaluation of the Evidence," *The Leadership Quarterly*, 14 (2003): 807–834.

Eagly, Alice H. and Mary C. Johannesen-Schmidt. "The Leadership Styles of Women and Men," *Journal of Social Issues*, 57(4) (2001): 781–797.

Eberwein, Wolf-Dieter and Karl Kaiser (eds.), *Germany's New Foreign Policy: Decision Making in an Independent World* (Basingstoke: Palgrave, 2001).

Egle, Christoph and Reimut Zohlnhöfer (eds.), *Die zweite Große Koalition: Eine Bilanz der Regierung Merkel 2005–2009* (Wiesbaden: Verlag für Sozialwissenschaften, 2010).

Eichhorn, Joachim Samuel. *Durch alle Klippen hindurch zum Erfolg: die Regierungspraxis der ersten Großen Koalition, 1966–1969* (Munich: Oldenbourg, 2009).

Ekardt, Felix, "Die rechtliche Energiewende seit 2011 – ein klima-, naturschutz- und landnutzungsbezogener Erfolg?" in Bundesministerium für Umwelt, Naturschutz und Reaktorensicherheit, *4. Jahrbuch nachhaltiger Ökonomie: Die Energiewende als gesellschaftlicher Transformationsprozess*, Marburg, 2014.

Elgindy, Khaled. "The Middle East Quartet: A Post-Mortem," Analysis Paper No. 25, Saban Center, Brookings Institution, February 2012.

Elson, Diane. "Gender Mainstreaming and Gender Budgeting," European Commission/DG Education, Brussels, March 4, 2003.

Elomäki, Anna. *The Price of Austerity: The Impact on Women's Rights and Gender Equality in Europe* (Brussels: European Women's Lobby, 2012).

Engert, Stefan. "A Case Study in 'Atonement': Adenauer's Holocaust Apology," *Israel Journal of Foreign Affairs*, 4(3) (2010): 111–122.

Eran, Oded. "Turkey and the European Union: An Israeli Perspective," *Israel Journal of Foreign Affairs*, 2(2) (2008): 65–71.

Featherstone, Kevin. "External Conditionality and the Debt Crisis: The 'Troika' and Public Administration Reform in Greece," *Journal of European Public Policy*, 22(3) (2015): 295–314.

Fischer, Sabine. "EU Sanktionen gegen Russland: Ziele, Wirkung und weiterer Umgang," *SWP Aktuelle*, 26 (2015).

"Die EU und Russland, Konflikte und Potenzial einer schwierigen Partnerschaft," *SWP-Berlin* (2006).

Fix, Liana. "Leadership in the Ukraine Conflict: A German Moment," in Niklas Helwig (ed.), *Europe's New Political Engine: Germany's Role in the EU's Foreign and Security Policy* (Helsinki: Finnish Institute of International Affairs, 2016), pp. 111–131.

Forsberg, Tuomas. "From Ostpolitik to 'Frostpolitik'? Merkel, Putin and German Foreign Policy towards Russia," *International Affairs*, 92(1) (2016): 21–42.

Fox, E. M. and L. Urwick (eds.). *Dynamic Administration. The Collected Papers of Mary Parker Follett* (London: Pitman, 1940).

Francoeur, Claude, Réal Labelle, and Bernard Sinclair-Desgagne. "Gender Diversity in Corporate Governance and Top Management," *Journal of Business Ethics*, 81 (2008): 83–95.

Gaffney, John. "Leadership and Style in the French Fifth Republic: Nicolas Sarkozy's Presidency in Historical and Cultural Perspective," *French Politics*, 10(4) (2012): 345–363.

Gardner Feldman, Lily. *The Special Relationship between West Germany and Israel* (Boston, MA: Allen & Unwin, 1984).

Germany's Foreign Policy of Reconciliation. From Enmity to Amity (Lanham, MD: Rowman & Littlefield 2012).

"What's in a Name? The German–Israeli Partnership: Is It a Special Relationship, a Friendship, an Alliance or Reconciliation," *AICGS* (March 6, 2014).

Gaus, Günther. *Wo Deutschland liegt–Eine Ortsbestimmung* (Hamburg: Hoffmann & Campe, 1983).

Gawl, Erik and Bernd Hansjürgens. "Projekt 'Energiewende': Schneckenstempo und Zickzackkurs statt klare Konzepte für die Systemtransformation?" *ZBW: Leibniz-Informationszentrum Wirtschaft*, 5 (2013): 283–288.

Gawel, Erik and Klaas Korte. "Regionale Verteilungswirkungen und Finanzierungsverantwortung: Bund und Länder bei der Strom-Energiewende," in Thorsten Müller and Hartmut Kahl (eds.), *Energiewende im Föderalismus* (Baden-Baden: Nomos, 2015), pp. 145–186.

Geissel, Brigitte. "Innovative Potenziale von Politikerinnen," *Aus Politik und Zeitgeschichte* 31/32 (2000): 24–29.

Genovese, Michael, A. (ed.). *Women as National Leaders* (London: Sage, 1993).

Georgi, Viola B. "Jugendliche aus Einwandererfamilien und die Geschichte des Nationalsozialismus," *Aus Politik und Zeitgeschichte* 40/41 (2003): 40–46.

Gerard, Alison and Sharon Pickering. "Gender, Securitization and Transit: Refugee Women and the Journey to the EU," *Journal of Refugee Studies*, 27(3) (2013): 338–359.

Glaesner, Katje. "Angela Merkel – mit 'Soft Skills' zum Erfolg?" *Aus Politik und Zeitgeschichte*, 50 (2009): 28–34.

Gradl, J. B. *Deutschland als Aufgabe* (Cologne: Wissenschaft & Politik, 1986).

Gréboval, Cécile (ed.). *Ticking Clocks: Alternative 2012. Country-specific Recommendations to Strengthen Women's Rights and Gender Equality in the EUROPE 2020 STRATEGY* (Brussels: European Women's Lobby, 2012).

Greiffenhagen, Martin and Sylvia Greiffenhagen. *Ein schwieriges Vaterland – Zur politischen Kultur der Bundesrepublik Deutschland* (Frankfurt: Fischer, 1981).

Grubb, Michael, Thomas L. Brewer, Misato Sato, Robert Heilmayr, and Dora Fazekas, "Climate Policy and Industrial Competitiveness: Ten Insights From Europe on the EU Emission Trading System," Climate and Energy Paper Series, July 2009.

Gusev, Alexander and Kirsten Westphal. "Russian Energy Policies Revisited: Assessing the Impact of the Crisis in Ukraine on Russian Energy Policies and Specifying the Implications for German and EU Energy Policies," Stiftung Wissenschaft und Politik, Berlin, December 2015.

Guzansky, Yoel. "Israel's Periphery Doctrine 2.0: The Mediterranean Plus," *Mediterranean Politics*, 19(1) (2014): 99–116.

Hagemann, Steffen and Roby Nathanson. "Germany and Israel Today: Linked by the Past, Divided by the Present," Bertelsmann Stiftung, Berlin, January 2015.

Hall, Peter A. "The Economics and Politics of the Euro Crisis," *German Politics*, 21(4) (2012): 355–371.

Hancock, Ange-Merie. "When Multiplication doesn't Equal Quick Addition: Examining Intersectionality as a Research Paradigm," *Perspectives on Politics*, 5(1) (2007): 63–79.

Hansel, Jana, *Zonenkinder* (Reinbeck: Rowohlt, 2004).

Achtung Zone: Warum wir Ostdeutschen anders bleiben sollten (Munich: Piper, 2009).

Harnisch, Sebastian and Hanns W. Maull (eds.). *Germany as a Civilian Power? The Foreign Policy of the Berlin Republic* (Manchester University Press, 2001).

Haury, Thomas. "Die DDR und der 'Aggressorstaat Israel' – Das 'unschuldige Deutschland' im Nahostkonflikt," *Tribüne*, 173 (2005): 202–215.

Häussling, Josef von, Klaus Held et al. *Drei Fragen zu Deutschland–58 Antworten* (Munich: Albrecht Knaus, 1985).

Heckel, Margaret. *So regiert die Kanzlerin. Eine Reportage* (Munich: Piper, 2009).

Heidenreich, Gert. *Die Gnade der späten Geburt* (Munich: Piper, 1986).

Heise, Arne. "Governance Without Government or: The Euro Crisis and What Went Wrong with European Economic Governance," University of Hamburg, August 2012.

Heisenberg, Dorothee. "Merkel's EU Policy: 'Kohl's Mädchen' or Interest-Driven Politics?" *German Politics and Society*, 24(1) (2006): 119–133.

Heith, Diane J. "The Lipstick Watch: Media Coverage, Gender and Presidential Campaigns," in Robert P. Watson and Ann Gordon (eds.), *Anticipating Madam President* (Boulder, CO: Lynne Rienner, 2003), pp. 123–130.

Hennicke, Peter and Paul Welfens. *Energiewende nach Fukushima – Deutscher Sonderweg oder weltweites Vorbild?* (Munich: Oekom, 2012).

Henninger, Annette and Angelika von Wahl. "Das Umspielen von Veto-Spielern. Wie eine konservative Familienministerin den Familialismus des deutschen Wohlfahrtsstaates unterminiert," in Christoph Egle and Reimut Zohlnhöfer (eds.), *Die zweite Große Koalition: Eine Bilanz der Regierung Merkel 2005–2009* (Wiesbaden: Verlag für Sozialwissenschaften, 2010), pp. 361–379.

Hermann, Christoph. "Crisis, Structural Reform and the Dismantling of the European Social Model(s)," *Economic and Industrial Democracy*, 36 (2014): 1–18.

Heubner, Thomas. "Nation und Nationalität – Staatsbürgerschaft: DDR – Nationalität: Deutsch – oder wie entwickeln sich Nationen?" *Junge Generation*, 35(10) (1981).

Hildebrand, Jan. "Dezentralität und Bürgerbeteiligung – Die Energiewende im Föderalismus aus Sicht der Akzeptanzforschung," in Thorsten Müller and Hartmut Kahl (eds.), *Energiewende im Föderalismus* (Baden-Baden: Nomos, 2015), pp. 129–144.

Hill, Fiona and Clifford Gaddy. *Mr. Putin: Operative in the Kremlin* (Washington, DC: Brookings Institution, 2013).

Hillebrand, Rainer. "Germany and its Eurozone Crisis Policy: The Impact of the Country's Ordo-Liberal Heritage," *German Politics & Society*, 33(1/2) (2015): 6–24.

Hirschman, Albert O. "Exit, Voice and the Fate of the German Democratic Republic," *World Politics*, 45 (1993): 173–202.

Hirsch, Rudolf and Rosemarie Schuder. *Der gelbe Fleck: Wurzeln und Wirkungen des Judenhasses in der deutschen Geschichte* (Berlin: Rütten & Löning, 1987).

Historikerstreit: Die Dokumentation der Kontroverse um die Einzigartigkeit der nationalsozialistischen Judenvernichtung (Munich: Piper, 1987).

Hofmann, Jürgen. *Ein neues Deutschland soll es sein: Zur Frage nach der Nation in der Geschichte der DDR und der Politik der SED* (Berlin: Dietz, 1989).

Holtz-Bacha, Christina. "Politikerinnen-Bilder im internationalen Vergleich," *Aus Politik und Zeitgeschichte*, 50 (2009): 3–8.

Höreth, Marcus. "A Successful Failure? The Contested Implications of Germany's Federal Reforms," *German Politics*, 17(4) (2008): 408–423.

Horst, Patrick. "Koalitionsbildungen und Koalitionsstrategien im neuen Fünfparteiensystem der Bundesrepublik Deutschland," *Zeitschrift für Politikwissenschaft*, 20(3/4) (2010): 327–408.

Huber, Joseph. *Die verlorene Unschuld der Ökologie* (Frankfurt: Fischer, 1982).

Hubert, Agnès and Maria Stratigaki. "Assessing 20 years of Gender Mainstreaming in the EU: Rebirth from the Ashes?" *Femina Politica*, 2 (2016): 21–36.

Hübner, Kurt. "German Crisis Management and Leadership: From Ignorance to Procrastination to Action," *Asia Europe Journal*, 9(2) (2012): 159–177.

Humphreys, Andrea. "Die Grünen and the Israeli–Palestinian Conflict," *Australian Journal of Politics and History*, 50(3) (2004): 407–419.

Huenteler, Joern, Tobias S. Schmidt, and Norichika Kanie, "Japan's Post-Fukushima Challenge: Implications from the German Experience on Renewable Energy Policy," *Energy Policy*, 45 (2012): 6–11.

Huß, Christian. "Durch Fukushima zum neuen Konsens? Die Umweltpolitik von 2009–2013," in Reimut Zöhlnhofer and Thomas Saalfeld (eds.), *Politik im Schatten der Krise. Eine Bilanz der Regierung Merkel, 2009–2013* (Berlin: Springer, 2014), pp. 521–553.

Inbar, Efraim and Eitan Shamir. "'Mowing the Grass': Israel's Strategy for Protracted Intractable Conflict," *Journal of Strategic Studies*, 37(1) (2014): 65–90.

Jansen, Mechthild (ed.). *Frauenwiderspruch – Alltag und Politik* (Cologne: Pahl-Rugenstein, 1987).

Janssen-Jurreit, Marie Louise. *Lieben Sie Deutschland? Gefühle zur Lage der Nation* (Munich: Piper, 1985).

Jarausch, Konrad H. (ed.). "Introduction," in *United Germany. Debating Processes and Prospects* (New York: Berghahn, 2013), pp. 1–21.

Kantor, Rosabeth Moss. *Men and Women of the Corporation* (New York: Basic Books, 1977).

Karapin, Roger. "Climate Policy Outcomes in Germany: Environmental Performance and Environmental Damage in Eleven Policy Areas," *German Politics & Society*, 30(3) (2012): 1–34.

Karl, Terry Lynn. *The Paradox of Plenty: Oil Booms and Petro-States* (Berkeley: University of California Press, 1997).

Kent, Thomas W., Carrie A. Blair, Howard F. Rudd, and Ulrich Schuele, "Gender Differences and Transformational Leadership Behavior: Do Both German Men and Women Lead in the Same Way?" *International Journal of Leadership Studies*, 6(1) (2010): 52–66.

Koelbl, Herlinde. *Spuren der Macht. Die Verwandlung des Menschen durch das Amt* (Munich: Knesebeck, 1999).

Köhler, Anne and Volker Ronge, "Ein Test auf Wiedervereinigung? Die Reaktion der Bundesdeutschen auf die Übersiedlerwelle aus der DDR von Frühjahr 1984," *Deutschland Archiv*, 18(1) (1984): 52–59.

Kolinsky, Eva. "Political Participation and Parliamentary Careers: Women's Quotas in West Germany," *West European Politics*, 14(1) (1991): 56–72.

Kolinsky, Eva and Hildegard Maria Nickel. *Reinventing Gender: Women in Eastern Germany since Unification* (London: Frank Cass, 2003).

Konrad, Alison, Vicki Kramer, and Sumru Erkut, "The Impact of Three or More Women on Corporate Boards," *Organizational Dynamics*, 37 (2008): 145–164.

Koopman, Paul L., Deanne N. Den Hartog, Edvard Konrad et al. "National Culture and Leadership Profiles in Europe: Some Results from the GLOBE Study," *European Journal of Work and Organizational Psychology*, 8(4) (1999): 503–520.

Kornelius, Stephan. *Angela Merkel. Die Kanzlerin und ihre Welt* (Hamburg: Hoffmann & Campe, 2013).

Korte, Karl-Rudolf. "Solutions for the Decision Dilemma: Political Styles of Germany's Chancellors," *German Politics*, 9(1) (2000): 1–22.

Kraushaar, Wolfgang. *Wann endlich beginnt bei Euch der Kampf gegen die heilige Kuh Israel? Über die antisemitischen Wurzeln des deutschen Terrorismus* (Reinbeck: Rowohlt, 2013).

Krick, Eva. "Regieren mit Gipfeln-Expertengremien der Großen Koalition," *Zeitschrift für Politikwissenschaft*, 20(2) (2010): 123–268.

Kryshtanovskaya, Olga and Stephen White. "Putin's Militocracy," *Post-Soviet Affairs*, 19(4) (2003): 289–306.

Kuhn, Thomas S. *The Structure of Scientific Revolutions* (University of Chicago Press, 1962).

Kundnani, Hans. *Utopia or Auschwitz. Germany's 1968 Generation and the Holocaust* (New York: Columbia University Press, 2009).

Kuran, Timur. "Now Out of Never: The Element of Surprise in the East European Revolutions of 1989," *World Politics*, 44(1) (1991): 7–48.

Lachenicht, Susanne. "Mythos Trümmerfrau? Trümmerräumung in Heilbronn (1944–1950)," *Heilbronnica*, 2, Beiträge zur Stadtgeschichte, Stadtarchiv Heilbronn, 2003, pp. 319–360.

Lahnstein, Manfred. *Die Gefesselerin: Wie Die Große Koalition Sich Selbst Blockiert* (Bergisch Gladbach: Verlagsgruppe Lübbe, 2006).

Land, Rainer. "East Germany, 1989–2010: A Fragmented Development," in Konrad H. Jarausch (ed.), *United Germany. Debating Processes and Prospects* (New York: Berghahn, 2013), pp. 104–118.

Lang, Sabine. "Gender Equality in post-Unification Germany: Between GDR Legacies and EU-level Pressures," *German Politics*, forthcoming 2017.

Lang, Sabine and Birgit Sauer. "Does Federalism Impact Gender Architectures? The Case of Women's Policy Agencies in Germany and Austria," *Publius: The Journal of Federalism*, 43(1) (2012): 68–89.

Lange, Bernd-Lutz. *Mauer, Jeans and Prager Frühling* (Berlin: Aufbau, 2006).

Langguth, Gerd. *Angela Merkel* (Munich: DTV, 2005).

Laruelle, Marlene. "Russia as a 'Divided Nation': From Compatriots to Crimea. A Contribution to the Discussion on Nationalism and Foreign Policy," *Problems of Post-Communism*, 62(2) (2015): 88–97.

Lau, Mariam. *Die Letzte Volkspartei. Angela Merkel und die Modernisierung der CDU* (Munich: Deutscher Verlagsanstalt, 2009).

Lauber, Volker and Lutz Mez. "Three Decades of Renewable Electricity Policies in Germany," *Energy and Environment*, 15(4) (2004): 599–623.

Leinemann, Jürgen. *Die Angst der Deutschen. Beobachtungen zur Bewußtseinslage der Nation* (Reinbeck: Rowohlt, 1982).

Lemke, Christiane. *Die Ursachen des Umbruchs. Politische Sozialisation in der ehemaligen DDR* (Opladen: Westdeutscher, 1991).

Leo, Annette. "Keine gemeinsame Erinnerung: Geschichtsbewusstsein in Ost und West," *Aus Politik und Zeitgeschichte*, 40/41 (2003): 27–32.

Lolos, Sarantis E. G. "The Effect of EU Structural Funds on Regional Growth: Assessing the Evidence from Greece, 1990–2005," *Economic Change and Restructuring* (Wiesbaden: Springer, 2009).

Lübbe, Hermann. "Der Nationalsozialismus im politischen Bewußtsein der Gegenwart," *Historische Zeitschrift*, 236 (1983): 579–599.

Ludewig, Damian. "Die Energiewende finanzieren und beschleunigen durch den Abbau umweltschädlicher Subventionen," 4. *Jahrbuch nachhaltiger Energie* (Marburg: Metropolis, 2014), pp. 357–376.

Macartney, Huw. *The Debt Crisis and European Democratic Legitimacy* (Basingstoke: Palgrave, 2013).

Maier, Charles S. *The Unmasterable Past. History, Holocaust, and German National Identity* (Cambridge, MA: Harvard University Press, 1998).

Makarychev, Andrey. "A New European Disunity: EU–Russia Ruptures and the Crisis in the Common Neighborhood," *Problems of Post-Communism*, 62(6) (2015): 313–315.

Makarychev, Andrey and Sergei Medvedev. "Biopolitics and Power in Putin's Russia," *Problems of Post-Communism*, 62(1) (2015): 45–54.

Mandell, Barbara and Shilpa Pherwani. "Relationship between Emotional Intelligence and Transformational Leadership Style: A Gender Comparison," *Journal of Business and Psychology*, 3 (2003): 387–404.

Marco, Allegra and Paolo Napolitano. "Two States or Not Two States? Leadership and Peace Making in the Israeli–Palestinian Conflict," *Mediterranean Politics*, 16(2) (2011): 261–278.

Markovits, Andrei. *The Politics of the West German Trade Unions: Strategies of Class and Interest Representation in Growth and Crisis* (Cambridge University Press, 1986).

Marten, Kimberly. "Informal Political Networks and Putin's Foreign Policy: The Examples of Iran and Syria," *Problems of Post-Communism*, 62(2) (2015): 71–87.

Mauerer, Marcus, Carsten Reinemann, Jürgen Maier, and Michaela Maier, *Schröder gegen Merkel. Wahrnehmung und Wirkung des TV-Duells 2005 im Ost-West-Vergleich* (Wiesbaden: VS Verlag, 2007).

Marx-Feree, Myra. "Angela Merkel: What Does it Mean to Run as a Woman?" *German Politics & Society*, 24(1) (2006): 93–107.

Matthijs, Matthias. "Powerful Rules Governing the Euro: The Perverse Logic of German Ideas," *Journal of European Public Policy*, 23(3) (2016): 375–391.

Maull, Hanns W. "German Foreign Policy, Post-Kosovo: Still a 'Civilian Power'?," *German Politics*, 9(2) (2000): 1–24.

Maull, Hanns W. and Sebastian Harnisch (eds.). "Analysis: Foreign Policy of the Grand Coalition: Base Line and First Assessment," *Foreign Policy in Dialogue*, 7/18 (2006).

Meier, Birgit. "'Nachts, wenn der Generalsekretär weint' – Politikerinnen in der Presse," *Aus Politik und Zeitgeschichte*, B-50 (2009): 9–15.

Meier, Franz Josef. "The Security and Defense Policy of the Grand Coalition," in Marco Overhaus, Hanns W. Maull, and Sebastian Harnisch (eds.), "Foreign Policy of the Grand Coalition: Base Line and First Assessment," *Foreign Policy in Dialogue*, 7/18 (2006).

Merkel, Angela (ed.). *Der Preis des Überlebens – Gedanken und Gespräche über zukünftige Aufgaben der Umweltpolitik* (Stuttgart: Deutsche Verlags-Anstalt, 1997).

Merkle, Susanne. "Personalisierung und genderspezifische Berichterstattung im Bundestagswahlkampf 2013 – 'Ausnahmefall' Angela Merkel oder typische Frau," in Christine Holtz-Bacha (ed.), *Die Massenmedien im Wahlkampf. Die Bundestagswahl 2013* (Wiesbaden: Springer, 2015), pp. 217–247.

Miethe, Ingrid. "Women's Movements in East Germany: Are We in Europe Yet?" in Konrad H. Jarausch (ed.), *United Germany. Debating Processes and Prospects* (New York: Berghahn, 2013), pp. 154–170.

"Die 89er als 68er des Ostens: Fallrekonstruktive Untersuchungen in einer Frauenfriedensgruppe der DDR," in Annegret Schüle, Thomas Ahbe, and Rainer Gries (eds.), *Die DDR aus generationsgeschichtlicher perspektive eine Inventur* (Leipzig: Uni-Verlag, 2006), pp. 355–376.

Miller, Bernhard and Wolfgang C. Müller. "Managing Grand Coalitions: Germany 2005–09," *German Politics*, 19(3/4) (2010): 332–352.

Mishra, Robin. *Angela Merkel – Machtworte: Die Standpunkte der Kanzlerin* (Freiburg: Herder, 2010).

Mitrakos, Theodore. "Inequality, Poverty and Social Welfare in Greece: Distributional Effects of Austerity," No. 174, Bank of Greece, Athens, February 2014.

Mitscherlich, Alexander and Margarete Mitscherlich. *Die Unfähigkeit zu trauern: Grundlagen kollektiven Verhaltens* (Munich: Piper, 1967).

Moersch, Karl. *Sind wir denn eine Nation? Die Deutschen und ihr Vaterland* (Bonn: Bonn Aktuell, 1982).

Mohanad, Mustafa and As'ad Ghanem, "The Empowering of the Israeli Extreme Right in the 18th Knesset Elections," *Mediterranean Politics,* 15(1) (2010): 25–44.

Momtcheva, Veneta. "The German EU Council Presidency (January–June 2007) and the Further Development of Transatlantic Relations," George C. Marshall European Center for Security Studies, Garmisch-Partenkirchen, July 2007.

Monstadt, Jochen. "Urban Governance and the Transition of Energy Systems: Institutional Change and Shifting Energy and Climate Policies in Berlin," *International Journal of Urban and Regional Research,* 31(2) (June 2007): 326–343.

Moore Jr., Barrington. *On the Social Origins of Dictatorship and Democracy: Lord and Peasant in the Making of the Modern World* (Boston, MA: Beacon Press, 1966).

Moser, Tilmann, "Die Unfähigkeit zu trauern: Hält die Diagnose einer Überprüfung stand? Zur psychischen Verarbeitung des Holocaust in der Bundesrepublik," *Psyche,* 46 (1992): 389–405.

Müller, Patrick. "The Europeanization of Germany's Foreign Policy toward the Israeli–Palestinian Conflict: Between Adaptation to the EU and National Projection," *Mediterranean Politics,* 16(3)(2011): 385–403.

Müller-Brandeck-Bocquet, G., C. Schukraft, N. Leuchtweis, and U. Keßler (eds.). *Deutsche Europapolitik: Von Adenauer bis Merkel* (Stuttgart: Springer, 2010).

Müller-Vogg, Hugo. *Angela Merkel: Mein Weg* (Hamburg: Hoffmann & Campe, 2005).

Murray, Donald A. *Democracy of Despots* (Montreal: McGill-Queens University Press, 1995).

Murswieck, Axel. "Angela Merkel als Regierungschefin und als Kanzler-Kandidatin," *Aus Politik und Zeitgeschichte,* B-51 (2009): 26–32.

Mushaben, Joyce Marie, "Anti-Politics and Successor Generations: The Role of Youth in the West and East German Peace Movements," *Journal of Political and Military Sociology,* 12 (1984): 171–190.

"Reflections on the Institutionalization of Protest: The Case of the West German Peace Movements," *Alternatives: Journal of World Policy,* 11(4) (1984): 519–539.

"Swords to Plowshares: The Church, the State and the East German Peace Movement," *Studies in Comparative Communism,* 17(2) (1984): 123–135.

"Cycles of Peace Protest in West Germany: Experiences from Three Decades," *West European Politics,* 8(1) (1985): 24–40.

"A Crisis of Culture: Social Isolation and Integration among Turkish Guestworkers in the German Federal Republic," in Ilyan Basgoz and Norman Furniss (eds.), *Turkish Workers in Europe: A Multidisciplinary Study* (Bloomington, IN: Indiana University Press, 1985), pp. 125–150.

"Grassroots and *Gewaltfreie Aktionen*: A Study of Mass Mobilization Strategies in the West German Peace Movement," *Journal of Peace Research,* 23(2) (1986): 141–154.

"Innocence Lost: Environmental Images and Political Experiences among the West German Greens," *New Political Science*, 14 (1986): 39–66.

"Youth Protest and the Democratic State: Reflections on the Rise of Anti-Political Culture in Prewar Germany and the German Federal Republic," *Research in Political Sociology*, 2 (1986): 171–197.

"Peace and the National Question: A Study of the Development of an 'Association of Responsibility' between the two Germanys," *Coexistence: A Review of East–West and Development Issues*, 24 (1987): 245–270.

"The Other Democratic Deficit: Women in the European Community Before and After Maastricht," in Paul Michael Lützeler (ed.), *Europe after Maastricht: American and European Perspectives* (Providence, RI: Berghahn, 1994), pp. 251–275.

"Second-Class Citizenship and its Discontents: Women in United Germany," in Peter Merkl (ed.), *The Federal Republic of Germany at 45* (New York: New York University Press, 1995), pp. 80–98.

"The Rise of Femi-Nazis? Women and Rightwing Extremist Movements in Unified Germany," *German Politics*, 5(2)(1996): 240–275.

"Concession or Compromise? The Politics of Abortion in United Germany," *German Politics*, 6(3) (1997): 69–87.

From Post-War to Post-Wall Generations. Changing Attitudes towards the National Question and NATO in the Federal Republic of Germany (Boulder, CO: Westview Press, 1998).

"Collective Memory Divided and Reunited: Mothers, Daughters and the Fascist Experience in Germany," *History and Memory* (1999): 1–34.

"The Politics of Critical Acts: Women and Leadership in the European Union," *European Studies Journal*, 15(2) (1999): 51–91.

"Die Lehrjahre sind vorbei! Re-Forming Democratic Interest Groups in Eastern Germany," *Democratization*, 8(4) (2001): 95–133.

"Ost–West Identitäten: Generationen zwischen Wende und Wandel," *Berliner Debatte INITIAL*, 12(3) (2001): 74–87.

"Girl Power: Women, Politics and Leadership in the Berlin Republic," in James Sperling (ed.), *The Federal Republic of Germany at Fifty-Five* (Manchester University Press, 2004), pp. 183–205.

"Memory and the Holocaust: Processing the Past through a Gendered Lens," special issue, *History of the Human Sciences*, 17(2/3) (2004): 147–185.

"Girl Power, Gender Mainstreaming and Critical Mass: Women's Leadership and Policy Paradigm Shifts in Germany's Red–Green Coalition, 1998–2002," *Journal of Women, Politics, and Policy*, 27(1/2) (2005): 145–182.

The Changing Faces of Citizenship: Integration and Mobilization among Minorities in Germany (Providence, RI: Berghahn Books, 2008).

"Madam Chancellor: Angela Merkel and the Triangulation of German Foreign Policy," *Georgetown Journal of International Affairs*, 10(1) (2009): 27–37.

"Up the Down Staircase: Redefining Gender Identities through Ethnic Employment in Germany," *Journal of Ethnic and Migration Studies*, 35(8) (2009): 1249–1274.

"Educating for Citizenship: Re-assessing the Role of Islamic Instruction in German Schools," *Politics & Religion*, 3 (2010): 518–552.

"From Ausländer to Inländer: The Changing Faces of Citizenship in Post-Wall Germany," *German Politics & Society*, 28(1) (2010): 141–164.

"The Best of Times, the Worst of Times: Angela Merkel, the Grand Coalition and 'Majority Rule' in Germany," *German Politics and Society*, 34(1) (2016): 1–25.

Nestle, Uwe. "Does the Use of Nuclear Power Lead to Lower Electricity Prices? An Analysis of the Debate in Germany with an International Perspective," *Energy Policy*, 41 (2012): 152–160.

Neubert, Ehrhart. *Geschichte der Opposition in der DDR, 1949–1989* (Berlin: Links, 1997).

Neumayer, Eric and Thomas Plümper. "The Gendered Nature of Natural Disasters: The Impact of Catastrophic Events on the Gender Gap in Life Expectancy, 1981–2002," *Annals of the Association of American Geographers*, 97 (2007): 551–566.

Niclauß, Karlheinz. "Kiesinger und Merkel in der Großen Koalition," *Aus Politik und Zeitgeschichte*, B-16 (2008): 3–11.

Niedermayer, Oskar (ed.). *Die Parteien nach der Bundestagswahl 2009* (Wiesbaden: Springer, 2011).

Niethammer, Lutz. *Die volkseigene Erfahrung: Eine Archäologie des Lebens in der Industrieprovinz der DDR* (Berlin: Rowohlt, 1991).

Ofer, Dalia and Lenore J. Weitzman (eds.). *Women in the Holocaust* (New Haven, CT: Yale University Press, 1998).

Öko-Insitut e.V. *Energiewende. Wachstum und Wohlstand ohne Erdöl und Uran* (Frankfurt: Fischer, 1980).

Oliver, Tim and Michael John Williams. "Special Relationships in Flux: Brexit and the Future of the US–EU and US–UK Relationships," *International Affairs*, 92(3) (2016): 547–567.

Olsen, Jonathan. *Nature and Nationalism: Right-Wing Ecology and the Politics of Identity in Contemporary Germany* (New York: St. Martin's Press, 1999).

"Leadership and Inter-party Relations in Grand Coalitions: Comparing Angela Merkel and Kurt Georg Kiesinger," *German Politics*, 20(3) (2011): 342–359.

Pallade, Yves P. *Germany and Israel in the 1990s and Beyond: Still a "Special Relationship"?* (Frankfurt: European University Studies, 2005).

"Antisemitism and Right-Wing Extremism in Germany: New Discourses," *Israel Journal of Foreign Affairs*, 2(1) (2008): 66–67.

"Delegitimizing Jews and the Jewish State: Anti-Semitism and Anti-Zionism after Auschwitz," *Israel Journal of Foreign Affairs*, 3 (2009): 63–69.

Papadopoulos, Theodoros and Antonios Roumpakis. "The Greek Welfare State in the Age of Austerity: Anti-social Policy and the Politico-economic Crisis," *Social Policy Review*, 24 (2012): 203–227.

Pardo, Sharon. "Going West: Guidelines for Israel's Integration into the European Union," *Israel Journal of Foreign Affairs*, 3(2) (2009): 51–62.

Parker Follett, Mary. *Creative Experience* (New York: Longmans, Green, 1930).

Peisl, Anton and Armin Mohler (eds.). *Die deutsche Neurose–Über die beschädigte Identität der Deutschen* (Frankfurt: Ullstein, 1980).

Petersen, Peter. *Sind wir denn noch zu retten? Der Bundestagsabgeordnete schreibt an seinen 19-jährigen Sohn, der sich Sorgen um die Zukunft macht* (Stuttgart: Burg, 1984).

Petmesidou, Maria. "Statism, Social Policy and the Middle Classes in Greece," *Journal of European Social Policy*, 1(1) (1991): 31–48.

Pirani, Simon, Jonathan Stern, and Katja Yafimava, "The Russo-Ukrainian Gas Dispute of January 2009: A Comprehensive Assessment," Oxford Institute for Energy Studies, February 2009.

Pollack, Detlef. *Politischer Protest. Politisch alternative Gruppen in der DDR* (Opladen: Leske & Budrich, 2000).

Power, Benjamin E. "The Berlin Connection: Locating German–Iranian Relations within the Current Understandings of Post-Unification German Foreign Policy," *Journal of International Relations*, 10 (2008): 12–21.

Primor, Avi. "Peeling Günther Grass' Israeli Onion," *Israel Journal of Foreign Affairs*, 6(2) (2012): 101–106.

Putin, Wladimir, with Natalija Geworkjan and Andrei Kolesnikow. *Aus erster Hand. Gespräche mit Wladimir Putin* (Munich: Heyne, 2000).

Radkau, Joachim. *Aufstieg und Krise der deutschen Atomwirtschaft, 1945–1975* (Hamburg: Rowohlt, 1983).

Radmacher, Anne (ed.). *"Ich bete jeden Tag, bitte laß uns bleiben": 14 Porträts asylsuchender Frauen aus aller Welt* (Munich: Goldmann, 1993).

Rehberg, Karl-Siegbert. "Ost–West," in Stephan Lessenich and Frank Nullmeier (eds.), *Deutschland, Eine gespaltene Gesellschaft* (Bonn: Bundeszentrale für politische Bildung, 2006), p. 219.

Reichel, Peter. *Vergangenheitsbewältigung in Deutschland: Die Auseinandersetzung mit der NS-Diktatur in Politik und Justiz* (Hamburg: Beck'sche Reihe, 2007).

Reimer, Franz. "Die Energiewende und die Kompetenzordnung des Grundgesetzes," in Thorsten Müller and Hartmut Kahl (eds.), *Energiewende im Föderalismus* (Baden-Baden: Nomos, 2015), pp. 69–98.

Resing, Volker. *Angela Merkel. Die Protestantin* (Leipzig: St. Benno, 2009).

Reuth, Ralf Georg and Günther Lachmann. *Das erste Leben der Angela M.* (Munich: Piper, 2013).

Riesenbichler, Alexander and Kimberly J. Morgan. "From 'Sick Man' to 'Miracle': Explaining the Robustness of the German Labor Market During and After the Financial Crisis 2008–2009," *Politics & Society*, 40(4) (2012): 549–579.

Rinke, Andreas. "Wie Putin Berlin verlor: Moskaus Annexion der Krim hat die deutsche Russland Politik verändert," *Internationale Politik*, 69(3) (2014): 33–47.

Rochau, Ludwig August von. *Grundsätze der Realpolitik angewendet auf die staatlichen Zustände Deutschlands* (1853).

Roesler, Jörg. "Privatization in East Germany," *Europe Asia Studies*, 46(3) (1994): 505–517.

Rohnstock, Katrin (ed.). *Stiefschwester: Was Ost-Frauen und West-Frauen von einander denken* (Frankfurt: Fischer, 1994).

Roll, Evelyn. *Die Erste. Angela Merkel's Weg zur Macht* (Reinbek: Rowohlt, 2005).

Rommelspacher, Birgit. *Dominanzkultur. Texte zu Fremdheit und Macht* (Berlin: Olanda, 2006).

Roßnagel, Alexander. *Bedroht die Kernenergie unsere Freiheit* (Munich: C. H. Beck, 1983).

Royo, Sebastian. "How Did the Spanish Financial System Survive the First Stage of the Global Crisis?" *Governance* (2012): 1–26.

Rubery, Jill and M. Karamessini (eds.). *Women and Austerity: The Economic Crisis and the Future for Gender Equality* (Abingdon: Routledge, 2013).

Rüdig, Wolfgang. "Negotiating the 'Berlin Mandate': Reflections on the First 'Conference of the Parties' to the UN Framework Convention on Climate Change," *Environmental Politics*, 4(3) (1995): 481–487.

Rudzio, Wolfgang. "Informelles regieren – Koalitionsmanagement der Regierung Merkel," *Aus Politik und Zeitgeschichte*, B-16 (2008): 11–17.

Runge, Irene. *Ausland DDR. Fremdenhass* (Berlin: Dietz, 1990).

Rüther, Günther. "Politische Kultur und innere Einheit in Deutschland," Konrad Adenauer Stiftung, Sankt Augustin, 1995.

Sauer, Joachim. "Die Kunst war, morgens noch in den Spiegel schauen zu können," *Humboldt Kosmos*, 96 (2010).

Schaeffer-Hegel, Barbara, Helga Foster, and Helga Lutoschat (eds.). *Frauen und Macht: Zum Wandel der politischen Kultur durch die Präsenz von Frauen in Führungspositionen* (Pfaffenweiler: Pfaffenweiler Press, 1995).

Scharpf, Fritz W. "After the Crash: A Perspective on Multilevel European Democracy," MPIFG Discussion Paper, Max Planck Institute, Cologne, 2014.

"No Exit from the Euro-Rescuing Trap?" MPIFG Discussion Paper 14/4, Max Planck Institute, Cologne, 2014.

Schelkle, Waltraud. "A Tale of Two Crises: The Euro Area in 2008/09 and in 2010," *European Political Science*, 10 (2011): 375–383.

"Policymaking in Hard Times: French and German Responses to Economic Crisis in the Euro Area," in N. Bermeo and J. Pontusson (eds.), *Coping with Crisis: Government Reactions to the Great Recession* (New York: Russell Sage, 2012), pp. 130–162.

Scherzer, Landolf. *Die Fremden: Unerwünschte Begegnungen und verbotene Protokolle* (Berlin: Aufbau, 2002).

Schick, Gerhard. "Why the Green New Deal is a Response to the European Debt Crisis," Green Political Foundation, Berlin, October 25, 2011.

Schild, Joachim. "Mission Impossible? The Potential for Franco-German Leadership in the Enlarged EU," *Journal of Common Market Studies*, 48 (2010): 1367–1390.

Schimany, Peter. "Migration und demographischer Wandel," BAMF, Forschungsbericht 5, Berlin, 2008.

Schmid, Harald. "Reform und Geschichte: Das Beispiel der ersten Großen Koalition 1966–1969," *Zeitschrift für Politikwissenschaft*, 20(3/4) (2010): 291–325.

Schmoeckel, Reinhard and Bruno Kaiser. *Die vergessene Regierung. Die Große Koalition 1966 bis 1969 und ihre langfristigen Wirkungen* (Bonn: Bouvier, 1991).

Schneider, Peter. *Der Mauerspringer* (Darmstadt: Luchterhand, 1982).

Scholz, Sylka (ed.). *"Kann die das?" Angela Merkels Kampf um die Macht* (Berlin: Dietz 2007).

Schreurs, Miranda A. "German Perspectives on Ecological Modernization, Technology Transfer and Intellectual Property Rights in the Case of Climate Change," American Institute for Contemporary German Studies, Policy Report No. 45, Washington DC, 2010, pp. 61–77.

Schreurs, Miranda and Sibyl Steuwer. "Der Koordinierungsbedarf zwischen Bund und Ländern bei der Umsetzung der Energiewende aus politikwissenschaftlicher Sicht," in Thorsten Müller and Hartmut Kahl (eds.), *Energiewende im Föderalismus* (Baden-Baden: Nomos, 2015), pp. 45–68.

Schreurs, Miranda A. and Yves Tiberghien. "Multi-Level Reinforcement: Explaining European Union Leadership in Climate Change Mitigation," *Global Environmental Politics*, 7(4) (2007): 19–46.

Schreyer, Michaele and Lutz Mez. "Erene: European Community for Renewable Energy," 3, Heinrich Böll Stiftung, Berlin, June 8, 2009.

Schroeder, Klaus. "Das Zusammenwachsen Deutschlands und die Kosten der deutschen Einheit, " *Politische Studien*, Themenheft 1 (2010).

Schuch, Gereon, Julian Pänke, Malte Brosig et al. *Gegenwart der Vergangenheit: Die politische Aktualität historischer Erinnerung in Mitteleuropa* (Baden-Baden: Nomos, 2007).

Schulz, Irmgard, Diana Hummel, Claudia Empacher et al., "Research on Gender, the Environment and Sustainable Development: Studies on Gender Impact Assessment of the Programmes of the 5th Framework Program for Research, Technological Development and Demonstration," Institut für sozial-ökologische Forschung, Frankfurt, 2001.

Schumacher, Hajo. *Die Zwölf Gesetze der Macht. Angela Merkels Erfolgsgeheimnisse* (Munich: Heyne, 2007).

Schumpeter, Joseph. *Capitalism, Socialism and Democracy* (New York: Harper & Row, 1942).

Schwarz, Hans-Peter. *Die Fraktion als Machtfaktor: CDU/CSU im Deutschen Bundestag 1949 bis heute* (Munich: Pantheon, 2009).

Schwarz, Patrick (ed.). *Angela Merkel, die Unerwartete – wie Deutschlands erste Kanzlerin mit der Zeit geht* (Hamburg: Edel, 2011).

Simon, Anette and Jan Faktor. *Fremd im eigenen Land?* (Gießen: Psychosozial-Verlag, 2000).

Simon, Herbert A. *Administrative Behavior: A Study of Decision-Making Processes in Administrative Organization* (New York: Macmillan, 1947).

Sonne, Werner. *Staatsräson? Wie Deutschland für Israels Sicherheit haftet* (Berlin: Propyläen, 2013).

Spellerberg, Annette. *Alltagskultur in Ost-und Westdeutschland: Unterschiede und Gemeinsamkeiten* (Berlin: Wissenschaftszentrum Berlin, 1994).

Spender, Dale. *Time and Tide Wait for No Man* (London: Pandora Press, 1984).

Sperling, Valerie. "Putin's Macho Personality Cult," *Communist and Post-Communist Studies*, 49(1) (2016): 13–23.

Spiegel Spezial. *Das Profil der Deutschen. Was sie vereint, was sie trennt*, No. 1 (1991).

Stefes, Christoph H. "Bypassing Germany's *Reformstau*: The Remarkable Rise of Renewable Energy," *German Politics*, 19(2) (2010): 148–163.

Stock, Wolfgang. *Angela Merkel: Eine politische Biographie* (Munich: Olzog, 2000).

Strand, Trude. "Tightening the Noose: The Institutionalized Impoverishment of Gaza, 2005–2010," *Journal of Palestine Studies*, 43(2) (2014): 6–23.

Stratigaki, Maria. "Gendering the Social Policy Agenda: Anti-discrimination, Social Inclusion and Social Protection," in Gabriele Abels and Joyce Marie Mushaben (eds.), *Gendering the European Union: New Approaches to Old Democratic Deficits* (Basingstoke: Palgrave Macmillan, 2012), pp. 169–186.

Strauss, Kayla. "Land Policies in Tokyo: Implications of the 2011 Tohoku Disaster," Honor's thesis, University of Missouri-St. Louis, December 31, 2011.

Streek, Wolfgang and Lea Elsässer. "Monetary Disunion: the Domestic Politics of Euroland," Max Planck Institute for the Study of Societies 14/17, Cologne, 2014.

Strömbom, Lisa. "Identity Shifts and Conflict Transformation: Probing the Israeli History Debates," *Mediterranean Politics*, 18(1) (2013): 79–97.

Stulberg, Adam N. "Out of Gas? Russia, Ukraine, Europe, and the Changing Geopolitics of Natural Gas," *Problems of Post-Communism*, 62(2) (2015): 112–130.

Tekin, Beyza Ç. "Rethinking the Post-National EU in Times of Austerity and Crisis," *Mediterranean Politics*, 19(1) (2014): 21–39.

Teti, Andrea and Gennaro Gervasio. "The Unbearable Lightness of Authoritarianism: Lessons from the Arab Uprisings," *Mediterranean Politics*, 16(2) (2011): 321–327.

Thomas, Ralf, Henrik Scheller, and Rudolf Hrbek (eds.). *Die bundesstaatliche Kompetenz- und Finanzverteilung im Spiegel der Föderalismusreform I und II* (Baden-Baden: Nomos, 2009).

Thompson, Mark R. and Ludmilla Lennartz. "The Making of Chancellor Merkel," *German Politics*, 15(1) (2006): 99–110.

Thränhardt, Dietrich. *Die Arbeitsmigration von Flüchtlingen in Deutschland: Humanität, Effektivität, Selbstbestimmung* (Munich: Bertelsmann, 2015).

Tibi, Bassam. *Europa ohne Identität, Die Krise der multikulturellen Gesellschaft* (Munich: Bertelsmann, 1998).

Töpfer, Klaus (ed.). *Deutsche Energiewende: Eine Gemeinschaftswerk für die Zukunft* (Berlin: Ethik Kommission Sichere Energieversorgung: 2011).

Töpfer, Klaus and Ranga Yogeshwar. *Unsere Zukunft. Ein Gespräche über die Welt nach Fukushima* (Munich: C. H. Beck, 2011).

Tucker, Joshua A. "Enough! Electoral Fraud, Collective Action Problems, and Post-Communist Colored Revolutions," *Perspectives on Politics*, 5(3) (2007): 535–551.

Umpfenbach, Katharina and Stephan Sina. "Analysis of the German Federal Government's National Renewable Energy Action Plan," Heinrich Böll Stiftung, Berlin, October 2010.

Umsland, Andreas. "Berlin, Kiev, Moskau und die Röhre: Die deutsche Ostpolitik im Spannungsfeld der russisch-ukrainischen Beziehungen," *Zeitschrift für Außen- und Sicherheitspolitik*, 6(3) (2013): 413–428.

United Nations. United Nations Framework Convention on Climate Change, Report of the Conference of the Parties on its First Session, Berlin, March 28–April 7, 1995, published June 6, 1995.

Urban, Susanne Y. "Representations of the Holocaust in Today's Germany: Between Justification and Empathy," *Jewish Political Studies Review*, 20(1/2) (2008).

Venohr, Wolfgang (ed.). *Die deutsche Einheit kommt bestimmt!* (Bergisch Gladbach: Gustav Lübbe, 1982).

(ed.). *Ohne Deutschland geht es nicht–7 Autoren zur Lage der Nation* (Drefeld: SINUS, 1985).

Vivoda, Vlado. "Japan's Energy Security Predicament post-Fukushima," *Energy Policy*, 46 (2012): 135–143.

Wahl, Angelika von. "A 'Women's Revolution from Above'? Female Leadership, Intersectionality, and Public Policy under the Merkel Government," *German Politics*, 20(3) (2011): 392–409.

Walter, Stephan. *In unruhiger Zeit: Reden und Aufsätze aus drei Jahren deutscher Einheit* (Bonn: Parerga, 1994).

Weidenfeld, Werner. *Ratlose Normalität–Die Deutschen auf der Suche nach sich selbst* (Osnabrück: Interfrom, 1984).

(ed.), *Nachdenken über Deutschland* (Cologne: Wissenschaft & Politik, 1985).

Weizsäcker, Richard von. *Die deutsche Geschichte geht weiter* (Munich: Deutscher Taschenbuch Verlag, 1985).

Wensierski, Peter. *Von oben nach unten wächst gar nichts: Umweltzerstörung und Protest in der DDR* (Frankfurt: Fischer, 1986).

Wensierksi, Peter and Wolfgang Buscher (eds.). *Beton ist Beton: Zivilisationskritik aus der DDR* (Hattingen: Scandica, 1981).

White, Stephen and Ian McAllister. "The Putin Phenomenon," *Journal of Communist Studies and Transition Politics*, 24(4) (2008): 604–628.

Wickel, Martin. "Klimaschutz auf Länderebene," in Thorsten Müller and Hartmut Kahl (eds.), *Energiewende im Föderalismus* (Baden-Baden: Nomos, 2015), pp. 187–202.

Wiliarty, Sarah. "Angela Merkel's Path to Power: The Role of Internal Party Dynamics and Leadership," *German Politics* 17, No.1 (2008): 81–96.

The CDU and the Politics of Gender in Germany: Bringing Women to the Party (Cambridge University Press, 2010).

Winkler, Gunnar (ed.). *Sozialreport 2004. Daten und Fakten zur sozialen Lage in den neuen Bundesländern* (Berlin-Brandenburg: Trafo, 2004).

Winter, Gerd. "The Rise and Fall of Nuclear Energy Use in Germany: Processes, Explanations and the Role of Law," *Journal of Environmental Law*, 25(1) (2013): 95–124.

Wittlinger, Ruth. "The Merkel Government's Politics of the Past," *German Politics and Society*, 26(4) (2008): 9–27.

German National Identity in the Twenty-first Century. A Different Republic After All? (Basingstoke: Palgrave Macmillan, 2010).

Woodward, Alison E. "From Equal Treatment to Gender Mainstreaming and Diversity Management," in Gabriele Abels and Joyce Marie Mushaben (eds.), *Gendering the European Union: New Approaches to Old Democratic Deficits* (Basingstoke: Palgrave Macmillan, 2012), pp. 85–103.

Worbs, Susanne, Antonia Scholz, and Stefanie Blicke. *Die Optionsregelung im Staatsangehörigkeitsrecht aus der Sicht von Betroffenen* (Berlin: Bundesamt für Migration & Flüchtlinge, 2012).

Würzel, Rüdiger K. W. "Environmental, Climate and Energy Policies: Path-Dependent Incrementalism or Quantum Leap?" *German Politics*, 19(3/4) (2010): 460–478.

Yoder, Jennifer. "Truth without Reconciliation in post-Communist Germany: An Appraisal of the Enquete Commission on the SED Dictatorship in Germany," *German Politics*, 8(3) (1999): 59–80.

"An Intersectional Approach to Angela Merkel's Foreign Policy," *German Politics*, 20(3) (2011): 360–375.

"From Amity to Enmity: German–Russian Relations in the Post Cold War Period," *German Politics and Society*, 33(3) (2015): 49–69.

Young, Brigitte. *Triumph of the Fatherland: German Unification and the Marginalization of Women* (Ann Arbor, MI: University of Michigan Press, 1999).

Yuval-Davis, Nira. "Intersectionality and Feminist Politics," *European Journal of Women's Studies*, 13(3) (2006): 193–209.

Zieger, Gottfried, Boris Meissner, and Dieter Blumenwitz (eds.). *Deutschland als Ganzes. Rechtliche und historische Überlegungen* (Cologne: Wissenschaft & Politik, 1985).

Zimmer, Matthias. "Der Staatsräson der Bundesrepublik Deutschland vor und nach 1989," *Zeitschrift für Außen- und Sicherheitspolitik*, 6(2) (2009): 291–294.

Zimmermann, Hubert. "No Country for the Market: The Regulation of Finance in Germany after the Crisis," *German Politics*, 21(4) (2012): 484–501.

Zohlnhöfer, Reimut and Thomas Saalfeld (eds.). *Politik im Schatten der Krise: Eine Bilanz der Regierung Merkel, 2009–2013* (Wiesbaden: Springer, 2015).

Zöllner, Reinhard. *Japan, Fukushima und Wir. Zelebranten einer nuklearen Erdbebenkatastrophe* (Munich: Judicium, 2011).

Index